Marrying in South Asia

Marrying in South Asia

Shifting Concepts, Changing Practices in a Globalising World

Edited by

RAVINDER KAUR
RAJNI PALRIWALA

Orient BlackSwan

MARRYING IN SOUTH ASIA: SHIFTING CONCEPTS, CHANGING PRACTICES IN A GLOBALISING WORLD

ORIENT BLACKSWAN PRIVATE LIMITED

Registered Office
3-6-752 Himayatnagar, Hyderabad 500 029, Telangana, India
e-mail: centraloffice@orientblackswan.com

Other Offices
Bengaluru, Bhopal, Chennai, Guwahati, Hyderabad, Jaipur, Kolkata, Lucknow, Mumbai, New Delhi, Noida, Patna, Vijayawada

First published by Orient Blackswan Private Limited 2013
This paperback edition 2018

ISBN 978-93-5287-273-2

027212

Typeset by
Le Studio Graphique, Gurgaon 122 001
in Minion Pro 10.5/12.6

Map cartographed by
Sangam Books
(An imprint of The Agricultural Development Commercial Credit And Industrial Investment Company Private Limited)

Printed at
Yash Printographics

Published by
Orient Blackswan Private Limited
3-6-752 Himayatnagar, Hyderabad 500 029, Telangana, India
e-mail: info@orientblackswan.com

Remembering Leela Dube
A pioneer in the field
And a source of inspiration

Contents

Part 5: *Love and Conjugality in and Beyond Marriage*

Part 6: *Legal Interventions and Activism*

Tables, Figures and Map

Tables

Figures

Map

Editors' Acknowledgements

This volume has been a long time in the making, not least because of the pre-occupations of the editors. We thank our contributors for their patience, not only with the delay, but also with repeated requests for clarifications and details to do with the nitty-gritty of publication. We started work on this volume with a conference held in late 2008. At that time, Shalini Grover was part of our organising and editorial team. Due to other personal and professional commitments, she had to withdraw from the collaboration, to our loss. We appreciate the thought and time she gave to the volume in its initial period.

The conference itself would not have taken place without substantial financial support from the United Nations Children's Fund (UNICEF), Delhi office, and additional funding from the Indian Council of Social Science Research (ICSSR), the Japan Foundation and the Indian Institute of Technology Delhi (IIT-D). Much of the success of the conference, and thence the possibility of what we hope will be a valuable addition to research in the area of marriage, was due to a range of people, which, at times, becomes invisible as publication becomes a reality. This includes the discussants, all of whom had seriously engaged with the papers they commented on, those who presented papers that for one reason or another could not be included, and the large number of interested participants, who remained with us throughout the three days. Most important was the team of enthusiastic research scholars from our respective institutions—the Department of Humanities and Social Sciences, IITD, and the Department of Sociology, University of Delhi—who took in hand the logistics and rapporteuring of the conference.

As we were preparing for the conference, we decided to compile a bibliography of work in the area, which in the course of time became an annotated bibliography, supported by UNICEF, Delhi, and which played its own role in the production of this volume. Michelle Bolourchi, Shruti Chaudhry and Anindita Mazumdar helped pull that effort together.

A word of thanks to the anonymous referee and the team at Orient BlackSwan for their efforts in bringing this volume to fruition.

A final acknowledgement to IIT-D and the University of Delhi for infrastructural support and the time we were able to extract to work on the book.

Publishers' Acknowledgements

Extracts from a table in Lham Dorji, *Sergamathang Kothkin and Other Bhutan Marriage Customs*, Thimphu: The Centre for Bhutan Studies, 2003, appearing in chapter 2 of this volume, reproduced with permission from Lham Dorji. © Lham Dorji.

Two essays in this volume have been published in the *Asian Journal of Women's Studies*. They have since been edited, reworked and updated. For permission to reproduce copyright material in this volume, the volume editors and publishers wish to make the following acknowledgements:

Janaki Abraham, '"Why Did You Send Me Like This?": Marriage, Matriliny and the "Providing Husband" in North Kerala, India'. Originally published in *Asian Journal of Women's Studies* 17 (2): 32–65.

Shalini Grover, '"Purani aur Nai Shadi": Separation, Divorce and Remarriage in the Lives of the Urban Poor in New Delhi'. Originally published in *Asian Journal of Women's Studies* 17 (1): 67–99.

Introduction

Marriage in South Asia: Continuities and Transformations

Rajni Palriwala and Ravinder Kaur

Weddings in South Asia are getting bigger and fatter, along with media and middle-class angst over a perceived rise in divorce. One may ask if this is all that is left to marriage in South Asia—an event and its denial? Reports of what are called 'honour killings'—violent attempts to prevent self-choice or inter-caste marriage—are also frequent, in North India and Pakistan. The 'age of consent' is once again under debate in India. Are these reiterations of the institutional nature of marriage or actions taken to bulwark a normative practice threatened as never before? Or do they, conjointly, ask us to rethink the theoretical models with which we have looked at marriage? Are these the effects of modernity, capitalist development, globalisation, and individualisation, or are they themes long present? What is happening to marriage outside the media glare or is that at all a possibility in today's world? A wide array of questions is evoked when examining the complexities of changes and continuities in marriage in South Asia.

Despite new public imaginations of marriage, love/self-choice marriage has not replaced arranged marriages; nor has divorce replaced lifelong marital unions. Not all iterations of marriage 'rules', which remain important signifiers of caste identity and community culture, require defence or rest on visible violence. Marriage and its gendered domesticity are significant in individual and familial aspirations for sexual and social intimacies and in life trajectories.

Yet, economic processes and globalisation have affected spousal selection, marriage prestations, and the articulations of desire; they cannot help but affect the inner workings of conjugality. Marriage and its termination has long been a site for state intervention and the point of entry for concerted efforts at gendered social reform. As social anthropologists and sociologists, in whose disciplinary histories constructions of marriage have been critical, these issues confront us. Literary scholars, too, are relooking at their imaginaries of love, intimacy and marriage. For scholars of other disciplines such as economics and demography, marriage either did not figure in their discourses or was simply a fact, rather than a process. Yet, they too are turning their attention to marriage.[1] Drawing from various disciplines and asking diverse questions, the essays in this book address the simultaneity of apparent flux and change with the hegemonic and gendered normativity of marriage.

The Institution of Marriage: Shifting Frameworks

In looking for recent work on marriage, at first sight it appeared as if we were in a desert. Perhaps the paucity of research could be related to Fortes' (1962) musings? He asked if there was anything new to add, empirically or theoretically, to the study of marriage other than work on procedures of spousal selection. The questions and assumptions that had driven earlier anthropological and sociological work on kinship, marriage and family globally have also underlain studies done in the subcontinent. Along with caste, religion, and village, the latter were taken to be the principles of social organisation. The shifts from structural functional (Srinivas 1952; Karve 1953) to structural (Dumont 1957, 1966; Madan 1975) and subsequently to cultural (Fruzzetti 1982; Inden and Nicholas 2005; Das 1976) frameworks led to new analytical insights (Uberoi 1993). Schenider's critique (1984) of the biological premises, ethnocentrism, and implicit 'orientalism' of kinship studies had concluded that there is no transcultural category called kinship. According to Stone (2001), this account froze kinship studies in the US academy. This does not, however, explain the apparent dearth of work on the subcontinent, where many studies remain oblivious of his critique. A quick scan of books published in the 1980s and 1990s, in which kinship and marriage figure, suggests a trend of extending extant frameworks to hitherto understudied groups, such as 'tribes', 'remote' communities, and non-Hindus. It could be, then, that the formalistic and legalistic models which permeated kinship studies, critiqued by Bourdieu (1977), is more pertinent in explaining the decline in interest. If rules are taken as a sufficient description of marriage and kinship, once the former are known, there would be little to understand other than deviance. Thus, much work in Pakistan, particularly as the Islamic character of its society was asserted, tended to focus on issues of state and religious law or the extent of the prevalence or otherwise of the formal rules of preferential kin marriage (Palriwala 1994).

On closer investigation, what comes to the fore is that the study of marriage had not disappeared, but been displaced. The study of kinship practices and marriage strategies—rather than of official rules and ideology—entails intensive fieldwork, for which funding has not been easily available, inside or outside academia. As economic growth and population control became central ideologies in development and state policy, demographic change and reproductive behaviour became privileged foci of funding. Social demographers explored the correlations between marital sexual behaviours, reproduction strategies, contraception, age at marriage, and fertility levels with family patterns, mobility, education, urbanisation and female empowerment.[2] In frameworks that rarely distinguish between rules and practice, surveys continue to address deviance, anomy, and the 'impact' of modernity. However, some of these studies also look at marital strategies, extended family/kinship relations, and institutional dimensions of marriage in understanding the behaviours they focus on (Fricke et al. 1986). Family being the assumed site of care and welfare in government policies across most of the subcontinent, the debate around the 'decline' of the extended family-household is another area in which marriage enters (Shah 1989; Agarwal and Panda 2007; Madan 1993).

Another steady thread of scholarship, globally, has been through the new focus on women's voices and on gender, resonating with Yanagisako and Collier's (1987) call for a unified analysis of gender and kinship. Earlier analyses of marriage have been examined through the prism of gender (Das 1975; Dube 1986). Thus, in discussing structures of work, family, and marriage, Jeffery and Jeffery (1996) narrated how young women looked at their lives. Kapadia (1993) looked at cross-cousin marriage from the point of view of the bride/wife and the pressures inimical to this practice, while Palriwala (1991) analysed residential practices focusing on female mobility rather than the permanence of the patrilineage. Many of these studies looked at the ideology, dynamics, and practices of marriage rather than simply at structure and form. What these and other studies examined more directly was how the historical entrenchment of capitalism had favoured patrilocal systems and male inheritance and thereby affected gender equations in marriage and the domestic sphere (Ram 1992). This is also reflected in social and cultural histories (Arunima 2003; Sangari and Vaid 1989; Oldenburg 2002). In looking at the gendered implications of colonial interventions in class, caste, and community relations, as well as cultural tropes entwined with law and legal practices, marriage was brought to the fore.[3]

In what sense is the institutional character of marriage invoked, in this volume as well as in the wider academic discourse? How does it shape the subjective and structural contours of individual and collective action? Given a discourse that suggests that fluidity has become paramount with globalisation, it becomes all the more necessary to delineate this issue. Sociologically, whether it is arranged by others or chosen for love by the individuals to be wedded, marriage is a structured and patterned set of social relations and practices. It is embedded in norms and values regarding what marriage should be and is. There are explicit social prescriptions and sanctions by public bodies, the state, religion, and community. At the minimum, a marriage makes legal and public, even if not always socially accepted, an intimate relation between two individuals.[4] It thereby imbricates the 'public' in the personal and makes public order vulnerable to the vagaries of what may be viewed as purely individual intimacies.

The latter is also so because in many cultures and certainly in much of South Asia, a marriage is articulated as more than an ongoing relationship between two individuals. It establishes a tie between two social groups such as family-households, lineages, or clans and, at times, reiterates an already existing tie between them. Whether viewed primarily as a contract or a sacrament, marriage establishes a relationship between more than just the two in the conjugal pair. In other words, marriage is an alliance in structuralist and political terms, entailing affinal relations. All this can be congruent with self-choice or love marriage, depending on what the named and valued social groups are.

Importantly, marriage is a social institution in the manner in which it gives social sanction and legal recognition to the filial tie. This is not only through a parentally arranged match and in affinal relations. Rather, marriage legitimises children of the married couple and thus carries implications for the continuity and boundaries of these groups; for inheritance and status, access to resources, labour, care and support. It is this dimension that provides impetus to the control of marriage of individuals by their natal families and their communities. Further, marriage is an institution to the extent that it remains significant in official value and in practice as the basis for family-households. Even when marriage does not result in continuous cohabitation, it has implications for responsibilities, rights, and expectations in the everyday life of the married, their kin and their children. It is not only '... the law [that] sees marriage as a fundamental social institution whose stability is necessary for the care of the young and the aged, for the protection of women, and for the well-being of society as a whole' (Derrett 1978: 163–64; also cited in Uberoi 1995: 323). Even if that stability is difficult to achieve in practice, it is part of the espoused social values and cultural beliefs cutting across many classes, communities, and regions in South Asia. The inequalities of marriage, domesticity and society remain interwoven, and as with all institutions, particularly those that pervade society and have a hegemonic sway, marriage excludes; it marginalises those who fall outside its parameters or never enter it. In speaking of the last, Borneman highlights the spectres and embodied lives of the unmarried, the divorced, the homosexual, and the widowed (1996: 229).

These multiple aspects of the institutional character of marriage indicate the complexity we confront when we try and map directions of continuity and change. One commonality through which this complexity is addressed here is by a focus on practices, social relations, and agency, with 'official' ideologies and norms either questioned or showing signs of being recast, forming a backdrop, or being reiterated. It is important to note that officialising strategies (Bourdieu 1977) may mask diversity as well as change or the new value assigned to 'modernity' may justify them.

When we started looking at the debates regarding the nature and dimensions of change in marriage and family relations in South Asia, the need for a volume that pulled together some of the ideas on the dimensions considered became apparent. One of the first issues was if we could sensibly speak of marriage across the breadth of South Asia. What comprised it into a region? There is, of course, the facticity of its geo-politics, with the Himalayas and its passes to the north, the oceans to the south; the contemporary formation of the South Asian Association for Regional Cooperation (SAARC). There is a long economic history of overland and maritime trade networks traversing this area. Its one-time centrality in the global intercourse was fragmented by a common subjugation to colonialism, mostly British. With the arrival of the latter and the later decades of capitalist development, movement of goods and people from the subcontinent reached new volumes and different parts of the globe. The effects of colonial rule were such that even those countries that formally remained outside could not remain untouched, with an apparent introversion that was possibly new to them, such as Nepal and Bhutan.

Most critically, these geographic, economic, and political contours and passages also made for cultural transactions, which cut across and made the region. South Asia is home to a bewildering array of religions and communities, dispersed, intermingled, interacting, holding themselves apart, and jostling for power and domination. Silent or visible resistance to the power and norms of hegemonic combines and class differentiations adds to the diversity in practice. Social groups of varied depth claim cultural uniqueness; that they follow their own rules in marriage, family, and personal rituals and life. There have also been emulations and common cultural and structural processes that bring them together (Trautmann 1981). In fact, with contemporary processes of globalisation and assertions of ethnic and religious identity, both these trends have intensified. Anthropologists have long looked at the region, defined as both less (excluding Malé) and more (including Myanmar) than the current lines drawn. They have drawn comparisons across the region and attempted to draw out structural unities (Dumont 1966; Tambiah 1973; Cohn 1987; Mandelbaum 1988). The cultural and religious significance of marriage rules and practices, marital transactions, and family-household have held an important place in much of this discussion.

It is in such historical and scholarly contexts that we relook at marriage across South Asia. While there is no way in which we could adequately cover the geographical and cultural areas that constitute it, we try to capture some sense of that vastness. One concern was not to make the earlier mistake of allowing the practices of dominant or visible social groups to become the implicit exemplar and paradigm on which the analyses would be based. A second problematic was that in addressing our concerns, we had to ensure that we neither lose sight of the important insights and analyses of earlier frameworks and studies, nor get caught in their web. This volume then represents a shift from earlier frameworks that often erred on the side of assuming the universality of upper caste and/or elite ideologies and collapsed practices into rules. Taking into account the salience of the rules and ideologies of dominant groups in self-representation and aspirations, the essays here focus on practices and the multiple, disparate, incoherent ideologies of family and marriage that influence individual and group choices. A third benchmark arose from our reading of many past studies that tended to look at marriage and family, work and economics, politics and law in separate essays except when summarising the 'impact of industrialisation, urbanisation, and modernity' (Goode 1970). Much of the last discussion explicitly abjured a cultural and political economy perspective, and worked within a Parsonian and modernisation framework. It centred on the idea that the extended family was being replaced by the nuclear family-household and arranged marriage was giving way to love and individual choice. Rather than assuming unidirectional change or unidirectional causality, the attempt in this volume is to capture the dialectics of the changing institution of marriage and the dynamics of marriage practices on the one hand and shifts in economy, polity, society, and family on the other, all affected by globalisation processes. Thus, changing opportunities for work, fracturing of communities by violence, new institutional structures that deal with the end of marriage, new modes of matchmaking with the availability of new technologies and new imaginings of conjugal and intimate relationships, mostly heterosexual but also involving same-sex partners, are drawn in.

Finally, tracing women's voices, gender, and contours of intimacy, rather than the mere fact of marital or other intimacy are important dimensions of the framework of this volume. As indicated earlier, gender has been central to most of the work done in the area of marriage, kinship and family in the last two decades. Issues of marital prestations and dowry, marital violence and the condition of widows for women's rights and value in society, as well as the mutual construction of kinship-marriage-family and gender ideologies have been examined. Yet, though the negativities of contemporary marriage for women have been a focus in earlier work, there has been little work on conjugality itself, on the dimensions of emotion, sexuality, support, and care which the fact of marriage is taken to frame. Agency in marriage then often appears only as male violence or parental suppression or self-choice. How and why do men and women desire or not desire marriage; what is it that not being married denies them; why do marriages persist in the face of conflict and how do individuals and groups deal with the end of marriage, whether by divorce or death? While this volume cannot address all these issues, the concern is to look simultaneously at the internal and external processes that make the institution of marriage and it implications for those in and out of it.

Renewing Tradition and Diversity

Attempts to analyse change or continuity in marriage, family, or kinship are vitiated at the start if the manifold cultures and local variants in the articulated rules and values pertaining to marriage are not kept in mind. Diversity in marriage practices has long been grist for the anthropological mill, even as (both structural functional and structuralist) theorisations were directed at understanding underlying universal structures. In the south Asian and in particular the Indian context, these diversities were ordered into more localised patterns or structures. The arguments of Karve (1953), Dumont (1966), and Yalman (1971) were divergent as were their units of analysis and mappings. Yet, their common concern was to find 'the similarity in principles and the underlying identity in the essentials of the structure' (Yalman 1971: 8). Caste endogamy and hypergamy emerged as important organising principles in much of these works, which tended to focus on Hindus, their norms, and dominant practices.[5] Three critical distinctions figured repeatedly in these research works. One was the preference for consanguineous marriage such as cross-cousin and uncle-niece marriage among castes in South India, or parallel and cross-cousin marriage among Muslims as against the north Indian Hindu rule that proscribed marriage between close kin of varying degrees—from the seventh to the untraceable (clan). The second was that post-marriage residential rules among many matrilineal and bilateral groups in the Malabar, in the Northeast and in Sri Lanka, were not in accordance with a simple patrilocality. The third was the variation in marriage prestations between dowry and bride-price, which Tambiah (1973) mapped across the subcontinent, but which otherwise tended to be peripheral in the search for the structural features of marriage.

Yet, there is a range of diversities that has not been mapped even though the diversity of articulated rules is the most easily narrated. One reason was the dominance of the upper-caste Hindu and the tribe in the sociological and anthropological imaginations of India. Thus, in this volume, Abraham discusses the Thiyyas who were matrilineal but patrilocal, different from the dominant matrilineal, matrilocal Nayars, who have been the focus of much anthropological work. Another factor was that conjugal relations and their implications for women was a dimension of analysis for only a few scholars such as Karve (1953), Gough (1959), and later Dube (1986).

As gender gained importance in social science scholarship, the north-south divide in marriage practices gained analytical significance. Along with women's work patterns, constructs of this diversity were deployed to explain regional demographic patterns in sex ratios, age at marriage and female empowerment or the lack of it (Miller 1981; Dyson and Moore 1983). Today, the divergences in the gendered implications of this geo-cultural divide are being questioned as caste ideologies, the proscription or acceptance of widow remarriage, and domestic violence are examined (Ram 1992; Agarwal and Panda 2007) and presumptions associating gender equality and female autonomy with close kin marriage queried (Philips, this volume; Abraham, this volume). It becomes important then to recognise and find ways to move beyond descriptions of levels of diversity and homogeneity.

Mapping and analysing practices and strategies of marriage, especially their divergence from dominant norms, is not easy. It is known that whatever the rule, demography and internal stratification have meant a high rate of non-consanguineous marriages among groups who preferred cousin marriage (Trautmann 1981; Palriwala 1994). The imperative of the fit between practice and rule has never been universal across social groups. To this are added intra-group shifts in the strength of the imperative. How can we decide whether the exigency of this rule has grown or diminished among communities such as the south Indian Muslim *khandan* discussed by Vatuk (this volume)? Religion alone, is not what gives it symbolic force. For them strategies of consanguineous marriage maintain community identity and secular prestige within the community. With their small numbers, increasing geographic dispersal and internal differentiations they hold this identity and prestige dear. In addition, they believe that close-kin marriage enables conjugal compatibility and better adjusted families. Women may also prefer consanguineous daughters-in-law in the hope of labour (Ramamurthy, this volume) or care (Vera-Sanso 1999). That close-kin marriage constrains dowry has become a factor in sustaining consanguineous marriage for some (Vatuk, this volume; Joshi et al., this volume), but a reason to avoid it among the upwardly mobile. Kapadia (1993), for one, pointed to the weakening of the imperatives of the preferential rule by dowry, even as the ideology of kinship in which kin marriage is embedded may remain in place.

The greater class differentiation and the emergence of substantial middle classes affect the ways in which traditions of marriage are or are not changing. That lived experiences of marriage vary substantially by class and not only by caste, ethnicity or religion is captured in studies conducted in the nineties. The earlier focus on elite rules makes for difficulties in tracing change. In reading Grover (this volume), one wonders how much of the acceptance of and resistance to separation, divorce and remarriage among non-elite groups is new and how much a continuity of earlier non-documented practices. How much is it a diversity which could not be acknowledged or was silenced as unnecessary in understanding global principles or structures? There has, of course, long been an argument that among the non-elite, the lower castes, tribes, and the non-Hindu[6], divorce and remarriage are accepted and practised and widows are not stigmatised (Kolenda 2003; Parry 2001; Ilaiah 2001).[7] With modernisation and the spread of Hindu middle-class values of monogamy and chastity, this argument continues, these practices are endangered, while middle-class, upper-caste ideologies are renewed. Kumar's essay (this volume) on the Kolams, a tribe in east Maharashtra, does in part support this argument. Chuki's overview (this volume) of regional, class, and religious diversity and change in Bhutan, however, raises questions about the earlier autonomy of women as well as of simple readings of current directions of change or continuity. A new diversity seems to be emerging related to class and differential claims to modernity and individual fulfilment as well as claims of community, identity and the valorisation of tradition.

The various essays suggest that the articulated rules of partner selection have become muddied with the espousal of new 'modern' values of 'love' and 'choice'. These values may, however, work to strengthen the institutional nature and value of marriage (Lessinger, this volume; Kaur with Dhanda, this volume). This can be of particular significance through the role of marriage in boundary maintenance, i.e. endogamy within caste, community or class. On the one hand, this process works through the assertion of distinct identity and marriage rules. On the other, community boundaries appear to become porous in long distance marriage (Kaur 2004), in the practices of the urban working class (Lessinger, this volume; Grover, this volume) or a new transnational middle class (Kaur with Dhanda, this volume). Yet, marriage is the strategy not just for ensuring a working domesticity, but a strategy for upward mobility and/or class endogamy. This gives all the more force to the demand for a homogeneity within diversity—the aspiration and desire for the legal right to marry for those who have so far been seen beyond its pale, such as the gay subjects of Tellis' research (this volume).

Diversity in practice, continuation of tradition, and homogeneity of trends appear simultaneous when we look at age at marriage, a continuing concern to social scientists and policy-makers.[8] The actual practice varies with community and class within each country and there is a common trend of a rising age at marriage. Child marriage persists, however (Sagade 2005). Based on large data sets, as is true for much of the demographic work on marriage, Amin and Das (this volume) argue that early marriage in Bangladesh is not just a carryover from the past. It is a contemporary strategy to avoid or give a lesser dowry. Another take on the persistence of the 'tradition' of early marriage is that suggested by Andrist et al. also in this volume. They relate it to the clear gap between marriage and continuous cohabitation, a consequence of the ritually marked deferral of consummation among many social groups across the subcontinent. This custom has a contradictory impulse in contemporary times: it allows the performance of gendered scripts in accordance with traditional norms of marriage simultaneous with the fulfilment of modern goals of women's education.

Marital Prestations, Weddings, and Beyond

Among themes which have received substantial attention during the last two decades is that of marriage payments, in terms of the shift from bride-price to dowry, the spread of dowry, changes in its form, and the implications for women's value, gender relations, and marital relations (Palriwala 2009; Bradley et al. 2009). Studies have elaborated the manner in which the effects of dowry and the cultural compulsions of marital prestations are experienced throughout a women's life, starting even before birth.[9] Given that there is a large and continuing body of work on marital prestations, we have not focused on the issue in this volume. A brief discussion, however, is apposite to the questions we raise. Marriage practices are changing in the face of dowry. Contradictory processes emerge: endogamous and hypergamous compulsions lead to acceptance of dowry demands; with the desire for dowry, close-kin marriage is given the go-by; in long-distance marriages endogamous rules may be violated simultaneous with the ability to avoid dowry (Kaur 2004). The debate on dowry, as female inheritance, takes on a new meaning today as large dowries may accompany the marriage of educated, urban daughters, or as migrant women negotiate better marriages for themselves due to their ability to pay dowries they have earned for themselves (Gallo 2008). Educated women may see dowry as a substitute if a share in ancestral property remains elusive, either due to law or practice. Across most religious communities, few women exercise their legal rights to parental property. They do not wish to jeopardise their relationship with their brothers—an implicit but important source of support in case of marital difficulties. Even as workers and earners, the significance of dowry and marriage as markers of women's value is sustained.

Analytically and socially, the ritual and symbolic dimensions of marriage are where tradition is asserted, though the performance may carry meanings other than in the past. Along with dowry, expenditure on marriage celebrations has been increasing and marriage ceremonies have become extended rather than abbreviated, particularly among the upper and middle classes. In making the wedding and thence the marriage, the matchmaker, the priest and the notary have now been joined by the photographer or videographer (Abraham 2010). The latter not only records the marriage for posterity, the created record lends the marriage legitimacy and reifies the 'correct performance of rituals'. Of equal if not greater importance has been the influence of popular media in creating or perpetuating a homogenised 'ideal' and 'idealised' wedding (Uberoi 1998). The occasional proclamations of caste bodies against excessive marriage expenditure remain just that for the conspicuous display of wealth serves as an expression of new or old status (Palriwala 2009; Kalpagam 2008). The commercialisation of weddings in a culture in which marriage remains of supreme importance is supported by a market-oriented economy in which 'tradition' is a source of profit.

The discussions on dowry have been particularly tied to the issue of 'bride burnings' and has both enabled and obscured the issue of marital violence. Women's groups have been active on both issues, though unevenly so, across time and place (Palriwala 2009). Importantly, there has been a tendency for studies to focus on the violence per se. Unwittingly perhaps, this feeds into the idea that this violence is a pathology rather than embedded in the cultural and political economy of contemporary marriage, kinship and gender. A critique of the perceived 'normality' of marriage and gender practices has entered the frame in some studies of 'honour killings' seen primarily in certain regions of the subcontinent such as parts of Pakistan and northern India (Chowdhry 2007; Hossain and Welchman 2006; Saheli 2007; Kaur 2010). This violence is directed towards young women or couples, who are seen as violating norms of endogamy or exogamy or resisting the social control of marriage by choosing their own partners and defying parental and community authority in the process.

Economies of Marriage and Work

In understanding contemporary marriage, it is necessary to move away from simple modernisation theses to a political and cultural economy of marriage. Systems of production, work organisation, class structures and caste hierarchies underwrite and are made through cultural arrangements for social reproduction. Capitalist development and globalisation have affected and used forms, dynamics and strategies of marriage and implicit and explicit conjugal contracts. In the process, gender equations, conjugality and love also get re-written.

In plantation economies and small-holder farming, the imperatives to marry are changing with economic transformations and shifts in the labour force, but remain significant to all generations especially where extended family-household norms have social, cultural, and material value (Philips this volume; Ramamurthy, this volume). Marriage controls and harnesses a woman's sexuality and gives rights to her labour, her earnings and linked benefits. Specific marriage forms carry cultural value, but also have instrumental importance, whether by assuring housing (Philips) or specific skills (Ramamurthy).

Women's value as workers and earners is exploited by parents, in-laws or by relatives for whom they may be preferred brides. Rather than lose labour and income, a daughter's marriage may be delayed (Still 2011; Lessinger, this volume). Or the girl's labour is acquired through the promise of marriage or marriage expenses (Ramamurthy, this volume). The economics of kin and non-kin marriages are debated. On the one hand, class endogamy, dowry or labour needs may take precedence over kin obligations. On the other hand, the possibility of deferment of economic exchanges may encourage kin marriage (Joshi et al., this volume). This is not without discussion, however, of a match in terms of compatibility and personal happiness, as Vatuk (this volume) also found.

The values and ideologies of love, romance and self-choice in marriage are evident everywhere, and new work spaces appear to be particularly conducive to new imaginings. Many of the women studied by Lessinger (this volume), employed in Chennai's garment factories, have entered 'love marriages', weakening the authority of the older generation (Dharmalingam 1994). Parental consent remains important, however, and may depend on implicit economic reasoning as well as the importance of family values and ties. Indeed the desire for marriage is embedded in the hopes of both a sexual and a familial life, enabling thereby the contradictory pulls of conjugal and filial intimacies. Some poor parents condone and even encourage such self-arranged marriages. They are relieved of the onus of matchmaking and giving dowry, seen also in the 'love *kaliyaanam*' among Sri Lankan Muslims (De Munck 1996) and the urban poor in Kolkata (Sen et al. 2009). That the new freedoms are not an unalloyed joy for women is evident when working women are subjected to the suspicions of husbands or prospective suitors. Their romantic relationships are considered morally questionable, especially if they do not end in marriage (Hettiarachchy and Schensul 2001; Philips, this volume).

The conflict between the lure or necessity of work and fulfilling marital and maternal obligations is largely discussed as a problem faced by middle-class women across South Asia. It is as much if not more, a problem faced by poor women who go out to work. Male unemployment and consumption aspirations make women's earnings important in family strategies. Yet, let aside equality, the sharing of domestic responsibilities largely remains a distant dream. An independent income with freedom and access to a world beyond the marital home can be compensation for some women. Anwar's discussion (this volume) of the various strata of employed middle class women in Karachi highlights an issue that deserves attention: the re-negotiations of domestic responsibilities between spouses and within the extended family (Mukhopadhyay and Sudarshan 2003). Through her study we learn that children are mostly taken care of by relatives (maternal and paternal); however, women feel less obligated if they depend on servants and not on family members for child care. While this contrasts with the findings of other studies and conventional wisdom that family members are the preferred replacement carers, it draws attention to another aspect of intimate relations. The repeated assertion of the strength of family and kinship is simultaneous with the knowledge that these are relationships that must not be overburdened. This is especially true for women who do not conform to gendered norms in domestic roles.

Making a Marriage

Are contemporary marriages modern or democratic? The prior question we must ask is, 'What is a modern marriage?' If we take self-choice and pre-marital courtship as the defining criteria, as do young residents of Thimpu, Bhutan (Chuki, this volume) and many others, can we see a trend towards modernity in South Asia? Or are there diverse modernities? One route to addressing this question is by observing the changes in matchmaking and examining how they reflect changes in the expectations from and desires in marriage of families and couples. In such an attempt, essays in this volume pay attention to strategies of parents in arranging marriages but also to those of the marrying individuals.

Two kinds of changes can be delineated here—in matchmakers and in the criteria of matchmaking. Both sets of changes have been driven by a variety of factors: migration, urbanisation, rising educational levels and greater socio-economic differentiation within traditionally endogamous groups. The majority of marriages continue to be arranged by parents or older siblings, relying on the extended family, acquaintances, work colleagues, neighbours and other individuals who they come into contact with. If no suitable match is found, they turn to other intermediaries such as marriage bureaus, fairs, newspaper matrimonial advertisements and, more recently, internet-based marriage websites (Kaur with Dhanda, this volume).

Majumdar (2009) shows how urbanisation and the decline of the traditional Bengali *ghatak* (the matchmaker) led to the rise of newspaper advertisements for matchmaking among the colonial and post-colonial urban middle class of Kolkata. The 'modernised' matchmaking mode, however, was also accompanied by the emergence of a new domesticated model for Bengali women, a demand for dowry and decline in women's status. Studies of newspaper advertisements and website profiles reveal gendered changes with a growing emphasis on the physical attractiveness of women. This reproduces the normative distinctions in the roles and attributes of women and men. Earlier matchmaking criteria such as caste, language, region and religion continue, even with a new stress on class indicators such as education, occupation and income (Chauhan 2007; Shukla and Kapadia 2007; Kaur with Dhanda, this volume).

With globalisation, diasporic communities desirous of 'traditional' marriages have grown. Retaining ties back home and re-stitching communities fractured by migration are important goals of transnational marriages (Palriwala and Uberoi 2008; Maunaguru, this volume). Different means are used to do so. Tamil Sri Lankans depend on kinship networks and professional agents to provide details of prospective partners as well as overcome immigration hurdles. Non-resident Indians tap into anonymous internet sites that bring together couples from the same community residing in various parts of the globe. In the process, caste, religious and national identities are imbricated in new professional identities and aspirations.

Over the decades, arranged marriage has begun to accommodate the increasing role and interest of the marrying individual in spouse selection. This entails a much more complex process of matching familial and individual goals (Kalpagam 2008; Donner 2002; Fuller and Narasimhan 2008; Kaur with Dhanda, this volume). Self-arranged (or love) marriages are not as rare anymore; it is at the two opposite ends of the economic spectrum—the working and upper classes—that they seem more frequent. While there is some ethnographic work on such marriages among the working poor and middle classes, there is much less work on upper-class love marriages, perhaps signalling the difficulties of doing fieldwork among the upper classes. The factors driving love marriages among different social classes are often quite different. An unstudied aspect of such marriages is the extent to which they cross boundaries of caste, region, religion and language, and whether these crossings break earlier social rigidities.

Love and Conjugality in and beyond Marriage

Rubin's (1975) critique of kinship studies centered on the heteronormative 'exchange of women' that underlay its theorisation and models. A more general critique of structuralism questioned the reduction of social persons to ciphers—mere signs, rather than active agents. Subsequently, studies that privileged practice and agency as keys in sociological understanding examined the making of marital matches as a critical dimension in the (re)making of structures (Bourdieu 1977). However, the internal workings of a marital relationship—both institutionalised and structured expectations of conjugality—and the experience and emotion of that relationship tended not to be at issue (except in the event of the breakdown of marriage, see next section). From today's vantage point, with gender and sexuality taking centre-stage in marriage discourse, it is amazing that there was so little focus by the social scientists on the meanings and contours of intimacy and desire (Trawick 1990). This had a lot to do with the assumption of a 'normative conjugality' (Abraham, this volume) in a functioning marriage—a hegemonic, heterosexual model. It also had much to do with viewing experience as individual and emotions as subjective. Not only were they perceived as difficult to study other than through attitudinal surveys or psychological studies,[10] but were also seen as telling us little of significance in delineating structures.

A number of essays in this volume make a foray beyond the mere fact of conjugality, some directly, some indirectly. They look at its various elements as well as the changing contours of emotion and desire which it encompasses. The social and cultural expectations that the two spouses have of each other and which society has of them as a couple vary with rules and practices of descent and inheritance. Thus, the 'providing husband' has been part of the marital ethos of the matrilineal Thiyya. Among matrilineal and bilateral groups, even where ideologies of the male breadwinner and household head or virilocality and the providing husband operate, a woman's rights to property and/or her right of return and residence in her natal home were important in the experience of conjugality (Abraham, this volume). More easily than in patrilineal contexts, women could draw on the support of natal kin within and beyond marriage. This was also true in close-kin marriage or where the natal kin of the spouses lived in close proximity (Kolenda 1967, 1968; Grover, this volume) or where divorce was not stigmatised (Kumar, this volume). Another aspect, discussed by Kumar is his finding among the Kolam tribe of eastern Maharashtra that despite the hope for sexual fidelity, infidelity is accepted. In easing the problems of insecurity and economic vulnerability, the space for negotiation within the marriage altered and thence the experience of conjugality did as well.

The everyday expectations and experience of conjugality work, perhaps increasingly so, within or under the shadow of models projected by the elite, the powerful and the media. Thus, the diverse conjugal models that communities upheld may be derogated, as was the case among various tribes as also polyandrous groups in the Himalayas (see Chuki, this volume) and among the Nayars. In the face of conjoined Victorian and Brahmanical values and the colonial project, values of individual, male property rights went hand-in-hand with a stress on the co-resident, nuclear, conjugal family unit, male authority, and lifelong monogamy and fidelity on the part of the women. The practice of conjugality, however, still diverges from the dominant model. Class is a critical factor. Among the middle class, family mobility goals or women's aspirations for a life beyond the home may deny the 'male breadwinner' model in practice, while retaining it as a value in the everyday of conjugality (Anwar, this volume). For the poor, the idea of a 'providing husband' is denied in both practice and articulation (Lessinger, this volume; Grover, this volume). Even in communities who value co-residence as an essential aspect of conjugality and familial relations, it may not be possible for the poor or new migrant. For poor women, the public acknowledgement of a socially sanctioned male partner is critical in their desire for a marriage, but so is the emotional confidence and support that a sexual companionship provides. Grover finds that a serial monogamous practice may emerge, with separation and remarriage entailing a careful balance of social criticism and approval.

Marriage and conjugality are also about support and care and the absence of either may be experienced as the absence of the proper emotion towards the partner (Lemons, this volume). The instrumental and the emotional are not distinct in conjugality or in the hopes of family life. The gendered division of labour, which heterosexual marriage remains tied to, is linked to social and material aspirations, ideas of a good marriage, and expressions of love. It is perhaps with this realisation that some young Bhutanese assert that the quality of the conjugal relationship and women's position were not very different in love or arranged marriage (Chuki, this volume).

Notions of love marriage and individualisation are intertwined and have gained a political valency. They are linked to democracy and modernity—love being viewed as an emotion that is about free, individual choice. Rather than family expectations and community norms, love is to provide the basis of marriage, thereby ensuring a personally satisfying conjugality. In their discussions on love and love marriage, three of the contributors—Lessinger, Grover and Tellis—address both the institutional patterning and public sanctioning of personal, sexual relations and the experiential and emotional expectations of that relationship. Economic independence on the part of either the woman or man may enable them to flout familial pressures and enter a love marriage. Where this is not the case or where familial ties are still intact, the burden of conforming to the norms of a properly arranged marriage falls on the young bride. She realises that her conjugal relationship remains embedded in family and the dictates of survival (Ramamurthy, this volume; Lemons, this volume). Young Tamil women who work in the garment industry want love, and also want marriage with contradictory views on whether it is love or marriage which is more important (Lessinger, this volume). Evidentially, love marriage is also about instrumentalities; self-arranged is a better description as the match avoids the costs of the properly arranged marriage, ensures a legal, conjugal tie that 'traditional' ways cannot succeed in ensuring (Kaur with Dhanda, this volume) and provides an escape from a natal family in which men were not fulfilling the contract of support (Lessinger, this volume). The hegemonic nature of the ideology that sexual love is proper love only when embedded in marriage and that marriage is the basis of social citizenship becomes apparent even when we move beyond heteronormative relationships. As Tellis finds, the aspiration of many of his gay informants, as also gay rights advocates and academics, is of a conjugality embedded in the institution of marriage. It would appear that the legality of the latter, the conjugal division of roles and of practices, indeed the emotional model of marriage, are difficult to question except in their links to heterosexuality and caste/community boundaries.

Activism and Legal Interventions

The British colonial state separated personal from criminal and civil laws in the parts of the subcontinent under its direct rule (i.e. excluding only Nepal and Bhutan). The assumption was that personal law derived from community and religious law. This rested to a large extent on the articulation of an apparent separation of a domain wherein the state was the warrantor of public order and one where community values were to prevail. In fact, each drew on the authority of the other where convenient—order in the private and order in the public being integral to each other. Thus, the regulation of inheritance, adoption, marriage, divorce and guardianship were not untouched or unchanged, as we see in Abraham's discussion of the matrilineal communities of Malabar. Victorian values entered into the administering of 'personal' laws and their legislation, particularly in their intersection with spheres under the jurisdiction of criminal law.[11] What has been less recognised is the existence of a range of practices, formal and informal, contrary to 'official' and dominant views. Holden's (2008) study in central India argues that separation and customary divorce have been less uncommon than have been recognised in lay and academic discourses.[12] Essays in this volume also draw our attention to procedures that lie outside the formal legal system (Lemons), but wherein people vie to demonstrate the sanction of state institutions (Grover).

At various times, nationalist and women's movements as well as religious and caste associations agitated for legal reform or a reiteration of tradition, often recast or reinterpreted, in the domain of marriage. Issues of the legal age at marriage and age of consent, polygamy, marriage prohibitions, dowry and domestic violence have been raised. Ideas of the naturalness and sanctity of kinship, heterosexual marriage and the conjugal tie, and familial relations as well as of custom and tradition have often been in conflict with concerns regarding women's rights and gender equality. Social unease due to perceived trends in family and divorce, as well as activist mobilisations have focused on the issues at stake at the end of marriage—widows' rights to property and remarriage, divorced women's rights to residence, maintenance, division of property and wealth transferred at marriage or accumulated during its life, guardianship, and fears of weakening patriarchal control. Among most Hindus, in India and in Nepal, a ritual stigma reinforces the social stigma of widowhood (Habakazi, this volume; Chen 1998). The possibilities of remarriage vary with caste and region despite social reform and women's movements. The Shah Bano case in 1984 brought much of this discussion to a head. It was an important reminder that marriage and the process of ending or living outside marriage remain closely tied to issues of identity and community, in particular, religion and caste. Crucially, what is also evident from various studies is that despite differences in personal law and religious sanctions there is a commonality across community lines in the experience of divorced (and widowed) women (Jeffery 2001; Hossain 2003).

What becomes evident in many of the essays in this volume is the power of marriage and the dread of what lies outside it; that they are deeply embedded, and indeed support a gendered cultural and political economy. Rights to residence and parental property do make a difference to women, as Abraham's discussion of the matrilineal Thiyya brings out, though the idea of the 'providing husband' is strong. More widely, however, the absence of secure rights to property—whether as daughters or wives—and women's lack of access to and cultural restrictions on their engagement in paid employment, cuts across caste, religion and most sub-regions. The abjurement of paid work for women has become part of the ethos of the upwardly mobile among those groups in which it was not an issue earlier—such as tribes and Dalits—while property is not available to men or women in these groups. Thus, the economic dependence of women, the sanctity of marriage, and the social stigma attached to widowhood and divorce are central to the cultural politics of marriage in South Asia.

This brings us to a constant issue: ambiguity and inconsistency as characteristics of agency in the intimate sphere and particularly of female agency, given that in the present world the personal continues as its main locale.[13] Lemons, in her essay, recounts a case wherein the wife complains of years of willful abandonment by her husband. Yet, she expresses her readiness to live with him should he return. Working-class Dalit women in Delhi may exercise freedom in leaving unsatisfactory marriages, but are constrained by community norms, and their informal re-marriages are highly unstable (Grover, this volume). This ambivalence is evident at the end of a marriage but also runs through its life. Thus, middle-class women in Karachi, married in traditionally arranged marriages, are concerned with being good wives, mothers and daughters-in-law. They also desire the personal satisfaction and pocket money for individual indulgences that paid work outside the home brings them, but admit to the fact with hesitation (Anwar, this volume). Indian middle-class professional women widen their horizons in spouse selection by encouraging parents to post their profiles on marriage websites (Kaur with Dhanda, this volume). Young Bhutanese want romance but with security (Chuki, this volume).

Unpacking agency is a complex process. Kalpagam (2008), for instance, makes the point that 'choice' need not be read necessarily as self-choice or love marriage, but also the ability to say no to a particular match. In a reflexive essay on resistance in contemporary Hindu arranged marriages, Chawla (2009) portrays 'silence' and what she calls 'material embodied resistance' as strategies of middle-class urban women. They redefine marriage for themselves while continuing to live in joint families. Agency and choice can only be understood contextually.

Many activists in South Asia emphasise that bad marriages abound and excoriate the current patriarchal contract embedded in marriage. Yet, as Tellis writes, marriage as an institution is rarely questioned. A variety of women's organisations and feminist groups have intervened in demanding legal reform, but also in providing legal aid and in arbitrating marital disputes and breakdown. Negotiation, rather than confrontation or explicit rejection, is the favoured strategy, even when women are in court. Basu (this volume) found that women appointed as social workers in the family courts in Kolkata saw themselves as protagonists of women's rights enabling individuals to return to their marriages, even previously violent ones.

None of this can be surprising in itself, given the nigh universality of marriage and the extent to which women and persons of marginalised sexualities desire marriage or the right to it. Instead, it points us to at least two persisting debates, other than the ambiguities of agency in the personal sphere discussed above. These have direct implications for policy and activism. One is regarding the workings of the legal pluralities that informal arbitration procedures create and whether these loosen or reify the gendering of the institution of marriage, as discussed in Basu's and Grover's respective essays.

The other is whether social change can be led by legal reform (Mazumdar 2000; Menon 1999). Globally, state law is critical in acknowledging a marriage and the rights and protections that accrue to individuals in the making or dissolution of marriage, even as legalised marriage may be on the decline in many cultures. In South Asia, law and state policy are pre-eminent sites in the battle for new mores and possibilities in gender and social relations (Mody 2008) in which governments and administrators subvert state law in the name of social values claimed by community hegemons (Chowdhry 2007). Given its intermeshing with the public order, those who contest the gender regime cannot but call on the state to match its rhetoric with concrete action, despite the knowledge that the state's interests may not be conducive to a reworked personal order.

The discussions in various essays indicate that struggles toward a new social and legal contract in marriage need to go hand-in-hand and also enable life outside marriage for those who so choose. Attempts to institute a new model *nikahnama* may appear of marginal efficacy in the face of women's economic dependence and the social values upheld in informal religious courts (as also in the family courts). They do, however, create a new language and knowledge (Lemons, this volume). They act in the social, if not the legal, sphere. Habakazi elaborates on the attempts by Ekal Mahila Samuha, an NGO representing single women to 'empower' widows in Nepal by confronting cultural and social discriminations through widows' groups and by accessing government programmes for training and economic opportunities. She points to the paradox that appears both inevitable and self-created; in working with the cultural signs of marriage and auspiciousness that had discriminated against widows, are their efforts condemned to reinforce them? This suggests another concern. Is it possible to retain marriage as an institution or a relationship without the social, sexual, economic, cultural and political hierarchies that have been integral to it thus far?

Conclusion: Whither Marriage?

Can we see a trend towards the democratisation of marriage as more people choose their own partners through pre-marital courtship, and as the termination of unhappy marriages through divorce becomes more common? Do trends in contemporary south Asian marriage reflect multiple modernities? Positive answers to these questions would certainly be in keeping with liberal, middle-class expectations and behaviours displayed in English magazines and society pages of newspapers. It is nowhere near the whole picture. Rather, we need to factor in the institutional dimensions and practice of marriage, as well as the internal dynamics and experience of the relationship.

What comes to the fore is both the stickiness of rules in 'intimate practices' and their role in mediating socio-economic processes such as labour organisation in agriculture, aspirations to work or consumption, rights to and acquisition of property, or the making of transnational communities—the cultural and political economy of marriage. The interpolations of marriage and gender relations may be shifting, but the languages and forms of tradition are invoked. The institutional hierarchies of marriage are not external to modernity. The decriminalisation of homosexuality in India is too recent for us to be able to know its implications.[14] Studies of non-marriage and the never married, intimacy inside and outside marriage, homosocial, homosexual, and (non-marital) heterosocial bonds are few. Yet, research on widows and on divorce indicates the continuing hegemony of marriage as a pre-condition for social citizenship, especially for women. Practices of spousal selection and parental authority, ideas and practices of conjugality and ideals of domesticity, among other aspects, demonstrate the centrality of the institution and relationships of marriage to strategies of life, mobility and healing in South Asia.

The introduction and this volume examines how marriage may be affected by varied socio-economic and political processes, some of which are captured in the shorthand term of globalisation: the increased migration of men and women, both voluntary and in the face of civil war, new commercialisations and globalisation in agriculture, the expansion of the middle class and the rise of consumerism, the growing involvement of middle-class women and poor young women in non-household paid work in cities, the advent of new communication technologies and new support groups, activism on issues of gender equality and alternative sexualities, fuelled partly by AIDS-related funding and partly by a wider access to and circulation of cultural and political ideas of individual choice and rights. The last have a long genealogy in varied social movements. The difficulty that we track is that directions of change, for what they are, are not unilinear. Indeed, trends are infinitely more complex than the dual society which Srinivas (1993) saw as emerging in India. Whether there is an increasing or lessening diversity in practice or ideology, and less or more space for alternative models and practices need further exploration.

Notes

[1] See Bloch et al. (2004), Banerjee et al. (2009), Mathur (2007) among others.

[2] See the numerous annotations in Chaudhry et al. (2010) on such applied research in Bangladesh, Pakistan and Nepal.

[3] See Chandra (2008), Chowdhry (1994, 2007), Oldenburg (2002), Majumdar (2009) for some examples of analyses that focus on colonial influence in the legal interpretation of the rights of wives, widows, or daughters and the privileging of the subordinate role of the 'economically unproductive' woman.

[4] See Gough (1959) for an early debate on defining marriage.

[5] See Palriwala (1994) for a more elaborate discussion of this issue; also see Uberoi (1993: 45–49).

[6] The Hindu was taken to include Sikh and Jain, but not the Buddhist in the north, east or south of the subcontinent. Muslims were barely acknowledged in this line of argument.

[7] This is in addition to practices on the 'margins of Hindu marriage' (Harlan and Courtright 1995).

[8] The legal minimum age for marriage in all south Asian countries has changed and today ranges between 21 for men and 18 for women (Bangladesh), 18 for both (Bhutan, India, Nepal, Sri Lanka), and 16 for women and 18 for men in Pakistan.

[9] Dowry and marriage prestations have been and continue to be of interest to social scientists.

[10] For a recent contribution by a psychologist, see Sandhya (2009).

[11] See Chandra (2008) on the restitution of conjugal rights; Chowdhry (1994) on widows' rights to inheritance; Mani (1998) on the practice of *sati*.

[12] This is also true for non-extended family-household living, such that imputed trends of a decline need to be complicated.

[13] Khandelwal's questioning (2009) of the binary of love and arranged marriage mapped on to North America and South Asia respectively suggests the complexity of agency in the 'personal', shaped through the interweaving of desire, pragmatic concerns and institutional factors.

[14] In late 2013, the Supreme Court upheld the law criminalising homosexuality.

References

Abraham, Janaki. 2010. 'Wedding Videos in North Kerala: Technologies, Rituals, and Ideas about Love and Conjugality'. *Visual Anthropology Review* 26 (2): 116–27.

Agarwal, Bina, and Pradeep Panda. 2007. 'Toward Freedom from Domestic Violence: The Neglected Obvious'. *Journal of Human Development* 8 (3): 359–88.

Arunima, G. 2003. *There Comes Papa: Colonialism and the Transformation of Matriliny in Kerala, Malabar, c.1850–1940*. New Delhi: Orient Longman.

Banerjee, Abhijit, Esther Duflo, Maitreesh Ghatak, and Jeanne Lafortune. 2009. 'Marry for What: Caste and Mate Selection in Modern India'. *NBER Working Paper* No. 14958.

Blanchet, Therese. 2008. 'Bangladeshi Girls Sold as Wives in North India'. In *Marriage, Migration and Gender*, ed. Rajni Palriwala and Patricia Uberoi. New Delhi: SAGE Publications.

Bloch, F., S. Desai, and V. Rao. 2004. 'Wedding Celebrations as Conspicuous Consumption: Signalling Social Status in Rural India'. *Journal of Human Resources* 39 (3): 675–95.

Borneman, John. 1996. 'Until Death Do Us Part: Marriage/Death in Anthropological Discourse'. *American Ethnologist* 23 (2): 215–35.

Bourdieu, Pierre. 1977. *Outline of a Theory of Practice*. Cambridge: Cambridge University Press.

Bradley, T. E. Tomalin, and M. Subramaniam (eds). 2009. *Dowry: Bridging the Gap Between Theory and Practice*. New Delhi: Women Unlimited.

Chandra, Sudhir. 2008. *Enslaved Daughters: Colonialism, Law and Women's Rights*. New Delhi: Oxford University Press.

Chaudhry, S., A. Majumdar, R. Kaur, and R. Palriwala. 2010. '*Marriage in Globalizing Contexts: Exploring Change and Continuity in South Asia: An Annotated Bibliography*'. Mimeo. New Delhi: UNICEF.

Chawla, Devika. 2009. 'I Will Speak Out: Narratives of Resistance in Contemporary Indian Women's Discourses in Hindu Arranged Marriages'. *Women and Language* 30 (1): 5–19.

Chauhan, Richa. 2007. 'Seeking a Suitable Match: Economic Development, Gender, and Matrimonial Advertisements in India'. In *Recent Studies on Indian Women: Empirical Work of Social Scientists*, eds. Kamal K. Misra and Janet Hubry Lowry, Jaipur: Rawat Publications.

Chen, Martha. 1998. *Widows in India*. New Delhi: Sage Publications.

Chowdhry, Prem. 2007. *Contentious Marriages, Eloping Couples: Gender, Caste, and Patriarchy in Northern India*. New Delhi: Oxford University Press.

———. 2004. 'Private Lives, State Intervention: Cases of Runaway Marriage in Rural North India'. *Modern Asian Studies* 38 (1): 55–84.

———. 1994. *The Veiled Women*. New Delhi: Oxford University Press.

Cohn, Bernard. 1987. *An Anthropologist Among the Historians and Other Essays*. New Delhi: Oxford University Press.

Collier, J. F., and S. J. Yanagisako (eds.). 1987. *Gender and Kinship: Essays towards a Unified Analysis*. Stanford: Stanford University Press.

Das, Veena. 1976. 'Masks and Faces: An Essay on Punjabi Kinship'. *Contributions to Indian Sociology* 10 (1): 1–30.

———. 1975. 'Marriage among the Hindus'. In *Indian Women*, ed. Devaki Jain. New Delhi: Publication Division, Ministry of Information and Broadcasting, Government of India.

De Munck, Victor. 1996. 'Love and Marriage in a Sri Lankan Muslim Community: Towards a Re-evaluation of Dravidian Marriage Practices'. *American Ethnologist* 23 (4): 698–716.

Derett, J. D. M. 1978. *The Death of a Marriage Law: Epitaph for the Rishis*. Durham, NC: Carolina Academic Press.

Dharmalingam, A. 1994. 'Economics of Marriage Change in a south Indian Village'. *Development and Change* 25 (3): 569–90.

Donner, Henrike. 2002. 'One's Own Marriage: Love Marriage in a Calcutta Neighbourhood'. *South Asia Research* 22 (1): 79–94.

Dube, L. 1986. 'Seed and Earth: The Symbolism of Biological Reproduction and Sexual Relations of Reproduction'. In *Essays on Power and Visibility: Essays on Women in Society and Development*, ed. L. Dube, E. Leacock, and S. Ardener. Delhi: Oxford University Press.

———. 1974. *Sociology of Kinship: An Analytical Survey of the Literature*. Bombay: Popular Prakashan.

Dumont, L. 1966. 'Marriage in India. The Present State of the Question III: North India in Relation to South India'. *Contributions to Indian Sociology* 9:90–114.

______. 1957. 'Hierarchy and Marriage Alliance in South Indian Kinship'. *Occasional Papers of the Royal Anthropological Institute of Great Britain and Ireland* 12. London: RAI.

Dyson, T., and M. Moore. 1983. 'On Kinship Structure: Female Autonomy and Demographic Behaviour in India'. *Population and Development Review* 9 (1): 35–60.

Fortes, Meyer. 1962. 'Introduction'. In *Marriage in Tribal Societies*, ed. Meyer Fortes. Cambridge: Cambridge University Press.

Fricke, Tom, Sobiha H. Syed, and Peter C. Smith. 1986. 'Rural Punjabi Social Organization and Marriage Timing in Pakistan'. *Demography* 23(4): 489–508.

Fruzzetti, Lina M. 1982. *The Gift of a Virgin: Women, Marriage and Ritual in a Bengali Society*. New Brunswick, NJ: Rutgers University Press.

Fruzzetti, Lina, and Akos Ostor. 1984. *Kinship and Ritual in Bengal: Anthropological Essays*. New Delhi: South Asia Books.

Fuller, C. J., and H. Narasimhan. 2008. 'Companionate Marriage in India: The Changing Marriage System in a Middle-Class Brahman Subcaste'. *Journal of the Royal Anthropological Institute* 14:736–54.

Gallo, Ester. 2008. 'Unorthodox Sisters: Gender Relations and Generational Change in Malayali Transnational Marriages' in Rajni Palriwala and Patricia Uberoi (eds). *Marriage, Migration and Gender*. New Delhi: Sage Publications.

Goode, W. J. 1970. *World Revolution and Family Patterns*. New York: The Free Press.

Goody, J., and S. J. Tambiah. 1974. *Bridewealth and Dowry*. Cambridge: Cambridge University Press.

Gough, K. 1959. 'Brahmin Kinship in a Tamil Village'. *American Anthropologist* 8 (5): 826–53.

Grover, Shalini. 2012. *Marriage, Love, Caste & Kinship Support: Lived Experiences of the Urban Poor in India*. New Delhi: Social Science Press.

Harlan, Lindsey, and Paul Courtright (eds.). 1995. *From the Margins of Hindu Marriage: Essays on Gender, Religion and Culture*. New York: Oxford University Press.

Hettiarachchy, T., and S. Schensul. 2001. 'The Risks of Pregnancy and the Consequences among Young Unmarried Women Working in a Free Trade Zone in Sri Lanka'. *Asia Pacific Journal* 16 (2): 125–40.

Holden, Livia. 2008. *Hindu Divorce: A Legal Anthropology*. Aldershot: Ashgate.

Hossain, Kamrul. 2003. 'In Search of Equality: Marriage Related Laws for Muslim Women in Bangladesh'. *Journal of International Women's Studies* 5 (1): 96–113.

Hossain, Sara, and Lynn Welchman (eds.). 2006. *"Honour": Crimes, Paradigms and Violence against Women*. New Delhi: Zubaan.

Ilaiah, Kancha. 2001. *Why I am Not a Hindu: A Sudra Critique of Hindutva Philosophy, Culture and Political Economy*. New Delhi: Samya (an imprint of Bhaktal and Sen).

Inden, Ronald, and Ralph Nicholas. 2005. *Kinship in Bengali Culture*. New Delhi: Chronicle Books.

Jeffery, Patricia, and Roger Jeffery. 1996. *Don't Marry Me to a Plowman! Women's Everyday Lives in Rural North India*. Boulder, Colorado: Westview Press.

Jeffery, Patricia. 2001. 'A Uniform Customary Code? Marital Breakdown and Women's Economic Entitlements in Rural Bijnor'. *Contributions to Indian Sociology* 35 (1): 1–32.

John, Mary, Ravinder Kaur, Rajni Palriwala, Saraswati Raju, and Alpana Sagar. 2008. *Planning Families, Planning Gender: The Adverse Child Sex Ratio in Selected Districts of Madhya Pradesh, Rajasthan, Himachal Pradesh, Haryana and Punjab*. Bangalore: Books for Change for ActionAid and IDRC.

Kalpagam, U. 2008. 'Marriage Norms, Choices and Aspirations of Rural Women'. *Economic and Political Weekly* 42 (21): 53–63.

Kapadia, Karin. 1993. 'Marrying Money: Changing Preference and Practice in Tamil Marriage'. *Contributions to Indian Sociology* 27 (1): 25–51.

Karve, Irawati. 1953. *Kinship Organization in India*. New York: Asia Publishing House.

Kaur, Ravinder. 2010. 'Khap Panchayats, Sex Ratio and Female Agency'. *Economic and Political Weekly* 45 (23): 14–16.

———. 2004. 'Across Region Marriages: Poverty, Female Migration and the Sex Ratio', *Economic and Political Weekly* 39 (25): 2595–630.

Khandelwal, Meena. 2009. 'Arranging Love: Interrogating the Vantage Point in Cross-Border Feminism'. *Signs: Journal of Women in Culture and Society* 34 (3): 583–609.

Kolenda, Pauline. 2003. 'Living the Levirate'. In *Caste, Marriage and Inequality: Studies from North and South India*, ed. Pauline Kolenda. Jaipur and New Delhi: Rawat.

———. 1968. 'Region, Caste and Family Structure: A Comparative Study of the Indian 'Joint' Family'. In *Structure and Change in Indian Society*, ed. M. Singer and B. Cohn. New York: Wenner-Gren Foundation for Anthropological Research.

———. 1967. 'Regional Differences in Indian Family Structure'. In '*Regions and Regionalism in South Asian Studies: An Exploratory Study*', ed. Robert I. Crane. Durham, NC: Duke University Press.

Madan, T. N. 1993. 'The Hindu Family and Development'. In *Family, Kinship and Marriage in India*. ed. Patricia Uberoi. New Delhi: Oxford University Press.

———. 1975. 'Structural Implications of Marriage in North India: Wife-givers and Wife-takers Among the Pandits of Kashmir'. *Contributions to Indian Sociology* 9 (2): 217–44.

Majumdar, Rochona. 2009. *Marriage and Modernity: Family Values in Colonial Bengal*. New Delhi: Oxford University Press.

Mandelbaum, David. 1988. *Women's Seclusion and Men's Honour: Sex Roles in North India, Bangladesh and Pakistan*. Tucson: University of Arizona Press.

Mani, Lata. 1998. *Contentious Traditions: The Debate on Sati in Colonial India*. Berkeley: University of California Press.

Mathur, Divya. 2007. *What's Love Got to Do with It? Parental Involvement and Spouse Choice in Urban India*. Available at SSRN: http://ssrn.com/abstract=1655998 or http://dx.doi.org/10.2139/ssrn.1655998. Accessed on: 22 March 2013.

Mazumdar, V. 2000. '*Political Ideology of the Women's Movement's Engagement with Law*', Occasional Paper 34. New Delhi: Centre for Women's Development Studies.

Menon, N. 1999. 'Introduction'. In *Gender and Politics in India*, ed. N. Menon. New Delhi: Oxford University Press.

Miller, Barbara D. 1981. *The Endangered Sex: Neglect of Female Children in Rural North India*. Ithaca: Cornell University Press.

Mody, Perveez. 2008. *The Intimate State: Love Marriage and the Law in Delhi*. New Delhi: Routledge.

Mukhopadhyay, S., and R. Sudarshan. 2003. *Tracking Gender Equity under Economic Reforms*. New Delhi: Kali for Women.

Nongbri, Tiplut. 2000. 'Khasi Women and Matriliny: Transformation in Gender Relations'. *Gender, Technology and Development* 4 (3): 359–95.

Oldenburg, Veena. 2002. *Dowry Murder: The Imperial Origins of a Cultural Crime*. New Delhi: Oxford University Press.

Palriwala, R. 2009. 'The Spider's Web: Seeing Dowry, Fighting Dowry'. In *Dowry: Bridging the Gap between Theory and Practice*, ed. T. Bradley, E. Tomalin, and M. Subramaniam. New Delhi: Women Unlimited.

———. 1994. *Changing Kinship, Family, and Gender Relations in South Asia: Processes, Trends, and Issues*. Leiden: Women and Autonomy Centre (VENA), Leiden University.

———. 1991. 'Transitory Residence and Invisible Work: A Case Study of a Rajasthan Village'. *Economic and Political Weekly* 26(48): 2763–77.

Palriwala, R., and P. Uberoi. 2008. *Marriage, Migration and Gender*. New Delhi: Sage Publications.

Parry, Jonathan. 2001. 'Ankalu's Errant Wife: Sex, Marriage and Industry in Contemporary Chattisgarh'. *Modern Asian Studies* 35 (4): 783–820.

Ram, Kalpana. 1992. *Mukkuvar Women: Gender Hegemony and Capitalist Transformation in a South Indian Fishing Community*. New Delhi: Kali for Women.

Rubin, Gayle. 1975. 'The Traffic in Women: Notes on the Political Economy of Sex'. In *Toward an Anthropology of women*, ed. Ranya R. Reiter. New York: Monthly Review Press.

Sagade, Jaya. 2005. *Child Marriage in India: Socio-Legal and Human Rights Dimensions*. New Delhi: Oxford University Press.

Sandhya, Shaifali. 2009. *Love Will Follow: Why the Indian Marriage is Burning*. New Delhi: Random House.

Sangari, Kumkum, and Sudesh Vaid. 1989. *Recasting Women: Essays in Indian Colonial History*. New Delhi: Kali for Women.

Saheli. 2007. 'Talking Marriage, Caste and Community: Voices from Within'. Report, New Delhi: Saheli.

Schneider, David M. 1984. *A Critique of the Study of Kinship*. Ann Arbor: University of Michigan Press.

Sen, Samita, Nandita Dhawan, Madhurima Mukhopadhyay, Nilanjana Sengupta, and Diya Dutta. 2009. *Re-negotiating Gender Relations in Marriage: Family, Class and Community in Kolkata in an Era of Globalisation: A Report*. Kolkata: School of Women's Studies, Jadavpur University.

Shah, A. M. 1989. 'Parameters of Family Policy in India'. *Economic and Political Weekly* 24 (10): 513–16.

Shukla, Sonal, and Shagufa Kapadia. 2007. 'Transition in Marriage Partner Selection Process: Are Matrimonial Advertisements an Indication?', *Psychology and Developing Societies* 19 (1): 37–54.

Srinivas, M. N. 1993. *On Living in a Revolution and Other Essays*. USA: Oxford University Press.

———. 1952. *Religion and Society among the Coorgs of South India*. Oxford: Clarendon Press.

Still, Clarinda. 2011. 'Spoiled Brides and the Fear of Education: Honour and Social Mobility among Dalits in South India'. *Modern Asian Studies* 45 (5): 1119–46.

Stone, L. 2001. 'Introduction: Theoretical Implications of New Directions in Anthropological Kinship'. In *New Directions in Anthropological Kinship*, ed. Linda Stone. Boulder: Rowman and Littlefield Publishers.

Tambiah, S. J. 1973. 'Dowry and Bridewealth and the Property Rights of Women in South Asia'. In *Bridewealth and Dowry*, ed. J. Goody and S. J. Tambiah. Cambridge Papers in Social Anthropology, No. 7. Cambridge: Cambridge University Press.

Trautmann, T. 1981. *Dravidian Kinship*. Cambridge: Cambridge University Press.

Trawick, M. E. 1990. *Notes on Love in a Tamil Family*. Berkeley: University of California Press.

Uberoi, Patricia. 1998. 'The Diaspora Comes Home: Disciplining Desire in *DDLJ*'. *Contributions to Indian Sociology* 32 (2): 305–36.

———. 1995. 'When is a Marriage Not a Marriage? Sex, Sacrament and Contract in Hindu Marriage', *Contributions to Indian Sociology* 29 (1–2): 319–45.

——— (ed.). 1993. *Family, Kinship and Marriage in India*. New Delhi: Oxford University Press.

Vera-Sanso, Penny. 1999. 'Dominant Daughters-in-law and Submissive Mothers-in-law? Cooperation and Conflict in South India'. *The Journal of the Royal Anthropological Institute* 5 (4): 577–93.

Yalman, Nur. 1971. 'On Land Disputes in Eastern Turkey'. In *Islam and its Cultural Divergence*, ed. G. Tikku. Urbana, IL: University of Illinois Press.

Yanagisako, J., and J. Collier. 1987. 'Towards a Unified Analysis of Gender and Kinship'. In *Gender and Kinship: Essays Towards a Unified Analysis*, ed. Collier, J., and J. Yanagisako. Stanford: Stanford University Press.

1

Change and Continuity in Marital Alliance Patterns

Muslims in South India, 1800–2012

Sylvia Vatuk

Introduction

This essay will address three questions about changing marriage patterns, in contemporary South Asia. First, to what extent are South Asians moving away from traditional systems of parentally arranged marriage and towards a system of personal choice? Second, how are the criteria for evaluating the suitability of a match—whether for oneself or for one's son or daughter—changing? And third, are traditional rules regulating marriage choice being adhered to or relaxed? For example, do marriages today conform strictly to the principles of endogamy (e.g., of the caste, linguistic region or kin-group) and exogamy (e.g., of the village, the *gotra* [patrilineal clan], or the kindred)? Is the prevalence of customary preferential marriages (such as for Dravidian-type cross-cousin and uncle-niece marriages among Hindus or for close consanguineal kin among Muslims) holding steady, or is it on the decline?

There is indeed considerable evidence from South Asia of an increasing prevalence—especially among urban, Western-educated young people—of the so-called 'arranged love marriage', in which parents allow themselves to be persuaded to approve their children's choice of a mate and then proceed to put on a wedding that resembles in every other respect the one they would have organised had they themselves made the match in the traditional manner. Even in families where parents continue to take the primary initiative in choosing mates for their children, both daughters and sons are being allowed to exercise more control over the choice of a spouse than they could in the past (Donner 2002, 2008). These new practices have been associated with such trends as declining birth and death rates, rising ages at marriage, higher levels of education for both sexes, greater economic prosperity (for some groups within the population), a growing middle class, the increased entry of women into the labour force, and widespread internal and international migration associated with a globalising economy.

Although some researchers have noted that in certain social settings marriages of personal choice are becoming increasingly prevalent (Parry 2001), the notion that marriages based solely or primarily on romantic attraction between young people of opposite sexes are replacing on a significant scale those arranged by parents—except perhaps among a very small minority of South Asians—does not appear to be well-supported by the available evidence. The very concept of the so-called 'love marriage' still carries considerable negative valence for most people in the region. It suggests to many the likelihood of illicit sexual intimacy having occurred and implies that the union was entered into against the wishes of one or both sets of parents. Therefore, couples who have married 'for love' will typically try to downplay or conceal this aspect of their personal history when speaking about their marriage. If the pair belongs to different castes or religious communities, parental consent to the match is indeed unlikely and the couple may be ostracised—or worse—by their families, kin and caste community (Chowdhry 2004; Mody 2008). Furthermore, because most people still regard romantic attraction as providing a weak foundation for a long and stable marital relationship, love marriages are widely believed to be at a high risk of failure. This belief may become a self-fulfilling prophecy, since such couples typically lack the kind of social support that those whose marriages were arranged can call upon when problems of adjustment or economic difficulties arise.

Marriage in a South Indian Muslim Family

Most scholars agree on the general direction of change in marriage patterns in today's globalising world, i.e. toward more participation by young people in the choice of their own spouses and some widening of the pool within which mates are being sought, through a relaxation—though not complete abandonment—of earlier limits on eligibility for marriage. But observers have noted wide variation within the south Asian population insofar as the specific nature and extent of the changes taking place is concerned. I will examine the issue here, with reference to the experience of members of a large extended family (a *khandan*, in Urdu) of south Indian Sunni Muslims of the Nawwayat *qaum* (community) (D'Souza 1955; Wala 1976). In 1801, the founding ancestor of this khandan was appointed *Diwan* (chief financial officer) in the court of the Nawwab of Carnatic in Madras (now Chennai). After 1855, the Carnatic Nawwabi was dismantled by the British and some of the khandan founder's descendants left Madras to seek employment in Hyderabad. After the Partition of India a few men of the extended family joined the Muslim exodus to Pakistan and others followed later, forming the core of what is now a substantial settlement of khandan members in that country. In the 1970s, several young men left India and Pakistan to study and/or work in Great Britain, North America and the Middle East, and thereafter the rate of emigration rapidly increased. Those who settled abroad brought parents, siblings and other close kin to join them.[1] Today, the khandan members—now numbering somewhere between 1000 and 1500 persons—are found in many parts of the world. Yet, they maintain a high degree of social unity, through frequent travel back to their home countries and by the use of modern forms of communication such as cell phones, instant messaging, email, webcams and social networking sites such as Facebook.

I have been engaged for many years in a long-term study of the past nine or ten generations of this family (Vatuk 1990, 1994, 1996, 1999). My sources include genealogical records (*shajre*) that document their ancestry at least as far back as the fourteenth century.[2] Their family archives also contain daily journals, letters and biographies of deceased khandan members, both published and unpublished. Many of the latter were written in the mid-twentieth century for family magazines that also contain many essays about the khandan's history, and about current social and political events and issues.

In 1983–84, I carried out ethnographic research among members of this family in Hyderabad. In 1988, 1989 and 1992, I made briefer visits to Chennai and spent nine months there in 1998–99. On two research trips to Hyderabad in 2001 and in 2005–06, I was able to reconnect with members of the family living there. Over the years, I have also been in contact by letter and in person with some khandan members living in India and in the US, and in this way have obtained considerable information about their and their relatives' marriages, migration patterns, educational attainments and occupational choices, though not in a systematic manner. Though the more recent information is not as complete and detailed as the archival and ethnographic data collected in the 1980s, it is sufficient to enable me to make some generalisations about continuity and change in marriage alliance patterns within the khandan, to suggest some of the possible reasons for those patterns, and to compare my findings with the observations of scholars who have studied marriage alliance patterns among other south Asian Muslim immigrant groups in the US and Great Britain.

I will show that the manner in which marriages are arranged have undergone considerable change over the past thirty or forty years and young people of both sexes are now given somewhat more opportunity to provide input into the choice of a life partner. At the same time, one cannot say that the system of arranged marriage is being rapidly replaced by one in which young people choose their own mates. What one does observe is an increasing number of arranged love marriages, in which an educated daughter or son has found someone of appropriate religious and social background, and then the two have approached their respective parents for permission to marry.

As far as adherence to traditional preferences for close-kin marriages are concerned, here again the extent of change is minimal. Khandan endogamy is still widely practised. Even though some have been willing to accommodate to the desires of children who have found someone of suitable religious and social background whom they would like to marry, parents generally still prefer that they be the ones to arrange the marriages of their offspring. And in doing so, they typically try to match up their sons and daughters with cousins or other close relatives, if at all possible, rather than actively looking beyond the extended family circle for suitable spouses.

Marriage Arrangements in the Past

Marriage alliance strategies have always played an important role in this khandan, as parents tried to ensure not only that their children attained full adult status and continued the family line, but that the family's existing social and kinship networks were strengthened and sometimes extended outward, often with an eye towards possible concrete benefits for the young people involved, for the parents themselves and for the khandan as a whole. In the past, young people were not considered capable of making their own choice of a life's partner or even of participating in the deliberations leading up to it. The practice of early betrothal and the customary segregation—even within the extended family household itself—of potentially marriageable post-pubertal young people of the opposite sex, ensured furthermore that in most cases they would neither have any basis upon which to choose their own life's partners nor be even tempted to try. Parents and grandparents took full responsibility for identifying potential mates and negotiating the terms of the marriage, typically without even discussing the matter with the young people concerned.

Occasionally, according to family lore, a young man did make his wishes known in the matter of his marriage. It is said of one prominent khandan ancestor that when he was in his early teens a daughter was born to one of his aunts. As soon as he saw the new baby he said that he wanted her to become his wife when she grew up; a wish that was eventually realised and they are remembered today as having been a devoted couple. More often, however, if a young man expressed a desire to marry a particular cousin his wishes were disregarded and he was married to someone else instead. Sometimes the bride chosen by his father is said to have won the young man's heart once they were married and they lived happily ever after. Other marriages begun in this manner were less successful. Similar issues rarely, if ever, arose where a daughter was concerned. For a girl to show interest in marrying a particular man—or even to display an overt interest in the progress of the search for a suitable husband—would have been regarded as shamefully immodest. Should the knowledge of their daughter's attraction to a male relative come to the notice of her parents, it would be hushed up immediately and another match quickly arranged, in order to forestall the possibility of a family scandal and the ruin of her reputation.

The Muslim Preference for Close-Kin Marriage

Among Muslims, marriageability is determined in terms of a two-fold classification of all members of the opposite sex into the categories *mahram* and *namahram* (from the Arabic *haram* meaning sacred or forbidden). These kinship categories correspond to customary concepts governing the gendered allocation of space. Mahram are those men with whom a respectable Muslim woman may freely associate, the only men who may enter the private female space of her home. They include her closest consanguineal kinsmen: father (and other direct ascendants), brother, son (and other male descendants), parents' brother and sibling's son. None of them may marry or have sexual relations with her.[3] The namaharam category is a residual one. It encompasses all other persons of the opposite sex, whether relative or stranger. Direct contact between a woman and any namahram man is carefully limited and controlled, if not avoided altogether, to preserve her privacy and ensure her chastity. It is from among some carefully delimited segment of a woman's namahram that a suitable husband will be sought for her.[4]

In the Middle East, marriage to close kin is very common and is indeed preferred by most Muslims, even though it is not specifically prescribed by their religion (Bourdieu 1977; Holy 1989; Gingrich 1995). Several ethnographic studies of south Asian Muslim communities have also reported a preference for marriage to consanguineal relatives (Vreede-de Stuers 1968; Das 1973; Jacobson 1976; Mines 1976; Pastner 1979, 1981; Jeffery 1979; Donnan 1988; Alvi 2007).[5] A recent analysis of National Family Health Survey data on almost 10,000 Indian Muslim women found that 22 per cent were married to relatives within the second-cousin range (Hussain and Bittles 2000), while two large-scale surveys of a total of 7600 women in Pakistan show an even higher rate of close-kin marriage. Sixty per cent of the women in the sample were married to relatives and 80 per cent of those couples were first cousins (Hussain and Bittles 1998).

The practise of marrying almost exclusively within a relatively small circle of close relatives is characteristic of this khandan as well. Family genealogies confirm that in the past the khandan was practically a closed, endogamous group. Marriages to first cousins (of all kinds) as well as to second and more distant cousins were very common. Marital alliances frequently reflected agreements between siblings or first cousins, made years ahead of time, to join their respective children or grandchildren in marriage, or to marry the child of one to the grandchild of the other. Such arrangements were sometimes made when the couple was very young; occasionally the prospective bride was still an infant.

Much of the theoretical literature on Muslim marriage in the Middle East focuses on trying to explain the preference for patrilateral parallel-cousin marriage—i.e. marriage of a man to his father's brother's daughter.[6] In this khandan, marriage to the patrilateral parallel-cousin is rarely cited as a specific preference and such marriages, while not uncommon, do not constitute a majority of all unions. But I have been told that a man seeking a wife for his son ought to first consider his own brother's daughter—that is, assuming that their relative ages are appropriate.[7] To put it another way, brothers are felt to have a special obligation towards one another where the marriages of their respective offspring are concerned. This is not so much a matter of a young man's 'right' to be given his father's brother's daughter (*cacazad bahen*) in marriage, but rather that he has an unwritten 'duty' to offer to marry her, especially if she does not have other suitors, in order to avoid the possibility that she will remain unmarried or that her marriage will be unduly delayed (Bourdieu 1977). Of course, this does not mean that the principle is invariably carried out in practice.

This notion that it is incumbent upon the parents of sons to see to it that the daughters of their close kin (and of their siblings, in particular) are suitably married before they seek elsewhere for a daughter-in-law is generalised beyond the set of brothers and other sibling pairs, though it naturally has somewhat greater force for them than it does for more distant kinsmen. The argument is sometimes made explicitly in discussions about the pros and cons of young men of the khandan marrying unrelated, *ghair khandan* (outsider) women. People say, 'If our boys don't marry our girls, who else will do so?' Thus, instead of expressing their marriage preferences in terms of specific kinship relationships—cacazad bahen, for example—a quasi-spatial metaphor is employed: to marry 'within' the khandan rather than 'outside' it. The possessive adjective *zati* (one's own) is sometimes used in this connection, as in the phrase *zati larka* (one of our own boys), in contrast to *bahar ka larka* (an outside boy).

Marrying Outside

In earlier generations, arranged marriages rarely joined a khandan man or woman to a non-relative.[8] And almost never was a marriage arranged with someone outside the Nawwayat fold. According to a 1904 book written by a Nawwayat on a related khandan and considered by contemporary members of the family to be the definitive work on Nawwayat social organisation and customs, the Nawwayats observe endogamy very strictly. He writes:

> Adherence to the principle of equality in marriage [*kufu*[9] *ki pabandi*] is this qaum's chief characteristic ... [T]he way in which the Nait qaum adheres to [this principle] is not seen in any other qaum in Hindustan ... However wealthy or however noble the ancestry of the other party, if he is not of the Nait qaum, then under no circumstances will a girl be given to him nor taken from him. This has the fortunate consequence that up to the present day the [pure] pedigree [*nasab*] of the qaum has been maintained. (Wala 1904/1976: 58–59, translated from the original Urdu by the author)

Note that the author speaks as if the entire Nawwayat qaum constituted the relevant endogamous unit, although in fact most marriages (in his own extended family as well as in the khandan of which I am writing here) were, in practice, confined to a very much smaller circle of close kin.

I should note that whereas marriages were almost never 'arranged' between a khandan man and a non-Nawwayat woman, occasionally a man whose first *khandani* wife had died chose a non-Nawwayat woman to be his second wife. More rarely, a married man contracted a polygynous marriage with a non-Nawwayat woman while his first wife was still alive. Polygynous unions were very rare in this khandan—there are no examples of a man married to two khandani women at the same time. In most cases, second wives in polygynous unions came from Muslim families of lower social class or were of Hindu background, converted to Islam before marriage.[10] Although there were some exceptions, the outsider-wife was typically set up by her husband in a separate household and had limited social interaction with khandan women. Genealogies confirm that the children of such women were seldom married to full-blooded members of the khandan. Instead, they married others of similarly mixed descent or were wed to ghair khandan relatives of their non-Nawwayat mother. Their descendants, in turn—no doubt as a result of having infrequent intimate contact with members of the khandan—usually disappeared from family records after a generation or two. By thus excluding, the offspring of such irregular unions from marriage relations—in practice, though not through the operation of any stated rule—the accepted khandan pedigree remained pure while an avenue still remained open for that small minority of men who were so inclined to establish marital unions and father children with outsider women.

The second decade of the twentieth century saw some loosening of khandan endogamy, for a variety of reasons that I do not have space to go into here.[11] In this period, several marriages were arranged between young men of the family and ghair khandani women. The first marriage of this kind took place in Hyderabad in 1914. In the following decade, two or three other men were married outside the khandan. But it was not until the next generation that arranged marriages with ghair khandani women began to occur with some frequency. Unlike in the past, by attending and participating in the associated wedding festivities, and by interacting with the couple thereafter on the same basis as with other married couples, members of the khandan gave social recognition and approval to unions with outsider women in a way that their ancestors had not done. These new outsider brides were not subject to the same social marginalisation that had been imposed upon those brought into the family as second wives in the nineteenth and early twentieth centuries. This was largely due to the fact that their marriages had been properly arranged by the young man's parents and were not unions of personal choice. Furthermore, the women invariably came from respectable (*sharif*) Muslim families whose social status was equivalent to the groom's own. This change in the way these outsider women were treated also reflected broader changes occurring within the khandan in this period. By this time, the khandan was becoming a much less exclusive and insular social group in other ways as well. This process both contributed to and was facilitated by an increasing prevalence of outside marriages.

The idea of giving a girl in marriage to an outside boy took somewhat longer to gain acceptance. It was not until 1934 that the first arranged marriage of this type took place; another was celebrated in 1937. However, in both cases the men belonged to the Nawwayat qaum. Furthermore, the second man was actually a distant relative, descended from the khandan founder's younger brother, who had married an unrelated Nawwayat woman back in the late eighteenth century. In the 1950s, a few khandan daughters were given in marriage to men from respectable, non-Nawwayat families and such matches continue to be made from time to time, especially by families living outside India.

Marriage Arrangement in the Khandan Today

Today, marriage ages within the khandan—as among middle-class Indians more generally—are significantly higher than in the past. Few young people—female or male—get married before reaching their twenties and most brides and grooms have at least a high school, if not a college, education and perhaps further professional training. Consequently, they are generally kept informed as the process of matchmaking proceeds and are usually given the opportunity to express their views and perhaps even reject candidates that their parents are considering. Sons are able to take a more active role in this process than are daughters, as it is still thought inappropriate for a girl to show excessive interest in the matter of her marriage. She is certainly not expected to be too outspoken in expressing her opinion about the men who are being considered as possible husbands for her. But there are indirect ways by which a girl can make her views known. Should she be strongly opposed to a particular match, her feelings are likely to be honoured. But, although young people certainly participate to a far greater degree than in the past in the search for a mate, and are more able to discuss with their parents what kind of qualifications they would prefer their future spouse to have, marriages based primarily on personal choice are still not the usual pattern.

Sometimes cousins or other close kin who have encountered one another at family gatherings, such as weddings, or when visiting one another's homes with their parents, are attracted to one another, though usually without having had much opportunity to interact privately. One of the pair, usually the man, may gather the courage to mention his feelings to a sister or to his mother, who will then tactfully make it known to his father and, if the parents have no strong objections to the match, they will try to determine the inclinations of the girl's family in an indirect and tactful way. Assuming that the latter indicate a willingness to give their consent, a formal proposal of marriage may follow.

There have also been occasional arranged love marriages that came about when two young people became acquainted at school or at work and persuaded their respective parents that they be allowed to marry. Thus, one young woman from Chennai, who had completed a professional degree at an institution in another city, married a college classmate with the full cooperation of both of their families. He belongs to the khandan of the former Carnatic Nawwabs, who had originally come to the Madras Presidency from northern India. Many of the bride's nineteenth-century ancestors had occupied high positions in that Nawwabi court, but had never had any previous marital connections with the royal family. Soon after the wedding the bride came to the United States for post-graduate study and her husband joined her a year later. Both are currently working and raising their children there.

Two other young women of the khandan whom I know, both brought up in North America by immigrant parents from India and/or Pakistan, have had arranged love marriages to young Muslim men of south Asian background whom they met in high school or college. Neither husband is a Nawwayat, but both come from educated, professional families and, like their wives, grew up outside of the Indian subcontinent. One young man of the khandan who came to the United States to study, and later found employment there is said to have married (with parental approval) the sister of a male friend—presumably one whom he had met (or seen) at the friend's home or at a wedding or other community gathering.

I know of no case in which a young couple fell in love and married without their parents' permission. Much earlier, at a time when very few khandan members had ever travelled to the West,[12] two young men—now in their sixties—came to the United States as students and eventually met and married non-Muslim American women. These are the only examples of which I am aware of khandan marriages contracted outside of the Muslim fold. Both men married in the United States, where they still live. I do not know what their families' reactions to those men's marriages were at the time, but certainly today they and their American wives and children are fully-accepted members of the khandan's diasporic community, keeping in regular touch with khandan relatives in India and elsewhere by phone and the internet, and often attending khandan weddings and other social gatherings, both in the vicinity of their homes and in other North American locales.

A Continued Preference for Close-Kin Marriage

There is some evidence that in India today many communities that formerly practised caste endogamy, village exogamy or preferential kin marriage and the like, have begun to expand their marriage networks, as new criteria for mate choice begin to replace old ones. Fuller and Narasimhan (2008), for example, find that Tamil Brahmans, who formerly practised cross-cousin marriage, today generally prefer to seek mates among unrelated families, though they still adhere in most marriages to caste endogamy and descent group exogamy, and care is still taken to match the prospective couple's horoscopes. Educational and occupational qualifications now play a larger role than they did in the past when assessing the relative desirability of prospective candidates for marriage. Young people of both sexes—but especially boys—are concerned about a potential mate's physical appearance, something that was never taken into consideration in former times. The desire to obtain employment overseas for one's son through the influence of a prospective bride's father, or to obtain a green card by marrying a woman who is a US citizen, may also enter into the calculations when a prospective match is being considered. And it stands to reason that one has a better chance of finding someone with the desired qualifications if one is willing to expand the pool of eligible candidates, rather than confine oneself to a small number of persons closely related in a particular way.

In this khandan, however, the long-standing preference for marrying close relatives persists up to the present day. Many khandan families still place a priority on finding an endogamous match for their child, if at all possible.[13] It is a particular concern for some of those living in Canada, the US or other Western countries that their children, growing up in the diaspora, are at risk of becoming overly influenced by Western ways, and as a consequence, will begin to 'date' members of the opposite sex and eventually want to select their own spouses, ignoring the guidance of their families. Some parents have succeeded in forestalling such possibilities by arranging their children's—especially their daughters'—marriages at fairly young ages with close relatives living in India, Pakistan or Saudi Arabia. For example, one such marriage about ten years ago joined a young woman, born and raised in New Jersey and just graduated from high school, to her father's brother's son, a college graduate from Chennai. After the wedding, which was held in India, he applied for a spousal visa to come to the US. At first, they lived with her family while she attended a nearby college. She did exceptionally well in her studies, despite giving birth to a child within the first two years of marriage. Later her parents arranged to have her younger brother marry a young relative from Chennai, who also came to live with the family as soon as her visa came through.

One set of Chennai brothers, some of whom live in the US, has managed to arrange marriages for several of their offspring to relatives from India from within their immediate kindred. The men's parents are first cousins; their respective wives are from different Hyderabadi families that also belong to the khandan. A few years ago, one of these men married his son to the daughter of a woman whose mother's sister is married to one of his brothers. On the same day, the two families celebrated the engagement of two of the bride's cousins (mother's sisters' daughters) to two cousins (father's brother's sons) of the groom. Calculating the relationship in the most direct way, the two fiancées, as well as the bride, were second cousins of their prospective grooms. But, given the complicated pattern of intermarriage that had already taken place among their ancestors, over many generations, they were, like most khandan men and women, related in a multitude of other ways as well.

Khandan members give a number of reasons for continuing to prefer close-kin marriage. First, there is a feeling that, generally speaking, a marriage to an outsider is riskier than marriage within the family. There is felt to be a greater chance that spouses coming from different backgrounds and lacking shared values and outlook on life will fail to adjust to one another. Although there have been very few cases in which an outside marriage resulted in separation or divorce—and at least one divorce happened between spouses who were related—this notion contributes to the reluctance of some khandan members to go out of the way to make an alliance with an unrelated family. The risk of marital maladjustment and discord is seen to be greatest when a man comes from India to marry an unrelated woman brought up in North America. One such marriage, contracted in the late 1980s between a khandan man whose father was deceased and a young Muslim woman from a different qaum raised in the US, can be cited as a case in point. The young man, motivated at least in part by the prospect of bettering his employment prospects through emigration, had responded to a matrimonial advertisement placed by the girl's parents in a Hyderabadi Urdu newspaper. The wedding was performed in India, after which the bride and her family returned to the US. Only after he joined them there did he learn that his bride, who had recently started college, had been unwilling to get married so young and, furthermore, felt that she had little in common with her India-raised husband. His economic dependence on her family once he arrived in the US did not help matters. The marriage was soon dissolved, but the man remained in the US. He was later persuaded by his mother and other relatives to remarry. He is now happily married to a second cousin who was born and grew up, as he did, in Hyderabad.

Another reason to prefer khandan endogamy is the relative ease of finding a suitable candidate, arranging a match and negotiating the financial and other details of the agreement and subsequent celebration of the wedding, when both spouses belong to the khandan. Of course, sometimes one's options during such a search or in the course of the negotiations are hampered by the inevitable tensions that develop over time within any large extended family, either because of earlier disagreements and perceived slights, or other contentious incidents from the past. But it is, nevertheless, a great advantage that when seeking a suitable spouse within the khandan the parents of the prospective groom or bride[14] already know or can easily find out all that they want to know about the prospective spouse's education, occupation and earnings, personal abilities, temperament and habits. These matters typically require extensive research when an unrelated candidate is being considered and often, even then, the most careful inquiries may fail to turn up the most damaging facts!

Economic Factors Favouring Close-Kin Marriage

The financial transactions that accompany a Muslim marriage in India, as in the diaspora, also favour close-kin marriage. The first of these is the *mahr*, a gift of money or valuables that every Muslim groom must promise in the marriage contract to transfer to his bride. In this khandan it is customary to give a small, standard amount—usually INR 640—as mahr. But many Muslims of equivalent social and economic stratum are accustomed to offer several thousand rupees or more (Vatuk 2007). Among Indian Muslims, the mahr is almost never handed over at the time of marriage. It is usually stated in the marriage contract (*nikahnama*) that its payment will be deferred (*muwajjal*), with the understanding that the wife may claim it at any time during the marriage and that it must, in any event, be paid to her upon divorce or widowhood. Since divorce is generally considered to be much more likely if the partners are unrelated, a man taking a ghair khandani bride may be compelled to commit himself to a much larger mahr than he would have to offer if he married a cousin.

A few years ago, the engagement of a Nawwayat man (of a different and unrelated khandan) to a young Hyderabadi Pathan woman, both of whom had been brought up in America, was broken off because of a serious disagreement over the mahr. His family insisted on offering only a token amount, in line with their customary practice, whereas her parents demanded that he offer USD 25,000. They reasoned that, in case of a divorce, she should have enough money to maintain herself for at least a year. But the prospective groom's family was unwilling to alter their stand, doubtless not only because they felt that the girl's family's demand was excessive, but also because it offended them that the other party was raising the possibility of a divorce even before the wedding had been solemnised!

The other significant material transaction associated with a Muslim marriage in South Asia is the dowry (*jahez*). Under Muslim law, the prospective bride's parents are not required to present any substantial gifts to the man she is to marry or to his family. But in the Indian subcontinent the originally Hindu custom of giving an elaborate dowry is widely practised among Muslims as well, and the amounts transferred on such occasions have escalated in recent decades. This khandan, however, has largely avoided participation in the trend toward extravagant dowries. For one thing, it conflicts with a long-standing family tradition of adhering to a simplified and strictly Islamic ritual regimen in connection with marriage. In endogamous marriages it is thus customary for the bride's family to give the groom only a ring and a set of clothes to wear during the wedding ceremony. Nowadays, an amount of cash sufficient to purchase this wedding outfit—or to have one tailored—may be given instead. On the other hand, parents contemplating a ghair khandan match for their daughter must be prepared for the possibility that they will be subjected to demands for additional cash, jewellery, household goods, furniture and appliances or even, in some cases, a motorcycle or car for the groom-to-be.

Where the roles are reversed and a bride is being sought for a son, it is conceivable that some young men would find it appealing to marry into a ghair khandan family that is accustomed to giving a generous dowry when a daughter is wed. However, though I have not been able to verify this with data from actual marriages, khandan men and women with whom I have discussed the matter uniformly insist that they do not take dowries when their sons marry—whether the bride is an outsider or not. In this connection, one older woman once remarked to me jokingly, 'that is why our educated boys are regarded as great bargains in today's marriage market!'

There are other, perhaps, more important reasons why arranging a marriage for one's daughter with an outside groom can be disadvantageous. In such unions, the bride is inevitably going to be under pressure to become fully incorporated into her husband's family. As a result, she will probably be unable to maintain as close a relationship with her parents and other natal kin as they—and she—would like. This becomes an issue even if the couple take up residence in the same city as her parents. A woman's husband and in-laws, even under the best of circumstances, are understood to have the right to determine how much time a daughter-in-law may spend with her own family. They may limit her opportunities to visit or even to communicate with her parents and siblings, both because they need her labour for housework, cooking and eventually child care, and also because they want her to adjust as quickly as possible to their way of living and to shift her emotional loyalties accordingly.

There is also a more remote, but still real, possibility that a daughter who is married to an outsider may not be treated as well by her husband and in-laws as she would be in an intra-khandan marriage. If she should find herself being abused, it may be difficult or impossible for her to communicate her problems to her parents and seek their help. The fact that so large a proportion of marriages nowadays involve emigration for the bride or the groom—or both—further increases the risk of marrying one's daughter outside of the khandan. When she is living so far away, her parents back in India or Pakistan have no easy way to learn what is happening in her marital home or to intervene on her behalf if they discover that she is having difficulties. I was told about one such case, in which a girl came from Pakistan to join her US-based ghair khandani husband and his parents. Soon they all began to physically and psychologically abuse her. Khandan relatives living in the same city became aware of the situation but felt unable to intervene or even to maintain frequent direct contact with her, for fear of inciting her in-laws' anger and aggravating her situation even further.

If the husband is a cousin, on the other hand, the likelihood of one's daughter being mistreated by him or his family is considered to be minimal or non-existent. It is not customary within the khandan to place any restrictions upon a young married woman's access to her natal relatives. So, even if problems should arise in an endogamous marriage, it is a relatively simple matter for her parents or brothers to keep an eye out for her welfare and intervene if they deem it necessary. And even if a young woman, married to a relative, moves overseas there are usually enough khandan members living in the same country and even the same general vicinity who will be in regular contact with her and in frequent communication with the family back in India and can keep her parents abreast of her domestic situation.

Ideological Factors in the Persistance of Kin Marriage

Having drawn attention to all of the purely practical and instrumental motivations for the persistence of the practice of close-kin marriage, it would be a mistake to discount the force of the ideology of purity of blood which played such an important role in the past in determining marriage choices for members of this khandan. Among those who claim descent from their founding ancestor, it has long been a mark of distinction to be able to trace one's connection to him through all lines of descent from the founding ancestor. The term *najib ut-tarfain* (noble on both sides) describes those members of the khandan who have no outside ancestry, whose descent line is pure (*khalis*) of any outside admixture. One hears khandan members speak sometimes of the fact that their pedigree (*nasal*) has been preserved (*mahfuz*) for many generations, kept separate (*alag*) from all unrelated descent lines. Those who are najib ut-tarfain share the same blood (*khun*) and are believed also to share certain transmitted qualities (*khassiat, khisal*) that can be lost or diluted through marriage with outsiders. Among their many good qualities are certain special abilities (such as intellectual prowess) and physical traits (such as fair skin and a relatively tall, slender build) but, more importantly, such moral traits as honesty, simplicity, religiosity and self-respect.[15]

Those who are of pure descent in this sense constitute in a substantive and symbolic sense the core of the khandan. They sometimes refer to themselves, or are referred to by others whose ancestry is mixed to some degree, as *khas khandan ke log*, the real, particular, special or genuine khandan people. Today, most—though not all—of those who boast such ancestry have spouses whose ancestry is similarly unsullied by out-marriage and have arranged or intend to arrange their children's marriages within the same core group. By so doing they enact the most crucial behavioural sign of loyalty and commitment to the preservation of the khandan as a distinctive and viable social and cultural unit.

The issue of the transmission of qualities through the blood has become a somewhat sensitive one in recent decades. At a time when many social forces have been propelling a move toward a more extensive network of marital alliances, scientific knowledge about the presumed deleterious effects of close-kin marriage has also been spreading. Indeed, a genetic study of the khandan conducted by a local university team back in the 1960s had become very controversial within the khandan, contributing to feelings of unease and ambivalence among some members of the khandan, about the possibly negative consequences of khandan endogamy. Nowadays, one occasionally hears quasi-genetic arguments used to support the view that close-kin marriage is harmful and that it would be better, for the health of one's (yet-to-be born) offspring, to marry out. Such arguments are not infrequently used by young men to justify a preference for marrying an unrelated girl rather than a cousin. Of course, they may also have other motives for voicing genetic objections to marrying a close relative: the strange and mysterious, unknown ghair khandan girl may seem a more romantic choice!

Others hotly contest the genetic argument against marrying endogamously. Some deny that their traditional practice could lead (or has ever led) to genetic defects. Or they point out that even if genetic principles do in fact operate in the way that scientists claim, it is better to keep on marrying endogamously so as to continue to replicate the family's desirable traits! If this also means that a few hereditary defects will be passed on to the next generation, it is better that these be the relatively mild ones, like poor eyesight, that are already known to be carried within the family. It is much more risky, they contend, to begin engaging in marital exchange with khandans of whose bad qualities one is unaware!

Comparisons with Other South Asian Muslims

Since the largest number of khandan members living outside of South Asia reside in North America, and since these are also the people with whom I am most familiar, it would be useful to try to compare this khandan with other Muslims of south Asian origin living in the US and Canada. Are they unique in continuing to practise close-kin marriage, or is this marriage pattern typical of all south Asian Muslims in the diaspora? Regrettably, there are few, if any, data upon which to base a satisfactory answer to this question. A handful of sociological studies of American Muslims (Leonard 2003; Schmidt 2004) and one book and several articles that deal specifically with south Asian Muslims (Mohammad-Arif 2002, 2009) have been published in the last decade. There are also several monographs on South Asians in North America, more generally (Bacon 1996; Leonard 1997; Lessinger 1995; Rayaprol 1997; Rudrappa 2004). With the exception of Mohammad-Arif's 2009 article, none of the cited works discusses issues of family and marriage within the diasporic south Asian Muslim community in any detail.

However, there is somewhat more information available on marriage alliance patterns among south Asian Muslims in Great Britain, where several researchers have reported finding a high incidence of close-kin marriage among Pakistani Muslim immigrants (Werbner 1990; Shaw 2001; Charsley 2003). Shaw, for example, found that 76 per cent of the husbands and wives in her sample of 70 marriages in the Pakistani community of Oxford were consanguineally related to one another and 59 per cent of them were first cousins. Interestingly, she also found that young Pakistani immigrants were even more likely than their parents or grandparents to have married a first cousin. This suggests that in the diaspora consanguineous marriages, rather than declining in frequency, may be on the rise (Shaw 2001: 315–16, 318–19)! The reasons that Shaw and the other scholars have cited for the persistence of consanguineous marriage among Pakistanis and for its apparent rise in frequency among immigrant families are similar to those that I have put forward here to account for the patterns I have observed among diasporic Nawwayats.

Conclusion

I have shown here how patterns of marital alliance have changed over several centuries in one Muslim family from southern India and have linked these changes with corresponding changes in the social and economic conditions within which the family has found itself in different times and places. Throughout its history there has been a strong and recurring tendency to favour marriage to close kin, rather than to people outside of one's own family circle, however that circle may be defined or conceptually bounded at any given point in time. Even today, when so many forces of change in South Asia seem to favour the development of extensive social networks rather than inwardly-oriented repetitions of earlier established marital alliances, the people of this khandan continue to find cousin-marriage safe, congenial, useful, convenient and ideologically satisfying, as they make their way in the global world that they now inhabit.

Notes

[1] This is not possible for most of those working in the Middle East, since those countries allow very few foreign workers to bring family members with them and, in any case, require them to return home once their terms of employment have ended.

[2] In the late nineteenth century much of this information was consolidated by a grandson of their common ancestor in an unpublished Persian manuscript (Madini 1871–72) and in the mid-twentieth a woman living in Hyderabad began putting together a biographical register of both living and deceased members of the *khandan*. She added to it as relatives were born, married and died, keeping it up-to-date until shortly before her death in 1984 (Majid 1984).

[3] A man's *mahram* are his corresponding female kin: mother, sister, daughter, etc. After marriage, a man and his wife become mahram to one another and to their respective immediate family members.

[4] For further details concerning the prohibited degrees and other requirements for a valid marriage in Islam, see Hidayatullah and Hidayatullah (1990: 223–34).

[5] Some more recent converts from Hinduism continue to follow their former caste customs in adhering to *gotra* (patrilineal clan) exogamy and prohibitions on marriage to those non-patrilineal kin who are classified as *sapinda* (Jamous 2003).

[6] For an extended discussion of the issues, see Holy (1989).

[7] There were very few violations of the rule that the husband should be older than the wife. Out of 321 marriages contracted by khandan members between 1175 and 1949—in which the marriage age of both partners is known—only seven wives were older than their husbands. In all but two of these marriages the age difference was less than one year. Both of those in which the age difference was greater than this were unions of personal choice. Only after some initial opposition had the young people involved been able to gain their respective families' assent to their marrying. For a more detailed analysis of changing ages at marriage and age differences between spouses, see Vatuk (2002: 250–51).

[8] Though I was not always able to trace out the relevant kinship links, there is likely to have been some distant kin connection between the spouses even in those marriages that appear not to conform to the endogamic pattern.

[9] The Arabic word *kufu* means likeness, similarity or equality. It is an important principle of Islamic marriage law that the husband's family's social status be at least similar, if not superior, to that of the wife's.

[10] Such women are referred to in family genealogical records as *naumuslim* (new Muslim).

[11] See Vatuk (1994, 2002) for detailed discussions of these matters, with analyses of figures documenting changes over time in the khandan's demographic and educational profiles.

[12] For centuries both male and female ancestors of the khandan had been regularly undertaking the pilgrimage to Mecca, and in the twentieth century some travelled to other parts of the Middle East, including Turkey. But it was not until after the Second World War that any member of the khandan ventured to Great Britain, Europe, North America or other Western countries.

[13] Of course, those whose ancestors already include one or more outsiders are more likely than those descended on both sides from the khandan founder to be open to the possibility of marrying their children outside of the khandan.

[14] Traditionally, the boy's family takes the initiative in these matters. The formal marriage proposal is sent in his name. But there are also indirect ways of letting it be known that one is seeking a groom for one's daughter.

[15] For a more detailed discussion on these notions, see Vatuk (1996).

References

Alvi, Anjum. 2007. 'India and the Muslim Punjab: A Unified Approach to South Asian Kinship'. *Journal of the Royal Anthropological Institute* 13 (3): 657–78.

Bacon, Jean. 1996. *Life Lines: Community, Family, and Assimilation among Asian Indian Immigrants*. New York: Oxford University Press.

Bourdieu, Pierre. 1977. *Outline of a Theory of Practice*. Cambridge: Cambridge University Press.

Charsley, Katherine. 2003. 'Rishtas: Transnational Pakistani Marriages'. Unpublished Ph.D. dissertation, University of Edinburgh.

Chowdhry, Prem. 2004. 'Caste Panchayats and the Policing of Marriage in Haryana: Enforcing Kinship and Territorial Exogamy'. *Contributions to Indian Sociology* 38 (1 and 2): 1–42.

Das, Veena. 1973. 'The Structure of Marriage Preferences: An Account from Pakistani Fiction'. *Man* n.s. 8 (1): 30–45

Donnan, Hastings. 1988. *Marriage among Muslims: Preference and Choice in Northern Pakistan*. Delhi: Hindustan Publications.

Donner, Henrike. 2008. *Domestic Goddesses: Maternity, Globalisation and Middle-class Identity in Contemporary India*. Aldershot: Ashgate.

———. 2002. '"One's Own Marriage": Love Marriages in a Calcutta Neighbourhood'. *South Asia Research* 22 (1): 79–94.

D'Souza, Victor. 1955. *The Navayats of Kanara: A Study in Culture Contact*. Dharwar: Kannada Research Institute.

Fuller, C. J., and Haripriya Narasimhan. 2008. 'Companionate Marriage in India: The Changing Marriage System in a Middle-class Brahman Subcaste'. *Journal of the Royal Anthropological Institute* 14 (4): 736–54.

Gingrich, Andre. 1995. 'The Prophet's Smile and Other Puzzles: Studying Arab Tribes and Comparing Close Marriages'. *Social Anthropology* 3 (2): 147–70.

Hidayatullah, M., and Arshad Hidayatullah. 1990. *Mulla's Principles of Mahomedan Law*. Nineteenth edition, Bombay: N. M. Tripathi Private Ltd.

Holy, Ladislav. 1989. *Kinship, Honour and Solidarity: Cousin Marriage in the Middle East*. Manchester: Manchester University Press.

Hussain, R., and A. H. Bittles. 2000. 'Sociodemographic Correlates of Consanguineous Marriage in the Muslim Population of India'. *Journal of Biosocial Science* 32 (4): 433–42.

———. 1998. 'The Prevalence and Demographic Characteristics of Consanguineous Marriages in Pakistan'. *Journal of Biosocial Science* 30 (2): 261–75.

Jacobson, Doranne. 1976. 'The Veil of Virtue: Purdah and the Muslim Family in the Bhopal Region of Central India'. In *Family, Kinship and Marriage Among Muslims in India*, ed. Imtiaz Ahmad. New Delhi: South Asia Books.

Jamous, Raymond. 2003. *Kinship and Rituals among the Meo of Northern India*. New Delhi: Oxford University Press.

Jeffery, Patricia. 1979. *Frogs in a Well: Indian Women in Purdah*. New Delhi: Vikas Publishing House.

Leonard, Karen. 2003. *Muslims in the United States: The State of Research*. New York: Russell Sage Foundation.

———. 1997. *The South Asian Americans*. Westport, CT: Greenwood Press.

Lessinger, Johanna. 1995. *From the Ganges to the Hudson: Indian Immigrants in New York City*. Boston: Allyn and Bacon.

Madini, Maulvi Ahmad-ul. 1871–72. 'Tarikh-i Ahmadi' [Persian]. Unpublished manuscript.

Majid, Amat-ul. 1984. 'Biographical Register' [Urdu]. Unpublished manuscript.

Mines, Mattison. 1976. 'Urbanisation, Family Structure and the Muslim Merchants of Tamilnadu'. In *Family, Kinship and Marriage Among Muslims in India*, ed. Imtiaz Ahmad. New Delhi: South Asia Books.

Mody, Perveez. 2008. *The Intimate State: Love-Marriage and the Law in Delhi*. London: Routledge.

Mohammad-Arif, Aminah. 2009. 'Au-delà de l'endogamie et de la mixité: les mariages endogames mixtes chez les musulmans indo-pakistanais aux États-Unis'. *Diasporas: Histoire et Sociétés* 15:68–82.

———. 2002. *Salaam America: South Asian Muslims in New York*. London: Anthem Press.

Parry, Jonathan. 2001. 'Ankalu's Errant Wife: Sex, Marriage and Industry in Contemporary Chhattisgarh'. *Modern Asian Studies* 35 (4): 783–820.

Pastner, Carroll McC. 1981. 'The Negotiation of Bilateral Endogamy in the Middle Eastern Context: The Zikri Baluch Example'. *Journal of Anthropological Research* 37 (4): 305–18.

———. 1979. 'Cousin Marriage among the Zikri Baluch of Coastal Pakistan'. *Ethnology* 18 (1): 31–47.

Rayaprol, Aparna. 1997. *Negotiating Identities: Women in the Indian Diaspora*. New Delhi: Oxford University Press.

Rudrappa, Sharmila. 2004. *Ethnic Routes to Becoming American: Indian Immigrants and the Cultures of Citizenship*. New Brunswick: Rutgers University Press.

Schmidt, Garbi. 2004. *Islam in Urban America: Sunni Muslims in Chicago*. Philadelphia: Temple University Press.

Shaw, Alison. 2001. 'Kinship, Cultural Preferences and Immigration: Consanguineous Marriage among British Pakistanis'. *Journal of the Royal Anthropological Institute* 7 (2): 315–34.

Vatuk, Sylvia. 2007. 'The "Cancer of Dowry" in Indian Muslim Marriages: Themes in the Popular Rhetoric from the South Indian Muslim Press'. In *Living With Secularism: The Destiny of India's Muslims*, ed. Mushirul Hasan. New Delhi: Manohar Publishers and Distributors.

———. 2002. 'Older Women, Past and Present, in an Indian Muslim Family'. In *Thinking Social Science in India: Essays in Honour of Alice Thorner*, eds. S. Patel, J. Bagchi, and K. Raj. New Delhi: Sage Publications.

———. 1999. 'Family Biographies as Sources for an Historical Anthropology of Muslim Women's Lives in Nineteenth-Century South India'. In *The Resources of History: Tradition, Narration and Nation in South Asia, Études Thematiques* 8: 153–72, ed. J. Assayag. Paris and Pondichery: École française d'extrême Orient and Institut français de Pondichery.

———. 1996. 'Identity and Difference or Equality and Inequality in South Asian Muslim Society'. In *Caste Today*, ed. C. Fuller. New Delhi: Oxford University Press.

———. 1994. 'Schooling for What? The Cultural and Social Context of Women's Education in a South Indian Muslim Family'. In *Women, Education, and Family*

Structure in India, eds. C. C. Mukhopadhyay, and S. Seymour. Boulder: Westview Press.

______. 1990. 'The Cultural Construction of Shared Identity: A South Indian Muslim Family History'. *Social Analysis* 28:114–31.

Vreede-de Stuers, Cora. 1968. *Parda: A Study of Muslim Women's Life in Northern India*. Assen: Van Gorcum.

Wala, Aziz Jang. [1904] 1976. *Tarikh-un Nawwayat*. Second edition. Hyderabad: Wala Akaidami.

Werbner, Pnina. 1990. *The Migration Process: Capital, Gifts and Offerings among British Pakistanis*. Oxford: Berg.

Marriage in Bhutan

At the Confluence of Modernity and Identity

Sonam Chuki

Introduction

This essay is an exploratory study of the changing concepts and practices of marriage in contemporary Bhutan. Lying in the foothills of the Himalayas, agriculture is the main occupation, providing livelihood to 67 per cent of the population in 2007, but contributing to less than 19 per cent of the Gross Domestic Product (National Statistics Bureau 2010: 74). The country's key sources of revenue are electricity and tourism. New businesses and industries, and the expansion of civil service, higher education and infrastructure have meant a range of new occupations, an increase in the urban population, continuing inequalities, and growing social and economic mobility.

A country that was never colonised, Bhutan has had a continuing and strong political emphasis on the preservation of its cultural identity. The last is derived largely from two main Buddhist ethnic groups: the Ngalong of the west and the Sharchop of the east, jointly known as the Drukpas. A third main ethnic group is the Lhotsampa of the south, an ethnic Nepalese population predominantly Hindu with a small portion of Christians (Turner et al. 2011: 189). Since March 2008, Bhutan has been a constitutional monarchy, with one party elected to most seats in the national assembly. The formal change in the political system has not meant a break in the development and policy discourse and ethos of the state. This is summed up in the idea of Gross National

Happiness—a balance between material and emotional happiness—and the maintenance of Bhutanese cultural values. However, sections of Bhutanese society voice the worry that the latter may be lost as social norms change with the impact of commercial globalisation and the adoption by urban youth of 'Western' ideas and lifestyles.

Modern education, including university education, and particularly that of women has been an important factor of change. New channels of information and communication, including the Internet and mobile phone have also had an effect. Singer's (1972) studies on tradition and modernity in India are illuminating in this context. There has always been (indigenous) innovation and, furthermore, modernity does not simply replace 'tradition'. Most crucially, ongoing and new practices, often initiated among privileged groups who see themselves as 'modern', are claimed and contested as being both modern and traditional. This process engenders trends of change, furthered as these concepts and practices redefine each other and travel beyond the 'modernising' elite. In Bhutan, the state has played a critical role in the construction of and attempts to assert a unique cultural identity and associated practices, while also initiating technological and educational modernisation. This gives particular salience to the intermeshing and mutual reconstruction of 'traditional' and 'modern' practices and concepts pertaining to the institution of marriage.

Scholarly or literary writings on Bhutanese kinship, marriage and social life are scanty. This essay draws on these materials, but more extensively on interviews, participant observation and reports in the print media[1], to explore continuities and shifts in various dimensions of marriage. Though most of the informants resided in the capital city, Thimphu, they had active and ongoing kin ties in different parts of the country. They included 12 men and 12 women, between 24 and 84 years of age, and of varied marital status. They were predominantly Buddhist with one Hindu, one Christian and one atheist. Other than one retiree, one home-maker, and three farmers, all were employed and most were middle class. Some of the last, migrants to Thimphu, were of old noble families, but most were 'commoners' and not elite.

Traditionally, in Buddhist Bhutan, there were four caste groups: *Gyal Rig* or the royal caste, *Je-Rig* or the ministers/noble caste, *Mang-Rig* or the common people and *Dheul-Rig* or the butchers, who were at the bottom of the caste hierarchy. The first two castes were the landowners, with position, rank and privileges in rural society and at the court. There was a belief that the people were born in a privileged caste because of their good deeds in a previous life and would have a good heart. One informant, Dorji, who had a monastic education and taught law in the capital, defined good heart as 'someone who recognises the *dharma* (Buddha's teachings or religious law), believes in the law of *karma* (one's actions in this and past lives, which determine one's destiny), cares for and respects parents and siblings.' Though some informants questioned the equation of high caste and good heart, this understanding did act as a justification for the social status and wealth of those of the high castes. Today, the elite is no longer exclusively from the high castes, though many are related to the royal family or claim to be descendents of ancient 'noble families'. Members of big business houses in urban areas and owners of land, cattle and big houses in rural areas also fall into the elite.

Two-thirds of the informants had completed secondary or a higher education that was imbued with 'Western' thought and culture as was the new media they increasingly accessed. They narrated and reflected on their own marriages and that of their contemporaries, parents and children, who lived in various parts of the country. They also spoke of radical trends evident in Thimphu, such as live-in relationships among young, urban, working professionals and online dating. Informants' responses on changing marriage practices were strongly embedded in beliefs and statements regarding moral, religious and social values, linking the group to tradition and recognition of the individual to modernity. They opined on the (non)desirability of specific trends and social change in general. The analysis has been framed by these attitudinal themes.

Within the small, face-to-face communities of village society, people were embedded in the family and its network. Kin were tapped at sickness, death, and in paying off debts and they asserted a social and moral pressure. Parents, elder siblings, grandparents, and immediate kin arranged and decided on an individual's marriage. Across ethnic groups, marriage was considered a sacred institution, valued and respected. Not all marriages were happy or successful, but spouses remained together rather than harm the reputation of their kin, since a separation or divorce was viewed as immoral.

Varied marriage practices were in vogue among the different ethnic groups. These included preferential cross-cousin marriage, child marriage, polygyny and polyandry. There were differences in rules and in practice between elites and commoners and between Buddhists and Hindus. The emphasis on arranged marriage was apparently contradicted by a practice of courtship prevalent particularly in eastern and central Bhutan, exoticised as 'night hunting'. Continuities in attitudes and practices in each of these features are discussed in the sections that follow, starting with those documented traditions that many informants were uneasy with.

Traditional Marriage Rules and Practices

First-Cousin Marriage

According to Dorji (2003), the preferred marriage among the Sharchop is with the first cross-cousin and then more distant cross-cousins, while parallel-cousin

Map 2.1: Map of Bhutan Showing the Major Ethnic Groups by Region

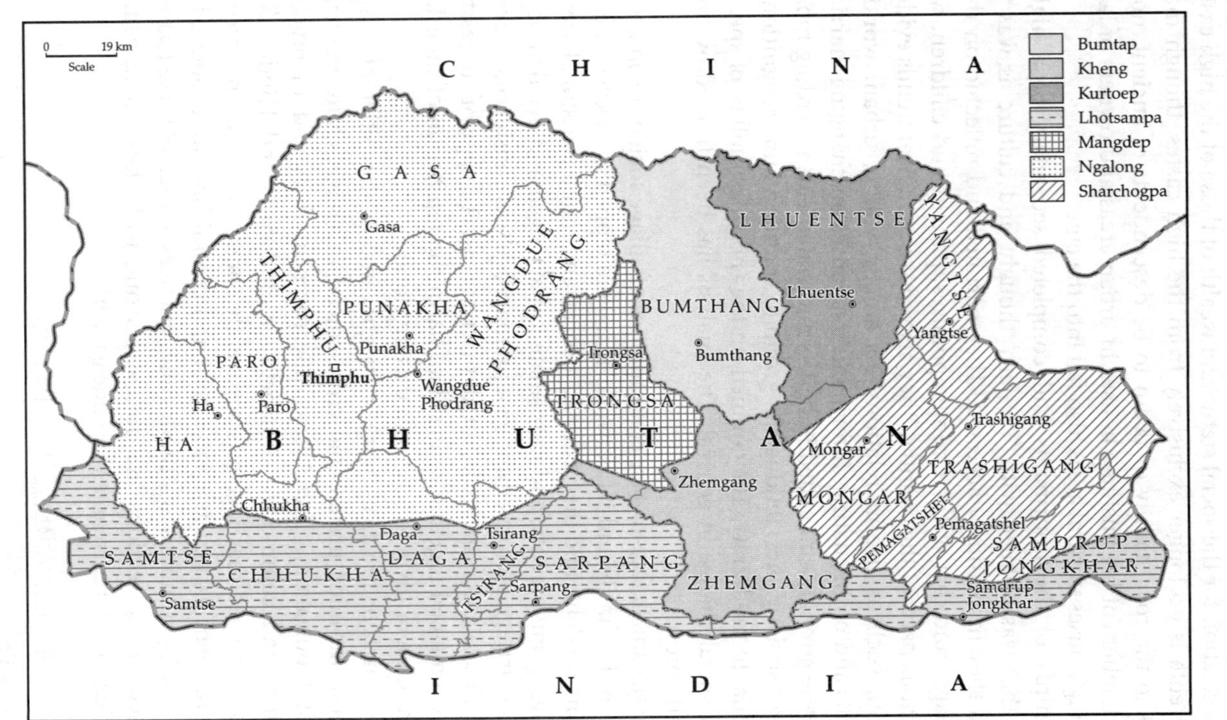

Note: © Government of India, Copyright 2018

1. The responsibility for the correctness of internal details rests with the publisher. 2. The external boundaries of India agree with the Record/Master Copy certified by Survey of India. 3. The spellings of names in this map have been taken from various sources.

marriage was considered the equivalent of brother-sister incest. *Sergamathang* refers to the first cross-cousin (mother's brother's daughter or father's sister's daughter) among the Sharchop and literally means golden cousin (ibid.: 23–24). The terms for cross-cousins are also that for affines: *mathang* is female cross-cousin and sister-in-law, and *kothkin* is male cross-cousin and brother-in-law. In the related Buddhist groups of Kurteop and Kheng (of the north-east and centre respectively) too, first cross-cousins are reserved for each other as children. However, in western Bhutan such marriages are taboo.

Dorji argues that cousin marriage was a bonding factor in creating communal identity and social organisation, and it determined social status by preserving family wealth and lineage and, thereby, caste. The practice is linked to the value given to endogamy and the idea of 'bone'. 'It is believed that marriages between same "bones" ensure purity of the descent. Families' status is differentiated according to "bone quality"' (2003: 31). In one contemporary case, an eldest daughter was married to her only male cross-cousin of the first degree, her mother's brother's son, who was 14 years her senior. It was an arrangement made by the girl's maternal grandfather and uncle in order to preserve the 'pure' blood lineage, which they claimed went back to the Tibetan royalty. She was especially groomed for him, an incarnate lama in the Mahayana Buddhist tradition, and received a traditional religious education. Her sisters address their brother-in-law as brother, while giving him the respect due to an incarnate lama and brother-in-law.

Dorji's household survey on the preference and prevalence of cross-cousin marriages in two selected *gewogs*[2] of Mongar district in eastern Bhutan is illuminating. The gap between stated marriage rule and practice is prevalent in most preferential systems (Trautmann 1982). It is the contrast between the two blocks in the same district, which is of interest to our discussion and may be an indication of directions of change.

TABLE 2.1: Preference and Prevalence of Cross-cousin Marriages in Two Blocks of Mongar District

	Kenkhar gewog	*Mongar gewog*	*Total*
Number of households surveyed	90	90	180
Number of people preferring cross-cousin marriage	89	82	171
Number of people preferring non-cousin marriages	1	8	9
Number of cross-cousin marriages	44	26	70
Number of non-cousin marriages	143	196	339

Source: Dorji (2003: 25), reproduced with permission.

Dorji concludes that the greater prevalence and preference of the practice in the Kenkhar gewog is because of its distance from modern life. Kenkhar gewog is one of the remotest blocks in Bhutan and it takes more than three days to reach there on foot. Mongar Gewog, however, is located close to the east-west highway and the district headquarters, with direct links to modern, urban life. It has access to the regional hospital, school, market, and banking and telecommunication facilities. Dorji (2003) argues that modern knowledge regarding the ill effects of consanguineous marriage must have been a factor in the reduced practice. This factor was also cited by one of my informants who, despite his traditional Buddhist education, considered cousin marriage 'immoral and unhealthy'. Tenzin, another informant, said that cousin marriage had come to be seen as 'shameful' in his village. These expressions may be seen as justifications of changes in marriage practices other than the decline in cousin marriage. Tenzin had used such arguments in his refusal to marry his cousin, who remained embittered with him. He also confirmed Dorji's (ibid.) findings in attributing the decline in cousin marriage 'to young people arranging their own life partners' and their desire to marry for love.

As Dorji's (2003) data shows us, cross-cousin marriage remains the stated ideal in both blocks; hence, further explanations for the varied shift in practice have to be sought. The decline in the practice may be linked to the occupational and economic differentiation of kin groups and the local community, and its effects on the criteria of eligibility (Kapadia 1995).[3] Cousins 'left behind' may no longer be a good match. In such a context, non-cross-cousin marriage enables class endogamy and upward mobility.

Polygyny and Polyandry

Polygyny and Polyandry are continuing practices among the northern Buddhists, the rural and urban, and across classes. Sororal polygyny (sisters marrying the same man) is preferred, marriage to two women being the most common. Economic and social purposes as well as practical convenience are cited as the motivating factors. The southern Hindus practice polygyny, but not polyandry, and sororal polygyny is rare.

Fraternal polyandry in which brothers share a wife is common amongst the Bjops and the Brokpas, nomadic herding communities living in the sub-alpine regions in the north-west (Laya—a block located in north of Gasa district in western Bhutan) and north-east (Merak and Sakteng—blocks located in north of Trashigang district in eastern Bhutan). These Buddhist groups have a distinct language, and economic and cultural practices. Dorji (2003) argues for the functionality of the system, given an ecology and economic organisation that divide family members, especially men, between summer pastures, highland and lowlands, cattle-keeping and trade. It also keeps land and cattle within a household.[4] However, fraternal polyandry not only facilitates household management and a better standard of living but also, as in Levine's (1988) study of the Nyinba in Nepal, it is in keeping with societal ideals of fraternal friendship, a 'good family man' and a powerful household that enables political power.

Inheritance is patrilineal, but the elder brother tends to inherit a larger portion of the land (Pain and Deki 2004: 427).[5] Though he dominates the family, brothers take turns in spending time with the wife. She becomes the nodal point of the family and knows who the father of each child is. Polyandry was also practised among rural elites and nobles of eastern Bhutan with the similar intent of preventing the fragmentation of family wealth and maintaining status. One husband would work as a courtier in the Royal Court,[6] another might engage in trade and one would stay back at home with the wife. The wife would make occasional visits to the husbands living away from the main home and had to have excellent personal skills to ensure good relations with and amongst the brothers.

Child Marriage

Arranged marriages are conducive of child marriage, found among the rural elite in northern Bhutan, Hindus in southern Bhutan, and also among other Buddhists and Hindus.[7] In Dzongkha, the national language, and in local dialects it is called *chung ngyen*, literally meaning small marriage. Parents agree to marry off their children once they are physically and mentally mature, but the age at marriage could be as low as 12 years. According to an unnamed interviewee cited in Dema (2009), the recently enacted legal age for marriage of 18 has little relevance among nomadic groups in Laya. For neighbours and relatives, who meet at the summer pastures, this is an opportune time to marry off their children. Young brides, between the ages of 10 and 16, are sent to their husband's home to manage domestic chores (ibid.: 1, 2).

The Sacredness of Marriage

Trends of change and diversity of views were discernible with regard to the idea of the sacredness of marriage. For those who affirmed the idea, there was a range of meanings—religious, moral and social—through which they upheld marriage as an institution and a lifelong relationship. For both Hindus and Christians, love, passion, children and family life were necessarily tied to marriage, which was a religious rite and duty. For Buddhists, the religious character was more indirect and complex. Informants explained it in terms of their understanding of aspects of Buddhist philosophy. Dorji, the informant mentioned earlier, commented, 'human life is the foundation of *choe* and *jigten*, religion and secularism'. Another informant pointed to the belief that it takes eons to be born as a human being, *melu rimpoche* (making human life rare and precious). Marriage, which will give birth to a new human life, a rare gift, is thence sacred. Marriage was also described as the union of *thap* and *sherab*, of Skilful means and Wisdom, the first being male and the second female. The connection between spouses is described in terms of karma, and deeds in a previous life. Tobgay, an informant, said, 'I and my wife met as a result of previous karma' and he asserted that nothing can break their relationship as long as their karmic connection is alive. In such interpretations, whatever the changes in society and economy, the institution of marriage must be respected.

There were non-religious dimensions to the idea of the 'sacredness' of marriage, emphasising it as socially essential. One, which we have discussed earlier, is the significance of endogamous marriage in preserving and continuing 'blood' and 'bone', caste, ethnicity and thence status and society itself. That marriage defines a person's place in society is an idea and a social norm that children are socialised into, particularly important for the elite. The sacredness of marriage is tied to the importance of having children. This entails mundane concerns—children as a person's social security, especially in illness and death—that along with religious connotations bring commoners within the ambit of the value. The notion of marriage as a life-long relation is also glossed in moral terms not tied to any one religion—it is the basis of a happy family life and demands respect, trust and faith. In this is inserted an ethic that there is a difference between sexual relationships within and without marriage.

Some informants rejected marriage as sacred because of their personal experiences of unhappy marriages and faithlessness or that 'marriage is a game for the Bhutanese', as one informant, Meto, observed. They had become cynical about the institution of marriage. Others cited positive and negative features of marriage and continued to uphold the institution on grounds of functionality rather than the religious. Some informants were rueful that the material dimension and purpose had become even more important in match-making and the life of a marriage resulting in the derogation of the 'sublime and religious' purpose of marriage.

A number of informants decried the rules of caste/lineage endogamy in a manner that critiqued marriage as a religious institution. The decline of lineage, caste, and tribe endogamy has accompanied the questioning of the sacredness of marriage as well as arranged marriages to which we turn after discussing the variations in practice between the elite and commoners.

THE WEDDING AND THE MARRIAGE: ELITE AND COMMONER VARIATIONS

Two main features demarcate elite and commoner marriage among the Buddhists and the Hindus. The first is the emphasis on class-caste endogamy, in the case of the elite, and ethnic endogamy among the commoners. For the Hindus, inter-caste marriage among the upper castes has become acceptable, though not preferred, but marriage between a 'high' and 'low' caste was still not recognised. Among Buddhists, family history, the original home towns, wealth, education and the astrological calendars (both Chinese and Tibetan) of the proposed pair are matched. Gazom, a librarian, stated, 'If the elites ever marry commoners, it is like the story of Romeo and Juliet'. Traditionally, maintenance of the pure bloodline was 'imposed' among the upper castes and this fostered the practice of cross-cousin marriage.[8] Travers' study of the matrimonial strategies of the Tibetan aristocracy between 1880 and 1959 reveals that despite an occasional marriage outside the exclusive group, maintenance of prestige and respect for the endogamy rule were of primary concern (2008: 1, 15). Nowadays even the members of the royal family marry outside the 'pure bloodline'.

The second difference between the elite and the commoners is with regard to the wedding, which is observed with elaborate and expensive formalities among the elite and with minimum ceremony among commoners. After completing the marriage talks, in which the bride and the groom are consulted, the elite again consult astrologers to fix the date and time of the ceremony. The not-so-well-off find basic astrological information in newspapers. A marriage ritual is then conducted, depending on convenience, at either the bride's or groom's home. In Buddhism, there is no religious ritual specifically dedicated to marriage. The wedding among the elite is a mix of local practices, elaborate prayers conducted by monks, and secular celebration.

Social status demands a grand ceremony of *shudrel phuensum tshogpa* (auspicious seated lines), a ceremony that is also performed on occasions other than marriage. Guests must be seated in neat, straight lines and served fruits and sweets as symbols of *tendrel* (good luck and prosperity). Eleven to 21 items are served, starting with oranges, a symbol of fertility.[9] The senior members of the family, who were involved in the marriage talks in the first place, orate on the significance of the marriage. The *lapa marchangi genpai tendrel* (ritual of holding wine), follows next. The bride and the groom drink from the same cup in the presence of the family, relatives and friends, symbolising they are of the same family. After this, the family and friends present *khaddar* (silk scarves of auspiciousness) to congratulate the bride and groom, and join in drinking, eating and traditional dances. Particularly in urban areas, elite families may hold a grand modern party instead of a ceremony. The rich and powerful, who are expected to present expensive gifts, are invited. The gifts help the young couple in setting up their new home and thereby offset the costs of the celebrations.

In rural Buddhist society, both the elite and the commoners hold a simple ceremony, with invitees presenting the khaddar to the couple and a small bamboo container of locally brewed wine towards the celebrations. Traditional, conservative commoners invite monks for a purification ritual and prayers, the extent depending on the resources of the parents and the betrothed couple.

Among Hindus the marriage rituals include a *puja* (ritual of worship) at the groom's home and the celebrations, which last for three days, at the bride's. The religious ritual is critical to legalising the marriage. Elite Hindu families also spend a lot of money on the wedding, inviting guests from their varied social network.

The grand marriage ceremony acts as a pressure to keep the couple together. Tshendu, thinking of an unhappily married friend, said that 'pompous marriages have obligations for the bride and the groom to live up to the celebrations. Even if you are not happy, you cannot move out of the marriage, it binds you like a stick'. 'Having a tendrel is more an aristocratic system and is not common for the ordinary people', said another informant. A commoner's marriage may not be anything more than just the community's acceptance, in the course of time, of a couple who has been living together as husband and wife. Not just Buddhists in the rural east, west and centre, but migrants to Thimphu also follow this practice. In such marriages, little attention is said to be paid to the family background. They are often associated with the 'looking for a maiden' custom, post-marital residence in the home of either of the partners, and easy divorce.

Pain and Pema argue that the absence of ritual causes instability in marriage and suggest the latter as an important factor behind matrilineal inheritance of land in parts of Bhutan (2004: 431). Pelzom, a pious Buddhist who grew up in the rural east, where her parents still reside, disagreed. She said that in the ceremony-less marriage, 'the couple comes in front of the society'. The society, witness to the marriage, can be called on for assistance during bad times, can demand that the couple remain together, and even provide legal assistance to the 'wronged' partner. Therefore, the marriage may not be as loose as it appears to be. This is important for marriages made through the custom of 'Looking for a Maiden', as we will soon discuss.

Since 1964, the Bhutanese marriage law demands a wedding certificate to legalise the marriage. A trend has surfaced for Buddhist and Hindu urban, middle-class couples to visit a court, obtain a legal marriage certificate, and host either a lunch or a dinner party for their family and friends, who bring gifts. The legal certificate may be obtained only because it is required by the government in situations such as children's school admission, scholarships and job transfers. In some cases, a marriage certificate is obtained after some years of living together.

The last is becoming popular amongst young people in modern, middle-class families, drawing both on the tradition of the ceremony-less marriage of commoners and elite ideas of Western lifestyle. Views on this emergent idea and practice are mixed. In the opinion of some, it trivialises marriage and the sexual relationship, and evades responsibility. They suggest that the practice of live-in allows for exploitation of women ('Bhutanese men use and dump them and look for better ones', as one informant said), promiscuity, unsafe sexual practices and their associated risks. Others, however, see it as a rational choice for young working professionals, who are economically independent and who wish to focus on their careers and not start a family too early. Both Kado (a Buddhist) and Dhan (an atheist) argued that the practice allows partners to get to know each other and decide on the feasibility of marriage. Even though his relationship ended, one informant claimed it taught him 'how to manage money, home, shop and even how to behave with the neighbours'. Though some opined that mutual understanding was all that was required to make the relationship work, some of this view were also worried about the 'misuse of partners' and unwanted pregnancies.

One important difference with the earlier practice of ceremony-less marriages, as another informant pointed out, was the absence of the social witness and legal protection. The couple now had to solve their problems on their own, with no support, especially as rural parents often did not know that their children were in a live-in relationship. This highlights how marriage is embedded in wider relationships. Ceremony-less marriage and live-in relations also take us back to our earlier discussion on perceptions of marriage as a sacred institution. Thus, our discussions so far has been issues in arranged and love marriages. We now focus on evaluative views on the two.

Love Versus Arranged Marriages

As discussed at the start, cross-cousin marriage and child marriage, endogamy of 'blood', caste, ethnicity, and practices such as polygamy and polyandry are closely linked to arranged marriage. According to a number of informants, arranged marriages are dominant, particularly in villages. In the villages of eastern Bhutan, it may be between children of neighbours if not of kin; in other parts, despite being a closely connected society, the young couple are likely to be strangers to each other at first. Some say that women who are illiterate or school drop-outs see this as the best option in their life. Arranged marriages also ensure caste endogamy for the Hindus. However, the discussion on commoners' marriage, for whom 'blood' and class endogamy is not critical, indicates long-standing alternative practices.

As with the idea of the sacred, arranged marriage implies a relationship not only between the spouses, but a relationship between families and emphasises inter-generational ties. An important perception upholding arranged marriage, as elaborated by various informants, is that parents know their children and through their experience and wisdom will come to a good match for them, ensuring personal, social and economic compatibility. Not only are the latter important, these marriages are embedded in a circle of social support, and the parents take on practical responsibilities such as that of raising the grandchildren. It is these perceptions as well as a rejection of child marriage, new aspirations following education and new ideas of romance that are leading to divergent and troubled views on arranged marriage.

Informants narrate stories of arranged marriages that were 'successful', thanking the wisdom of the match-maker—a parent, elder sibling or uncle. Social backgrounds and incomes of the pair were similar and the personalities were a 'perfect' complementary match. It was striking that in these stories either the wife was cool and patient or accepted that her husband made the decisions, even as he respected and consulted her on her views. The stories of unhappy arranged marriages, on the other hand, were ones in which the wife came from a richer family or the match-makers had not learnt enough about the prospective partners and the man turned out to be a wastrel or the woman had hidden a pre-marital pregnancy. Others pointed out that interference from the parents when there are marital problems, rather than being a social support, can in fact further complicate matters. In cross-cousin alliances, couples may have to remain in unhappy situations or else families may be torn apart.

Even informants of a similar age were divided in their opinions of arranged and love marriages. Some said that the choice of the partner can be left to the wisdom of the parents, who are to be obeyed, respected and revered. Gazom, describing her own marriage, and others talking of their observations, suggested that in a well arranged match, love will follow the wedding. One informant interpreted a Bhutanese saying, '*Nyen bu da bumi loden*'—marriage is the son's and daughter's wish—to argue for love marriage, but with parental guidance, including advice on astrological compatibility. Dema, another informant, drew on the idea of karma to point out that it was not possible to know whether somebody would have a love or arranged marriage.

Others suggested that parents have not understood that the world has changed and their children have changed, that matches that do not take into account the latter's new ideals, aspirations and interests lead to unhappy marriages. For some, resistance was primarily to early marriage as they wished to pursue higher education and marry only after getting jobs, by when they would also not be amenable to an arranged match. Dhan, an informant, questioned the concept of marriage itself, yet hoped for a love marriage, inspired by his elder sister's happy inter-religious marriage—between a Hindu and a Buddhist. Successful self-choice or love marriages were recounted in both rural and urban settings. The four rural informants, all farmers on the outskirts of Thimphu, described their own marriages and that of others in their village in these terms.

Yet, love marriages were not always accepted. Gazom's parents, who had themselves fallen in love and married, arranged her marriage with a man other than the one she was in love with. Kizom's first marriage angered her kin. Her husband, a primary school headmaster in her village, was not of her own ethnic and religious community. Strong parental objections and even ostracism by the community could follow in such cases. Informants narrated tales of parental intervention in preventing or breaking up love marriages due to religious, caste or class differences that were thought to jeopardise status. Critics of love marriage said that such incompatibilities inevitably led to problems in these marriages and did not allow for a harmonious family life. This was not Kizom's view, though her own inter-community marriage had ended when her husband left her. 'Many of the village girls competed to have him as their husband,' commented Kizom, adding that because of her illiteracy she was unable to 'fight back the woman who intervened in their marriage.'

Many of the informants who had had love marriages did not have an articulated rejection of marriages arranged by their elders. However, ideas of romance and love and constructions of an ideal marriage were elaborated by those who argued for self-choice. Affection, care, cooperation, honesty and understanding, compatibility based on common interests, effective communication, trust, advisor-companion-best friend, soul mate, pure love are among the ideals that were voiced. These views subtly pushed love marriages into a domain of individuality that earlier self-choice marriages did not emphasise. Much greater demands were being placed on the individual, inter-personal relationship even as the idea of 'finding one's life partner' expressed the continuing investment in the institution of marriage.

Perhaps it was this that led to the disenchantment with love and love marriage, noticeable in the narrations of a number of men. Tsulthrim, thinking over his own experience, said that pure love was driven out by differences in background. Tshendu commented that 'in love marriage, feelings and things can change with time. Love can fade'. Partners changed after the marriage, becoming very different from what they were like during the courtship—becoming a wastrel or taking to religion. A number of informants felt that often physical love had been paramount in the idea of love and that young people were possessive and did not take time to understand each other. They argued that these were the factors behind divorce and suggested a trend towards increasing divorce concomitant with the trend towards love marriage.

For many, their notions of romance were tempered by a touch of realism and social desires. One feature, common across much of the sub-continent, is the wish for a traditional wedding that signifies parental acceptance, simultaneous with the idea that parents should not intervene in the relationship. Seldon was not disillusioned with love, but suggested that marriage entails responsibilities and if it is to work, sacrifices have to be made. Her husband had an affair, which she forgave as neither wanted to give up on the marriage. Lhekzom attributed the success of her marriage to the positive lessons she learnt from her first, failed marriage. Dechen mentioned that she and her husband have their own share of arguments. She feels there is a loss of identity and privacy for women even in love marriage, and that it is women who make sacrifices for the sake of the husband and the children. This may be compounded if, as Kamal said, when speaking of his own self-arranged marriage, men want their wives to have their mother's characteristics!

For Seldon, Lhekzom and Dechen the quality of the conjugal relationship and women's position was not really different in arranged and love marriages. Further, 'even in a successful love marriage, the couples struggle to make a living, raise a family and survive. In such a situation, the couples have no time to relax and experience love'. Starting from the other end, informants had suggested that love develops in a well-arranged marriage. They also pointed to cases where a love relationship was arranged into a marriage. Kamal had been introduced to his wife by friends and they chose to marry though they did not experience 'romantic love'. There were cases of active intervention by the senior generation who would push a couple to marry because they were in a relationship or because one of them had expressed love for or courted the other.

Concerns regarding compatibility, common interests, getting to know each other, affection and trust, suggest that a necessary condition for love or self-arranged marriage to become a practice are opportunities for hetero-social interaction. A couple must be able to spend time together without the immediate pressure of marriage. College education has provided one such possibility. Many of the cases narrated, including that of Seldon, was that of a high school or college romance. Others were office romances, meetings with common friends, or interaction while working in the fields, at weddings, village festivals and other such occasions. Lack of such opportunities, as informants pointed out, acted as a break on self-choice marriages in conservative communities like the southern Bhutanese Hindus. Young and not-so-young people were drawing on both traditional and modern forms to meet and court prospective lovers and spouses—the custom of 'looking for a maiden' and online dating. In the last section of this essay, we discuss dimensions and implications of both these forms, with expressed ideas of traditional and modern marriage in the background.

Courtship: Old and New Practices

Looking for a Maiden

The long practised courtship custom of 'looking for a maiden', that appears to contrast with arranged marriage has received attention in the media and in studies. It has been both romanticised and demonised. Its advocates see it as an open expression of love, leading to a self-chosen, intimate, and sexual relation, courtship, and then marriage. Critics view it as an exploitative practice, wherein girls and women are subjected to sexual harassment and even rape.

'Let us go for a stroll', 'youth on stroll', and 'strolling for women' are other terms by which it is referred to in various dialects. The custom has been and is practised in rural settings in all regions of Bhutan,[10] but is particularly part of non-elite culture in the east and centre. Tshendu recounted that 'looking for a maiden' had led to the marriages of half the people in his village in eastern Bhutan. There was a broad sequence of activities that this custom built on. Girls and boys met and interacted while farming or collecting firewood, dried leaves and fodder in the woods. They got to know each other in the course of these activities and could subsequently socialise after the day's work. Through secret signals between a young woman and man, attracted to each other, she would indicate her readiness to open the door should her lover visit at night. In time, they or their parents would decide that they must marry, which, as outlined earlier, could be with minimum ritual and residence in either partner's natal home.

The local terms had a positive connotation, but the male initiative that they embraced was a precursor to the contemporary shifts and controversies in the custom. It is now known more popularly as 'night hunting'[11] and its relevance and implications have become a topic for discussion among the educated. There was a noticeable gender divide in the views of the informants. According to Kizom and Lhekzom, it was a game young men played so as to enjoy physical sex without responsibility. Since there was no concept of rape in eastern Bhutan, sexual harassment of girls was not acknowledged. The doors and windows of the homes of the village poor were not strong, the traditional wooden latch could be opened from outside, and men could enter uninvited. At times, parents woke up and drove such intruders out. Girls would sleep near elderly women to deter young men. Kizom said that she remained safe because she was physically strong and could fight unwanted advances.

Given that it is a legitimate path to marriage, young women are kept on the razor's edge between encouraging flirtations to achieve a desired marriage, deflecting harassment and losing their reputation. The prevalent idea that the more attractive girl is visited by more men could easily slip into the label of promiscuity, making a marriage more difficult for her. A number of the informants spoke of women who had children outside marriage as a result of 'looking for a maiden' liaisons and the difficulties that they and their children faced. The problem, usually, arose as the father did not accept the liaison as a marriage and the children as his. Penjore, however, does not agree that the children suffer any legal or social disability, and he relates this to sanctions of the small community of his field study as well as the 1980 Marriage Act, which obliges men to pay child maintenance for children born outside marriage (2009: 147–49).

Dorji, Tenzin and Raju were among the male informants who spoke in favour of the custom. It provided a platform for courtship, cross-sex joking and socialising, and getting to know a possible marriage partner. Traditionally, 'shyness of sexual expression' was absent. They insisted that theirs was not a culture in which women or girls are bullied and that it was difficult to enter into a house uninvited. Whether or not this was true in the past, many suggest that with electricity, glass windows and modern door latches, men cannot hide and can be found nowadays. Dorji's own marriage was through this approach of courtship. Tenzin saw it as a route to love marriage and out of arranged and cross-cousin marriage, even while acknowledging that it could be misused.[12] A number of men narrated how the term was also used to describe the night-time 'hunt' by groups of young men for girls to 'have some fun' with. Kado saw this to be a consequence of changing norms of non-marital sexuality: it had not been a taboo earlier, but nor had casual sex been acceptable.

In drawing together the diverse views and stories, what emerges is that the traditional custom was a form of flirtation and courtship that was intended to lead to marriage. That it did not always do so was accepted, more for men than for women. The latter suffered, not because it was known that they had had pre-marital sexual relations, but because of the label of promiscuity. It also made them vulnerable to forced and unwanted sex. Thus, this open expression of individual love and intimacy was not based on gender equality, though social sanctions in small communities provided a modicum of security to children born outside marriage. Many rural women and urban and rural men continue to take this route to meet, get to know and court possible marital partners, not always in keeping with earlier rules of cousin marriage and endogamy. This traditional form has become a part of contemporary life, especially with changing aspirations and desires that followed increasing geographical and economic mobility. The mobility, however—with its implications for the breaching of community and class endogamy—has also created many of the difficulties.

Students from nearby colleges, truck drivers and civil servants on rural tour are more eligible as husbands than local farmers, and a route out of the hard labour of village life. Young women are happy to be 'courted' by these 'outsiders', who, however, may have a temporary relationship in mind. These men 'succeed' by promising marriage, but are themselves looking for a 'better' marriage or have a wife elsewhere. Their desperate attempt to seek the woman's consent to sexual intimacy is captured in the saying, *San phamai phazhing yang bee, ngazi gongphai khab yang me thun*, meaning 'even parental land will be given at night; not even a needle from a lapel will be left behind in the morning'. Penjore (2009) also found that 'false promises of marriage' had become linked to the custom, though he argues that the girls can always protect themselves since the activity takes place at their homes (ibid.: 113, 115–16, 149). His conclusion was based on the views of his mostly male respondents, for few women were ready to talk to him about the custom (ibid.: 4–5, 146). Critically, local community sanction has little force for such passing outsiders.

Female aspirations and agency as well as male hubris are all part of the contemporary practice, if not also of the traditional form, as illustrated by the following, apocryphal case. This was an instance in which social gossip is used to bring state law into the process to the advantage of the woman.

> A young woman, about 16 years old, who had dropped out of high school, was living with her married, elder sister. The latter invited a civil servant posted in their block for dinner to their village home. She served the food late so that it was no longer possible for him to walk back home. At night, she sent her younger sister to the room in which she had prepared his bed. The man was happy to sleep with the young woman and returned to his home in the morning, with no sign of returning any time soon. After a couple of weeks, the elder sister warned the man that he should marry her sister or she would file a case of rape under the new laws according to which her sister was underage. Village gossip and public knowledge of the incident made this a real threat, so the man married her. However, he neglected her and planned to leave her once she completed 18 years to fulfil his own dream of marrying an 'educated and glamorous woman'. Meto, the narrator, critical of young rural women who accepted the custom of 'looking for a maiden', said that civil servants refer to this incident as the 'trap game' and adds, 'But the couple have now compromised with each other and are living a happy life. They are glued together. He spends less time with his friends.'

Online Dating

Young urban men and women spend time in online chat rooms while at work, at home and from cyber cafes. In Tsulthrim's words, 'I did it for the sake of fun and chatted with nameless and faceless identities. I don't mind socialising'. Online chatting even helped him improve his typing speed, he points out! Many informants and their friends and relatives used online chat rooms as a platform to date, make friends, court and perhaps find a marriage partner. Even without meeting face-to-face, they 'can find out if they are compatible and if not, would stay as friends'. It could give women the initiative in deciding whether to take a relationship further or not. People usually met online as strangers, but occasionally through mutual friends. For young people, online dating has opened the world to romance: Kamal's daughters had met their husbands online, one a Hindu from India and one a Buddhist living in the US. Both the marriages are inter-community, but it was the younger daughter's to an Indian Hindu that he had resisted initially and still worries about, because of the 'conservative social norms that are harsh on women' in India. For his elder daughter, it was a second marriage, and she decided to remarry only because the man accepted her daughter from her first marriage. Though they met and dated online, some relatives had put them in touch with each other.

However, stories of disappointment and cheating were as frequent as stories with successful and happy ends (Editorial 2008). Sad endings were foretold, suggested one informant, as young people seemed to 'blindly fall in love at first sight', or rather first chat, and assume that marriage was the natural end. Despite traditional, rural social gatherings and modern, urban parties, cross-gender socialising of young people where intimacy is not oriented to possible marriage, is not easy or common. The dangers cited more often were that of 'faceless and nameless identities', who could lie and cheat, or the 'addiction to flirtation' without social control. Some informants, such as Dhan, had created false identities and persona to conduct one or more online flirtations. When the woman wished to meet him in real life, an appointment was made but not kept. Some ignored and pretended not to know the person when they realised that he or she was nothing like what they had described themselves to be online. Others decided that an online date had nefarious or material ends in mind, rather than a romantic connection. Some spoke of how they suffered heartbreak when they discovered that the 'friend' was not who he said he was, or had another long-standing relationship or marriage and they themselves were just 'time pass'. 'It is difficult to find a person who is wife or husband material online', said Meto. Many of these informants were of the view that the stories of online dating leading to marriages were only in movies and newspapers. Yet, online dating has become a social practice for educated urban youth, driven by the desire for flirtation, and even more by the hope of a romantic love leading to marriage.

Conclusion

In delineating marriage patterns in Bhutan, both continuities and the remaking of tradition are evident, as is the recasting of modernity. Thimphu can be viewed as a microcosm of the country, but also containing an avant garde. The informants, whatever their age, related not only their own experiences, but also that of their kin, neighbours, friends and colleagues of various ages and from varied ethnic groups and regions. They spoke of values and practices that called on ideas of a unique cultural identity and the centrality of the social group and tradition, even as they spoke of individual desires and strategems to make a life of love, marriage and family. Thus, arranged marriages were to provide the desired love relationship and love marriages were not only to be a lifelong fulfilment of individual desire and bonding, but were to be embedded in traditional social networks and identity. Marriages brought generations together even as they separated them in their aspirations. Weddings could be both modern and traditional, religious celebrations and secular parties.

This intermeshing of ideas and practices of tradition and modernity were in part possible because of the fluidity in both. This was based on the diversity of practice that each contained—ethnic and religious in tradition, in the sources and possibilities in the modern, with status and class as aspects of both. It was also based on an unnoticed continuity of ideas between traditional values and the modern. Most critical in the latter was the common emphasis on the institution of marriage, a harmonious family life, and the gendered model of the conjugal relationship. Though women were educated and in new occupations and despite flexibility in traditional post-marital residence, the expectation that they would ensure that the marriage worked was common to both. While the link between endogamy and the sacredness of marriage was questioned, new secular and religious interpretations upheld support for endogamy. Aspirations for self-choice and individual self-love could cite traditional practices such as 'looking for a maiden' and ceremony-less weddings to culturally embed their radical choices.

The contradictions and growing divergence in views, the divide between the old and the new could, however, be too deep to cross. Men and women differed in their views of traditional practice and its modern translations. The urban young and those educated in the 'modern' values contrasted with the villagers and nomads in the north and the west, the Hindus in the south, and the traditional elite in their neighbourhood in their romantic desires and advocacy of individual choice over social group and marital practices. While it remains a question as to whether the young are the trendsetters or will remain a small section, today, the practices claimed as custom and those highlighted as the new deeply influence each other.

Notes

[1] The fieldwork was conducted in 2008–09. My own family's marital history informs the study, such that my personal engagement in Bhutanese society has meant a constant struggle to see along with and beyond my own subjectivities. Interviews at the first meeting took the form of 'story-telling' or life history narratives.

[2] A group of villages make up a *gewog* or block. It is the lowest unit of administration and government in the country.

[3] Kapadia (1995) has discussed such factors in the decline of cousin marriage in South India.

[4] These motivations have been discussed in a range of writings on polyandry and polygyny among non-Buddhist groups, including Mazumdar (1962), Berreman (1963), and Gupta (1990).

[5] There are commonalities also with the Sherpa in Nepal studied by Ortner (1978) and groups across the border in Tibet.

[6] From 1900 till late 1940s, the Royal Court was located in central Bhutan. Many courtiers spent long periods away from their native homes to serve the monarch.

[7] The Hindus, many of Nepali origin, also follow caste endogamy, but do not have a dowry system.

[8] Till the late 1940s, bone monitors from the Royal Court visited the districts and the villages once in three years to check that there had been no 'mixing white and black bones'. If there was such a marriage, a fine was imposed and the couple was forced to divorce.

[9] The belief is that just as a single orange, when peeled, has many small fruits, so also a couple will be blessed with many children.

[10] Penjore (2009) points to a similar custom among Sherpa communities in Nepal and the matrilineal Na in Yunnan, South-East China.

[11] There are various theories as to how this name was given to this custom, ranging from the predatory practices of public school and college boys to the ethnocentric view of outsiders. Penjore (2009), who undertook an ethnographic study of the custom in a village in central Bhutan, suggests the last theory.

[12] That the traditional form could be the path to non-conventional matches parallels Ahearn's (2002) finding that the traditional form of elopement among the Magar in Nepal could result in 'extremely inappropriate' marriages.

References

Ahearn, Laura M. 2002. *Invitations to Love: Literacy, Love Letters and Social Change in Nepal*. Ann Arbor: University of Michigan Press.

Berreman, G. 1963. *Hindus of the Himalayas: Ethnography and change*. Berkeley: University of California Press.

Dema, Tashi. 2009. *The Child Brides of Laya*. Thimphu: Kuensel.
Dorji, Lham, 2003. *Sergamathang Kothkin and other Bhutanese Marriage Customs*. Thimphu: The Centre for Bhutan Studies.
Editorial. 2008. 'Beware of the Cyber Criminal'. *Kuensel City Bytes* 2 (30). 26 July.
Gupta, J. 1990. 'Class relations, family structure, and the bondage of women. In *Structures and Strategies: Women, Work and Family in Asia*, ed. Leela Dube and Rajni Palriwala, 151–73. New Delhi: SAGE.
Kapadia, K. 1995. *Siva and her Sisters: Gender, Caste, and Class in Rural India*. Oxford: Westview Press.
Levine, Nancy E. 1988. *Dynamics of Polyandry, Kinship, Domesticity and Population on Tibetan Border*. Chicago: The University of Chicago Press.
Mazumdar, D. N. 1962. *Himalayan Polyandry: Structure, Functioning and Culture Change, A Study of Jaunsar Bawar*. Bombay: Asia Publishing House.
National Statistics Bureau, Royal Government of Bhutan. 2010. *Statistical Year Book, 2010*. Available at: http://www.nsb.gov.bt/index.php?id=13; Accessed on: 21 June 2011.
Ortner, Sherry B. 1978. *Sherpas Through Their Rituals*. London: Cambridge University Press.
Pain, Adam, and Pema Deki. 2004. 'The Matrilineal Inheritance of Land in Bhutan', *Contemporary South Asia* 13 (4): 421–35.
Penjore, Dorji. 2009. *Love, Courtship and Marriage in Rural Bhutan: A Preliminary Ethnography of Wamling Village in Zhemgang*. Thimphu: Galing Printers and Publishers.
Singer, Milton. 1972. *When a Great Tradition Modernises: An Anthropological Approach to Indian Civilisation*. New York: Praeger Publishers.
Travers, Alice. 2008. 'Exclusiveness and Openness: A Study of Matrimonial Strategies in the Dga'Idan Pho brang Aristocracy (1880–1959)'. In *Journal of the International Association of Tibetan Studies*, ed. Jose I. Cabezon and David Germano, Issue 4, at the Tibetan and Himalayan Library.
Trautmann, T. R. 1982. *Dravidian Kinship*. Cambridge: Cambridge University Press.
Turner, Mark, Sonam Chuki, and Jit Tshering. 2011. 'Democratization by decree: the case of Bhutan', *Democratization*, 18 (1): 184–210. Available at: http://dx.doi.org /10.1080/13510347.2011.532626. Accessed on: 24 January 2011.

Transgressions, Accommodations and Change

Configuring Gender and Sexuality within Marriage Practices of the Kolams

Pushpesh Kumar

Introduction

I begin this essay with the traditional bridewealth practices among the Kolams of eastern Maharashtra, who practised hoe cultivation till the end of 1930s. Ester Boserup (1910–99), an economist who studied developing countries comparatively is perhaps the first scholar to emphasise a significant link between patterns of subsistence agriculture and forms of marriage payments to delineate the implications of this correlation for the quality of gender relations (Boserup 1970). She describes female and male systems of farming based on the predominance of a female or male workforce. The former prevailing in Africa and parts of South-East Asia and the latter in Asia, the Arab worlds and parts of Latin America, representing a striking contrast to each other in modes of agriculture: shifting and plough; in marital exchange: bridewealth and dowry; and in gender norms: relaxed and flexible in the former, while stricter and firm in the latter. While bridewealth societies might entail greater a work burden for women with their central role in agriculture, it simultaneously means more freedom of movement and relative economic independence for them. In contrast to this, societies practising dowry not only transfer wealth to the groom and his kin and make the wife dependent on the husband, but also exhibit norms of female veiling, seclusion between sexes, high female mortality and even practices like female infanticide. Women's role as producer is downplayed in plough economies, and they are perceived more as an instrument to reproduce male children to perpetuate the male line. Though Boserup (ibid.: 50) appears to be wary of the oversimplification in this distinction between hoe and plough societies, she nonetheless finds it valuable to work out this correlation to highlight qualitatively different gender norms in two different subsistence agricultural economies. Following Boserup, Jack Goody (1988)[1] made the questions of control over the body and sexuality of women rather central to his analysis. He argued that bridewealth, prevalent in Africa, transferred reproductive rights in the woman to the man whose kin have paid bridewealth. Unlike Eurasian societies with plough economy and marked social differentiations showing particular concern over women's purity and virginity, societies in Africa relatively lacked social differentiation and did not exercise similar control over female sexuality. Goody is simultaneously concerned with changes in productive systems and in kinship institutions through a shift in marital exchange with a simultaneous qualitative transformation of existing gender relations.

I try to demonstrate that traditional hoe cultivation among the Kolams and their bridewealth practice entailed a lack of class differentiation and fostered egalitarian gender norms. The ideology of kinship never emphasised virginity and purity of women. Gender egalitarianism substantially continues and despite shift to plough agriculture the latter remains inconsequential in altering gender norms, because it neither generates surplus nor has it become the sole source of subsistence for the majority of the Kolam families of this region. While delineating the gender-egalitarian practices, I do not wish to argue that traditional Kolami kinship entailed a complete lack of gender hierarchy. The sexual division of labour along with elaborate rules of menstrual taboo have been rather unchanging, and men assert their physical prowess through hunting and the ritual sacrifice of animals from which women are debarred. This, however, does not mean that Kolam women are subordinate in every sphere. On the contrary, both women and men have enjoyed several sexual freedoms—those listed by Goody for hoe societies with bridewealth practices, which include pre-marital sex, relatively free mixing of the sexes, widow re-marriage, divorce and extra-marital liaisons. The first part of the essay underlines the traditional bridewealth practice among the Kolams, which accords equal status to bride-givers and bride-takers and entails flexible post-marital residential arrangements. The second part consists of the empirical evidence of transgressions of prescribed sexual norms by men and women and their accommodation in the everyday life of the community. The third and last sections of the essay are about the changing ethos among some Kolam households due to the access to cash and surplus which might affect the existing forms of marital exchange with corresponding shifts in sexual norms. Ethnographic data for the present study is collected from the tribal village of Jawarla, in Kinwat Tehsil of Nanded district in eastern Maharashtra between 2003 and 2005.

The Kolams

The Kolams are a Scheduled Tribe, identified as one of the 'primitive'[2] groups by the Government of India (Shashi 1994: 80). They are distributed mainly in Yeotmal, Osmanabad, Chandrapur, Gadhchiroli and Nagpur districts of Maharashtra, and Adilabad district of Andhra Pradesh (Singh 1998: 1767). Though Singh has not included Nanded district of Maharashtra in his account, the Kolams also reside in several villages along the hill and forest areas of Kinwat tehsil, one of the most backward tehsils of Nanded district.

The Kolams weave *tople* (baskets) of different sizes and *tatte* (bamboo walls) for which there is perennial demand in the rural economy (Kumar 2006a). They speak their own dialect, Kolami, apart from Telugu and Marathi, and practice cross-cousin marriage. Trautmann (1995: 11–12) includes Kolami in the Dravidian group of languages; kinship terminology and its semantics reveal close proximity to the structure of Dravidian kinship terminologies. Every Kolam *pod* (settlement) has a *guri* (temple) of *Bhimaiyyak*, the chief deity of the Kolams.

The Kolams of Jawarla Village

Jawarla village, where the study was conducted, is referred to as a *adivasi che gaon* (tribal village), because of the greater numerical strength of Gonds and Kolams, the two tribal communities. There is no upper-caste group in the village and the number of lower and middle castes remains insignificant. There are two Kolam pods—the Pulsi pod and the Kazi pod—both located away from the main village and towards forested hillocks. The Kolam population is 255, distributed over 44 households in these two pods. The majority of households are nuclear, adult sons establishing separate households within few months of their marriage. A joint family is only maintained in cases when there is a single son and/or when the size of land is relatively large since family labour plays a vital role in cultivation on the family farm. This, however, is a recent phenomenon as settled agriculture is only a few decades old.

There is minimal education and literacy in the community, especially in the older generations. Despite state initiatives to establish *ashram shala*s (tribal schools) in the village, there is no young man who has successfully completed secondary education. A household survey (conducted by this author) of the two pods in 2005 revealed a mere 8 per cent female literacy with male literacy pegged at 25 per cent. Migration in search of livelihood is very low compared to Gonds and other caste groups in the village.

Absence of Private Property among the Kolams

Kolams have historically been a property-less community. In Furer-Haimendorf's accounts of Adilabad tribes (1945: 62, 96), the Kolams are depicted as hapless victims of the Nizam government's forest policies:

> The Kolams are a tribe of shifting cultivators who possessed until recently neither plough nor cattle; even today, many of them subsist by hoe-cultivation on hill slopes ... Except for a few Kolams ... who have taken to independent plough cultivation, the members of this tribe possess no cattle and as a rule not even goats, sheep or pigs, chickens and dogs being their only domestic animals. (ibid.: 96)

Jawarla Kolams have sustained themselves through bamboo weaving. Elderly Kolams do remember some cultivation on hill slopes in the remote past when millet seeds were spread to grow on their own. There was no concept of private ownership then. Acquisition of land and settled agriculture began some 40 years ago when the Kolams were compelled to leave their old settlement located at the south-western boundary of the village. The police suspecting Naxalite activities used to raid the Kolam settlement very often;[3] to escape police intrusion the Kolams moved towards forested hillocks in two different directions. In their newly-settled areas, the Kolam families cleared some forest land and began cultivation. At that time, none of them owned bullocks or bullock carts. By 2000, some 60 per cent of the Kolam households possessed a small tract of land and the other 40 per cent continued to remain landless. The landowner families lacked *pattas* (legal entitlement of ownership in agricultural land) and hence could not benefit from state agricultural subsidies to marginal and tribal farmers. The land owned by Kolams was uneven, stony and lacked irrigation facility. A few Kolam households owned brass utensils and cattle-wealth, mainly goats distributed by the government over the last few decades.

In mid-1990s, the Government of Maharashtra attempted to implement several income-generating schemes under the Integrated Tribal Development Programme (ITDP). These failed to bring the desired result due to official venality and lack of will to know the real needs of the community (Kumar 2003). The Kolams have also not been able to benefit from the reservation policies of the government for Scheduled Tribes, due to their lack of education. Only three of the 44 households of the Kolams were regarded as affluent as they produced surplus foodgrains, which they sold in the market. This affluence is attributed to the hard work of these respective families. This limited class differentiation in economic terms has not influenced material culture, sartorial styles, consumption patterns and lifestyle in substantial ways. The elite are still involved in manual labour and subsistence activities like others in their community.

One recent phenomenon which has made some impact on the lifestyle and material culture of some of the Kolam families is the hiring of young Kolam men by affluent Banjara[4] landlords on an annual contract basis. Under this arrangement, the hired Kolam man is given a fixed sum of grain and INR 20,000–25,000 per annum to work and supervise agricultural activities of the landlord on a full-time basis. This brings him into close proximity with affluent families and also ensures him some regular cash and foodgrains. It exposes him to the material culture of one of the dominant communities of the tehsil. A part of the cash income is spent on buying tape recorders, fancy denims, bicycles and gifts for family members. As will be brought out later in this essay, these young men have begun to arrange gifts on the occasion of their sister's weddings, which is a completely new phenomenon in their community.

Culture and economy among the Jawarla Kolams show remarkable continuity with the past. The Kolams engage in bamboo weaving, gathering, hunting, firewood selling, agriculture wage labour and cultivation with the help of family labour. Men, women and children work to ensure family survival. The forest continues to play a vital role in their subsistence economy. The attempt of local forest officials to restrict the community's access to forest bamboo has met with stiff resistance in recent times. Free access to bamboo enables Kolam families to earn a marginal profit through the investment of physical labour in fetching, processing, weaving and carrying the finished bamboo product to the market. Even today, one form of subsistence is not sufficient to guarantee family survival in the Kolami economy nor is one individual's work (Mies 1986).

Pod and Exogamous Units

Pods are inhabited by different phratries or exogamous groups. The phratries are called *deya*. They have no names but are described in numerical terms: 7 (*nali deya*), 6 (*aeed deya*), 5 (*aar deya*) and 4 (*yedd deya*). None of these exogamous units have been a corporate or property holding unit. They do, however, constitute affines to each other; the members of the same deya are related to each other through consanguineal bonds, whereas members of different deyas are cross-kin to each other. The co-existence of different exogamous units within a pod creates the possibility of intra-pod marriages. Members of different deyas within a particular generation are cross-cousins to each other. If the age equation is proper, i.e. a senior male and a junior female of are the same generation and of different exogamous units, then they are potential mates. It does not mean that all such potential mates will necessarily become marital partners.[5]

What I try to argue here is that the most central aspect of the pod as a cultural space is the division of its inhabitants between cross and parallel relationships from the ego's perspective. The cross-kin relation among the Kolams is often expressed in joking relationships between real and potential affines as in some other Dravidian groups (Yalman 1967: 334). The content of the joking relationship among the Kolams is generally sexual in nature. A man is found humorously teasing another senior kinsman in a MB (uncle, mother's brother) relationship by asking for the hand of the latter's daughter. A woman keeps telling a young man to become her son-in-law if the latter is in a cross relation to her daughter. There are several folk songs in which men are depicted as asking women to reveal their surnames so that the man will figure out the cross-parallel relation. These songs are always received with a giggle by the whole community. If men and women in cross-relation violate the prescribed sexual norms, it is generally tolerated or resolved through community meetings. In other words, the Kolams show considerable tolerance towards violation of prescribed sexual norms among the opposite sex cross-cousins. From both men's and women's point of view, this tolerance towards violations entails greater sexual freedom. The prescribed sexual norms discourage pre-marital sex, extra-marital liaison and incest, but the community has always shown tolerance towards them as the cases later discussed corroborate. There have been cases in the field village where a sexual liaison between men and women in a consanguineal relation has been either ignored or resolved through community consensus, even though the sentiment to punish violations of the incest taboo[6] is very strong in the community.

Bridewealth among the Kolams

There has been no specific term among the Kolams to describe bridewealth. Marriages have been solemnised with only a token gift called *aaher*, which is received by the bride's parents at the end of wedding. Aaher comprises a *lugde* (nine-yard sari) offered to the bride's mother and a *dhotre* (traditional lower apparel for men) given to the bride's father. Another lugde is given to the *appa* (FZ: father's sister), whose presence is compulsory during wedding rituals. It seems improper to equate this gift of apparel with bridewealth. If we consider it as bridewealth, it is very minimal (in comparison to cows, as in the case of the Nuer). Lack of even a modicum of wealth among the Kolams probably decreed that cost of marriage would be minimal and no wealth would flow from the groom's side. The major expenditure incurred by the groom's family is on the community feast following the end of wedding rituals; a feast traditionally including *mekeng muriyal* (goat meat) and *biyam* (rice). The marriage procession among the Kolams is called *penli mandi*. A Kolam bride arrives with her kin to the groom's place to marry him. This might involve some expenditure if the bride's natal home is located in a village which is far and not in walking distance and/or un-approachable by bullock cart. This expenditure is generally borne by the groom's family or sometimes shared by both the bride's and the groom's families together. In case the bride and the groom belong to the same village or same pod, this expenditure does not arise at all in the first place.

Symmetric Affinity and Women as Economic Providers

In the absence of any hypergamous lineage system, which is integral to much of North India and some of the Brahmanical castes of the Dravidian south (Yalman 1963; Dumont 1961: 84) and western India (Benei 1995), the Kolami culture exhibits egalitarian affinal norms. There is not a single ritual context that emphasises the superiority of bride-takers over the bride-givers. Dumont mentions that certain societies rank the wife-givers superior to the wife-takers, though women are not precisely equal to their husbands. Bloch (1989: 138) also highlights the complexity involved in kinship systems where hierarchy and equality are thoroughly mixed. In some ways, Kolami cultural ethos and gender norms reflect the above formulations of Dumont and Bloch.

As women are important economic providers in the household economy, marriage brings immediate productive and reproductive burdens for them. While men and women both engage in certain agricultural operations and bamboo weaving, women are almost solely responsible for gathering forest products and cutting, processing and selling the firewood. These two activities bring immediate cash to the household. Though women's reproductive labour is taken for granted by the Kolam men, the productive labour and contributions of cash through several economic activities carried outside the domestic domain are fully acknowledged by both men and women. Even in agricultural labour, women are involved in a variety of agricultural operations, viz. weeding, winnowing, spreading fertiliser around cotton plants, assisting men in spraying the fertilisers, clearing the unwanted grass and stalks from the agricultural field, and sowing. Harvesting millet and plucking cotton and matured beans of green gram and *Cajanus indicus* (Pigeon Pea, the Kolams call it 'togari dari') are feminine operations.

It is worth mentioning here that young girls begin to earn cash much earlier than their brothers through agricultural wage labour. Generally, a 12–14-year-old girl is hired by better off and even medium-size farmers in the village[7] to spread fertiliser around the cotton plant for which the village people give the explanation that young girls move very fast from one plant to another. The boys are hired only for ploughing, when they become 16 or 17 years old at that. Girls also begin to assist in child care and free their mothers from household work. Probably due to the vital role of girls in household subsistence, preference for a son seems to be irrelevant among the Kolams (Kumar 2006b). On the same note, I was told that a pregnant woman is given *khichadi* to eat which is prepared by boiling rice and lentils together. Kichadi is not the usual diet among the Kolams. As per the popular belief among them, if a pregnant woman is given khichadi to eat she will give birth to both son(s) and daughter(s) through successive pregnancies. All Kolam women say that they should get both daughters and sons.

In sum, it is not only that women contribute more to the subsistence economy, but this fact is also acknowledged by both men and women. However, there is a lack of recognition of the value of women's reproductive labour by men. Reproductive labour here includes cooking, cleaning, mud-plastering the house, washing, child care, and preparations for ritual and ceremonial occasions. In the perception of the community, the prospective brides are looked at as valuable economic actors and their departure from the natal home is considered as loss of this human resource. The bridewealth of wedding feast and gift and ceremonial expenditure by the groom's kin is justified by every member of the community as compensation of the loss. During the fieldwork which this essay draws on, an elderly Kolam man expressed his disgust at the idea of dowry and said, 'On the one hand, we get a new member which the bride's people lose, on the other, if you ask them to give money and goods, [it] will be fully unjust'. The perception of women as economic actors is also reflected in women's folk songs. In one of the folk songs the bride angrily reminds her brother about the contributions she has made to the household economy by handing over the sickle to him. The singers explain that the girl earns money for the family through weeding and bamboo work. This money goes to the natal family. After marriage she loses membership in her natal home[8] and she expresses her unease by reminding her brother of her contribution through her labour and cash.

The Kolam bride-takers accord very high status to the bride-givers at certain moments during the wedding ceremony, which further substantiates the acknowledgement of 'loss' and 'gain' of productive labour. When a marriage is about to begin, the bride along with the bride-givers proceed towards the *penli pandri* (marriage platform) where the groom's party is waiting for them. Here, before entering the penli pandri, the feet of the bride and the bride-givers are washed by the bride-takers in a ritual called *getalorupsar*. It is to be noted here that among the Kolams, it is the bride who goes to the groom's place along with her kin to marry. The bride's people enter the penli pandri in a *penli mandi* (procession). They are considered as special guests by the groom's party. The latter have to make all preparations so that no lacuna would remain in the hospitality and wedding arrangements. The last lines of one wedding song show that the arrangements of the groom's party is found wanting by the bride's parents. In these lines, the bride's parents refuse to sit on the *gona* (carpet). In the explanation of the singers, the bride's parents are special guests and they ask for some special treatment: instead of a gona they want a *palang* (wooden cot)—a very luxurious and rare article among the Kolams.

The superior status of the bride and her parents on ritual and ceremonial occasions does not mean gender equality. It does, however, reflect that the Kolams acknowledge women's contributions in the subsistence economy. The groom gains the right in the domestic and non-domestic labour of his wife. He also gets a sexual right in her. However, these rights are not absolute or in perpetuity among the Kolams. A woman can break away from a marriage and can come back to her natal home. She is easily accepted by the natal family. There is no stigma attached to *wegre pattam* (divorce). Re-marriage is allowed, but the woman loses her right in her children from her previous husband. In the village, there were women who had given up their children, preferring to enter into another marriage, while others had decided not to remarry for fear of losing their children (Kumar 2006b). However, no one can force a Kolam woman to enter into re-marriage against her will (Kolenda 1987).

Post-marital Residence among Kolams

Post-marital residential arrangements have occupied a great deal of attention in anthropological literature. In gender-sensitive ethnographies, patri-virilocal residence has been associated with powerlessness and weak bargaining power of women in the marital home (Agarwal 1997; Dube 1997; Palriwala 1996). Due to the predominance of nuclear households, Kolam women have relative freedom even when they move to their husband's village. Women who are married within their natal pod or village feel privileged in comparison to those who are married elsewhere, whom they pity. If not within their natal village, all women wish to marry into a village which is not far. During my fieldwork many Kolam women, who are born and married in the same pod, often mentioned, 'I am just coming from my brother's house after having a cup of tea' to express their contentment of having both the natal and marital homes in one place. In contrast, many men told me that one should marry a woman from a distant village so that the latter's brother could not interfere in case of conflict between the spouses. Men would emphasise the ideal norm of virilocality as per the norms of patrilineal kinship of the Kolams. In practice, since a substantial number of Kolam women have either intra-pod or intra-village marriage, the implications of such a norm remain more of an ideal. There are primarily two ways in which kinship norms allow uxorilocal post-marital residence. In the first instance, intra-pod marriages between men and women of different exogamous units allow women to remain in their natal place, though they form a new household with their husbands. Life-history narratives of several men and women reveal minimal variations in the incidence of intra-pod marriage across various generations. Such couples may build their hut near the woman's natal home rather than the man's, where both live in the same pod. There is a second and interesting way that a more explicitly uxorilocal household may be formed. Many women, who leave their natal village upon their marriage, return with their husbands after a few months of their marriage and construct a house alongside the hut of the woman's parents. Gondi and Kolami folk songs depict men's migration to their wife's natal home.[9] The family of Jamuna Bai and Bhuja Madawi is one where four generations of women have born, married and resided in the same pod. The genealogy and residential history of their family demonstrates the acceptance of intra-pod marriage and uxorilocal residence (Figure 3.1 below).

FIGURE 3.1: The Pre- and Post-marital Dwelling Places of the Family of Jamuna Bai and Bhuja Madawi

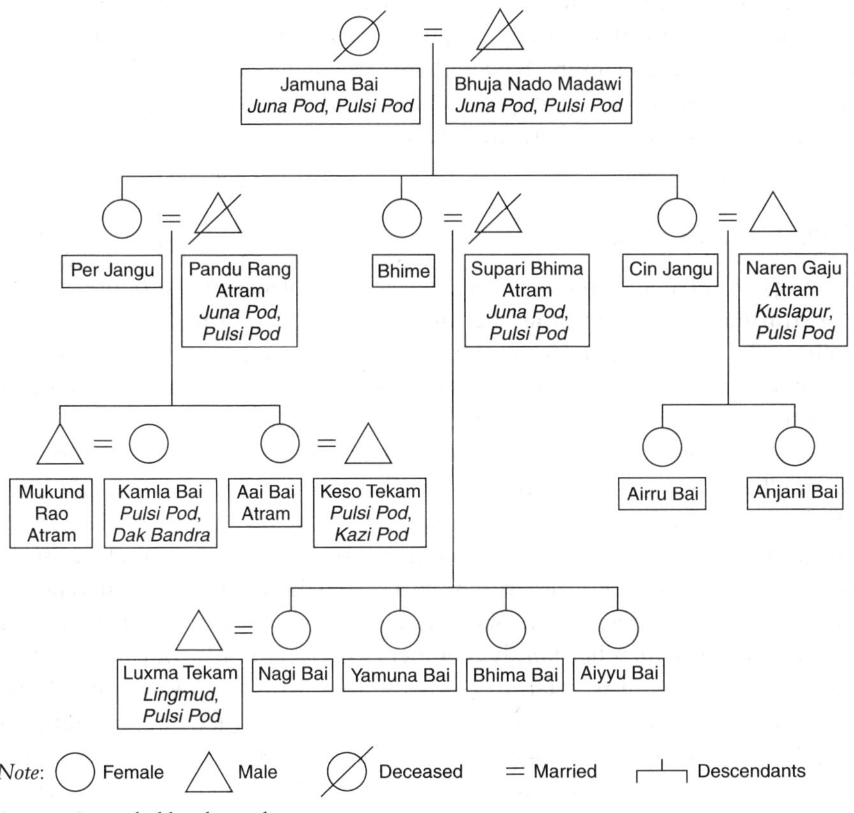

Source: Compiled by the author.

Jamuna Bai's natal home and marital home were in the same pod even after her marriage to Bhuja Madawi; the couple formed their own household by constructing a hut near Jamuna Bai's parents' house. The octogenarian couple lived to see their great grandchildren. The couple had three daughters: *per* (senior) Jangu, Bhime and *cin* (junior) Jangu. The husbands of Per Jangu and Bhime, both now widowed, were from the same pod. Bhime had moved with her husband to a hut they had constructed near her parental home. The third daughter, Cin Jangu, married into a different village, Kuslapur, but returned to her natal home with her husband, where they constructed a hut beside her parents' house. Per Jangu's daughter, Aayi Bai, is married to Keso Tekam of Kazi pod of the same village, Jawarla. She and her husband live with her mother; the husband is an *iltam seddin* (man who stays uxorilocally). Bhime's eldest daughter, Nagi Bai, and her husband, Luxma Tekam, from the neighbouring village of Limgud, also reside in Nagi's widowed mother's house, and he too is an iltam seddin. The other children are as yet unmarried. Thus, two alternative post-marital residential arrangements are evident: women who are married within their natal pod, but do not reside in their parental home after their marriage (Jamuna Bai and her three daughters under this category) and women who reside in their parental home along with their husband (Aayi Bai and Nagi Bai, here). There are several families of the second type in both the pods in Jawarla.

Sexual Transgression

Among the Kolams, a woman is not subjected to violence in case of pre-marital or extra-marital pregnancy as she might have to face in mainstream Hindu society. She is either married off to the man who is responsible for the act, or the man is heavily fined if he is found guiltier than the woman, as in a case narrated later here. The child, however, will bear the name of the biological father whom the mother identifies and can claim a share in the father's property when s/he grows up, even if the mother is not married to this man. At least, this is accepted in principle, though the Kolams being a property-less group, the question of asking for a share in family property does not generally arise. In some cases, the adult children from such a sexual liaison have chosen to ignore their claim to property. Bhim Bai (name changed) became pregnant during her early teens, which her family members discovered only four months into her pregnancy. She was asked to name the man who was responsible. Bhim Bai named a man of the Rajput clan from the village. Since inter-community marriage is usually discouraged, the man was asked to pay a fine of a few thousand rupees. Bhim Bai gave birth to a son and was later married to a man of her own community from the same village. In this case, the son carries the name of his social father, because his biological father belongs to a different community.

Recently, there are several cases where young unmarried girls have become pregnant. Sometimes the men who are held responsible for the pregnancy by the woman deny responsibility and flee the village in order to escape such marriage. So parents and kin of a girl think it proper that she have an abortion and the girls are taken to hospitals in the nearby town of Adilabad for this.[10] Despite public knowledge of the liaison and abortion, these girls have received offers of marriage. It may be pointed out that among the Kolams, it is the groom's family who has to approach a prospective bride's family with a marriage proposal. It is almost a stigma for the bride's family to approach a groom's family.

There are cases where the parents have not liked the love affairs of their daughters, but they had to marry off the daughter to the lover of her choice. Bagu Bai (name changed) of the Kazi pod had an affair with Rama (name changed) who was her classificatory cross-cousin residing in the same pod. Everybody in the pod knew that they were having an affair. Her parents did not approve, primarily because pre-marital sex is not approved of, but also because the man, according to them, was not hard-working and industrious. After a few months, it was discovered that Bagu Bai had become pregnant. The parents were ready to take her to a private hospital for an abortion, but she was reluctant and wanted to marry her lover. On the insistence of Bagu Bai, she was finally married to Rama. Now, after their marriage Rama continues with his lax attitude, hardly earning any money. Bagu Bai ekes out her livelihood by selling firewood and visits her parents' house very frequently. The parents pity her and support her with food and sometimes cash.

In another case, an unmarried Kolam girl from the main village was impregnated by a middle-aged man of the Pulsi pod. She was three months into her term when her family discovered that she was pregnant. The girl and the man belong to the same phratry and hence are blood relatives according to the kinship norms of the Kolams. The girl's father is elder to her impregnator and hence the latter is related to the girl as *kakond* (FyB: father's younger brother). Since it was a case of incest, they could not be married. The man was beaten up by her female kin, her mother and her FZs, who reside in the same village. The girl was then taken to the hospital of Adilabad city for an abortion. As far as I could gather by talking to her FZs, no one in the family and kin blamed the girl; they found the man solely guilty by virtue of being much senior in age and generation. The community men of Pulsi pod brought the matter to the Mahajan, the adjudicating authority in the community. The Mahajan fined the girl's family INR 1000 and the man was fined INR 3000. Evidently, pre-marital sex, though formally disapproved of, is not dealt with severely among the Kolams. The girl was not victimised because of the incestuous relation. On the contrary, she received support from her family and kin and the Mahajan fined her family less than her impregnator.

Though Kolams do not sanction extra-marital and pre-marital liaisons either, deviance from this prescribed norm is tolerated in everyday life. As some of the women told me, 'In a drunken state no one knows who is sleeping with whom'. I came across many Kolam women buying liquor from the shop of a Komati[11] in the nearby market at Mandwi. One of these women is Dame Bai (name changed) from Kazi pod, in her mid 30's and mother of three children. She has a passion for liquor, as the men and women of this pod confirm. She frequently shares liquor with her husband. On many occasions, when her husband is not available in the village she goes to the market and does not come back home. Everyone in the pod talks of her sexual conduct, but she does not face social ostracism on this account. To exemplify this, on the occasion of the festival of Bhimaiyyak, she was seen singing devotional songs with other women and cooking *garkalamba*[12] with them to offer to the deity. Once, however, she was severely beaten up by her husband. On inquiry, the women of the pod said that this was because she had taken grain from her house to buy liquor and not for her adulterous behaviour. Recently, after absenting herself from her husband's place for several months without informing anyone, leaving her children in his custody, she returned and the couple stay together.

There are cases of elopement, and in one case in a neighbouring village, a grandmother is married to her actual grandson and they are still living in the community. I was informed that this grandmother-wife would pull her grandson-husband to the dance floor during community singing and dancing on certain occasions; the latter feels shy and hesitant in front of others to dance with his wife, but the wife struts about having a young, handsome husband.

There are many more instances of transgression of sexual norms and their accommodation in everyday life of the community; transgressions, thus, do not lead to social ostracism and exclusion from community life.

Change in Egalitarian Ethos

Over the past several years, the cost of marriage has been increasing and brides' families have begun to arrange gifts for the bride, which mainly includes utensils. Steel and brass utensils constitute a very common gift item among caste groups of this region. Gonds, the dominant tribe, adopted this custom much earlier. Though it is less spectacular in the Jawarla village, Kolam interlocutors say that giving gifts to the bride has become very popular among the Kolams of the neighbouring Adilabad district in Andhra Pradesh. The reason cited is growing affluence among the Kolams due to the successful implementation of land distribution there and their subsequent adoption of some customs of Telugu caste groups.

As mentioned earlier, the Kolam boys of Jawarla, who serve on Banjara landlords' farms on a yearly contract basis, get a fixed sum of money and foodgrain per annum. These boys bought gifts for their sisters on the occasion of the latters' wedding. The natal family of Bali, an informant, is landless. A substantial part of the family's livelihood comes from selling bamboo products. Her brother works in the farm of a Banjara landowner in the nearby Mandvi village. At her wedding, he gave her gifts that included a water vessel, tray and jug made of brass, two dinner plates, two glasses, four bowls of steel, and a rack for keeping utensils. All marriageable Kolam girls of Jawarla, however, are not lucky to receive these goods of household use and the pace of transition to dowry would probably depend on the economic prosperity of Kolam households.

Earlier Kolam weddings had no specific ritual of giving gifts by the bride's kin; the parents of the bride being recipients of the aaher offered by the groom's family at the end of the wedding ritual. Now this ritual has expanded to include gifts to the bride from a range of her kin. So far items like a television set, furniture and cattle-wealth have not been given by the bride's kin in Jawarla, but one of the wedding songs present these aspirations. According to women singers, this is a new song added to the repertoire of wedding songs sung by them. It depicts a variety of items brought for the bride by her paternal and maternal kin on her wedding. The bride is in a sad mood as her membership from her parental group has come to an end, even if her mother's house is not far. Even in the case of divorce, a woman cannot regain membership of her natal deya (phratry), *pari* (clan) and *khanda* (lineage). The girl has to leave the *pita* (seating stand) of her own group and sit on that of her husband's group. She weeps and wails at this ritual separation from her parents' group. At this juncture, the singers try to pacify and console the girl by telling her of the gifts her paternal and maternal kin have brought for her. The kin sung about might include her maternal and/or paternal grandparents, her brother, brother's wife (*vanna*), FeB (father's elder brother) and his wife, FyB (father's younger brother) and his wife, and a host of others. The items include television sets, goats, cows, bicycles and other such things. This might reflect future dowry aspirations of the Kolams.

The cost of marriage is increasing for the groom's family also as they give an increasing volume of aaher to their kin. In traditional Kolami weddings, aaher was only offered to the bride's parents and *appa* (FZ) because of the latter's traditional ritual role. Over the past four or five years, the number of kin from the groom's side who are given gifts has expanded to include the groom's MZs (Mother's sisters), MM (Mother's mother), FZs (Father's sisters) and a host of other relatives. This might be the influence of neighbouring caste groups, particularly the middle castes like Malis, Reddis and Telis, as well as the lower-caste Boddhs, who customarily include a large number of kin and friends for gift-giving. In their case, gifts of apparel are also made, generally to female kin of the parents of both the groom and bride. Now Kolam women, particularly the groom's mother, boast of the large number of kin to whom they will give aaher.

Another reason for the increasing cost of marriage among the Kolams is the inclusion of small gold beads in the *poti* (wedding necklace), which the groom's family gives the bride. One of the wedding songs of Kolam women reveals their aspirations for silver jewellery, which they could barely afford in the past as well as in the present. Ironically, small gold beads in the poti is becoming almost a compulsory item in Kolami marriage! Many Kolam families (the groom's) are even buying a gold pendant to be threaded into the black-bead poti. In the wedding songs of Kolams, *wendi* (silver) is the precious metal desired by women, gold never figuring in the women's lyrics. The jewellery which the Kolam women wear, however, never had an element of silver; it is only aspired for. The poor Kolam women have to opt for aluminium jewellery to adorn themselves. The women referred to this metal as *german*.

The minimum cost of marriage in 2005 was INR 20,000–25,000 for a groom's family. Earlier, the cost of marriage included mainly the ceremonial feast; now, gifts and gold and a loudspeaker have become the new additions. In a recent case, a woman wanted divorce from her husband, but he did not want to divorce his wife. The matter was taken to the Mahajan. As the man had spent a lot of money on wedding gifts, rituals and the ceremonial feast, he asked his wife's family to repay the cost of marriage. The bride's family being poor was unable to pay this amount and the woman was forced to live with the husband as decided in the community. Thus, the growing cost of marriage may become an obstacle in women obtaining divorce.

Earlier, the wedding feast included only the community members. Now some Kolam households invite the entire village, further increasing the cost of marriage. Kishan Bhima Atram of Pulsi pod works as a peon in the ashram shala at Tulsi, a neighbouring village. Since he is earning a regular salary, the *soyerik* (betrothal) of his daughter in 2005 looked more expensive. A small colourful tent was erected, giving the impression of any mainstream cultural event. Earlier the Kolams would not even eat at the bride's place, because that was considered as taxing the bride's family. The Kolam men and women from the groom's side, who would come to the prospective bride's place for soyerik would carry food for themselves. Now these things are changing, albeit gradually. Atram had refreshments, including *murmure* (crisp or brittle rice) and salted biscuits, served to everyone on small pieces of papers torn off from the old notebooks of the children. He is the only lucky Kolam in the village to have a government job. His stay at the ashram shala and the interaction with teachers recruited from various communities, ranging from Brahmins to Marathas to Komatis, have influenced his and his family's lifestyle. He offered a gold ring to his prospective son-in-law.

To sum up, changes in marriage prestations seem to be reversing the earlier direction of gift-giving and may possibly lead to dowry. Dowry being associated with a lower value of brides or lack of recognition of their productive worth, thereby affecting the more egalitarian form of marriage, which has been the practice among the Kolams. The growing expenditure on marriage by the groom's side might also affect women's autonomy, such as in initiating and obtaining divorce as in the case discussed above. It simultaneously appears that the lesser degree of class differentiation and continuing diversity in subsistence activities together have kept the pace of transition to dowry rather slow. Bridewealth continues to be rather central to the cultural life of the community, along with many of the flexible gender norms listed by Boserup and Goody for hoe societies.

Notes

[1] Goody's (1988) work is interesting as he links marital payments with agricultural economies and attempts particularly to address control of women's body and sexuality in relation to them. He is not, however, very consistent and persuasive in the manner of contemporary feminist anthropologists. For example, he does not see dowry as problematical (ibid.: 6). Dowry for him is also a 'conjugal fund' providing security to women; he fails to see, for example, that the groom's kin could exercise considerable authority in transacting and controlling dowry. Feminist anthropological writings since the 1970s have emphasised the specific need to foreground women's agency in any ritual and institutional process, including marital transactions. Gayle Rubin's (1975) radical critique of dominant theories of kinship could be viewed as a landmark essay inspiring subsequent feminist writings in anthropology. For a critical feminist perspective on dowry in South Asia, see Sharma (1993).

[2] The term 'primitive' is consistently identified with anthropology (Hsu 1964: 169) since the late nineteenth century. The connotation of 'primitive' being inferior appears in the evolutionary theory of culture offered by E. B. Taylor (1881). 'Primitive' is now seldom used as an 'adjective' in anthropological texts and, as Hsu (1964) rightly points out, the political climate of the world today is simply unfavourable to the continued application of this term. In the present context, the use of the term 'primitive' for the Kolams is not my choice as an author. In 1975, the Government of India identified some more backward groups among the Scheduled Tribes as Primitive Tribal Groups (PTGs). Some 75 tribal communities have been categorised as PTGs in different states of India (Government of India 1980). In Maharashtra, there are three communities, viz. Maria Gonds of Chandrapur Gadhchiroli district, Katkaris of Thane district and

the Kolams residing in the eastern region of the state that have been considered as Primitive Tribes (Deogaonkar and Deogaonkar 2003: 10).

[3] The Adilabad district of Andhra Pradesh bordering Kinwat tehsil of Nanded district where the majority population belong to Scheduled Tribes and nomadic groups has also been a significant site of the Naxal movement since the mid-80s. The Naxal movement has been articulating rights of tribal groups, who are regarded as the original inhabitants of the region who were pushed to the wall by the 'clever' migrants from the plains, who were primarily from the Maratha caste and traditional business communities. The Naxal leaders, themselves from tribal and nomadic groups have shown empathy to and concern for fellow tribes and hence the police have been led to believe that tribal families shelter Naxal leaders. Since the Kolams and the forest are in close proximity, the police used to raid their homes suspecting that Naxalite leaders were being sheltered by the tribals.

[4] Banjaras are considered as nomadic tribes in Maharashtra and they are politically more influential than any other tribal groups. In the surrounding villages, many Banjara families are big landlords even though a majority of this group is poor.

[5] Sometimes the parents prefer to marry their children outside their pod. In some other instances, when the real affines reside in a different village and if it is already mutually agreed to marry the children to each other by close affines, it would mean that affinal ties within a pod are sidestepped.

[6] Men and women placed in the same phratry are considered to share the same *nettur* (blood) and sexual relation between them is strictly prohibited. This is evident in the way the Kolams meet and interact with any unknown or *suttam* (stranger) from their community. In such instances, they first ask about the latter's phratry. If it is found that the stranger(s) (either two individuals or a group in a face-to-face encounter) belong to the same phratry, they address each other as *dada* (brother) in case of male and *bai* (sister) in case of female. Sexual relations in such cases will amount to *pap taksaad* (sin). Sex is also tabooed between the ego and her MZch (mother's sister's child), even when the two (the ego and MZch) belong to different phratries. Female siblings might get married in different exogamous groups, but their children constitute parallel-cousins to each other and sexual relation is strictly tabooed in this case. Though incest is rare in the village, it is difficult to provide an explanation for the tolerance shown in such a case which needs further exploration. The Kolam interlocutors in the village always tried to avoid answering this ethnographic curiosity.

[7] It is a general practice in the village to hire girls of this age-group for this particular agricultural operation. The young girls, who perform this labour belong to the Kolam community and are also from poor Gond families in the village. Not only the affluent, but also the medium farmers irrespective of communities in the village, hire these girls for spreading fertiliser around cotton plants. Since the Kolams mostly do farming with the help of family labour, their own daughters and wives perform this feminine task.

[8] Even though there is no sharp distinction between women as 'daughters of the village' and 'brides of the village', as mentioned by Karve (1953) for other groups, and the bride may not be a complete stranger to the in-laws, the Gond and Kolam women in Jawarla lament their departure from their parental home. There are numerous heart-breaking songs that express the pain of severing of ties through marriage.

[9] Furer-Haimendorf (1945, 1948) has brought out this widely prevalent practice among the Gonds. This is also conspicuous among the Kolams. A popular Gondi song depicting a husband's migration to his wife's natal village is now available in cassettes and CDs, which are constantly played in the village. In the opening stanza of one song, the wife is provoking and inviting her husband to leave his village to settle in her *shedmiyar* (natal village). This accepted practice among Gonds and Kolams might change with the sedentarisation of Kolams as a result of housing and other welfare scheme of the government.

[10] As per the earlier norms, a girl upon being pregnant without marriage was to be married off to the impregnator. This still continues in the villages. In recent times, there is a simultaneous trend to abort the foetus in such cases. My key interlocutors attribute the growing number of abortions in recent times to the access to technology. Due to the opening of health services in the nearest city of Adilabad in Andhra Pradesh, the parents decide to abort the foetus and wait for a match of their own choice for their daughters

[11] Komatis are middle-caste business community in Maharashtra.

[12] *Garkalamba* is a sweet ritual food prepared from wheat flour and sugar. It is prepared on the occasion of the annual festival of Deb. Women sing religious songs in groups, and participate in kneading wheat flour and then frying it. They compulsorily take a bath and wear clean clothes. This is a feminine task and is considered auspicious by women and men, as the food is offered to the chief deity Bhimaiyyak.

References

Agarwal, Bina. 1997. 'Bargaining' and Gender Relations: Within and Beyond the Household. *Feminist Economics* 3 (1): 1–51.

Benei, Veronique. 1995. '*To Give or Not to Give: From Brideprice to Dowry in Maharashtra*'. Working Paper. Pondichery: French Institute of Pondichery.

Bloch, Maurice. 1989. *Ritual, History and Power: Selected Papers in Anthropology*. London: Athlone Press.

Boserup, Ester. 1970. *Women's Role in Economic Development*. London: Earthscan Publications.

Deogaonkar, Sashisekhar Gopal and Leena Deogaonkar. 2003. *The Kolam Tribals*. Delhi: Concept Publishing Company.

Dube, Leela. 1997. *Women and Kinship: Comparative Perspectives on Gender in South and Southeast Asia*. New Delhi: Vistaar Publications.

Dumont, Louis. 1961. 'Marriage in India: The Present State of the Question'. *Contributions to Indian Sociology* 5:75–96.

Furer-Haimendorf, Christoph von. 1948. *The Raj Gonds of Adilabad: A Peasant Culture of the Deccan*. London: Macmillan.

———. 1945. *Tribal Hyderabad: Four Reports*. Hyderabad: Government of Andhra Pradesh.

Goody, Jack. 1988. *Production and Reproduction: A Comparative Study of the Domestic Domain*. Cambridge: Cambridge University Press.

Government of India. 1980. *Report of the Backward Classes Commission* 1. New Delhi: Government of India.

Hsu, Francis L. K. 1964. 'Rethinking the Concept "primitive"'. *Current Anthropology* 5 (3): 169–78.

Karve, Iravati. 1953. *Kinship Organisation in India*. Poona: Deccan College Postgraduate and Research Institute.

Kolenda, Pauline. 1987. *Regional Differences in Family Organisation*. Jaipur: Rawat Publications.

Kumar, Pushpesh. 2006a. 'Kinship and Gender: A Study of the Kolams of Maharashtra'. *Doctoral Dissertation*. Delhi: Jamia Millia Islamia and the Institute of Economic Growth.

_______. 2006b. 'Gender and Procreative Ideology among the Kolams of Maharashtra'. *Contributions to Indian Sociology* 40 (3): 279–310.

_______. 2003. 'Response to Development Intervention: A Study of Kolams—A 'Primitive' Tribe in Nanded District'. *Report of the UGC Minor Project*. Nanded: SRTM University.

Mies, Maria. 1986. *Indian Women in Subsistence and Agriculture Labour*. Geneva: ILO.

Palriwala, Rajni. 1996. 'Negotiating Patriliny: Intra-household Consumption and Authority in Northwest India'. In *Shifting Circles of Support: Contextualising Gender and Kinship in South Asia and Sub-Saharan Africa*, ed. Rajni Palriwala and Carla Risseeuw. New Delhi: Sage.

Rubin, Gayle. 1975. 'The Traffic in Women: Notes on the "Political Economy of Sex"'. In *Toward an Anthropology of Women*, ed. Rayna R. Reiter. New York: Monthly Review Press.

Sharma, Ursula. 1993. 'Dowry in North India: Its Consequences for Women'. In *Family, Kinship and Marriage in India*, ed. Patricia Uberoi. New Delhi: Oxford University Press.

Shashi, S. S. 1994. *Encyclopaedia of Indian Tribes*. New Delhi: Anmol Publications.

Singh, K. S. 1998. *India's Communities: People of India National Series* 5. New Delhi: Oxford University Press.

Taylor, E. B. 1881. *Anthropology: An Introduction to the Study of Man and Civilization*. London: Macmillan and Company.

Trautmann, Thomas R. 1995. *Dravidian Kinship*. New Delhi: Vistaar Publications.

Yalman, Nur. 1967. *Under the Bo Tree: Studies in Caste, Kinship and Marriages in the Interior of Ceylon*. Berkeley: University of California Press.

_______. 1963. 'On the Purity of Women in the Castes of Ceylon and Malabar'. *The Journal of Royal Anthropological Institute of Great Britain and Ireland* 93 (1): 25–58.

Marriage Continuity and Change in Bangladesh*

Sajeda Amin and Maitreyi Das

Introduction

Marriage is a stable institution in Bangladesh in many ways, but rising dowry demands is a cause for concern. Marriage is universal, i.e. most men and women marry early and remain married throughout their adult lives. Although family law allows polygamy and divorce, polygamy is rare, and divorce occurs with moderate frequency. Marriages are usually arranged. Women marry at relatively young ages, at about 16 years.

Dowry is defined here as a translation of the Bangla word *joutuk*, commonly used to refer to payments demanded by the groom, or on behalf of the groom, from the bride and her family (Amin and Cain 1997; Rozario 2009; Amin et al. 2008). As noted in several studies on Bangladesh, dowry is not an established practice among Muslims. Respondents often use the word *dabi*, or even the English language translation of the word, which is 'demand', to refer to dowry (Rozario 2001; Naved et al. 2008; Lindenbaum 1981). In our use of the term with respondents, we have accordingly emphasised the demanded element of dowry. Legal definitions refer only to the exchange of dowry in cash or valued security, and do not mention other demands that may be made, such

* The authors gratefully acknowledge support from the United Kingdom Department for International Development through a grant to the Population Council. They thank Ashish Bajracharya for advice on the statistical analysis.

as for jobs, which is also a common practice (Ministry of Law 1980). Although there is no reliable evidence about the size of dowry relative to other types of transfers at marriages of other types, there is some evidence from the eastern region of India that dowry constitutes the major part of marriage transactions (Chowdhury 2008).

Bangladesh has a number of legal and social measures in place aimed at influencing or reforming marriage practices. Child marriage, defined as marriage below the age of 18 for girls and the age of 21 for boys, is banned. Dowry is illegal and punishable by law. Wedding parties exceeding a certain size are taxed as a way of limiting extravagant expenditure. A scholarship scheme is available for unmarried girls attending secondary school that is contingent upon a bond being signed by the girl's parents to guarantee that her marriage will not take place until the age of 18. A marriage registration system is in place as part of a strategy for enforcing laws regulating marriage. Members of development organisations, which number in the millions, recite these regulations and laws as part of their social awareness programmes. While these laws and policies are well known, there is relatively little evidence on whether or how these measures have influenced actual trends and practices (Amin, Diamond and Steele 1997).

This essay explores regional variations, cohort contrasts as a measure of trends over time, covariates of early marriage and dowry, and several key post-marriage outcomes to describe patterns of continuity and change in marriage in Bangladesh. We use detailed nationally representative data from Bangladesh to explore patterns of association with a view of promoting a more nuanced understanding of marriage in Bangladesh, and to identify social policy and strategies to promote more equitable gender norms in Bangladesh through healthier marriage practices. Many of the policy interventions described above are not based on a sound evidence base.

Trends in Marriage over Time

According to the 2004 Bangladesh Demographic and Health Survey (BDHS) (reported in NIPORT and ORC 2005), the median age at first marriage rose from 13.9 years for women in the age group 45–49 to 16.0 years for women in the age group 20–24. For these same cohorts, the proportion of women marrying very early, i.e. by age 15, declined by almost half over time, from 71 per cent (cohort age group 45–49) to 37 per cent (cohort age group 20–24). However, a comparison of the four BDHS surveys since 1993 reveals that an overwhelming majority of women, both in the past and at present, marry before the legal age of marriage. During the 1990s, the proportion marrying early dropped from 73 per cent in 1993–94 to 65 per cent in 1999–2000. The latest BDHS registers a reversal of trends and finds an actual increase to 68 per cent marrying below the age of 18 in 2004. Trends in the BDHS series indicate that while the incidence of very early child marriages has declined, the majority of women continue to marry below the age of 18 and the legal minimum age limits for men and women are routinely ignored (ibid.).

While demographic and economic surveys usually include questions on marriage age and marital status, questions on marital transactions are not commonly asked. Relatively little is known about dowry or other marriage transactions. Only a few small studies have explored the question of exchanges such as dowry in marriage. At least two studies have noted a switch from bride price (payment by groom to bride) to dowry (payment by bride to groom) that took place sometime in the 1960s (Amin et al. 1997; Lindenbaum 1981). Other anthropologists have noted a similar mention of the rise of dowry as perceived by villagers (White 1992; Rozario 1992). These reported changes are similar to trends observed in non-dowry societies in parts of India (Caldwell, Reddy and Caldwell 1983; Rao 1993).

As in the case of dowry, there are no national-level data on the exercise of women's voice in marriage. It is widely held, and has been reaffirmed by the findings of studies from all over Bangladesh, that most marriages are arranged (Cain, Khanam and Nahar 1979; Lindenbaum 1981; White 1992). A survey of rural adolescents living in Chapainawabganj, Chittagong and Sherpur districts shows that while 45 per cent of married female respondents said that they had no say in their marriage, 30 per cent reported that they were consulted, and 21 per cent reported that they chose their spouse but sought the permission of parents. Only 2.6 per cent reported deciding on their own (Amin et al. 2002a).

The Bangladeshi age pattern of marriage is anomalous in several ways. Exploring the association between age at marriage on one axis and fertility and schooling on the other, and performing regression analysis using BDHS data shows Bangladesh to be a significant outlier. Age at marriage is five years lower than what one might expect based on fertility levels (Figure 4.1). Demographers expect marriage change to typically precede fertility change based on the experience of most historical and contemporary societies. The association between female marriage age and education tells a similar story of an anomalous pattern (Amin et al. 2006).

What Explains the Rise of Dowry?

The three broad categories of explanations for the increase in dowry observed in Bangladesh are rising female competition (Amin and Cain 1997; Lindenbaum 1981), rising relative groom price (Mobarak et al. 2011), and dowry as a form of insurance against divorce (Ambrus et al. 2008). Amin and Cain (1997) argued that dowry arises as female competition increases because there is an

FIGURE 4.1: Relationship Between Female Age at First Marriage and Fertility Rate, Bangladesh and Selected other Developing Countries, Demographic and Health Surveys

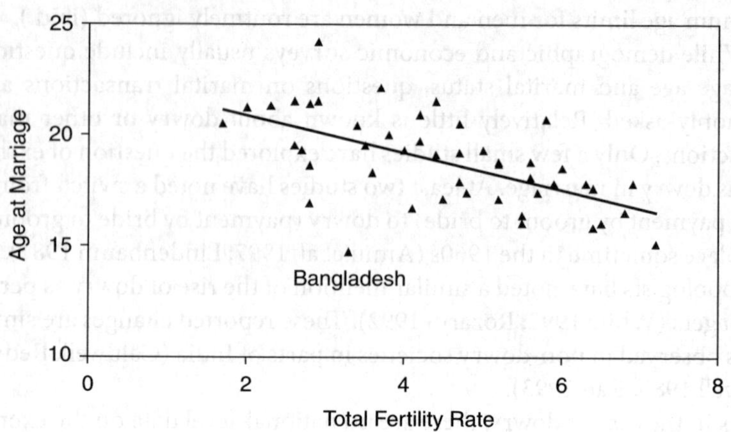

Source: Amin et al. (2006).

excess of brides for the number of available grooms. Arunachalam and Naidu (2008) presented evidence that correlated the rise of dowry to the introduction of family planning, which allowed women to control their fertility, thus reducing their reproductive potential as well as their value relative to grooms. Mobarak et al. (2011) found an association between the construction of river embankments and rising dowry, and argued that increased productivity of land in embankment-protected areas led to increased demand for grooms who hold that land. Lindenbaum (1981) argued that the rise of dowry was the result of economic diversification, which increased the desirability of the few men who could move out of farming and who then commanded more dowry. Joshi et al., in this volume, relates rising dowry to the decline of kin marriage. Similarly, Ambrus et al. (2008) attribute changes in the payment of dowry to changes in marriage registration, which may have led to the rise of reported dowry since registered marriages require an agreed upon *mehr* or dower for Muslim marriages.

Although there is no real consensus on the drivers of rising dowry, and even some dissonance on whether there is evidence of a clear rising trend in the practice (Ambrus et al. 2008), there is no dispute that dowry or marriage transactions are socially and economically important and are intriguing phenomena in Bangladesh. There is also relatively little convincing evidence on the consequences of dowry practice later in life.

Data Collection and Methodology

The World Bank Gender Norms Survey of 2006 (qtd. in World Bank 2008) was a nationally representative sample of 5000 adults, including 1500 married women in the 15–25-year age range, 1500 married women in the 45–59-year age range, 1500 married men in the 25–50-year age range, and 500 opinion leaders such as Union Parishad (UP) members and *imams/moulvis* (religious leaders). This essay uses only the results drawn from the female respondents. The sample was drawn in two stages. During the first sampling stage, 91 clusters (corresponding roughly to the lowest administrative unit, *mouza* or *moholla*, in rural and urban areas respectively) were selected as sub-samples of the 361 clusters included in the BDHS of 2004. During the second sampling stage, one adult from each household was selected. Out of the 49 adults interviewed in a cluster, roughly 16 were married women in the age group 15–25, 16 were married women in the age group 45–59, and 17 were married men in the age group 25–50. Interviews were conducted in April–May 2006.

Results

The Marriage Process

The World Bank Gender Norms Survey of 2006 offers a detailed portrayal of marriage practices in Bangladesh. The design of the survey also allows for regional comparison and an examination of change over time. It confirms our expectations, based on smaller studies, of dramatic change in some aspects of marriage, such as the giving of dowry and the registration of marriage. There is also evidence that much remains unchanged, such as the overwhelming majority of women who marry before the legal age, women who meet the husband for the first time on the wedding night, and women who begin marital life in the home of the husband's parents. There is also evidence of considerable diversity in marriage practices within the country. Particularly striking is the variation in dowry exchange practices documented in this survey.

Tables 4A.1 to 4A.7 provide some summary statistics of marriage indicators by age cohort and region. Overall, 20 per cent of all the women interviewed said that they had some say in the choice of husband when they were first married (Table 4A.1). There were important variations by cohort and region. Among older women (above age 45), the proportion was 14.2 per cent; the figure rose to 25.7 per cent for younger women (age 25 or under). There were large differences by region; among older women, the proportion saying that their opinion was taken varied from 3 per cent in Sylhet to 27.2 per cent in Barisal. Among the younger cohort of women who said that they had some say in the choice of their partner, the figures varied from 11.9 per cent in Khulna to 41.3 per cent in Barisal.

However, this measure of choice needs to be interpreted in the context of arranged marriages. Women may be consulted as to the timing of the marriage and about the man who has been selected as the husband, but this is not to say that they knew the husband before the wedding. 79.1 per cent of all respondents reported that they met the husband for the first time on their wedding night (Table 4A.2a). This pattern did not change much over time; it was 82.3 per cent for the older cohort and 75.9 per cent for the younger cohort. Most of those who reported knowing the husband said that they had known him since childhood; these are respondents who are married within the village or within the family. Women who are married to kin are mostly to a parallel or cross-cousin. Overall, only 9 per cent of women reported being married to kin. To put this finding in perspective, this figure is significantly lower than the proportions of women marrying kin in Egypt and Pakistan, as reported in the BDHSs. Within Bangladesh, kin endogamy is somewhat variable by region, being the lowest in Khulna at 6.3 per cent and the highest in Sylhet at 21.1 per cent for younger women. The proportion of respondents married to kin and the regional pattern relating to kin endogamy did not change over time (Table 4A.2b).

Reports of women's increasing choice in marriage may also be a function of rising marriage registration. Comparing older women to younger women, we observe a near doubling of marriages that are registered (Table 4A.3). The proportions are 44.1 per cent among older women and 85.2 per cent among younger women. The process of registration, among other things, requires documentation of the bride's consent to the marriage. While consent is always sought in a Muslim marriage (the bride says '*qabul*', i.e. she indicates her acceptance of the marriage contract), there is an added formality to this consent when it is written in a legal document. This additional formality may lead to women being more aware that they have given their consent to the marriage.

Overall, 27 per cent of marriages were reported to involve dowry demand (Table 4A.4), 7.7 per cent among the older cohort and 46.4 per cent among the younger cohort. For younger women, regionally, dowry ranged from 12.7 per cent in Sylhet (average amount demanded Tk. 19,000) to 65.3 per cent in Rajshahi (average amount demanded Tk. 17,237). The regional average amount demanded in dowry was highest among young women in Chittagong at Tk. 26,567 (Table 4A.5).

Finally, the survey respondents reported ages at first marriage that confirm a very early age pattern for the country (Table 4A.6). Overall, 52 per cent of all respondents were married before age 15. The figures ranged from a low of 20 per cent in Sylhet to a high of 66 per cent in Rajshahi. Data disaggregated by age cohort showed that such variations derive from a long-standing tradition.

In Sylhet, the proportion married before age 15 fell from 25 per cent for the older cohort to 14 per cent for the younger cohort. In Rajshahi, the proportion fell from 73 per cent among older women to 60 per cent among younger women. Since such high proportions of respondents reported early marriage, we use 15 rather than the legal age at marriage of 18, by when the vast majority are already married.

Table 4A.7 shows how dowry payments are associated with age at marriage. Dowry amounts paid by those who reported a dowry was paid at marriage increase considerably with age at marriage. While this age gradient is modest for the older cohort of women, the increase in dowry with age at marriage is much more pronounced among younger women, with women marrying at older ages (over 18) paying twice as much dowry as women who are married under age 16.

Covariates of Marriage Practices

To further explore the nature of marriage, in this section we analyse covariates of three marriage indicators: early marriage, payment of dowry, and whether women have any say in the choice of husband (Table 4.1). Education is measured so that women who have secondary level education or higher are compared to women who have less than secondary schooling. Family characteristics are measured by religious affiliation and the relative economic status of the bride's natal family relative to her marital family. Since this latter variable is strongly associated with economic status rankings, only the relative measure is included. Individual characteristics considered are the woman's own education and whether she and her spouse grew up in the same village. Other sources of regional variation are captured in regional dummy variables for each of the six divisions. The influence of urban-rural residence is captured by a separate variable.

All of the individual and family characteristics were in the expected direction. Women who have received some secondary education are less likely to pay dowry and are also less likely to be married young compared to women who have received less than secondary education. Women married to men in the same village are also less likely to pay dowry and are more likely to exercise choice in marriage compared to women who are married to men from a different village.

Urban-rural residence is neither significantly related to early marriage nor to whether dowry was paid. This non-difference is possibly explained by the fact that most recent urban migrants continue following the culture and tradition of their rural communities or places of origin, and may even go back to the village residence for a marriage. For example, Naved et al. (2001) report that female garment workers in Dhaka express a strong preference for marrying

TABLE 4.1: Relative Risks Associated with Covariates of Marriage Characteristics, Bangladesh Marriage and Gender Norms Survey, Married Women, 15–25 Years, 2006

	Paid any dowry	*Married young (<15)*	*Had a say in choice of spouse*
Respondent's education			
Less than secondary	1.00	1.00	1.00
Secondary plus	0.49**	0.23**	1.55**
Village endogamy			
Spouse from different village	1.00	1.00	1.00
Spouse from same village	0.62*	0.99	2.40**
Type of residence			
Urban	1.00	1.00	1.00
Rural	1.35	0.91	0.51**
Religion			
Non-Muslim	1.00	1.00	1.00
Muslim	0.79	1.51	2.09
Family economic status			
Same status	1.00	1.00	1.00
Natal family better off	1.23	1.51*	1.22
Husband's family better off	1.15	0.85	1.29
Division (Barisal omitted)		1.00	1.00
Chittagong	2.45**	1.07	0.97
Dhaka	2.00*	1.26	0.71
Khulna	1.2	1.7*	0.24**
Rajshahi	4.89**	2.45**	0.36**
Sylhet	0.35**	0.25**	0.23**

Note: Paid dowry: 1 = if any dowry paid; 0 = if no dowry paid.
Married early: 1 = married before age 15; 0 = married at age 15 or after.
Any say in choice of spouse: 1 = yes; 0 = no.
* significant at 0.05.
** significant at 0.01.
Source: Authors' calculations based on data from World Bank Gender Norms Survey of 2006.

men from their own home districts and describe their parents choosing their husband, even while they live highly autonomous lives and save to pay for their own dowry. Urban women are significantly more likely, than their rural counterparts, to report that they had some voice in choosing their spouse.

Muslim women are significantly more likely to be married young, but there are no other significant differences in payment of dowry or say in marriage choice by religion. Women whose natal family is better off than their marital family are also likely to be married young, but there is no difference in dowry or marriage choice.

The regional variables demonstrate that even allowing for family and individual characteristics, marriage norms tend to vary substantially across the country. The proportion of marriages involving dowry is almost five times as high in Rajshahi as in Barisal. Early marriage is also substantially more widespread in Rajshahi. The proportion of married women who paid dowry is very low in Sylhet and Barisal, and very high in Rajshahi. The factors behind these variations are not well understood.

It is possible that migration plays a role; both Sylhet and Barisal have long been migrant-sending areas. Migrants from Barisal are the dominant group in Dhaka, and they also tend to migrate to the Middle East as contract workers. Sylheti migrants are both temporary circular migrants and permanent settlers overseas. Poor landless peasants travel far to seek agricultural work during the annual inundation of the low-lying areas of Sylhet. Sylhet also has a long history of migration to the United Kingdom. The Sylheti Londoni—as they are known—retain strong marital ties with their home region, and all migrants tend to remit funds to families left behind. Since the prospect of migration through marriage to a Sylheti girl in London is considered a highly desirable match, migrant marriages may introduce a different dynamic into this marriage market. Our qualitative data from focus group discussions (FGDs) and interviews hint at the nature of such a dynamic. Almost every focus group in Sunamgonj, Sylhet, indicated that 'reverse dowry' is common if it provides grooms with legal entry into the UK. Sylhet traditionally has been a sending area for migrants to the UK and the Middle East. Young men especially aspire to migrate abroad, and marriage is an important route to migration. London-based girls and their families demand payment for a marriage that helps the groom to migrate.

Regional Variation in Dowry

To further explore factors explaining the considerable regional variation in individual-level analysis, we estimated nested multi-level models (Tables 4.2 and 4.3). The district of residence is defined as the community of relevance following previous work on spatial socio-demographic analysis (Amin et al. 1997; Amin et al. 2002b). The community variables constructed are categorised into two sets. The first set measures the economic characteristics of the community; including the proportion of respondents in the district who report having a bank account, the proportion reporting receiving remittances, the proportion of households that own agricultural land, the proportion of households that are ranked in the highest wealth quintile for the nation in terms of asset holdings, the proportion of adult women in the community having some secondary education, and the proportion of women currently working for cash or kind. The second set of variables measures values and attitudes in the community regarding the status of women. These include the proportion in the community who approve of violence against women, the proportion who say that they oppose women working outside the home, the proportion of women who observe *purdah* (the practice of seclusion of women) before marriage, and the proportion who support equal education for boys and girls. The models are estimated separately for each of the three outcomes of interest regarding marriage, the incidence of early marriage, and whether dowry was demanded and paid at the time of marriage. For each outcome, we first estimated a base model with individual variables only; we then introduced the two sets of economic and cultural variables, first on their own and then combined. We examined the coefficient estimates of each of the variables, as well as the change in a measure of the district-level variance estimated using the Mixed Effects Logit command in Stata, the statistical software package. The variances of the nested models are compared to assess whether these variables improve the relative explanatory powers of the model. Statistical significance is assessed by examining the Likelihood Ratio test.

TABLE 4.2: Nested Multi-level Mixed Effects Logit Model Predicting Payment of Dowry

Variables	*Base*	*Add economic variables*	*Add social conservatism variables*	*Final model*
FIXED PARAMETERS				
Individual-level Variables				
Respondent has some secondary education	0.648*** (0.095)	0.665*** (0.098)	0.642*** (0.094)	0.664*** (0.098)
Respondent's spouse is from same village	0.660*** (0.106)	0.655*** (0.105)	0.664** (0.106)	0.661*** (0.106)
Economic Status (Middle 40%) (Ref: Bottom 40%)	0.570*** (0.086)	0.579*** (0.087)	0.566*** (0.085)	0.574*** (0.086)
Economic Status (Top 20%) (Ref: Bottom 40%)	0.329*** (0.074)	0.335*** (0.076)	0.331*** (0.075)	0.332*** (0.075)
Area (Urban/Rural)	1.059 (0.193)	1.068 (0.197)	1.071 (0.192)	1.139 (0.209)

(Contd.)

(Table 4.2 Contd.)

Variables	*Base*	*Add economic variables*	*Add social conservatism variables*	*Final model*
Religion: Muslim	0.548** (0.147)	0.573** (0.154)	0.584** (0.157)	0.628* (0.170)
District-level Economic Variables				
Proportion of households owning agricultural land		1.160 (1.319)		0.400 (0.424)
Proportion of households in top wealth quintile		1.174 (2.067)		1.385 (2.417)
Proportion of adult women with some secondary education		0.264 (0.484)		0.103 (0.184)
Proportion of respondents owning a bank account		1.125 (3.244)		8.743 (23.763)
Proportion households receiving some form of remittance		0.126 (0.185)		0.403 (0.557)
Proportion of women currently working for cash or kind		4.036 (5.719)		1.507 (2.081)
District-level Social Conservatism Variables				
Proportion approving of violence against women			24.891** (35.095)	24.163** (37.576)
Proportion of women observing 'purdah' before marriage			0.059*** (0.062)	0.047*** (0.054)
Proportion who support equal education for boys and girls			0.112*** (0.095)	0.098*** (0.086)
Proportion who are opposed to women working outside the home			16.592 (28.477)	10.698 (18.012)
Constant	2.433** (1.087)	3.195 (2.722)	17.015*** (12.809)	41.179*** (46.398)

(Contd.)

(Table 4.2 Contd.)

Variables	*Base*	*Add economic variables*	*Add social conservatism variables*	*Final model*
RANDOM PARAMETERS				
Variance (^{2}) (Intercept: Between Districts)	1.158 (0.306)	0.973 (0.269)	0.816 (0.237)	0.679 (0.207)
LR Test vs. Logistic Regression (^{2})	152.36***	106.49***	82.40***	62.08***
Observations	1373	1373	1373	1373
Number of groups	51	51	51	51

Note: * Significant at 0.05.
** Significant at 0.01.
*** Significant at 0.001.

Source: Authors' calculations based on data from World Bank Gender Norms Survey of 2006.

TABLE 4.3: Nested Multi-level Mixed Effects Logit Model Predicting Early Marriage

Variables	*Base*	*Add economic variables*	*Add social conservatism variables*	*Final model*
FIXED PARAMETERS				
Individual-level Variables				
Respondent has some secondary education	0.369*** (0.052)	0.369*** (0.052)	0.362*** (0.051)	0.365*** (0.052)
Respondent's spouse is from same village	1.184 (0.177)	1.170 (0.175)	1.184 (0.177)	1.175 (0.176)
Economic Status (Middle 40%) (Ref: Bottom 40%)	0.605*** (0.087)	0.618*** (0.089)	0.625*** (0.089)	0.630*** (0.090)
Economic Status (Top 20%) (Ref: Bottom 40%)	0.322*** (0.072)	0.338*** (0.076)	0.341*** (0.076)	0.342*** (0.077)
Area (Urban/Rural)	1.074 (0.180)	1.031 (0.178)	1.030 (0.163)	1.070 (0.178)
Religion: Muslim	1.589* (0.443)	1.655* (0.459)	4.650* (0.451)	1.760** (0.483)

(Contd.)

(Table 4.3 Contd.)

Variables	Base	Add economic variables	Add social conservatism variables	Final model
District-level Economic Variables				
Proportion of households owning agricultural land		2.648 (1.974)		1.094 (0.715)
Proportion of households in top wealth quintile		0.647 (0.751)		1.786 (1.982)
Proportion of adult women with some secondary education		1.182 (1.453)		0.698 (0.788)
Proportion of respondents owning a bank account		1.909 (3.750)		3.539 (6.321)
Proportion households receiving some form of remittance		0.101** (0.101)		0.161** (0.143)
Proportion of women currently working for cash or kind		0.869 (0.821)		0.501 (0.441)
District-level Social Conservatism Variables				
Proportion approving of violence against women			4.314* (3.627)	2.948 (2.862)
Proportion of women observing 'purdah' before marriage			0.261** (0.170)	0.277* (0.203)
Proportion who support equal education for boys and girls			0.088*** (0.046)	0.076*** (0.043)
Proportion who are opposed to women working outside the home			2.020 (2.015)	2.957 (2.954)
Constant	0.867 (0.352)	0.740 (0.452)	4.888*** (2.555)	5.534*** (3.964)
RANDOM PARAMETERS				
Variance (^{2}) (Intercept: Between Districts)	0.391 (0.124)	0.300 (0.110)	0.165 (0.079)	0.129 (0.071)

(Contd.)

(Table 4.3 Contd.)

Variables	Base	Add economic variables	Add social conservatism variables	Final model
LR Test vs. Logistic Regression (^{2})	50.06***	25.20***	10.80***	7.09***
Observations	1373	1373	1373	1373
Number of groups	51	51	51	51

Note: * Significant at 0.05.
** Significant at 0.01.
*** Significant at 0.001.

Source: Authors' calculations based on data from World Bank Gender Norms Survey of 2006.

The general conclusions drawn from these models are as follows: there is significant district-level variation for both outcome variables in the absence of controls for district-level characteristics (Base Model in Table 4.2). Entering the set of economic variables reduces the variation collectively, as reflected in a lower variance estimate of the random parameter for the model as a whole. None of the economic indicators are significantly associated with outcomes indicating payment of dowry and early marriage. Thus, we conclude that the observed district-level indicators are not explained by the economic indicators considered.

The attitudinal measures were found to be highly significant in explaining variations in whether dowry was paid and for early marriage (second column in Table 4.2) and for whether marriage was early (third column in Table 4.3). Districts that ranked high in approval of violence had higher proportions of respondents paying dowry at marriage and contracting marriage at an early age. Similarly, districts that ranked high in the proportion of respondents advocating equal education for boys and girls were less likely to pay dowry and were less likely to have early marriage. In contrast, districts that ranked higher in the proportion of women respondents reporting purdah observance before marriage reported lower rates of dowry exchange and lower rates of early marriage. While the first two community attitudinal indicators are expected, i.e. dowry and early marriage are associated with socially conservative attitudes, the influence of purdah practice is surprising. It is possible that this association is attributable to rapidly spreading religious movements that advocate veiling for women and that also oppose dowry as an un-Islamic practice. These Islamic social movements also encourage the practice and study of Islam through frequent congregation and interaction, thus promoting social networking albeit in gender-segregated groups (Metcalf 1996). Social networking may have an independent influence on the marriage market by facilitating contact with wider social groups.

Marriage Characteristics and Life after Marriage

Next we consider responses to a set of questions about the respondents' present status and relate their replies to the women's own marriage characteristics. Table 4.4 shows the association between the eight indicators of women's control over their own lives in multiple dimensions. First, two questions assess the level of autonomous control over money by asking whether the respondent has any cash in hand and whether she has a bank account. Second, a question about an attitudinal variable assesses the respondent's own attitude towards gender inequality by seeking her opinion on whether boys or girls should have more or equal or less education. The variable is coded as one if the respondent thinks that boys should receive more education than girls. The next four questions assess a woman's autonomy and her ability to indulge in very small luxuries. These questions ask whether she can eat what she wants when she wants, whether she owns a lipstick, and whether she has eaten fruits and drunk milk in the past week. Finally, the respondent is asked if she has ever experienced domestic violence in her marriage.

As may be expected, for each of these indicators, having some secondary education is associated positively with women's position and status, indicating more control over their own lives. Women who have received some secondary education are significantly more likely to report having cash in hand and are more likely to have bank accounts than women with less education. They exhibit more gender-equitable attitudes and are considerably less likely to say that boys should have more education than girls. They are also more likely to report that they can eat as and when they want, implying that they do not need permission to do so. They are significantly more likely to own a lipstick, and they are also significantly more likely to say that they ate fruits and drank milk in the past week.

Four variables measure the nature of marriage: whether the woman married into a family that was better off than her natal family at the time of marriage; whether the woman was married before the age of 15; whether the woman had any say in the choice of her husband; and whether dowry was paid at the time of marriage. Responses were coded as women having a say in choice of husband, if the woman said that she had decided on her own or had been consulted at the time the marriage decision was made. Women who paid dowry were ranked in terms of the amounts paid into quartiles. Women who paid no dowry was the reference or comparison category. A respondent fell into the lowest quartile if her dowry was in the bottom 25th percentile of the dowry paid by all women respondents.

TABLE 4.4: Relative Risks Associated with Covariates of Women's Autonomy and Status, Bangladesh Marriage and Gender Norms Survey, Married Women, 15–25 Years, 2006

	Has cash in hand	*Has bank account*	*Boys more educated*	*Eats at will*	*Owns lipstick*	*Ate fruit last week*	*Drank milk last week*	*Has experienced violence*
Some secondary education (< sec. omitted)	1.22	2.55**	0.49*	1.93**	3.22**	1.90*	2.17**	0.81
Married before 15 (=> 15 omitted)	1.37	0.83	1.14	3.25**	0.65*	0.84	1.00	0.85
Any say in choice of husband (none omitted)	1.01	0.83	1.24	1.81	1.44	1.38	1.07	0.42
Dowry quintiles (none paid omitted)								
Lowest	1.06	0.29**	2.43**	0.75	0.82	0.31**	0.39**	0.88
Second	0.50*	0.85	0.98	0.44	0.53*	0.47**	0.49**	3.85*
Middle	0.56*	0.39**	1.17	1.20	0.85	0.64*	0.49**	2.67*
Fourth	0.39**	0.32**	1.53	0.30*	0.69	0.51**	0.51*	2.39
Highest	0.44**	0.91	1.22	0.57	1.88*	0.69	0.68*	1.25
Received remittances (none omitted)	1.72*	5.17**	0.83	0.83	1.44	1.26	1.25	0.95
Spouse from the same village (none omitted)	0.94	0.99	0.90	1.26	0.91	1.03	0.87	0.98

(Contd.)

(Table 4.4 Contd.)

	Has cash in hand	*Has bank account*	*Boys more educated*	*Eats at will*	*Owns lipstick*	*Ate fruit last week*	*Drank milk last week*	*Has experienced violence*
Rural (urban omitted)	0.77	0.54**	1.24	1.19	0.66*	0.73	0.99	1.01
Muslim (non-Muslim omitted)	0.99	1.13	2.31*	0.11*	0.31**	0.50	0.49*	1.95
Relative economic status (same omitted)								
Natal family better off	0.97	0.96	1.16	0.78	0.84	1.26	1.11	1.53
Husband's family better off	0.62*	0.98	2.48**	0.46**	0.89	1.07	0.91	1.35
Purdah before marriage	0.88	0.97	0.88	1.06	1.12	0.76	1.50*	1.44
Division (Barisal omitted)								
Chittagong	1.91*	0.38**	2.01	0.75	1.02	0.86	0.69*	0.92
Dhaka	2.10**	0.59*	0.55	0.64	1.12	2.14*	1.52	0.55
Khulna	2.49**	0.84	0.76	0.46	0.51**	1.88	1.28	1.63
Rajshahi	4.35**	0.76	1.03	0.41	0.70	1.83	1.17	0.09**
Sylhet	4.88**	0.68	0.03**	0.79	4.15**	0.94	0.36**	1.10

Source: Authors' calculations based on data from World Bank Gender Norms Survey of 2006.

Respondents were asked to report the relative status of their natal and marital families. The reference category is women who reported that their natal and marital families were of equal status. If the natal family was better off, the marriage was coded as marrying down; if the natal family was worse off, it was coded as marrying up. Women who marry up are significantly less likely to report having control over their own lives according to three of the eight indicators. Women who marry up are less likely to have cash in hand, are significantly more likely to say that boys should have more education, and are significantly less likely to say that they can eat as and when they want. The other indicators are not statistically significant. Women whose natal family is better off are not significantly different from those who marry equals on any of these indicators.

Dowry is significantly associated with six of the eight indicators of empowerment, with dowry payment being negatively associated with empowerment indicators, post-marriage. Generally, women who did not pay any dowry are better off (meaning, having more control) than women who paid dowry. Women who paid dowry were significantly less likely to have cash in hand relative to women who paid no dowry. Similarly, the association between paying dowry and having a bank account shows that those who paid dowry are less likely to have a bank account. The indicator that shows women who believe that boys should have more education reveals that only women in the lowest dowry quartile are significantly different. Respondents in all the other categories are more likely to say that boys should have more education, but those parameter estimates are not statistically significant. Relative to those who paid no dowry, women in the second dowry quartile (25th to 50th percentile) are significantly less likely to say that they can eat when they want, are less likely to own a lipstick, and are less likely to have eaten fruits or drunk milk in the past week. Women in all dowry-paying quartiles are less likely to say that they had drunk milk in the past week relative to those who reported paying no dowry. Women in the second and third dowry quartiles are significantly more likely to report being abused, relative to women who reported paying no dowry. Women in the highest quartile also report being abused, but the result is not statistically significant.

Compared to the two marriage indicators discussed above (dowry payment and marrying up or down), early marriage and say in the choice of husband are not strongly associated with women's control over various dimensions of their own lives. For marriage timing, three out of the eight indicators are significant, but none in the expected direction. It is generally assumed that early or child marriage will be associated with negative outcomes after marriage and that women who married early will be disempowered. These data show that women who married early are more likely to say that they have cash in hand compared to women who married at older ages. They are more likely to say that they can eat when and what they want, and are less likely to own a lipstick. Finally, only one empowerment indicator is significantly related to women having a say in choosing their husband. Women who said that they had some choice in this regard were significantly more likely to say that they could eat what and when they want.

Another indicator of marriage, i.e. whether the spouse grew up in the same village (village endogamy), did not prove to be significantly associated with any of the outcome variables. Some other household indicators that were included in the models are: whether the household was a remittance-receiving household, urban versus rural residence, and religious background. The two indicators pertaining to control over money—having cash in hand and having a bank account—are strongly significant for households receiving remittances, but other variables are not significantly associated. The urban effect is a bit counterintuitive; women in urban areas are less likely to own a bank account and are less likely to own a lipstick. The bank account indicator may be explained by the greater access to financial services enjoyed by women in rural areas because of the existence of micro-credit programmes. The lipstick indicator is harder to understand given that this cosmetic is more readily available in urban settings.

Relative to non-Muslims, Muslims are significantly more likely to say that boys should have more education than girls, and are less likely to eat what and when they want, are less likely to own a lipstick, and are less likely to have eaten fruits or drunk milk in the past week.

There are strong regional differences in only one of the indicators of women's control, i.e. women reporting having cash in hand. There are not many differences in the other indicators by region with the exception of Sylhet, which generally shows contradictory outcomes. Women in Sylhet seem to have more control in that they are more likely to have cash, are less likely to say that boys should have more education, and also are more likely to say that they own a lipstick, but are less likely to say that they drank milk in the past week. The reference category is Barisal.

To summarise, these results suggest that most marriage strategy indicators perform well in predicting women's control over their own lives. Women marrying into families that are better off generally do not fare well, suggesting that marrying up is not a good marriage strategy if the objective is to ensure that women retain control over these aspects of their lives. This may also be attributable directly to poverty; women in the poorest households have no choice but to marry an equal or up, and thus poor women, who are disadvantaged in the marriage market, may be driving this association. Not paying dowry is associated with generally positive outcomes relative to all categories of dowry payment, small or large, suggesting that paying dowry is also not a good way of ensuring that women maintain some control over their own lives. In the way that we have defined women's say in the choice of husband, we find that it is not strongly associated with women having control over their own lives. Most surprisingly, early marriage is not associated with less control. On the contrary, in the three indicators examined here, women who are married early indicate that they have more control over their own lives.

Conclusions

In this essay, we have explored the dynamics of continuity and change in marriage. To summarise, there is considerable evidence of persistence in early and arranged marriages and in the attendant living arrangements. There is widespread evidence of increasing dowry, although there is also substantial regional variation. The World Bank Gender Norms Survey of 2006 (qtd. in World Bank 2008) provides valuable new information on marriage practices in Bangladesh. It is the first survey to document patterns of marriage transactions and arrangements, levels of village endogamy, and post-marriage living arrangements. Questions pertaining to antecedents and post-marriage status also allow us to relate marriage characteristics to women's experiences after marriage.

We have also attempted to address the question of whether signs of continuity and change are interrelated. Is the persistence of early marriage merely a marker of a more traditional social context characterised by stronger patriarchal structures? We do not have a clearly affirmative answer to this question. In the parts of the country that are thought to be most progressive, for example, Rajshahi, age at marriage is the earliest and dowry is most widely prevalent. Regarding the areas where the lowest rates of dowry are reported, for example Barisal and Sylhet, we see that these provinces have both large and small proportions of marriage at an early age. We suggest that this situation may be related to the influence of migration, thus setting these areas apart from the rest of the country. Whereas in Rajshahi, where women have fewer children, are more likely to be involved in paid work, and are less likely to observe purdah, three out of every five marriages involve dowry. In Sylhet and Barisal, less than one in five marriages involves dowry. These two areas have the poorest health indicators, according to the Millennium Development Goals Report on Bangladesh (World Bank 2005). In Rajshahi and Chittagong, where dowry is also very widely prevalent, dowry is listed as one of the major societal problems. In Sylhet and Barisal, dowry is not perceived as being especially problematic. It is likely that poverty is a driver of part of this association.

Although the poor give small amounts, they are more likely to pay dowry than the wealthy (Amin et al. 2008).

Our analysis shows that dowry payment and village endogamy are consistently related to women having less control over their own lives. Somewhat surprisingly, not having a say in the choice of husband and even extremely early marriage are not similarly related to the exercise of control by women over their own lives. Much of the policy effort has focused on trying to change very early patterns of marriage out of a concern that early marriage has adverse later-life outcomes. While there is a good argument to be made for later marriage, trying to bring about this marriage reform while the practice of dowry continues to become more widespread defeats the purpose of the measure. Women would probably be better off with greater efforts being made to remove the incentives for dowry exchange rather than efforts being made at eradicating early marriage per se.

Any effort to change the prevailing dowry practices has to take into account the substantial regional variation in this social phenomenon. Early marriage, dowry exchange and marriage choice all vary across regions within Bangladesh, but the patterns of variation are different for each of the indicators and are not easily explained.

Finally, the data analysis shown here in terms of post-marriage covariates of marriage decisions reveals very consistently that secondary education is related to generally positive outcomes. Education in general is associated with a lower likelihood of paying dowry and with a lower likelihood of an early marriage. To the extent that marriage and dowry practices have changed, and are changing, it is clear that the greatest promise lies in linking these changes to girls' education.

The association with dowry prevalence and poverty (World Bank 2008) suggests that a full exploration of the determinants of early marriage needs to explicitly understand the economic aspects of marriage. While cultural patterns and preferences form part of the context, the economic underpinnings of marriage decisions cannot be ignored. The evidence strongly suggests that one of the enduring results of the rise of dowry has made previously latent economic dynamics more explicit.

Appendix: Marriage Characteristics by Age Cohort and Region, Marriage Survey, 2006

Table 4A.1: Per cent of Women who Reported They had a Say or Were Consulted When Their Husband was Chosen

Division name	*Older women*	*Younger women*	*All women*
Sample size (absolute numbers)	1431	1373	2804
Barisal	27.2	41.3	33.8
Chittagong	22.8	39.2	30.6
Dhaka	16.3	29.5	22.6
Khulna	2.9	11.9	7.8
Rajshahi	9.9	19.7	15.0
Sylhet	3.0	12.6	7.5
Total	14.2	25.7	20.0

Source: Authors' calculations based on data from World Bank Gender Norms Survey of 2006.

Table 4A.2a: Per cent of Women who Reported They First Met Their (First) Husband on Their Wedding Day

Division name	*Older women*	*Younger women*	*All women*
Sample size (absolute numbers)	1431	1373	2804
Barisal	81.8	66.8	74.7
Chittagong	86.0	77.1	81.8
Dhaka	78.0	72.4	75.3
Khulna	87.2	75.1	80.7
Rajshahi	83.5	83.7	83.6
Sylhet	81.8	67.0	74.9
Total	82.3	75.9	79.1

Source: Authors' calculations based on data from World Bank Gender Norms Survey of 2006.

TABLE 4A.2b: Per cent of Women who Reported they are NOT Related to their (first) Husband by Blood

Division name	*Older women*	*Younger women*	*All women*
Sample size (absolute numbers)	1431	1373	2804
Barisal	9.3	7.9	8.6
Chittagong	12.3	11.2	11.8
Dhaka	6.3	8.9	7.5
Khulna	6.6	6	6.3
Rajshahi	9.7	7	8.2
Sylhet	18.1	21.1	19.5
Total	9.2	9.0	9.1

Source: Authors' calculations based on data from World Bank Gender Norms Survey of 2006.

TABLE 4A.3: Per cent of Women who Reported their (first) Marriage was Registered

Division name	*Older women*	*Younger women*	*All women*
Sample size (absolute numbers)	1425	1360	2785
Barisal	50.1	87.9	67.9
Chittagong	52.6	82.5	66.9
Dhaka	45.9	86.4	65.2
Khulna	29.5	72.9	52.8
Rajshahi	33.8	89.9	63.7
Sylhet	66.7	89.4	77.2
Total	44.1	85.2	64.5

Source: Authors' calculations based on data from World Bank Gender Norms Survey of 2006.

TABLE 4A.4: Per cent of Women who Reported That a Dowry was Agreed upon or Paid at the Time of Marriage

Division name	*Older women*	*Younger women*	*All women*
Sample size (absolute numbers)	1431	1373	2804
Barisal	5.9	25.7	15.2
Chittagong	5.7	48.1	25.9
Dhaka	6.4	44.7	24.8
Khulna	5.6	34.2	21.0
Rajshahi	14.1	65.3	41.4
Sylhet	1.8	12.7	6.8
Total	7.7	46.4	27.0

Source: Authors' calculations based on data from World Bank Gender Norms Survey of 2006.

TABLE 4A.5: The Average Amount of Dowry that was Agreed upon at the Time of Marriage (Amount in Tk.)

Division name	*Older women*	*Younger women*	*All women*
Sample size (absolute numbers)	1431	1373	2804
Barisal	3687	13,556	11,428
Chittagong	57,723	22,562	26,567
Dhaka	7118	19,624	17,975
Khulna	8325	15,895	14,929
Rajshahi	3150	17,237	15,011
Sylhet	3209	19,000	16,826
Total	11,903	18,608	17,658

Note: US$ 1 ~ BD Taka 65.00 in 2005.
Source: Authors' calculations based on data from World Bank Gender Norms Survey of 2006.

TABLE 4A.6: Per cent Women who Were First Married before the Age of 15

Division name	*Older women*	*Younger women*	*All women*
Sample size (absolute numbers)	1431	1373	2804
Barisal	52	32	43
Chittagong	56	39	48
Dhaka	56	43	50
Khulna	67	49	57
Rajshahi	73	60	66
Sylhet	25	14	20
Total	59	45	52

Source: Authors' calculations based on data from World Bank Gender Norms Survey of 2006.

TABLE 4A.7: Average Amount of Dowry Paid by Age at Marriage, in Tk.

Age at marriage	*Older women*	*Younger women*	*All women*
Sample size (absolute numbers)	1431	1373	2804
<15	4602	21,215	18,973
16–18	13,132*	23,583	22,514
>18	5514*	42,146	34,321

Note: * less than 30 respondents reporting.
Source: Authors' calculations based on data from World Bank Gender Norms Survey of 2006.

REFERENCES

Ambrus, Attila, Erica Field, and Maximo Torero. 2008. '*Muslim Family Law, Prenuptial Agreements and the Emergence of Dowry in Bangladesh*'. BREAD Working Paper 179. Available at: http://ipl.econ.duke.edu/bread/papers/working/179.pdf. Accessed on: 11 January 2013.

Amin, Sajeda, and Luciana Suran. 2009. 'Terms of Marriage and Time-use Patterns of Young Wives: Evidence from Rural Bangladesh'. *Electronic Journal of Time Use Research* 6 (1): 92–108.

Amin, Sajeda, Alaka M. Basu, Rob Stephenson, and Lopita Huq. 2008. 'Marriage Considerations in Sending Girls to School in Bangladesh: Some Qualitative Evidence'. *Poverty, Gender, and Youth* Working Paper 12. New York: Population Council.

Amin, Sajeda, Alaka M. Basu, Rob Stephenson Nasheeba Selim, and Nashid Kamal Waiz. 2006. *Causes and Consequences of Early Marriage in Bangladesh: Background Report for Workshop on Programs and Policies to Prevent Early Marriage*. Dhaka: Population Council.

Amin, Sajeda, Simeen Mahmud, and Lopita Huq. 2002a. *Kishori Abhijan: Baseline Survey Report on Rural Adolescents in Bangladesh*. Dhaka: Ministry of Women and Children Affairs, Government of Bangladesh (Supported by UNICEF, Bangladesh).

Amin, Sajeda, Alaka M. Basu, and Rob Stephenson. 2002b. 'Spatial Variation in Contraceptive Use in Bangladesh: Looking beyond the Borders'. *Demography* 39 (2): 251–67.

Amin, Sajeda, and Mead Cain. 1997. 'The Rise of Dowry in Bangladesh'. In *The Continuing Demographic Transition*, eds. Gavin W. Jones, Robert M. Douglas, John C. Caldwell, and Rennie M. D'Souza, 290–306. Oxford: Clarendon Press.

Amin, Sajeda, Ian Diamond, and Fiona Steele. 1997. 'Contraception and Religious Practice in Bangladesh'. In *The Continuing Demographic Transition*, ed. Gavin W. Jones, Robert M. Douglas, John C. Caldwell, and Rennie M. D'Souza. Oxford: Clarendon Press.

Arunachalam, Raj, and Suresh Naidu. 2008. *The Price of Fertility: Marriage Markets and Family Planning in Bangladesh*. Available at: http://www-personal.umich.edu/~arunacha/AN_dowryfertility.pdf. Accessed on: 10 January 2013.

Cain, Mead, Syeda Rokeya Khanam, and Shamsun Nahar. 1979. 'Class, Patriarchy, and Women's Work in Bangladesh'. *Population and Development Review* 5 (3): 405–38.

Caldwell, J. C., P. H. Reddy, and Pat Caldwell. 1983. 'The Causes of Marriage Change in South India' *Population Studies* 37 (3): 343–61.

Chowdhury, A. R. 2008. 'Money and Marriage: A Fresh Look at Marriage Transactions in Rural India'. Ph.D. dissertation, Department of Sociology, Brown University.

Lindenbaum, Shirley. 1981. 'Implications for Women of Changing Marriage Transactions in Bangladesh'. *Studies in Family Planning* 12 (11): 394–401.

Metcalf, Barbara. 1996. 'Islam and Women: The Case of the Tablighi Jama'at'. *SEHR, 5 (1): Contested Polities*. Available at: http://www.stanford.edu/group/SHR/5-1/text/metcalf.html. Accessed on: 11 January 2013.

Ministry of Law, Government of Bangladesh. 1980. 'Dowry Prohibition Act of 1980'. Available at: http://bdlaws.minlaw.gov.bd/display_pdf_volume.php?alp=22. Accessed on: 11 January 2013.

Mobarak, A. Mushfiq, Randall Kuhn, and Christina Peters. 2011. 'Marriage Market Effects of a Wealth Shock in Bangladesh'. Unpublished paper. Available at: http://faculty.som.yale.edu/mushfiqmobarak/consanguinity_marriage.pdf. Accessed on: 11 January 2013.

National Institute of Population Research and Training (NIPORT) Mitra and Associates and ORC Macro. 2005. *Bangladesh Demographic and Health Survey 2004*. Dhaka, Bangladesh and Calverton, Maryland, USA: NIPORT and ORC.

Naved, Ruchira T., Margaret Newby, Sajeda Amin, and Lars A. Persson. 2008. 'Factors Associated with Physical Spousal Abuse of Women during Pregnancy in Bangladesh'. *International Family Planning Perspectives* 34 (2): 71–78.

Naved, Ruchira T., Margaret Newby, and Sajeda Amin. 2001. 'Female Labor Migration and Its Implication for Marriage and Childbearing in Bangladesh'. *International Journal of Population Geography* 7:91–104.

Rao, Vijayendra. 1993. 'Dowry "Inflation" in Rural India: A Statistical Investigation'. *Population Studies* 47 (2): 283–93.

Rozario, Santi. 2009. 'Dowry in Rural Bangladesh: An Intractable Problem?' In *Dowry: Bridging the Gap between Theory and Practice*, eds. Tamsin Bradley, Emma Tomalin, and Mangala Subramaniam. New Delhi: Women Unlimited.

———. 2001. 'Women and Poverty: Is Grameen Bank the Answer?' *Journal of Interdisciplinary Gender Studies* 6 (2): 60–82.

———. 1992. *Purity and Communal Boundaries: Women and Social Change in a Bangladeshi Village*. London: Zed Press.

White, Sarah C. 1992. *Arguing with the Crocodile: Gender and Class in Bangladesh*. Dhaka: University Press Limited.

World Bank. 2008. '*Whispers to Voices: Gender and Social Transformation in Bangladesh*'. Dhaka: World Bank. Available at: http://siteresources.worldbank.org/SOUTHASIAEXT/Resources/Publications/448813-1185396961095/4030558-1205418213360/bdgender2008.pdf. Accessed on: 10 January 2013).

———. 2005. '*Attaining the Millennium Development Goals in Bangladesh*'. World Bank Human Development Unit, South Asia Region. Available on: http://www-wds.worldbank.org/external/default/WDSContentServer/WDSP/IB/2005/07/06/000012009_20050706090851/Rendered/PDF/318460rev.pdf. Accessed on: 10 January 2013.

Negotiating Marriage*

Examining the Gap between Marriage and Cohabitation in India

Lester Andrist, Manjistha Banerji and Sonalde Desai

Introduction

Two connected observations often loom large in discussions about marriage in India. The first is that marriage for women on the subcontinent often occurs at a relatively early age and this is cause for concern because early marriage is thought to disempower women by reducing their access to education and thrusting adult responsibilities on them early in life. The second observation is that marriage in India is more or less universal (Tables 5.1 and 5.2) (Uberoi 1993), making the first issue all the more pressing.

Indeed, evidence suggests that while the average age at marriage in India has been increasing for both men and women, increases have been fairly slow, with much of the change coming through elimination of marriage for girls

* This study is based on the India Human Development Survey (IHDS) 2004–05 jointly organised by researchers at the University of Maryland and the National Council of Applied Economic Research (NCAER). The data collection was funded by grants R01HD041455 and R01HD046166 from the National Institute of Health to the University of Maryland. Part of the sample represents a resurvey of households which had been initially surveyed during the course of IHDS 1993–94 conducted by NCAER.

under 14 years of age rather than bringing about an actual delay in marriage for older teenagers or women in their twenties. In a 30-year period spanning from 1961 to 1991, on average, women's age at marriage increased only by about three years, from a mean age of 16 to about 19 years of age (IIPS and O.R.C. Macro 2000). In contrast, average age at marriage in neighbouring Bangladesh was delayed by a full year more during the same three decades (Islam and Ahmed 1998).

TABLE 5.1: Singulate Mean Age at Marriage of Women in India and Bangladesh, 1961–2001

	1961	*1971*	*1981*	*1991*	*2001*
India*	16.1	17.2	18.4	19.3	17.2
Bangladesh**	13.9	–	16.6	18.0	–

Source: Authors' calculations based on IHDS Data.
* 1961–2001: IIPS and O.R.C. Macro (2000); Desai et al. (2009, 2010).
** 1961–1991: Islam and Ahmed (1998).

TABLE 5.2: Percentage of Married Women Aged 20–24 in Various Developing Regions

Eastern/Southern Africa	66
Western/Middle Africa	79
Eastern Asia	46
Former Soviet Asia	54
Caribbean/Central America	56
South America	51
Middle East/North Africa	55
All-India	77
Rural India	83
Urban India	63

Source: See Table C-2 for India in Census of India (2001), Mensch et al. (2005) for other developing countries.

It is instructive to examine this slow change in marriage in the context of rapid changes observed in other areas of Indian life. The economy has grown annually at a rate of 7–9 per cent over the past 15 years, and education has expanded rapidly for all segments of the society (Desai and Kulkarni 2008). Indian families have also undergone rather dramatic changes, suggested by rapid declines in the Total Fertility Rate from 4.8 in the 1960s to 2.7 in recent years (IIPS and Macro International 2007). Thus, this relatively slow change in the average age at marriage is somewhat of a puzzle and one worth examining.

Originating out of a long tradition of village studies, much of the classic research on marriage in India is characteristically structural and places emphasis on detailing the rules associated with kinship and caste. Marital timing is tied up with questions such as who counts as a suitable marriage partner and whether there is a marriage squeeze. In this work, marriage is seen as often forming the key through which social relations are built, and the practices endorsed by those at the top of such hierarchies are conceived to have a determining influence on marital timing (Dube 1996, 2001; Dyson and Moore 1983; Karve 1965; Srinivas 1977; Uberoi 1993). Even when culture—in the form of norms and customs—is explicitly theorised to be the driving force behind changes in age at marriage, it is often treated as just another structure, as though a kind of static programmed human behaviour (Retherford et al. 2001). Despite the dynamism typically associated with culture, it has too often featured in these analyses as a kind of fossilised backdrop (Hammel 1990).

Accurately rendering the dynamism of culture in order to develop nuanced theoretical models for studying patterned behaviours related to marriage and family remains challenging, particularly in light of the privacy typically accorded to issues so close to families. Families may act from a particular set of dispositions or habitus, but their actions aggregate as patterns capable of continually modifying those dispositions. The corporate family[1] in India is certainly no exception and we think it serves as a useful site for gaining a better understanding of the slow pace of change in marital timing on the subcontinent.

Pierre Bourdieu (1977) first suggested that families can be understood as resting on systems of durable dispositions or habitus. The timing of a marriage, in these terms, is not a determination made by an aloof family in isolation from the community within which it is embedded; neither is timing wholly determined by the imperatives of class, caste and kinship typical of that community. Rather, the corporate family can be usefully recognised as an embodied agent, which is able to negotiate between the often competing demands placed on it.

In deciding on an appropriate time to arrange marriage for their sons and daughters—particularly daughters—parents are faced with competing demands; some push toward an early age at marriage and others toward a later age. For instance, if finding a good match depends on the availability of eligible candidates, then the pressure to find a match only mounts as a girl gets older and the pool of candidates dwindles. In addition, much has been written about the ability of families to avert harmful rumours about a daughter's alleged promiscuity through early marriage, thereby maintaining family honour or *izzat* (Caldwell et al. 1983; Caldwell et al. 1998; Lindenbaum 1981).

Although it is important to recognise this downward pressure, it is equally important to acknowledge the rather formidable pressure against early marriage. The Indian state, for instance, has explicitly banned child marriage, which it defines as under age 18 for women and under age 21 for men. Moreover, legal prohibition is reinforced in a pervasive print and visual media, which itself is but one feature of a much broader social discourse.

Thus, the central problematic facing research on marriage timing in India can be posed as two related questions: (1) How is 'optimal' timing for marriage established? (2) How do families negotiate competing demands regarding appropriate age at marriage?

Gender Performance and Marriage Timing

This essay argues that in concert with examining the corporate family as an embodied actor, paying particular attention to the performative dimension of gender offers a useful means of studying marriage patterns in an Indian context. Goffman (1976) first argued that men and women engage in a visible display of gender where a stylised mode of interaction may indicate deference or dominance. Then, nearly a decade later, a provocative paper by West and Zimmerman (1987, 2009) entitled, 'Doing Gender' appeared to simultaneously echo the work of Bourdieu (1977) on practice while further elaborating Goffman's central insight on gender as a performance.

In 'Doing Gender', West and Zimmerman relied on an ethnomethodological approach to argue for an understanding of gender, not as a finished or stable designation, but as an ongoing process that must be perpetually achieved. Thus, one cannot simply 'be' a gender but must 'do' gender and do it continually. Although she drew more explicitly from Bourdieu, this insight is also extant in Judith Butler's (1988) performativity theory and has taken hold in anthropology more generally under the banner of performance theory (Morris 1995). For instance, Steve Derné's conclusion based on fieldwork in northern India (1994, 2003) captures this theoretical perspective when he writes that 'in every interaction in which a husband gives his wife permission to go outside the home, he reconstitutes the normal state of affairs in which restrictions on women are necessary.' (Derne 1994: 210)

There is a synergy between performance theory and the classical social anthropology of M. N. Srinivas. Srinivas (1977) first identified the role of women as custodians of family status and caste purity and focused on the notion of 'sanskritisation', which he identified as the process through which castes manipulate their ritual status; they attempt to legitimise their upward mobility by embracing gendered practises such as prohibition of widow remarriage or by observing purdah. He also acknowledged that performances which attempt to manipulate or legitimate ritual status might also conflict with demands associated with modernisation and Westernisation. While Srinivas's work has been highly influential for several generations of scholars, it seems that his original insight on the performative aspect of caste mobility has been obfuscated by village studies, which largely emphasised the essential stability of caste structure.

But performance theory constitutes a departure from structuralism and is currently enjoying wide application. In a highly controversial essay titled 'Doing Difference', West and Fenstermaker (1995) argue that differences in terms of race, class and gender are performed and accomplished in local settings; Schein (1999) argues that the Miao minority in China create performances of modernity in order to challenge their status as backward cultural conservators. For our purposes, performance theory allows us to focus on the way in which social actors use culture to fabricate meaning in their lives, while at the same time responding to the normative demands of their communities (Kaufman 2004).

We argue that a notion of scripts that frame actors' day-to-day behaviour and yet are constantly modified as actors face competing demands, provides an interesting framework for a study of marriage in India.[2] Yet, travels across India reveal a broad diversity in scripts and the way gender is performed. Purdah, or *ghunghat*, is probably the most visible marker or public performance of gender and it varies from a sari pulled over the face to render women virtually invisible in north and central India, to a polite nod at segregation when an older relative is present in Gujarat, to a total absence of purdah in southern India. While purdah might be the most visible marker to an outsider, there are many other more subtle markers of gender segregation. In some parts of India, men and women regularly eat together, while in other parts, a gender segregated eating order is practised and it would be unthinkable for a young daughter-in-law to eat with her husband's father. Restriction on women's physical mobility is a third marker of gender segregation. In parts of India, women must seek permission from family elders before venturing outside the home, even when visiting a health centre.

It is important to note that, as has been reported in a host of demographic studies on the multidimensionality of gender inequality, gender segregation is not necessarily consonant with inequality in the household (Kishor 2000; Mason 1986). For example, secluded women may retain considerable power in the household, and women with considerable freedom of movement may not find this freedom translating into control over economic resources. For our work, the focus on gendered performances, which denote seemingly 'natural' differences and become the basis for gendered segregation, is particularly important.

Linking of gender scripts to age at marriage must also be viewed in the historical context of the late nineteenth and early twentieth century conflicts between the colonial state which set itself up as the protector of Indian women, and the nationalist movement which needed to articulate an alternative construction of Indian women in order to deflect the colonial discourse. The Opposition to the Age of Consent Act of 1891 represents the attempt to articulate such a construction (Heimsath 1962). This act set a minimum age for a 'consenting' bride at 12. However, nationalist Indians viewed this as an attack on Indian religious autonomy and a vigorous protest emerged led by a charismatic Indian politician, Lokmanya Balgangadhar Tilak. A subsequent increase of minimum age at marriage to 14 in 1929 in an act that came to be known as the Sharda Act also led to significant protests. Partha Chatterjee (1989, 1993) has written persuasively about the process through which the nationalist movement of the early twentieth century created a vision of Indian womanhood that was at once modest, decorous, spiritual and refined. This positioning of Indian women of refinement against their Western counterparts emerged as a response to the colonial state and a Western discourse which posited Indian women as dispossessed and subjugated. Tied up in the nationalist response to colonialism was the creation of a kind of gendered script, the performance of which would mark a distinct Indian womanhood.

Resistance to the colonial construction of early marriage may have attenuated after 60 years of independence, but other practical concerns certainly persist. One of the greatest concerns for most parents is to arrange a marriage for their daughter in a 'good' family where she would thrive. While the definition of 'good marriage' may vary across families, there is a nearly universal concern that nothing should damage the value of a daughter in the marriage market. Popular literature, films and the annals of social science, all emphasise a fear of women's sexuality—particularly among upper class and upper-caste families—and suggest a girl does not even have to be sexually active to be labelled promiscuous. Simple contact and platonic friendship with the opposite sex can be enough to damage her reputation and reduce her desirability to her prospective parents-in-law (Caldwell et al. 1983; Caldwell et al. 1998; Lindenbaum 1981).

Examining modernity in middle-class urban India, Derné (2003) notes the persistence of male preference for modesty and femininity, even under the onslaught of the global culture. Another study in Mumbai recorded young men's preferences for family-oriented, 'simple' wives, who 'respect elders' (Abraham 2001). The common thread of these findings seems to be a preoccupation with women's modesty that does not allow deviation from the normative age at marriage for women, while it is far more easily permitted for men (Leonard 1976). Thus, a long gap between puberty and marriage is seen as a risky period, encouraging parents to minimise this risk by arranging an early marriage.

However, this concern with women's sexual purity is neither universal nor predominant across class and geographic boundaries (Mandelbaum 1988; Papanek 1973). In line with Srinivas' notion of sankritisation, reification of women's modesty is the privilege of upper social classes, and higher caste status is often demonstrated through such reification (Dube 2001; Sharma 1980). Lower-class and lower-caste women rarely have the privilege of secluding themselves. Similarly, casual contact with men is viewed with much greater fear in certain areas of the country than others. We seek to better understand the role this fear of women's sexuality and immodesty plays in shaping marriage patterns via an examination of these differences across different cultural contexts. Fortunately for our purposes, India provides a fascinating laboratory of diverse practices, allowing us to examine whether early marriage is a part and parcel of other gender scripts that emphasise the importance of women's decorum and modesty.

Our focus on gender scripts emphasises a concern with public performance of modesty and implied control over women's sexuality, but is quite distinct from other approaches which aim to measure women's empowerment, such as their control over resources or their general power in household decision-making (Mason 1986; Mukhopadhyay et al. 1988). In line with earlier work, we argue that the median age at first marriage is lower in areas and in communities where there is a greater concern with women's sexuality indicated by greater segregation of men and women into separate spheres (Desai and Andrist 2010). Yet, while early marriage may be associated with scripts that prescribe greater gender segregation, it occurs within the context of a growing public consensus about the undesirability of child marriage. Parents are anxious to allow their daughters to mature before facing the pressures of married life and they worry about curtailing the educational attainment of their daughters. Since education is one of the most important claims to modernity in India, early marriage is not something parents enter into lightly. One of the interesting ways of reconciling these seemingly conflicting demands may be to arrange an early marriage, but one which delays consummation.

The Indian marriage system is characterised by a disjunction between formal marriage and cohabitation, and initiation of sexual activity. Historically, marriage was quite different from *gauna* or effective marriage, where the bride was sent to her husband's home to begin a married life; a gap between marriage and gauna has long been common for child marriages. Analysts recognise that this gap appears to serve a purpose. Basu (1993) argues that the gap often plays an important, if incidental, role in delaying the age of first birth[3]. Palriwala (1991) conceives of the family in a more instrumental manner and argues—based on field data collected in Rajasthan—that the gap is often drawn out by the woman's natal family for the purpose of retaining their daughters' labour for household production, even while forging ties with the conjugal family.

In contrast, we suggest that women's fertility and labour productivity only amount to part of the story. More than a pretence for retaining valuable labour, more even than a means of ensuring a mature age at sexual initiation, this tradition may also be used by parents to ensure their daughters' education, thereby positioning themselves as modern and upwardly mobile. The groom's family must also acquiesce for the process to work, but frequently a desire for this obvious marker of modernity—higher education—is shared by both parties.

Data

Results presented in this essay come from the India Human Development Survey (IHDS) 2005, spanning 41,554 households over all 25 states and union territories of India (with the exception of Andaman and Nicobar, and Lakshadweep). The survey was conducted by researchers from the University of Maryland and the National Council of Applied Economic Research and was funded by the US National Institute of Health. It was a nationally representative survey (Desai et al. 2009) specifically designed to study various dimensions of gender relations, and since the data were collected in structured interviews, considerable attention was directed to framing questions which would provide information that would meaningfully tap into women's experiences within the Indian context.

For this analysis, we restricted our sample to 27,930 ever married women in the age group of 25–49 for whom complete data was available. Results from the 2001 Indian census indicate that nearly 95 per cent of women are married by age 25 and restricting our sample to ever married women aged 25 and above allows us to minimise the selection bias due to the omission of women who marry late. These women were interviewed in their homes by female interviewers in the local language.

Marriage Patterns in Modern India

Given a lack of national information on marriage patterns in India, we start with descriptive statistics from IHDS. Table 5.3 shows that average age at marriage varies considerably across demographic characteristics among ever married women aged 25 years and above in our sample. Regional differences in age at marriage are striking, with average age being 15–17 years in some states like Jharkhand and Madhya Pradesh and a higher age at marriage in Punjab and Himachal Pradesh as well as in the southern states. Women in poor and less educated households often marry around 16 years of age while women from better off and more educated households get married around age 19–20 years. Average age at marriage is 19.3 years in metro cities and is considerably lower in less developed villages.

TABLE 5.3: Marriage and Cohabitation Patterns by Selected Characteristics for Women (Age: 25–49)

	Mean age at marriage	*% Not Cohabiting immediately*	*Mean age at cohabitation*
Full Sample	17.4	51.0	18.0
Women's Age			
25–29	17.6	48.0	18.1
30–39	17.4	50.0	18.0
40–49	17.3	53.0	18.0
Women's Education			
Illiterate	16.1	64.0	17.0
1–4 Standards	17.1	45.0	17.5
5–9 Standards	17.9	40.0	18.3
10–11 Standards	19.5	33.0	19.8
12 and Some College	20.7	31.0	20.9
College Graduate	22.6	24.0	22.8
Place of Residence			
Metro Cities	19.3	31.0	19.5
Other Urban Area	18.5	44.0	19.0
More Developed Villages	17.2	54.0	17.8
Less Developed Villages	16.5	56.0	17.3
Income			
Lowest Quintile	16.5	56.0	17.3
Second Quintile	16.7	55.0	17.4
Third Quintile	17.0	54.0	17.7
Fourth Quintile	17.6	48.0	18.2
Highest Quintile	19.0	40.0	19.4

(Contd.)

(Table 5.3 Contd.)

		% Not	
	Mean age at marriage	*Cohabiting immediately*	*Mean age at cohabitation*
Social Groups			
High-Caste Hindus	18.4	41.0	18.9
OBC	17.2	55.0	18.0
Dalit	16.5	55.0	17.2
Adivasi	17.1	54.0	17.7
Muslim	17.2	50.0	17.7
Other Religions	20.8	30.0	21.1
States			
Jammu and Kashmir	18.9	57.0	19.3
Himachal Pradesh	18.6	28.0	18.9
Uttarakhand	17.6	27.0	17.8
Punjab	19.7	37.0	19.9
Haryana	17.4	74.0	18.3
Delhi	19.2	45.0	19.6
Uttar Pradesh	16.1	72.0	17.5
Bihar	15.2	75.0	16.6
Jharkhand	17.4	54.0	17.9
Rajasthan	15.8	88.0	17.4
Chhattisgarh	16.0	87.0	17.1
Madhya Pradesh	16.0	59.0	17.0
North-East*	20.6	37.0	20.8
Assam	19.5	31.0	19.6
West Bengal	17.5	16.0	17.6
Orissa	17.9	13.0	18.0
Gujarat	18.2	69.0	18.9
Maharashtra, Goa	18.1	20.0	18.2
Andhra Pradesh	15.9	71.0	16.5
Karnataka	17.7	66.0	18.2
Kerala	20.9	21.0	21.0
Tamil Nadu	18.8	36.0	19.0

Source: Desai et al. (2010: 156–57).
Note: *North-East includes the states of Arunachal Pradesh, Manipur, Meghalaya, Mizoram, Nagaland, Sikkim and Tripura.

Not surprisingly, many of the young brides were physically immature and had not attained puberty at the time of marriage. For instance, in Bihar and Rajasthan, states with earliest age at marriage, around 25 per cent of girls had not attained puberty at the time of their marriage. At the same time, a focus on formal age at marriage may well be mistaken in a context where early marriage is not synonymous with early age at entry into a sexual union. As documented by many anthropologists, early marriage is often associated with a delay in consummation and the bride remains with her parents until a formal gauna or *bidai*[4] ceremony occurs. States with very early age at formal marriage also follow the custom of a gap of a year or more between gauna and marriage. Table 5.3 indicates proportions waiting at least six months following the wedding before cohabitation. In Bihar about 75 per cent of women waited for six months or more to begin living with their husbands as did about 88 per cent of women in Rajasthan. As Figure 5.1 shows, this waiting period is often associated with the relative youth and immaturity of the bride and tends to decline as the age at marriage increases. But it is important to note that regardless of the age at which formal marriage occurs, average age at which cohabitation or effective marriage begins is barely about 18–19 years in many states and even younger in others (Table 5.3).

FIGURE 5.1: Average Gap Between Marriage and Cohabitation, by Age at Marriage

Source: Desai et al. (2010: 149).

Table 5.3 indicates that the per cent not cohabitating immediately is highest for women who are illiterate (64 per cent) and lowest for college graduates (24 per cent). This seemingly contradicts our argument that the institution of gauna is used by families to pursue education; however, this is a simple cross tabulation that does not control for conflating factors such as caste, place of residence, level of income, and most importantly, for the purposes of this discussion, age at marriage. One can expect that lower the age at marriage, higher will be the gap between age at marriage and age at cohabitation, and young brides are likely to use this gap to pursue higher education. This complex three-way association is more easily examined in a regression framework. Controlling for other variables, including age at marriage, we find that women who are more educated are more likely to have a longer gap between marriage and gauna (Table 5.4). Table 5.4 also indicates that the age at marriage has a negative sign, which lends evidence to our hypothesis that it has an inverse relationship to age at cohabitation.

TABLE 5.4: Coefficients from Ordinary Least Squares Model Predicting the Gap between Marriage and Cohabitation

	Coefficients	*Standard error*	*Significance level*
Women's Education (*Reference category: Illiterate*)			
1–4 Standards	–0.0988	0.03	**
5–9 Standards	–0.0191	0.02	Not significant
10–11 Standards	0.167	0.03	**
12 and Some College	0.295	0.04	**
College Graduate	0.643	0.04	**
Age at Marriage	–0.177	0.002	**
Income	0.012	0.01	Not significant
Urban (*Reference category: Rural residence*)	–0.0511	0.018	**
Social Groups (*Reference category: High-caste Hindus*)			
OBC	0.213	0.02	**
Dalit	0.080	0.02	**
Adivasi	0.021	0.03	Not significant
Muslim	–0.207	0.03	**
Other religion	0.233	0.08	**

(*Contd.*)

(Table 5.4 Contd.)

	Coefficients	*Standard error*	*Significance level*
States (*Reference category: Jammu and Kashmir*)			
Himachal Pradesh	–0.104	0.11	Not significant
Uttarakhand	–0.377	0.09	**
Punjab	–0.151	0.09	**
Haryana	–0.029	0.09	Not significant
Delhi	–0.098	0.09	Not significant
Uttar Pradesh	0.395	0.07	**
Bihar	0.422	0.08	**
Jharkhand	–0.293	0.08	**
Rajasthan	0.781	0.08	**
Chhattisgarh	0.033	0.08	Not significant
Madhya Pradesh	0.099	0.08	Not significant
North-East*	0.016	0.09	Not significant
Assam	–0.051	0.08	Not significant
West Bengal	–0.336	0.08	**
Orissa	–0.369	0.08	**
Gujarat	–0.035	0.08	Not significant
Maharashtra, Goa	–0.324	0.07	**
Andhra Pradesh	–0.513	0.08	**
Karnataka	–0.296	0.08	**
Kerala	–0.015	0.08	Not significant
Tamil Nadu	–0.330	0.08	**

Source: Authors' calculations based on IHDS data.
Note: *North-East includes the states of Arunachal Pradesh, Manipur, Meghalaya, Mizoram, Nagaland, Sikkim and Tripura.
** $p \leq 0.01$

Most marriages are arranged. In spite of the Valentine's Day articles in English newspapers emphasising the importance of love in marriage among urban elites, in our sample only around 5 per cent of the women said they chose their husbands independently of their parents (Table 5.5). The rest reported a variety of arrangements through which their families made marriage decisions. Most reported a very limited contact with their husbands before marriage; 68 per cent met their husbands on the day of the wedding or shortly before; an additional 9 per cent knew their husbands for a month before the wedding. Only 23 per cent knew their husbands for more than a month when they got married. While educated women are more likely to have a longer acquaintanceship with their husbands, as Figure 5.2 indicates, even among women with college education, a long acquaintanceship before marriage is not normative. It is important to note that while the IHDS data were only collected from women, meaning that much of the discussion has necessarily focused on women's choices, a similar story could also be told for men, who have limited contact with their wives before marriage.

FIGURE 5.2: Women's Length of Acquaintance with Husbands before Marriage, by Years of Women's Education

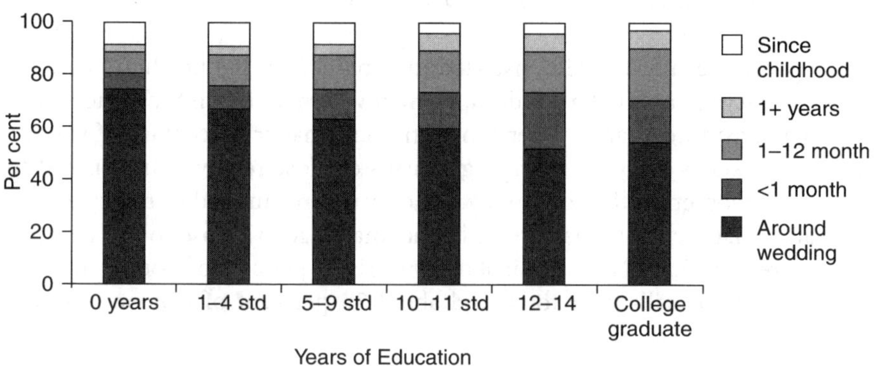

Source: Desai et al. (2010: 150).

Yet, despite the popular stereotype of women who are coerced into arranged marriages, about 65 per cent felt their wishes were considered in selecting their partners. One of the most striking changes seen in the data we examined regarding Indian marriage patterns is the extent to which the bride's consent is sought when making marriage arrangements. Table 5.5, for example, indicates that women between the ages of 25 and 30 were more likely to report having a say in choosing their spouse (24 per cent) and less likely to report being involved in an arranged marriage without their consent (35 per cent) than women from earlier birth cohorts. Indeed, nearly 6 per cent of women between the ages of 25 and 29 arranged their own marriages, as opposed to 4 per cent of women between the ages of 40 and 49.

While women appear to be more inclined than older cohorts to emphasise for themselves their choice and efficacy in determining their marriage partner, one can still argue that entrenched marriage patterns make some choices more probable than others. In parts of India, especially in the north, the practice

TABLE 5.5: Distribution of Marriage Types for Women (Age: 25–49)

	Type of marriage			
	Self-arranged	*Jointly-arranged*	*Parent-arranged with consent from the respondent*	*Parent-arranged without consent from the respondent*
Full Sample	4.96	34.96	22.21	37.86
Women's Age				
25–29	6.20	33.94	24.44	35.43
30–39	4.75	35.14	22.68	37.43
40–49	4.39	35.44	19.85	40.31

Source: Based on authors' calculations from Desai et al. (2009, 2010).

of exogamy prevails. As demonstrated in Table 5.6, in the northern states of Punjab, Haryana and Uttar Pradesh, women who married in the same village or town constituted barely 5 per cent. An even smaller percentage of women from these states reported marrying cousins or close relatives. In contrast to the north, women in the south may not only be encouraged to marry within the natal village, custom may prescribe that marriage to a close cousin or uncle is preferred. In Tamil Nadu, for instance, nearly 27 per cent of women married within the same village or town and about 30 per cent of women reported marrying a close relative.

TABLE 5.6: Percentage of Endogamy and Marriage to a Relation for Women (Age: 25–49), by State

	% of women married within the same village	*% of women married to a close relative or uncle*
Full Sample	13.70	11.70
States		
Jammu and Kashmir	23.10	20.50
Himachal Pradesh	10.50	0.40
Uttarakhand	7.70	0.80
Punjab	4.80	1.00
Haryana	2.90	1.50
Delhi	18.90	1.80
Uttar Pradesh	5.30	5.10
Bihar	6.10	5.80

(Contd.)

(Table 5.6 Contd.)

	% of women married within the same village	% of women married to a close relative or uncle
Jharkhand	8.40	6.10
Rajasthan	10.50	2.00
Chhattisgarh	6.90	1.10
Madhya Pradesh	10.40	4.10
North-East	41.80	2.60
Assam	27.40	1.20
West Bengal	20.40	3.60
Orissa	17.00	9.20
Gujarat	8.30	2.90
Maharashtra	12.20	26.20
Andhra Pradesh	16.70	29.40
Karnataka	11.70	23.20
Kerala	27.60	2.70
Tamil Nadu	27.10	29.50

Source: Desai et al. (2010: 159).

Gender Performance and Marriage

If age at marriage is a component of a gender script that views early marriage as a marker of decorum and propriety, we would expect it to coincide with other markers of gender performance. Specifically, we highlight the relationship between age at first marriage, on the one hand, and the practice of purdah, a gendered eating order during meal times, and the extent of restrictions placed on women's mobility.

Purdah or ghunghat is, as already pointed out, probably the most visible marker or public performance of gender. In the IHDS, women responded Yes or No to the question, 'Do you practise ghunghat/purdah/*pallu*?' While only about half of women between the ages of 25 and 49 reported they practised purdah, Table 5.7 demonstrates marked regional variation. Dividing India into northern and southern halves by the Satpura Hill Range, purdah practice is nearly ubiquitous in the northern states of Rajasthan, Madhya Pradesh and Bihar. Indeed 94 per cent of women claimed to practise purdah in Rajasthan and in the state of Bihar nearly 88 per cent of women claimed to do so. In contrast, women in South India practised purdah far less. In Tamil Nadu only 10 per cent of women claimed to practise it.

TABLE 5.7: Mean of Gender Performativity Variables for Women (Age: 25–49), by State

	% practising purdah	*% men and women who eat separately*	*% of women who are less mobile*
Full Sample	54.80	34.36	43.67
States			
Jammu and Kashmir	76.40	20.08	44.68
Himachal Pradesh	44.60	10.59	23.86
Uttarakhand	44.50	40.37	31.10
Punjab	32.30	23.07	36.56
Haryana	80.70	9.88	39.58
Delhi	43.20	14.16	27.63
Uttar Pradesh	87.10	70.05	51.80
Bihar	88.10	90.64	70.27
Jharkhand	58.60	53.94	59.72
Rajasthan	93.90	42.67	59.08
Chhattisgarh	57.60	46.65	59.15
Madhya Pradesh	92.70	48.80	53.70
North-East	27.80	4.78	30.38
Assam	67.60	33.46	51.23
West Bengal	69.50	25.00	40.21
Orissa	63.70	60.11	38.28
Gujarat	75.70	4.48	23.83
Maharashtra	37.50	17.54	22.52
Andhra Pradesh	12.30	7.44	33.00
Karnataka	11.90	26.46	38.30
Kerala	14.70	8.81	24.31
Tamil Nadu	9.70	14.74	25.38

Source: Based on authors' calculations from Desai et al. (2009, 2010).

Slightly less visible to public scrutiny are the behaviours of households associated with meal time, and in some parts of India, a gendered eating order is followed. The IHDS asked women, 'When your family takes the main meal, do women usually eat with the men? Do women eat first by themselves? Or do men eat first?' The options 'eating together' and 'varies' were coded together, while the options 'women first' and 'men first' were coded together. In the northern state of Gujarat only about 4 per cent of women reported that their household practised an eating order. Thus, while there is a less discernable north-south pattern in eating order, the percentage of families who ate separately during meal time was highest at 91 per cent in the northern state of Bihar. Neighbouring Uttar Pradesh followed with nearly 70 per cent of women reporting they practised an eating order in their families.

Finally, restrictions on women's physical mobility are yet another marker of gender segregation. We examined the prevalence of women seeking permission from family elders before leaving the home alone to visit health centres, friends or the local bazaar. For each of these three destinations interviewers asked women, 'Can you go alone?' (Yes or No).[5] Sixty-six per cent of respondents could travel unescorted to the local health centre (Desai and Andrist 2010), while 74 per cent of respondents could go to a friend's home alone. At 80 per cent, most women reported being able to travel alone to the local market or *kirana* (grocery) shop. Table 5.7 shows a dichotomous mobility variable, where women were counted as mobile if they could travel alone to all three destinations. Fifty-nine per cent of all women fit these criteria and 13 per cent reported they could not travel alone to any of the three destinations. In Bihar, about 30 per cent of women reported being able to travel unescorted to all three destinations and, in sharp contrast, 70 per cent of women in the North-East reported being similarly mobile.

Figures 5.3, 5.4 and 5.5 graphically state specific markers of gender performance by age at marriage. As the trend line indicates, the states with greater emphasis on gender performance are also states with lower age at marriage. In results not reported here, we have undertaken multivariate analysis

FIGURE 5.3: Age at First Marriage and Purdah, by State

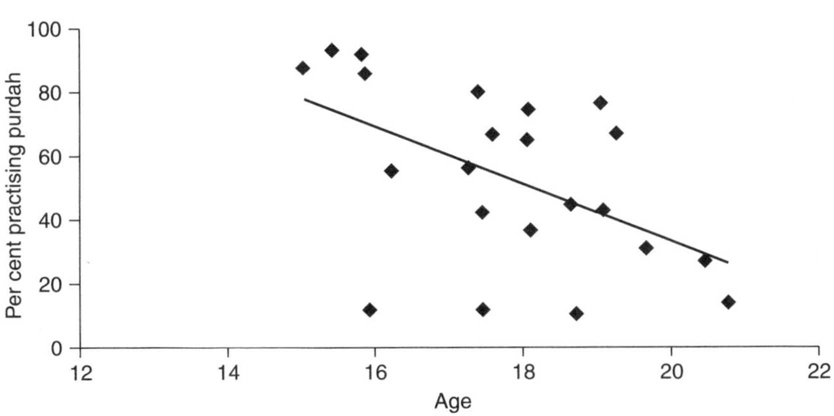

Source: Authors' calculations based on IHDS Data.

using hierarchical linear models that control for women's age, education, household economic status and place of residence (Desai and Andrist 2010). Even after controlling for these factors, the district-level gender performance indicators seem to be significantly associated with age at marriage.

These results suggest that in regions where gender segregation is more prevalent, early marriage is also preferred. This bolsters our argument that for women, early marriage is part of a pattern in which seclusion, segregation and modesty mark claims to refinement and status.

FIGURE 5.4: Age at First Marriage and Eating Separate, by State

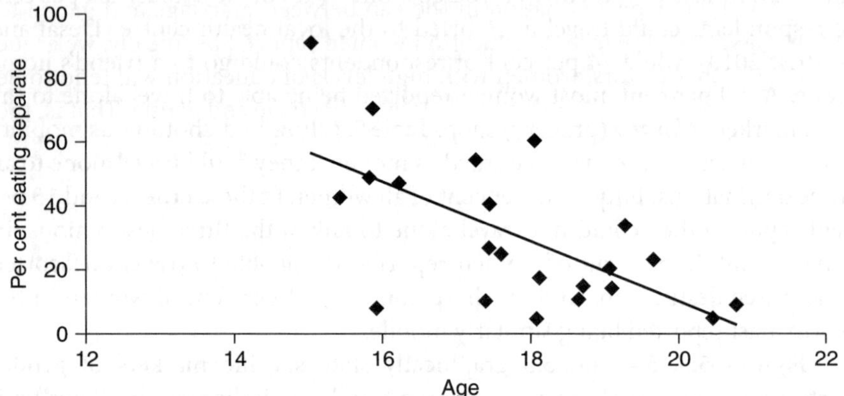

Source: Authors' calculations based on IHDS Data.

FIGURE 5.5: Age at First Marriage and Mobility, by State

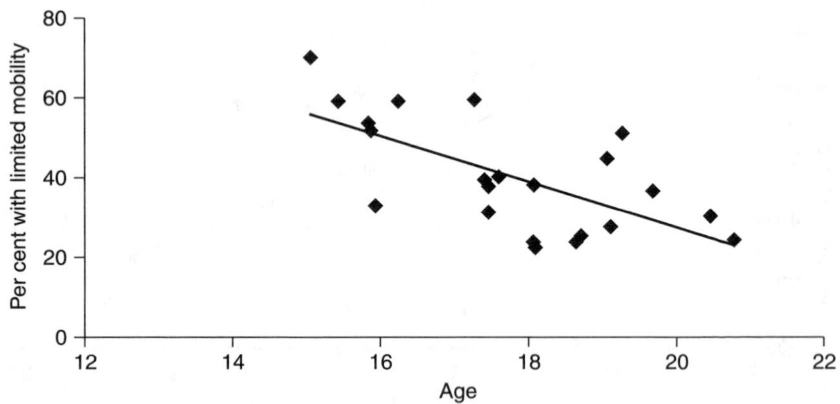

Source: Authors' calculations based on IHDS Data.

Competing Claims of Gender Performance and Modernity

In our theoretical discussion we noted that families are faced by competing demands of gender performance and modernity. Whereas Srinivas' notion of sanskritisation points to a process of leveraging caste status through emphasising behaviours associated with women's modesty and decorum, claims based on modernity emphasise such things as attaining high levels of education and a protected childhood. How families resolve the contradictions between these demands is an interesting empirical question and is the focus of our analysis. We suggest that a lengthy gap between marriage and cohabitation may be one avenue through which these competing claims may be resolved. Thus, one might expect variation in the gap between marriage and gauna to be associated with the level of education women report. Specifically, we argue that, net of other factors, women with high levels of education will tend to be women who report an extended gap between marriage and gauna. That is, the marriage-gauna gap allows families to project an impression of decorum and modesty for their daughters, while allowing them to attain higher levels of education.

In what follows we use ordinary least squares regression to analyse this gap between marriage and cohabitation and how it might vary with women's education levels.[6] Thus, our principle explanatory variable is the eligible women's education level, broken down into five discreet categories: 'illiterate', '1–4 years', '5–9 years', '10–11 years', '12 and some college' and 'college graduate'. The category 'illiterate' is dropped from the model and used as the reference category.

We include controls for caste, tribe and religion to mitigate the conflating effects of differential marriage and gauna patterns associated with these groups. As women living in an urban setting may be more inclined to seize upon and enact the prescriptions of scripts associated with modernity, we include a dichotomous variable indicating whether the eligible woman lived in an urban setting. As we have demonstrated throughout this essay, regional diversity in India is substantial. While states in India operate as administrative boundaries, they also approximate cultural and linguistic boundaries. Thus, we attempt to control for the conflating effects of that diversity by adding state dummies to the model. Finally, because we know age at first marriage is associated with the gap between marriage and gauna, we add age at first marriage as a control variable to the model.

After adding controls, the results indicate that higher education is associated with longer gaps between marriage and cohabitation. Note that this is not simply a wealth effect. Other variables measuring socioeconomic status and urban residence do not appear to be correlated with the gap between marriage and gauna once controls are added. It is only higher education that lengthens this gap.

Discussion

A son's or daughter's marriage is often a pivotal moment for an entire family, and the timing of this event is likely to receive careful thought and planning. Economic considerations certainly influence the timing of marriage. For example, increased expenses associated with a daughter's marriage may lead families to postpone the marriage long enough to accumulate the necessary resources (Caldwell et al. 1983). The timing of a daughter's marriage may also hinge on the marriage market or the depth of the pool of eligible bachelors (Kaur 2004). Although these frameworks have proven useful they are incomplete because, on the one hand, they suggest Indian families act in strictly economically rational terms and, on the other, what families actually do to influence the timing of marriage disappears altogether. In this essay, we have argued for an expanded notion of agency; one which acknowledges that families are simultaneously bound by the demands of dominant scripts but are relatively free to negotiate the way in which they respond to such demands.

What happens when the demands associated with one script seem to preclude one's ability to meet the demands of another? What happens when a woman is encouraged to retain respectability through an early marriage, even when an early marriage might preclude her ability to attain higher levels of education? The way in which this dilemma is often resolved is illustrated in a recent *National Geographic* article profiling child brides (Gorney 2011). In it, Shobha Choudhary, a 17-year-old girl from rural Rajasthan, discusses her marriage at age eight and her desire to pursue a college education. To achieve this goal, she believes she must delay gauna; yet at the same time, she is adamant that she cannot delay cohabitation forever and risk disgracing her parents.

Shobha's dilemma illustrates the central argument in this essay: namely, families are expanding the gap between marriage and gauna as a means of negotiating these competing demands. While families are certainly impacted by dominant scripts pertaining to appropriate enactments of gender, sexuality and modernity, their response has not been to either choose early marriage or late marriage. Instead, families have opted to have it both ways by often continuing to participate in early marriage while delaying the age of effective marriage or gauna. Adopting this theoretical orientation, then, can be seen as a move to bring the family back in as a central author of the social processes in which it finds itself immured.

Using survey data, we have demonstrated the usefulness of this theoretical perspective. We have shown that families very likely continue to be engaged in a process of sanskritisation, which M. N. Srinivas (1977) identified over

30 years ago. The data demonstrate the continuing pervasiveness of early marriage, purdah practice, restricted mobility for women and gendered eating order in India, suggesting that families continue to find it useful to enact these traditional scripts in order to legitimise—or position themselves for—upward mobility. At the same time, families continue to run up against demands which push for greater education. The results demonstrate that the gap between formal marriage and gauna is positively associated with the level of education for women, suggesting that this gap is being adapted as a means of increasing educational attainment and doing modernity.[7]

This essay joins recent scholarship, which grapples with understanding processes of social change in India. For instance, other studies have also focused on changing marriage patterns and have demonstrated that parent-arranged marriages are increasingly incorporating consent from the bride and groom (Banerji et al. 2008). As we have argued, while marriage patterns in India are certainly changing, and while they are certainly capable of continued change, we think it would be inaccurate to view these changes as evidence that India is incrementally moving toward Western-style marriage patterns. The process which involves negotiating the gap between marriage and gauna is far more dynamic than any process suggested by the notion of Westernisation.

Notes

[1] In this essay, we use the term 'corporate family' to refer to families which act as relatively coherent and autonomous economic and political entities.

[2] 'Scripts' as a theoretical concept bears notable resemblance to other work done on marriage patterns in India. Most recently, in her study of marriage norms in Allahabad district in Uttar Pradesh, U. Kalpagam (2008) makes use of the related concept of 'social disciplines'.

[3] Basu specifically writes about the period *aoni-jaoni*, a term mostly used in Rajasthan. We would like to thank the editors for pointing out that aoni-jaoni refers to a period after the *gauna* and not the period between the wedding and gauna. While this is an important distinction, we think Basu's argument might be relevant to the gap between marriage and gauna as well.

[4] The *gauna* or *bidai* is a relatively common practice in northern India and occurs after a period of time in which a young woman continues to live with her natal family after she has been formally married. Thus the gauna ceremony marks the occassion of final sending off a young woman to live with her husband and in-laws.

[5] A preceding question asked the respondent whether she needed to acquire permission to travel outside the home. In cases where women reported they did not need to acquire permission, interviewers often failed to ask whether she could 'go alone' to a particular destination. Because it is impossible to know whether women who did not need permission to go out were allowed to travel alone, we have opted to drop these records from the analysis. In total, there were 2379 such cases.

[6] The IHDS obtained information about first and second marriages. This analysis is restricted to age at first marriage

[7] Interestingly, the benefit of using this gap to increase educational attainment has also been noted by some activist groups and delayed cohabitation is seen as one of the objectives of programmes such as *Doosra Dashak* in Rajasthan.

References

Abraham, L. 2001. 'Redrawing the Lakshman Rekha: Gender Differences and Cultural Constructions in Youth Sexuality in Urban India'. *South Asia: Journal of South Asian Studies* 24:133–56.

Banerji, Manjistha, Steven P. Martin, and Sonalde Desai. 2008. 'Is Education associated with a Transition towards Autonomy in Partner Choice? A Case Study of India'. New Delhi: IUSSP Seminar on *Changing Transitions to Marriage: Gender Implications for the Next Generation.*

Basu, Alaka Malwade. 1993. 'Cultural Influences on the Timing of First Births in India: Large Differences that Add Up to Little Differences'. *Population Studies* 47 (1): 85–95.

Bourdieu, Pierre. 1977. *Outline of a Theory of Practice*. Cambridge Studies in Social Anthropology. Cambridge, New York: Cambridge University Press.

Butler, Judith. 1988. 'Performative Acts and Gender Constitution: An Essay in Phenomenology and Feminist Theory'. *Theatre Journal* 40 (4): 519–31.

Caldwell, John C., Pat Caldwell, Bruce K. Caldwell, and Indrani Pieris. 1998. 'The Construction of Adolescence in a Changing World: Implications for Sexuality, Reproduction, and Marriage'. *Studies in Family Planning* 29 (2): 137–53.

Caldwell, John C., P. H. Reddy, and Pat Caldwell. 1983. 'The Causes of Marriage Change in South India'. *Population Studies* 37 (3): 343–61.

Census of India. 2001. 'Table C-2: Marital Status by Age and Sex. Available at: http://censusindia.gov.in/Table_Published/C-series/C-series_link/C2_India.pdg. Accessed on: 1 July 2013.

Chatterjee, Partha. 1993. *The Nation and Its Fragments: Colonial and Postcolonial Histories*. Princeton Studies in Culture/Power/History. Princeton, N. J.: Princeton University Press.

_______. 1989. 'Colonialism, Nationalism, and Colonialized Women: The Contest in India'. *American Ethnologist* 16 (4): 622–33.

Derné, Steve. 2003. 'Arnold Schwarzenegger, Ally McBeal, and Arranged Marriages: Globalization on the Ground in India'. *Contexts* 2:12–18.

_______. 1994. 'Hindu Men Talk about Controlling Women: Cultural Ideas as a Tool of the Powerful'. *Sociological Perspectives* 37 (2): 203–27.

Desai, Sonalde, Amaresh Dubey, Brij Lal Joshi, Mitali Sen, Abusaleh Shariff, and Reeve Vanneman. 2010. *Human Development in India: Challenges for a Society in Transition*. New Delhi: Oxford University Press.

_______. 2009. '*India Human Development Survey: Design and Data Quality*'. IHDS Technical Paper 1. College Park, Maryland: University of Maryland.

Desai, Sonalde, and Lester Andrist. 2010. 'Gender Scripts and Age at Marriage in India'. *Demography* 47 (3): 667–87.

Desai, Sonalde, and Veena Kulkarni. 2008. 'Changing Educational Inequalities in India: In the Context of Affirmative Action'. *Demography* 45 (2): 245–70.

Dube, Leela. 2001. *Anthropological Explorations in Gender: Intersecting Fields*. New Delhi: SAGE Publications.

———. 1996. 'Caste and Women'. In *Caste: Its Twentieth Century Avatar*, ed. M. N. Srinivas. New Delhi: Penguin Publishers.

Dyson, T., and M. Moore. 1983. 'On Kinship Structure, Female Autonomy, and Demographic Behaviour in India'. *Population and Development Review* 9 (1): 35–60.

Goffman, Erving. 1976. 'Gender Display'. *Studies in the Anthropology of Visual Communication* 3:69–77.

Gorney, Cynthia. 2011. 'Too Young to Wed: The Secret World of Child Brides'. *National Geographic*. Accessed at: http://ngm.nationalgeographic.com/2011/06/child-brides/gorney-text, Accessed on: 25 July 2011.

Hammel, E. A. 1990. 'A Theory of Culture for Demography'. *Population and Development Review*. 16 (3): 455–85.

Heimsath, C. H. 1962. 'The Origin and Enactment of the Indian Age of Consent Bill, 1891'. *The Journal of Asian Studies* 21 (4): 491–504.

IIPS (International Institute for Population Sciences) and Macro international. 2007. '*National Family Health Survey (NFHS-3) 2005–2006*', *India: Volume 1*. IIPS: Mumbai.

IIPS and O.R.C. Macro. 2000. '*National Family and Health Survey (NFHS-2), 1998–99*', *India*. IIPS: Mumbai.

Islam, M. Nurul, and Ashraf U. Ahmed. 1998. 'Age at First Marriage and its Determinants in Bangladesh'. *Asia-Pacific Population Journal* 13 (2): 72–92.

Kalpagam, U. 2008. 'Marriage Norms, Choice and Aspirations of Rural Women'. *Economic and Political Weekly* 43 (21): 53–63.

Karve, Irawati Karmarkar. 1965. *Kinship Organisation in India*. Bombay: Asia Publishing House.

Kaufman, Jason. 2004. 'Endogenous Explanation in the Sociology of Culture'. *Annual Review of Sociology* 30: 335–57.

Kaur, Ravinder. 2004. 'Across-Region Marriages: Poverty, Female Migration and the Sex Ratio'. *Economic and Political Weekly* 39 (25): 2595–2603.

Kishor, Sunita. 2000. 'Empowerment of Women in Egypt and Links to the Survival and Health of their Children'. In *Women's Empowerment and Demographic Processes*, ed. H. Presser and G. Sen. Oxford: Oxford University Press.

Leonard, Karen. 1976. 'Women and Social Change in Modern India'. *Feminist Studies* 3(3–4): 117–30.

Lindenbaum, Shirley. 1981. 'Implications for Women of Changing Marriage Transactions in Bangladesh'. *Studies in Family Planning* 12 (11): 394–401.

Mason, K. O. 1986. 'The Status of Women: Conceptual and Methodological Issues in Demographic Studies'. *Sociological Forum* 1 (2): 284–300.

Mandelbaum, David G. 1988. *Women's Seclusion and Men's Honor: Sex Roles in India, Bangladesh and Pakistan*. Tuscon, Arizona: University of Arizona Press.

Mensch, Barbara S., Susheela Singh, and John B. Casterline. 2005. 'Trends in the Timing of First Marriage Among Men and Women in the Developing World'. *The Population Council Working Paper* 202. New York: Population Council.

Morris, Rosalind C. 1995. 'All Made Up: Performance Theory and the New Anthropology of Sex and Gender'. *Annual Review of Anthropology* 24 (1): 567–92.

Mukhopadhyay, Carol C., and Patricia J. Higgins. 1988. 'Anthropological Studies of Women's Status Revisited: 1977–1987'. *Annual Review of Anthropology* 17:461–95.

Palriwala, Rajni. 1991. 'Transitory Residence and Invisible Work: Case Study of a Rajasthan Village'. *Economic and Political Weekly* 26 (48): 2763–71.

Papanek, Hanna. 1973. 'Purdah: Separate Worlds and Symbolic Shelter'. *Comparative Studies in Society and History* 15 (3): 289–325.

Retherford, Robert D., Naohiro Ogawa, and Rikiya Matsukura. 2001. 'Late Marriage and Less Marriage in Japan'. *Population and Development Review* 27 (1): 65–102.

Schein, L. 1999. 'Performing Modernity'. *Cultural Anthropology* 14 (3): 361–95.

Sharma, Ursula. 1980. *Women, Work and Property in North-West India*. New York: Tavistock.

Srinivas, M. N. 1977. 'The Changing Position of Indian Women'. *Man* 12 (2): 221–38.

Uberoi, Patricia. 1993. *Family, Kinship and Marriage in India*. Oxford in India Readings in Sociology and Social Anthropology. New Delhi: Oxford University Press.

West, Candace, and Sarah Fenstermaker. 1995. 'Doing Difference'. *Gender & Society* 9 (1): 8–37.

West, Candace, and Don H. Zimmerman. 2009. 'Accounting for Doing Gender'. *Gender & Society* 23 (1): 112–22.

———. 1987. 'Doing Gender'. *Gender & Society* 1 (2): 125–51.

MARRIAGE, WOMEN AND WORK

The Estate Tamils in Sri Lanka's Tea Plantations

AMALI PHILIPS

INTRODUCTION

The Tamil residents on Sri Lanka's tea estates are the descendants of nineteenth-century labour migrants from South India brought during British colonial rule, to work the British owned and run coffee and tea plantations. From colonial beginnings, to land reform and nationalisation after independence in 1948, to the more recent privatisation of the plantations, the social and marital lives of the Tamils—who identify themselves as 'Estate Tamils'—have been sustained by the plantation capitalist agricultural production system using an almost captive labour force living in isolation from the country's other ethnic groups. These conditions gave rise to the consolidation and reproduction of marriage forms and practices that benefited plantation production, and labour and social reproduction. The mediating role of marriage, in linking the household and the plantation capitalist economy (Young, Wolkowitz and McCullagh 1981), entailed both 'subsistence reproduction', i.e. the work of human and labour reproduction, and 'extended reproduction', namely, the appropriation of women's labour by capital (Brennholdt-Thomsen 1981: 17; Mackintosh 1981: 8).

Tamil women on Sri Lanka's tea estates make up over 50 per cent of the plantation labour force and 90 per cent of them work as tea pluckers. Estate Tamil women have the highest work participation rates among all Sri

Lankan women in the formal economy. In the current situation of privatised plantations, Tamil women's contributions to both plantation production and household subsistence have increased, demonstrating the value of women's work to marriage and men's benefits from marriage. Women are emerging as the main 'breadwinners' among some estate families, since they work longer hours and earn higher incomes compared to men who are primarily involved in field maintenance which has low priority among private companies. New employment opportunities have also become available for educated young women, particularly in garment manufacturing factories that have emerged around the estates as part of the 200 Garment Factory Program introduced in the 1990s in different parts of the island to tap the labour of rural and estate women. Since the late 1970s, the Sri Lankan government has been promoting the migration of women to the Middle East in response to the demands for housemaids and care work in the Middle East. The estates are increasingly becoming recruiting grounds for the labour migration of married women. There has been no significant improvement, however, in Tamil women's status and standing within marriage. As generally the case in most of South Asia, the importance of Tamil women to marriage is culturally and ideologically under-valued, while the importance of marriage to women is culturally over-emphasised (Otoo-Oyortey and Pobi 2003; Reynolds 1980; Sweetman 2003).

This essay examines the continuities and changes in marriage forms and practices among the Tamils in colonial and contemporary tea estates, and explores the impact of economic liberalisation and privatisation of the tea estates on women's work and marriage. The first section discusses the colonial phase of globalisation and the establishment of British colonial plantations, which sets the context for examining the continuities and changes in Tamil marriage in contemporary plantations. The migration of Indians and the sex-selective nature of colonial recruitment and migration practices resulted in irregular unions and an unstable family life. The main shift occurred with the onset of tea cultivation and efforts of colonial planters to encourage the migration of single and married women for tea plucking work and to reproduce the plantation labour force. The second section describes the pragmatics of Tamil marriage within the contexts and constraints of estate work and living, and explores current transformations in women's work and marriage expectations in light of youth aspirations and new economic opportunities. The new employment opportunities for women under economic liberalisation are mainly in garment factories and in Middle-East employment. Tamil male youth form an urban underclass of daily-wage workers in the informal economy and service sectors, while the more enterprising among them are engaged in lucrative self-employment ventures outside the estates.

Colonial Plantations

The Sri Lankan plantations began as a labour-intensive and highly capitalised form of agriculture producing first coffee and then tea for competitive export markets. As a labour-intensive industry, the retention, control and reproduction of labour were crucial to the productivity of the plantations and the success of the enterprise. Marriage served a crucial role in the organisation of production and for balancing labour demand and supply.

The plantations were run as 'total institutions' (Goffman 1961), where work and residence were united in the same physical place with workers spending their entire lives from birth to death within the confines of the estates (de Silva 1982). The organisation of labour was pre-capitalist in nature, based on traditional divisions of caste and kinship and the sexual division of labour (de Silva 1982; Kurian 1998). The plantations were managed by the British planter, or *periya dorai* (big master), and his British assistant or *sinna dorai* (small master), while the Tamil *kanganie*s (labour supervisor) from the non-Brahmin upper castes served as supervisors and recruiters of mostly lower-caste Indian labour. As was the case in most of the British colonial plantations, women workers were at the bottom of the 'race, class and gender hierarchies' (Northrop 1995: 125). The recruitment of workers from largely homogeneous castes from the Tamil districts of South India facilitated labour organisation on the plantations, with labour gangs from similar caste and kin groups serving under a *silarai kangany* (minor supervisor) of the same caste who paid obeisance to the higher-caste head kangany above him (Kurian 1998: 68).

The need for immigrant labour for the early coffee estates, from the period between 1830 and 1867, arose from the social reluctance of and lack of economic incentives for the local population to become wage labourers (Ludowyk 1966). Colonial authorities and plantation entrepreneurs found a fertile source of cheap and docile labour among the impoverished and caste-marginalised Tamil communities in South India. The labour demands for coffee and tea differed in their gender balances, with coffee demanding predominantly male and seasonal labour, while tea required more women and a more permanent labour force. Labour migrations began with single and married men migrating to the plantations in Sri Lanka mostly as seasonal workers for coffee plantations, while the wives of married migrants remained in the villages to work as agricultural labourers and to care for family dependents (Omvedt 1980). The seasonal nature of coffee cultivation and Sri Lanka's proximity to South India enabled workers to return periodically to their families. Cultural restrictions also impeded the migration of single women or of married women who were unaccompanied by their husbands. The practice of child marriage reduced the numbers of unmarried single women who could migrate to the estates (Mangru 1987). This system appeared to be a convenient strategy for the planters who did not have to deal with the additional burden of providing support for families (Kurian 1984). As in other overseas plantations, planters discouraged both marriage and childbearing to keep costs down (Breman and Daniel 1992).

For the European planter, the ideal worker was the 'unencumbered' male (Breman and Daniel 1992) who was either single or unaccompanied by his wife, while in Tamil culture, marriage was the path to full adult status for a man (Jayaraman 1975). The European planters infantilised the 'incomplete' male worker by referring to him as *podiyan* or boy, regardless of his age or marital status (Breman and Daniel 1992: 284; Steuart 1906). Their communities in India (Daniel 1993) similarly stigmatised the village wives of absent male migrants because of their single status. Women who did join the early migrants to the coffee estates were separated into the 'respectable' married women, mostly from the upper castes, who kept to their esteemed roles as wives, and unattached single women who migrated to the estates to escape oppressive conditions at home. Hugh Tinker (1977: 5) describes these single women migrants as forming a 'sorry sisterhood' of prostitutes, widows, *devadasi*s (temple dancers), women abandoned by their husbands or escaping an oppressive marriage, and women kidnapped and duped by recruiting Tamil kanganies (de Silva 1982). As in the case of female migrants to Caribbean plantations, single women reportedly attached themselves to men at the ports of embarkation to avoid social stigma and to secure a marital relationship (Carter 1996; Tinker 1974).

The main references to marriage in colonial writings on Sri Lanka are with regard to the marital challenges faced by immigrant men because of a shortage of women on the estates (CO 101/131 1871; Kondapi 1951; Moldrich 1988). This sex imbalance led to what British planters essentialised as 'unnatural *cooly*[*ie*] practices' (Breman and Daniel 1992: 284) such as homosexuality, polygamy, multiple sexual partners, adultery, rape, infanticide (of illegitimate children), incest, suicides, and uxoricide due to jealousy and marital infidelity (Moldrich 1988). The practice of uxoricide seems to have existed in the natal villages of Indian migrants due to marital transgressions and sexual jealousies (Mangru 1987). Marital crimes and loose pairing were also exacerbated by the low sex ratio on the estates and by what Breman and Daniel (1992: 284) describe as workers' adaptation to 'capitalism's abnormal conditions'. Married men resolved the problem of absent wives by forming temporary liaisons with other woman for domestic and sexual services (Moldrich 1988). Early accounts on the coffee plantations in Sri Lanka describe women migrants as being 'brought over for a purpose little better than prostitution' (Ferguson's *Ceylon Directory 1866–67*, cited in Moldrich 1988: 97).

The living arrangements on the estates were not conducive to the development of stable marital relationships. The workers were initially housed in mud huts and temporary sheds which were replaced later by more permanent housing called the 'lines'—long buildings divided into single units measuring 10 feet by 12 feet linked by a common veranda in the front. Married men were reluctant to bring their wives to the estates because of the lack of privacy and the large number of single men in the lines known to proposition the wives of other workers. The same reasons discouraged married men from leaving their wives alone in the line rooms to seek medical attention in the hospitals located outside the estates (Moldrich 1988: 97).

The gender patterns of migration changed as the more seasonal coffee gave way to tea production, which required women for plucking and a more permanent labour force. Women were considered to be ideally suited for the labour-intensive but less-skilled work of tea plucking because of their 'nimble fingers' and their docile demeanour (Kurian 1998: 70). Family migration along with a quota for married female recruits ensured a steady and reliable work force (Jayaraman 1975). Another method employed by colonial officials was to encourage the migration of young, nubile women who would be potential child bearers (Northrop 1995; Peebles 2001). Over time, migrations became more permanent and women joined the inflow in increasing numbers. Between 1880 and 1910, the proportion of women rose to 45 per cent of the total migrant workers who came to the plantations in Sri Lanka (Guilmoto 1993: 114) compared to the ratio of one woman to 30 men during the coffee period (Moldrich 1988). The migration of families and the more or less balanced composition of the sexes led to more stable families on Sri Lanka's tea plantations (Jayaraman 1975) compared to the situation in the early coffee period and in contrast to most Caribbean countries, where irregular and unstable unions affected the stabilisation of family life.

Child labour 'influenced the income-fertility relationship' on the estates (de Silva 1982: 197) as children of both sexes could be put to work from the age of five with female children accompanying their mothers to the field and learning the art of plucking from their working mothers (de Silva 1982; Moxham 2003). Although infanticide (Cave 1900) and abortions (Breman and Daniel 1992) were common practices in the early coffee period, these practices declined during the tea period as parents came to realise the economic significance of child labour (Cave 1900: 185). Planter paternalism took the form of the provision of a 'welfare package in favour of childbearing' that included maternity and medical benefits, donations for childbirth and crèches for aiding working mothers (de Silva 1982: 343).

The availability of work on the plantations for young men and the allocation of separate line rooms for every family, enabled young men to break loose from their natal families by marrying young, and forming a separate nuclear family (Jeyaraman 1975). The proximity of extended family members, however, strengthened extended family ties over incipient nuclearisation. Patri-virilocal residence rules and bilateral-cross-cousin and close-kin marriages expanded the network of ties between families in different estates.

In contrast to the situation in many of the Caribbean countries (Carter 1996; Hollup 1993; Reddock 1998), the near homogeneous caste and regional affiliations of the migrants to Sri Lanka's plantations favoured the consolidation and maintenance of caste and sub-caste divisions over time through endogamous marriage practices. As Mary Steuart, a British visitor to Sri Lanka in the early twentieth century observed, 'This system of castes complicates not only work, but also marriage, for girls are compelled to marry into exactly the same caste as their own family.' (1906: 96) Caste sentiments were such that a high-caste head kangany would send his daughter to India to be married for lack of a suitable partner in the estates (ibid.: 63). Caste endogamy and close-kin marriages resulted in a high degree of relatedness within castes. While caste separation was not always easy, given the close residential arrangements and work requirements in the plantations, such a separation was achieved by clusters of kin and homogeneous castes being housed in contiguous line rooms in the expanding tea plantations of the late nineteenth and early twentieth centuries.

Contemporary Tea Plantations

The two main developments that have affected caste-kin demographics and the marriage pool of the estate Tamils are the disenfranchisement of all resident Indians and land reform measures both of which had disproportionate impacts on the estate Tamils. In 1948 and 1949, Sri Lanka passed citizenship laws that disenfranchised and made almost half-a-million Indians stateless and arranged their repatriation to India with the agreement of the Indian government. The nationalisation of the estates in the 1970s and land reform policies led to the displacement of many estate Tamils to the North and East—where Tamils of Sri Lankan origin mostly live—and to the ethnically diverse areas around Colombo, Sri Lanka's capital. Others left for India because of the ethnic violence targeting Tamils on the plantations. These outward movements reduced the population of Indians from 13 per cent at the dawn of independence to 4.6 per cent of the current Sri Lankan population of 20 million.[1] Eighty per cent of the 1.3 million 'Indian Origin Tamils' (official term for the Estate Tamils) live on the plantations (Balasundaram, Chandrabose and Sivaprgasam 2009).

Kinship and caste continue to define marriage patterns among the predominantly lower-caste and lower-class Tamils on the estates (Jayaraman 1975; Hollup 1994). The resilience of these two institutions requires an explanation that goes beyond normative and structural theorising. Lacking opportunities for social mobility and for expanding social ties outward, families have used traditional kinship and caste networks to adapt to work and life on the estates. In the following sections, I examine the pragmatics of close-kin marriage, caste endogamy and other forms of unconventional union in relation to external restrictions and individual preferences, and explore the changes in marriage expectations as estate youth attempt to expand their social horizons and work aspirations outside the estates.

Close-kin Marriage

The estate Tamils, like the other three ethnic groups in the Island, viz., the Sinhalese, Sri Lankan Tamils and Muslims have a Dravidian system of kinship and a preference for bilateral cross-kin and other close-kin marriages. Estate Tamils distinguish all forms of *conta kalyanam* (kin marriages) from *pirathy kalyanam* (marriages outside the kin circle). *Contathai patukapkurathu* (to preserve kinship) is the rationale given for kin marriage, and in the contexts of the day-to-day struggles of estate work and residence preserving *contam* (one's own) has practical and economic ramifications as a support system based on *anpu* (affection), reciprocity and mutuality. Preference for kin marriage may derive from individual self-interest as in the case of a bilateral maternal or paternal aunt activating her *urimai* (right/claim) when in need of domestic help which a daughter-in-law can provide, or from a mother's attempt to strengthen her consanguineal tie over her affinal one. A daughter might agree to a close-kin marriage to ensure kin support in the event of domestic violence, conjugal disputes, marital infidelity or economic difficulties. External constraints such as lack of dowry, 'saving face' in the case of out-of-wedlock pregnancy, caste endogamy due to the restrictive connubial practices of the upper castes and limited options for contracting marriages outside close-kin circles are also reasons for contracting close-kin marriages.

Male cross-cousins (real or classificatory) are not merely marriageable partners, but take on the role of moral guardians of their female kin and sometimes pursue the affections of their female wards. The proximity of kin living in contiguous lines facilitates close-kin marriages of the approved *murai* (type) inasmuch as it promotes marriages between parallel-cousins, which the Tamils describe as *murai mariya kalyanangal* (out-of-line marriages). Parallel-cousin marriages are the result of *virimbiya kalyanangal* (love marriages) and are neither given religious sanction nor ritualised through the *tali* (sacred thread symbolising marriage union) rite.

The main change in preferential marriage rules is among educated youth who have begun to raise concerns about the genetic consequences of close-kin marriages. Young women noted that these marriages seldom operate as insurance against domestic violence and marital fidelity and are a deterrent to leaving a bad marriage because of the existing kinship link. Estate youth also aspire to contracting non-kin marriages and marriages outside the estates as a vehicle for ending their dependence on estate livelihood (Hollup 1994). Educated young men are now beginning to speak of securing 'companionate marriages' (Parry 2001: 784, on North India), by which they mean 'affection and intimacy' and personal compatibility, and are becoming less interested in contracting close-kin marriages.

Marriage and Caste

Unlike the past, contemporary estates are caste-free in relation to organisational structures, the recruitment of kanganies and line-room accommodation. Marriage remains the central institution for the reproduction of caste divisions among the Tamils, and this is largely due to the material and political dominance of the higher castes and their restrictive caste-centred connubial practices, which lead to enforced caste endogamy among the lower castes. The numerical preponderance of PPC castes (Pallan, Parayan and Chakkilian), the three lower castes on the estates has contributed to the consolidation of caste divisions through endogamous marriage. The ethnic exclusiveness of the Sinhalese and Sri Lankan Tamils and class constraints operate as further impediments to the expansion of marital ties outside kin and caste circles and the social boundaries of estates. Caste restrictions are also reasons for the high degree of kinship relatedness between families in the estates. Yet, caste—and not sub-caste endogamy—is the main consideration in arranged marriages at present and this is largely due to demographic changes brought on by citizenship laws and the repatriation of many estate Tamils to India. These outward movements have largely affected the marriage pool of the upper castes, collectively known as Kudiyanavar, that are a minority on the estates. While the high population numbers of the lower castes enable the reproduction of castes through endogamous marriage, upper-caste families have had to widen their endogamous circles to include other high castes that were previously unmarriageable (Jayaraman 1975). There are greater restrictions on movement between India and Sri Lanka compared to the situation in the past, and few families have known relatives in India who could arrange marriages for their children. Given these demographic constraints, some upper-caste families have had to delay the marriages of their children—particularly daughters—until caste-appropriate matches could be arranged, which often means extending the search for suitable partners outside the estates. A daughter's marriage outside the caste has definite impacts on family honour compared to a son's cross-caste marriage. The tali worn by a married woman is specific to each caste and identifies the caste of the husband. Women marrying below their castes are thus constrained to carry the stigma of their marriages on their bodies (Jayaraman 1975). Cross-caste couples often suffer social ostracism, especially if the marriage is hypogamous or if the couple belonged to structurally distant castes. The loss of economic support generally affects women to a greater degree and many young women are reluctant to pursue a romantic interest if it involves a cross-caste relationship.

Saathi mari kalyanangal (inter-caste marriages), are largely the result of 'love marriages' and are contracted either as 'primary marriages'[2] or 'secondary marriages', but are not legitimated by the tali ritual (Hollup 1994: 258).

Unlike the older generation of estate Tamils, the estate youth are less likely to define their identity in caste terms and are thus, less encumbered by caste rules when choosing their own partners. Inter-caste marriages are increasing among migrant youth who take up employment and residence in the capital city of Colombo. These youth are often oblivious to caste affiliations and become conscious of caste only after becoming romantically involved with a person of a different caste (Balasundaram et al. 2009). Couples might react to parental objections to cross-caste marriages by eloping or committing suicide, but as Balasundaram et al. (ibid.) have noted the birth of children may also lead to eventual acceptance by family members.

Plural Unions

Plural unions and other forms of unconventional marriages have been associated with the lower classes and castes of India (Dumont 1966; Good 1991). Explanations for the casual nature of marriage among the lower classes range from the absence of status concerns and the relative equality of the sexes in marriage (Kapadia 1995; Parry 2001), to being 'exit strategies' among poor women and men in unhappy marriages, of spousal abandonment and/or economic circumstances (Grover 2009). While these explanations do have some validity in the case of the estate Tamils, the challenges surrounding estate work and living are also responsible for such flexible marital practices.

Plural unions range from sororal polygyny (with the wife's sister as an additional mate), associative polygyny (unrelated second mate) and plural unions of the leviratic type (with the wife of the deceased brother), as well as pre-marital and extra-marital relationships. All plural unions or 'secondary marriages' are 'illegitimate', whether or not they subscribe to caste or sub-caste endogamy[3], do not receive ritual legitimacy through the tali rite and cannot be registered as legal marriages under Sri Lankan laws. They usually draw disapproval from estate residents who consider these practices to be 'offences against the community' (Jayaraman 1975). However, previously flexible attitudes to sexual and marital relationships of the colonial plantation era may have changed as marriage and female sexuality are becoming more rigidly regulated and controlled for status reasons (Kurian 1998). However, as Parry's (2001) study of industrial workers in Chhattisgarh in North India, and Kapadia's (1995) work among poor agricultural communities in Tiruchi in South India indicate, these changes among lower income groups could be the result of upward mobility and the emulation of the marital and sexual conventions of the upper castes and classes.

In the past, the estate committees found on every estate, resolved disputes around adultery, plural unions and conjugal separation (Jayaraman 1975: 115). These committees functioned as traditional *panchayat*s with the right to regulate marriages and punish those who transgressed caste or marital rules. Customary rules applied in all cases of marital transgressions and ranged from the payment of fines imposed on the offending party and return of the *parisam* (bridewealth) money by the wife if she instigated separation or took up residence with another man, or return of the dowry in the case of the male offender. In some cases, the estate committee had prescribed expulsion of the offending parties from the estate. The estate committee's function as marital regulator seems to have diminished in recent years, removing thereby a traditional means of support available for women and men in cases of marital breakdown. Currently, kanganies, *talaivar*s (trade union leaders on the plantations) and community elders intervene to provide marriage counselling and bring pressure on married couples to reconcile their differences and remain in the marriage.

Married women who are victims of what they refer to as their husband's 'wayward ways' disapprove of secondary unions and bemoan their lack of and access to state laws and supports that other Sri Lankan women make use of in dealing with marital breakdown. This lack of state support is due to the ethnic marginalisation of Tamils and their citizenship status, which was resolved only in 2003. Women are often constrained to tolerate unfaithful husbands and plural unions for the sake of economic security, family harmony and the fear of abandonment. Women are in vulnerable situations whether or not they are willing or unwilling conscripts of male sexual and marital transgressions. Some women internalise patriarchal normative conventions about their wifely role that includes loyalty to husbands, producing children and supporting a husband who has saved them from a life of inauspiciousness by 'choosing' them as wives since 'women cannot live without husbands' (Philips 2005). The 'ideological enclosure' of marriage as a mechanism for regulating, privileging and protecting women results in various social exclusions (Borneman 1996: 228–29), as in the stigma attached to widowed, *maladi* (infertile), unmarried and divorced women. These social exclusions result in women accommodating a co-wife, forming a relationship with a married man, or privileging a man's right to form a polygynous union since it is a privilege granted by the gods.

Thus, Sevathi amma, aged 75, a child bride and mother, saw her infertility during the early years of marriage as the reason why her husband took his niece as a second wife. Manjula, aged 30, whose husband had raped her younger sister, tried to mitigate her husband's infraction by alluding to the 'special blood bond' between sisters (Busby 1995, on south Indian Tamils). 'It is difficult to live without a husband', noted Navamany, aged 49, a widow who has had a prolonged sexual partnership with her deceased husband's brother who is also a cross-cousin and lives with his primary wife and family on another estate. Shared living space in the increasingly overcrowded setting of the line rooms and extended family living are also responsible for many cases of consensual or forced sexual unions between cross-sex affines—as in the case of Sahadevan, aged 38, who lives with his wife and her sister whom he had impregnated while she was living with them (Philips 2005).

The migration of married women who work as care workers and housemaids in the Middle East has created new challenges for women and their marriages, a growing phenomenon of what might be called the 'absent-wife syndrome'. Sri Lankan female migrants to the Middle East share some common problems (Gamburd 2000) that range from on-the-job abuse by the some Middle Eastern employers to having their remittances splurged by their husbands on alcohol consumption and gifts to their mistresses. Husbands also question the sexual purity of their wives on their return because of the highly publicised experiences of sexual abuse of Sri Lankan female migrants. Divorce is not an easy option in the face of strong social pressures. While conjugal separation exists, not all women are predisposed to take this course of action in a community in which the status of being single brings few benefits. Women have also used Middle-East employment as an escape strategy to end a bad or unhappy marriage (ibid.).

Marriage and Work

Private managements, and natal and affinal families have a stake in Tamil women's labour. Since the 1990s, the emphasis of companies has been on short-term profits based on increased productivity and cutting costs in maintaining the plantation infrastructure and natural assets in good condition. From the point of view of the gender division of labour, this new emphasis has meant more tea plucking work for women and less maintenance work for men. Many Tamil men must now rely on the wages of wives and daughters from estate work.

Planters deploy the work of women to serve their production and labour needs, and these needs influence their recruitment and family planning strategies. The location of birth, estate residence and work experience are the eligibility criteria for hiring Tamil men and women as registered estate workers. The marriage of women does not disadvantage the labour needs of estate companies since out-marrying daughters replace in-marrying wives as women circulate between estates to live in patri-virilocal residence. Custom defines this pattern of labour circulation since *veetodu mappillai* (matrilocal husbands) have a lower status in the community. Planters accommodate such cultural rules by seldom hiring men to work on their wives' estates; the hiring of a new wife, however, is contingent on the husband's status as an estate worker in his natal estate. Managers with surplus labour have told me that they are more inclined to retain the services of young, single women since their employment would ensure their chances of being re-employed on their husbands' natal estate after marriage (Philips 2005). However, underemployment and the declining availability of maintenance work for men, and male outmigration for employment purposes, have led to a significant shift from patrilocal residence to uxorilocal residence (De Neve 2005, on Tamil Nadu). A man's choice of residence would now depend on his wife's employment or employability as an estate worker. Some managers even disregard the eligibility criteria when there is a shortage of labour as in the case of Renuka, aged 34, who was first a child domestic worker and then a factory worker before returning to work on her natal estate after marriage to support her unemployed husband and three young children.

Labour supply and demand are also managed by reproductive strategies that involve the efforts of both the Sri Lankan government and the plantation managements that sometimes work at cross purposes, particularly in the case of estates with a labour shortage. The government of Sri Lanka has been vigorously promoting family planning and the sterilisation of women is the most common family planning method on the estates. Estate managers, whose estates experience labour shortages, are not favourably disposed towards the family planning efforts of the government. Estates with surplus labour and/ or access to Sinhalese village labour, on the other hand, support government family planning policies. Some estate companies even subject in-marrying wives to pregnancy tests before hiring them to keep welfare costs low and to ensure the uninterrupted work of women.

Affinal households depend on the wage earnings and retirement benefits of their female affines. The timing of a son's marriage may often depend on the domestic work needs of a mother-in-law or the retirement of parents-in-law from estate work. As Jayaraman has noted, 'there is an economic motive in seeking a wife' (1975: 133). It is normal practice on the estates for husbands to collect their wife's wages and to exercise total control over the use of them. Husbands also insist on their wives reporting for work on a daily basis and not record absence since it would reduce their earnings. In some cases, the *peyer* (name, reputation, daily wages) women earn by meeting the daily plucking norm, i.e. poundage of tea leaves to be picked, have been manipulated by husbands who transfer the name to other workers to pay debts or claim favours from kanganies, conductors (weighing supervisors) and co-workers.

Apart from the guarantee of income, men have another stake in marrying a woman who is an estate worker. The resolution of the citizenship issue in 2003—with the passing of 'The Grant of Citizenship to Persons of Indian Origin Act, No 35'—has raised the question of future ownership of the line rooms. Given the uncertainty of work for men, the shortage of housing outside the estates and because estate work is a requirement for families to be entitled to their line-room residence, the onus is on women to continue working. The estates have also become safe havens for the Tamils due to ethnic violence and insecurity outside the estates. Parents approaching retirement age will arrange a marriage for a son who is not an estate worker in order to ensure their continued occupation of the line room after retirement. Some young women who had factory jobs before marriage had returned to the estates after marriage to work as tea pluckers in order to ensure a family's claim to estate housing. While educated young women prefer factory work to estate work, factory work is only a temporary option since marriage and the problem of finding cheap housing outside the estates forces them back into estate work. Husbands are also free to seek work outside the estates if their wives can stake their claims to estate housing.

A man's adult status is contingent upon marriage and a husband's status is usually defined by his provider role, which, given current employment trends, is precarious at best. 'Being strong' is a metaphor for status in the culture of the estate Tamils and the strength of a husband is dependent on fulfilling kinship obligations and demonstrating economic capability. Some husbands overextend themselves in their efforts to earn prestige through gift giving at life-cycle rituals such as marriage and female puberty and use their wife's wages for this purpose. Although women also consume and benefit from men's status displays, the direct beneficiaries of status strength are their husbands since it enables them to position themselves in the formal kinship network within the community.

Few unmarried women take up employment in the Middle East because of the cultural stigma attached to the migration of single women to overseas destinations. Married women insist that they go abroad to 'raise their heads', by which they mean enhancing their self-esteem, the respect of families and improving their families' living standards. Women use the earnings from the Middle East to renovate and expand line-room housing in anticipation of future ownership, to educate their children and to provide dowries to their daughters. These women are often the prime movers in their family's efforts to pull themselves out of poverty and to improve their economic circumstances (Philips 2005).

From the point of view of a woman's natal family, a daughter's work has a marriage-based investment in terms of securing a prospective spouse and eliminating the need for a cash dowry. Daughters are economic assets since they can become wage earners as soon as they reach the minimum age of seventeen, which is the age at which family members of both sexes can become registered workers under current labour laws that have made child labour illegal. Parents would register their daughters for estate work as soon as they reach the minimum age for employment since a daughter's employment becomes a surrogate for dowry in her marriage. Even estate managers try to employ young women, if they are efficient pluckers, in order to enhance their marriageability and to eliminate the need for dowry in their marriages.

Changing Facets of Marriage, Women's Work and Status Production

New employment opportunities and changes in income levels among some estate families are leading to what Hannah Papenek (1979) has called 'status production' work and attendant social differentiation between households. Status production involves the earnings and efforts of the whole family and is manifested in material and symbolic ways, including house renovations, sartorial changes among youth (Daniel 1996), conspicuous consumption, the acquisition of jewellery, electronic entertainment goods, and extravagant celebrations of marriage and puberty rituals, and an increase in the practice of dowry. These changes have trickle-down effects on poorer households who struggle to 'keep up with the Joneses'.

Patriarchal notions of family honour and shame associated with women and men's protective role over women are becoming more evident in male discourses around gender role constructions. Young men are patriarchal in limiting women's work and movements within the acceptable boundaries of 'female respectability', which in current perceptions is linked to appropriate jobs, taboos relating to cross-sex mixing and norms on female behaviour in public places. For instance, young men have begun to stipulate to their sisters and wives the types of work that a self-respecting woman can and cannot do while households with additional, non-estate-based incomes, tend to keep their wives and daughters out of estate work. Although young women are beginning to reject estate work for more 'respectable jobs' such as factory work, educated young women are also being pressured by family members not to secure any work at all, which is leading to the re-domestication of women. Keeping wives and daughters at home was a practice among the upper-caste kangany families in the colonial period (Steuart 1906), but it is increasingly emerging as a status symbol among upwardly mobile lower-castes and class families who attempt to Sanskritise their way of life. Parents negotiating a marriage and dowry for their daughter may stipulate as a condition of marriage that their daughter be kept at home after marriage, while a prospective groom and his family may claim a dowry by making a similar promise. Even men who have married above their caste adopt such status-enhancing practices in order to impress their affinal families and claim respectability by demonstrating economic strength. The dowry does not always guarantee a woman's confinement to the home however, since some women have noted that changing economic circumstances forced them to go back to work on the estates.

The control of female sexuality is also seen as necessary to challenge and reverse the commonplace stereotypes of the estate Tamils held by other ethnic groups that they are sexually lax, effeminate and morally irresponsible (Hollup 1994). Some families have begun to withdraw their daughters from school after puberty. Thus, Annamamy, aged 47, who is a tea plucker, pulled her pubescent daughter out of school to prevent her from cross-sex mixing and protect her from eve teasing which has become common on buses and in other public places. She plans to arrange an early marriage for her daughter to a groom who could support a non-working wife. The Labour Force Survey of 1996 indicated an increasing trend among the estate Tamils to delay marriages because of high rates of female participation in the estate labour force, youth education, lack of housing for married couples and the reluctance of men to marry until they find employment (qtd. in Dunham 1997: 30). However, if the recent trend of withdrawing girls from school after puberty continues, young girls may become likely candidates for early marriage, despite housing shortages and underemployment among male estate workers.

Traditional dowry demands and transactions, that are a compulsory feature of marriages in other south Asian communities, were never major issues among estate families because most families did not have much property other than jewellery, clothing and household items to provide as dowry. Bridewealth was a common practice in the past but the dowry practice seems to be growing among upwardly mobile families, among households with male family members employed outside the estates, and among households with women in overseas employment. The customary items constituting a woman's marriage gifts consist of seven items: *kudangal* (pots), *thodugal* (earrings), *mukuthi* (nose ring), *pathirangal* (utensils), *uduppu* (dress), *pai* (mat) and *kinnangal* (drinking glasses). The current situation is for a family of means to dower furniture, steel cupboards, 'showcases' (cabinets) and suitcases that are items of prestige and display. Upwardly mobile families provide electronic goods, cash and heavy pieces of jewellery as dowry. Investments in jewellery have increased among the estate Tamils, indicating a rise in disposable income. Although workers have no legal right to line-room ownership, there is an informal rule of transmitting such rights to sons. Line-room rights are endowed as dowry to daughters as 'residual heirs' in the absence of sons or if the sons are willing to transfer the rights to daughters.

The marital preferences of educated youth are changing and this has become another factor in driving dowry demands upwards. Educated males insist on marrying women who are not 'basket carriers', a derogatory reference to the baskets that female tea pluckers carry on their shoulders. This demeaning of women's work emerges from youth rejection of the stigma associated with estate work. The dowries demanded for non-working women are higher. Educated young women also show preference for marrying men who are not estate workers. The collection of cash and goods for dowry is also a strong motivation for married women to go abroad and work as housemaids, since it would increase a daughter's chance of marrying a non-estate worker or becoming a stay-at-home wife. Unmarried older sisters are also contributing to the dowry needs of their younger sisters as in the case of Jeyamangalam, aged 35, an unmarried single woman who has been twice to Kuwait and has been collecting dowry money for her school-going younger sisters who want to marry men working outside the estate. Jeyamangalam noted that the dowry for such grooms might go up to about SLR 50,000. While there are indications to suggest that women's employment and earnings have begun to undermine dowries among other Sri Lankan communities (Asian Development Bank 2004: 28), my own research suggests that emerging community discourses around women's non-work as a symbol of status and respectability may drive dowry demands upwards.

Concluding Remarks

There are two factors currently shaping marriage practices in Sri Lankan tea estates. The first is the impact that education is having on the employment aspirations of youth and their marriage preferences. The second factor is the status aspirations of upwardly mobile families who have benefited by economic liberalisation and alternative employment opportunities outside the estates. Both factors are having mutually reinforcing impacts on the marriage preferences of estate youth, on women's work and the practice of dowry.

In contrast to the older generation of workers or their less-educated counterparts, educated youth are not constrained to contract cross-cousin or close-kin marriages for pragmatic or normative reasons. Apart from their concerns about the genetic implications of such marriages, the youth are also looking to expand their matrimonial links outside the estates or with non-estate workers. Young, educated women neither see the marital benefits of kinship and close-kin marriages nor have such marriages led to gender equality within marriage, as evidenced by the reality of male domination, domestic violence and marital infidelity. Young men and women are also less concerned about caste identity and avoiding inter-caste marriages. Economic liberalisation has opened up new employment prospects outside the estates for estate youth and this has created new social spaces for youth to arrange their own marriages including inter-caste marriages.

Also, emerging income differences between households are resulting in status production work among upwardly mobile families who show their arrival in material and symbolic ways. In this context, women's work or non-work becomes a signifier of social status and respectability. While women are increasingly contributing to household status and mobility through estate work and new forms of employment outside the estates, economic prosperity and upward mobility are also leading to the domestication of educated daughters. The pattern that is emerging is for dowry to be linked to men's work and women's non-work since the dowries for non-working women are higher while a daughter's marriage to a man who is not an estate worker also requires a higher dowry. These changes not only entrench the practice of dowry as a compulsory requirement in arranged marriages, but also increase the need for daughters to be dowered at marriage both as compensation for their lack of income and as a signifier of the rising family status. The increasing practice of dowry among higher-income families has demonstration effects on low-income families, and dowry demands in the absence of rising incomes place great stress on many families in the estates who want their daughters married. Estate families seldom regarded daughters as economic burdens in the past, but women's non-work may lead to a change in community perceptions as families may come to regard daughters as financial liabilities rather than as economic assets.

The global forces that are leading to new work opportunities for young women and men, the upward mobility of some estate households and attendant 'status production' work are also undermining young women's position as wage earners. The domestication of women will lead to women's dependence on their husbands after marriage. Thus, youth education, new employment opportunities and status production have both empowering and disempowering impacts on women with the reordering and reactivation of traditional kinship, gender and marital relationships.

Notes

[1] See http://www.indexmundi.com/sri_lanka/demographics_profile.html (accessed on: 30 January 2013).

[2] I respectfully disagree with Dumont's position (1996) on this.

[3] I respectfully disagree with Dumont's position (1996) on this.

REFERENCES

Asian Development Bank. 2004. *Sri Lanka: Country Gender Assessment*. Manila.

Balasundaram, Sasikumar, A. S. Chandrabose, and P. P. Sivapragasam. 2009. 'Caste Discrimination among Indian Tamil Plantation Workers in Sri Lanka'. In *Casteless or Caste Blind: Dynamics of Concealed Caste Discrimination, Social Exclusion and Protest in Sri Lanka*, eds. Kalinga Tudor Silva, P. P. Sivapragasam and Paramsothy Thanges. Colombo, Chennai: Kumaran Book House.

Borneman, John. 1996. 'Until Death Do Us Part: Marriage/Death in Anthropological Discourse'. *American Ethnologist* 23 (2): 215–35.

Breman, Jan, and Valentine Daniel. 1992. 'The Making of a Coolie'. *Journal of Peasant Studies* 19 (3/4): 268–95.

Brennholdt-Thomsen, Veronika. 1981. 'Subsistence Production and Extended Reproduction'. In *Of Marriage and the Market: Women's Subordination in International Perspective*, eds. Kate Young, Carol Wolkowitz and Roslyn McCullagh. London: CSE Books.

Busby, Cecilia. 1997. 'Of Marriage and Marriageability: Gender and Dravidian Kinship'. *Journal of the Royal Anthropological Institute* 3 (1): 21–42.

Carter, Marina. 1996. *Voices from Indenture*. London and New York: Leicester University Press.

Cave, Henry. 1900. *Golden Tips*. London: Sampson Low, Marston and Company, Limited, St. Dunstan's House.

CO 101/131. 1871. '*Letter from the immigration agent to the colonial secretary Samuel Mitchell. Proportion of women to be maintained amongst emigrants from India to the colonies*'. Colonial Office.

Daniel, Valentine. 1996. *Charred Lullabies: Chapters in An Anthropography of Violence*. New Jersey: Princeton University Press.

———. 1993. 'Tea Talk: Violent Measures in the Discursive Practices of Sri Lanka's Estate Tamils'. *Comparative Studies in Society and History* 35 (3): 568–600.

De Neve, Geert. 2005. 'Weaving for IKEA in South India: Subcontracting, Labour Markets and Gender Relations in a Global Value Chain'. In *Globalizing India*, eds. Jackie Assayag and C. J. Fuller. London, New York: Anthem Press.

de Silva, S. B. D. 1982. *The Political Economy of Underdevelopment*. London, Boston and Henley: Routledge and Kegan Paul.

Dumont, Louis. 1966. 'Marriage in India: The Present State of the Question'. *Contributions to Indian Sociology* 7:77–98.

Dunham, David. 1997. *The Labour Situation on Sri Lanka's Tea Estates: A View to 2005*. Labour Economic Series, Colombo: Institute of Policy Studies.

Gamburd, Michelle Ruth. 2000. *The Kitchen Spoon's Handle: Transnationalism and Sri Lanka's Migrant Housemaids*. Ithaca and London: Cornell University Press.

Good, Anthony. 1991. *The Female Bridegroom: A Comparative Study of Life-Cycle Rituals in South India and Sri Lanka*. Oxford and New York: Clarendon Press, Oxford University Press.

Goffman, Irvin. 1961. *Asylums*. New York: Doubleday Anchor Books.

Grover, Shalini. 2009. 'Lived Experiences: Marriage, Notions of Love, and Kinship Support among Poor Women in Delhi'. *Contributions to Indian Sociology* 43:1–33.

Guilmoto, Christophe. 1993. 'The Tamil Migration Cycle'. *Economic and Political Weekly* 16 (23): 111–20.

Hollup, Oddvar. 1994. *Bonded Labour: Caste and Cultural Identity Among Tamil Plantation Workers in Sri Lanka*. Sri Lanka: Charles Subasinghe and Sons.

———. 1993. 'Caste Identity and Cultural Continuity among Tamil Plantation Workers in Sri Lanka'. *Journal of African and Asian Studies* 28 (1–2): 67–87.

Jayaraman, R. 1975. *Caste Continuities in Ceylon*. Bombay: Popular Prakashan.

Kapadia, Karin. 1995. *Siva and her Sisters: Gender, Caste and Class in Rural South India*. San Francisco: Oxford University Press.

Kondapi, C. 1951. *Indians Overseas (1838–1948)*. New Delhi: Indian Council of World Affairs.

Kurian, Rachel. 1998. 'Tamil Women on Sri Lankan Plantations: Labour Control and Patriarchy'. In *Women Plantation Workers*, eds. Shobhita Jain and Rhoda Reddock. Oxford and New York: BERG.

———. 1984. *State, Capital and Labour in the Plantation Industry in Sri Lanka 1834–1884*. Amsterdam: University of Amsterdam.

Ludowyk, Evelyn Frederick. 1966. *The Modern History of Ceylon*. London: Weidenfeld and Nicholson.

Mackintosh, Maureen. 1981. 'Gender and Economics'. *Of Marriage and the Market: Women's Subordination in International Perspective* eds. Kate Young, Carol Wolkowitz and Roselyn McCullagh, 1–15. London: CSE Books.

Mangru, Basdeo. 1987. 'The Sex-Ratio Disparity and Its Consequences under Indenture in British Guiana'. In *India in the Caribbean*, eds. David Dabydeena and Brinsley Samaroo. London: Hansib/University of Warwick, Centre for Caribbean Studies.

Moldrich, Donovan. 1988. *Bitter Berry Bondage: The Nineteenth Century Coffee Workers in Sri Lanka*. Kandy Sri Lanka: Co-ordinating Secretariat for Plantation Areas.

Moxham, Roy. 2003. *Tea: Addiction, Exploitation and Empire*. London: Constable and Co.

Northrop, David. 1995. *Indentured Labour in the Age of Imperialism 1834–1922*. Cambridge: Cambridge University Press.

Oishi, Nana. 2005. *Women in Motion: Globalization, State Policies, and Labour Migration in Asia*. Stanford: Stanford University Press.

Omvedt, Gail. 1980. 'Migration in Colonial India: The Articulation of Feudalism and Capitalism by the Colonial State'. *Journal of Peasant Studies* 7 (2): 185–212.

Otoo-Oyortey, Nana, and Sonita Pobi. 2003. 'Early Marriage and Poverty: Exploring Links and Key Policy Issues'. *Gender, Development and Marriage*. Oxford: Oxfam.

Papanek, Hanna. 1979. 'Family Status Production: The 'Work' and 'Non-Work' of Women'. *Signs* 4 (4): 775–81.

Parry, Jonathan. 2001. 'Ankalu's Errant Wife: Sex, Marriage and Industry in Contemporary Chhattisgarh'. *Modern Asian Studies* 35 (4): 783–820.

Peebles, Patrick. 2001. *The Plantation Tamils of Ceylon*. London and New York: Leicester University Press.

Philips, Amali. 2005. 'The Kinship, Marriage and Gender Experiences of Tamil Women in Sri Lanka's Tea Plantations'. *Contributions to Indian Sociology* 39 (1): 107–42.

Reddock, Rhoda. 1998. 'The Indentureship Experience: Indian Women in Trinidad and Tobago 1845–1917'. In *Women Plantation Workers*, eds. Shobhita Jain and Rhoda Reddock. Oxford and New York: BERG.

Reynolds, Holly. 1980. 'The Auspicious Married Woman'. In *The Powers of Tamil Women*, ed. Susan Wadley. Syracuse University: Maxwell School of Citizenship and Public Affairs.

Steuart, Mary. 1906. *Everyday Life on a Ceylon Cocoa Estate*. London: Henry J. Drane.

Sweetman, Caroline. 2003. 'Editorial'. *Gender, Development and Marriage*. Oxford: Oxfam.

Tinker, Hugh. 1977. *The Banyan Tree: Overseas Emigrants from India, Pakistan and Bangladesh*. Oxford: Oxford University Press.

_______. 1974. *A New System of Slavery: The Export of Indian Labour Overseas 1830–1920*. London, New York and Bombay: Oxford University Press.

Young, Kate, Carol Wolkowitz, and Roslyn McCullagh (eds.). 1981. *Of Marriage and the Market: Women's Subordination in International Perspective*. London: CSE.

Marriage, Labour Circulation and Smallholder Capitalism in Andhra Pradesh

Priti Ramamurthy

Introduction

The big news in Panipaadu village every summer is who has just got married.[1] In late June 2009, everyone was talking about Anand and Sandhya's marriage. College educated and personable, Anand was his Dalit parents' promise of a better future. Earlier that month, he had run away with Sandhya, a classmate and daughter of the village pastor. From Hyderabad, they had been summoned back by his father, Jayaraj, and returned 20 days later. A panchayat of nine Madiga, Dalit-Christian village elders was hastily convened to deliberate on what should be done. They recommended that a wedding be immediately performed. With the elders as witness, Anand tied a simple wedding pendant on Sandhya and with the ritual blessings of rice they were declared married. Ostracised by her parents, who had by then moved out of Panipaadu, Sandhya came to her in-laws' residence that night 'with just the sari she wore' and no dowry.

Three weeks later, when I first met Sandhya, she was hard at work doing *moggalu panni* (cross-pollinating buds by hand to produce hybrid cottonseeds) on Anand's family fields.[2] She had begun working alongside her mother-in-law, Satyamma, the very morning after her wedding. Well-versed in '[sewing] machine-stitching and computers', Sandhya had never before worked in the fields. As she recalled:

> My mother didn't let me do any work at my natal home .... At first I found this work difficult. My arms hurt, my back hurt. I felt it that first week. But I have no heart to stay home .... How many days will I be able to sit? I have to come back to this field. *Panni tappadu* [the work won't stop].

Sandhya's 'love' marriage is unusual in Panipaadu, where marriages are usually arranged by parents and kin. Even though it was within the Madiga caste (i.e. caste endogamous), the marriage had been preceded by the young couple's assertion of sexual desire and disregard of the normative strictures on pre-marital sex. Once 'Anand's spoiling of the girl', as Satyamma put it, had been socially regularised through marriage, Sandhya was trying to be a good daughter-in-law. On the day of my visit, the other daughter-in-law in their joint household—whose marriage had been conventionally arranged to Anand's younger brother, Moshay—had gone back to her natal home for a ritual visit. No one had so much as come to invite Sandhya back to hers. She had lost the respite of the natal home by her unconventional marriage.[3] But Sandhya herself reasoned, 'It will cost INR 100 to hire a labourer to do crossing work if I go. So I thought I'd stay. No, Anand didn't tell me to stay back. I decided to. My mother-in-law will find it difficult to manage all the house work and all the field work on her own'. By so doing, Sandhya demonstrated her commitment to the joint family, an ideological construction which privileges collective identity over the conjugal relationship between husband and wife (Uberoi 2003); she did so through labouring.

Jayaraj and Satyamma, Sandhya's in-laws, are smallholders, who cultivated hybrid cottonseed on a mere 70 cents (0.7 acre) in 2009. Formerly impoverished migrant labourers, for them, cottonseed is an aspirational crop; full of dreams of better futures for their sons as being *tellvi* (or worldly), and liberated from the unfree labour—'tied' to a big farmer till a debt is cleared—which Jayaraj had endured. With cottonseed came their hopes for the autonomy of self-cultivation, 'labouring for themselves', and of 'growing self-respect and dignity' as Madigas—members of a formerly untouchable caste community. These dreams can only be realised through family strategies to enable the circulation—the deployment and movement—of their labour and the re-working of labour relations through affect.

In this essay, I explore how marriage plays a critical role in different forms of labour circulation in smallholder households, like Jayaraj and Satyamma's.[4] The wider contributions of the essay are to, first, bring to the sociological literature on marriage a focus on agriculture, a context that is not usually considered a globalising one in India, but is, as we shall see, deeply so. Second, I focus on smallholder capitalism characterised so because smallholders are enmeshed in market relations, committing to contracts with agribusiness corporations and advancing capital accumulation on an extended scale.

Agricultural biotechnologies, like hybrid cottonseed and contract farming are at the heart of contemporary strategies of economic development world-wide.[5] In conversation with the economic literature on marriage, I show why rationalist arguments of marriage, which cast it in functional terms, fall short. My main contribution is to demonstrate how the contradictions of smallholder capitalism, in a now global context, relate to normative marriage preferences and kinship patterns. Contested practices and interpretations of consanguinity and opposite desires of parents for daughters and in daughters-in-law are illustrative of these contradictions. The relationship between prescriptive marriage preferences and the commodification of kinship is in flux: at times the continuity of marriage and kinship ideologies constrains the process and at others, they ease the process of commodification. As the form and content of labour relations within smallholder households change, the texture of labour relations emerges as affective elements of meaning, morality and value. The contours of family life under capitalism and how it is experienced by people in the global everyday are thereby discernable as 'structures of feeling: meanings and values as they are actively lived and felt ... not feeling against thought but thought as felt and feeling as thought: practical consciousness of a present kind in a living and interrelating continuity' (Williams 1977: 132).

Cottonseed Production: A Globalising and Gendered Context

Cottonseed production in India is a globalising context because cottonseed, the seed which is sown to grow cotton for fibre, is the first node in a global commodity chain. India has the largest area under cotton in the world, it is the second largest producer of cotton, and it is a major exporter of cotton fibre, textiles and apparel (Ramamurthy 2000, 2003, 2004). Cottonseed production in India is global also because 90 per cent of Indian farmers of all size classes, grow genetically modified cotton, more commonly called Bt cotton. Into each cell of Bt cotton, a gene, which is toxic to a major cotton pest when ingested has been inserted.[6] The cottonseed market in India is at the centre of the investment strategies of the biggest multinational seed companies, like Monsanto, Bayer and Dow, because the Indian market, valued at INR 2500 crores annually, is already twice the size of the US market in 2011. Their presence will grow even further in the next ten years (Monsanto 2007).

India is a particularly attractive market for multinationals, and the Indian seed companies that buy the patented gene constructs of these multinationals, because it is the only country in the world where cottonseed is hybridised or manually cross-pollinated on a commercial scale. Hybridisation protects the patented technology of corporations because hybrids do not reproduce genetically modified traits, such as bollworm toxicity, in subsequent generations. So, if a farmer stores and plants a Bt cotton hybrid seed the next year, he will reap a smaller yield and his cotton plants will have a much weaker capacity to repel the bollworm, and he will end up having to use pesticide on the plant at a high cost once again. It is hybridisation, not a 'terminator gene,' which protects gene patents and guarantees seed companies that Indian farmers will purchase their branded seeds afresh each season. This makes the process of hybridisation 'a perfect fit', as one Monsanto executive put it, for multinational and Indian seed corporations to protect intellectual property.

Hybrid cottonseeds are manufactured each season through the laborious process of manually cross-pollinating two varieties: the moggalu panni, also called 'crossing' work, done by Sandhya in the opening account. First, buds on the 'female' plant that will bloom the next day are emasculated, i.e. the petals and pollen-laden anthers are removed from the bud with one's thumb nail in a single twirl. This controls self-pollination. The emasculated bud is tagged. Then the next morning, pollen from 'male' parent flowers is dusted onto the stigma (the pollen receptacle) of each tagged bud on the 'female' plant.[7] Each hybrid cottonseed in the 15 million packets of cottonseed sold each year in India has been touched by human fingers at least four times: during emasculation, tagging, pollination and picking. I change the referent of hybridisation to floral sex work to draw attention to the symbolic linking of the natural to the social through processes of gendering (Ramamurthy 2010). Floral sex work—labour intensive and cheap or unpaid—for hybrid cottonseed production is, thus, not just a globalised context but a deeply gendered one which is integral to the reproduction of Indian and multinational capital on an extended scale.

Cottonseed Farming in Andhra Pradesh and Smallholder Capitalism

Andhra Pradesh state produced the most hybrid cottonseed in the country till 2007. Most of it is grown in the Raichur *doab*, the area between the confluent Krishna and Tungabhadra rivers in southern Telengana. For the last 30 years, from the 1980s to the early 2000s, cottonseed has been typically produced by large landholders (owning over 25 acres each) with assured access to water and hired labour. They are mostly 'settlers' who came to the area from the coastal Andhra region and are of the Kamma caste.[8] Cottonseed production is highly capital intensive and highly labour intensive; for a 3–4 acre plot of cottonseed, the size typically cultivated by large farmers, 20 to 30 labourers are hired to do floral sex work. Till 2006, cottonseed labourers on large farms were mainly children; over 70 per cent of them girls. *Seedu pillalu* (seed children), as they are called, were paid half to three-quarters the adult female wage and worked four to five hours longer. Most were migrants who stayed in the seed farmer's house for the three-month crossing period. Large farmers began abandoning cottonseed production in the 2000s, due to the activism around the use of child labour, the higher costs of labour, especially after the National Rural Employment Guarantee Scheme (NREGS) and the stagnant prices for seeds paid by seed companies.

In a significant shift since the early 2000s, smallholders—owning 5 acres or less of irrigated land—cultivate cottonseed on tiny plots of one-third to a half acre of land. Former floral sex workers themselves, smallholders grow cottonseed as an aspirational crop, with the anticipation of dignity, better futures for their children and class-leaping returns. Stories abound of neighbours who have netted INR 1 lakh from less than an acre of cottonseed.[9] This is not mere hype. Some households actually achieve this, making cottonseed the most profitable crop to grow by far. Men in white clothes, *pucca* (permanent) houses, colour TVs, motorbikes, auto-rickshaws, tractors and educated sons are all in evidence as icons of prosperity, possibility and self-respect. The successful cultivation of cottonseed is, however, far from assured. The desire to overcome past ignominies of caste discrimination makes cottonseed cultivation by formerly untouchable caste communities worthwhile, even if economic returns are risky and often low or zero (Ramamurthy 2011).

Research Context and Methodology

Panipaadu, a Raichur doab village of 500 households in Mahbubnagar district in the Telengana region of Andhra Pradesh, depends on agriculture for livelihoods. Nearly everyone owns land; 70 per cent are smallholders who have migrated out in search of dry-season work for generations, because this is in an arid part of the country. The main caste group in the village is Munnuru Kapu and a fourth of the population is of the formerly untouchable Madiga caste, of whom nearly all are Christian. The hundred or so cottonseed smallholders in Panipaadu mainly belong to these two castes.

This essay is based on fieldwork in Panipaadu in 2006, 2007 and 2009. Over 200 interviews and a detailed survey of 29 smallholder cottonseed households were conducted. Here, I mainly draw on interviews with four households. I also talked to large landholders, seed company agents and managers and government officials. This research is part of a larger study of gender and agrarian change over a period of more than two decades in four villages in Mahbubnagar district.

Gender, Marriage and Kinship in Panipaadu

Gender and marriage systematically structure life and everyday discourse in Panipaadu. The normative gender regime is apparent in the very term *aadavallu* for adult females. In Telugu, *aada* literally means 'over there' and *vallu* is for 'people', hence *aadavallu* signifies 'people from over there'. This spatialisation encodes patrilocality, the norm that women will move out of the natal home after marriage to take up residence in the home of their husbands and in-laws. It firmly puts in place compulsory heterosexuality as well: all females must marry and cohabit with males. Aadavallu is a sign that articulates sexed bodies with difference and makes processes of differentiation based on gender feel natural. Used in conversations, everyday and all the time, no one stops to think about the way it encodes power. 'With *aada-pillalu* (girls or daughters) we quarrel, with *aada-vallu* (wives or daughters-in-law) we're in trouble' is a common saying. The sign aadavallu, thus, indelibly shapes the ways in which reality is represented, imagined and acted upon.

Marriages are usually arranged by family and kin in Panipaadu when a girl is a couple of years past puberty.[10] Caste endogamy is preserved through marriage. A preference for village endogamy is expressed through the concept of *unduru ichinam*, 'we gave our daughter in marriage within our village'. Very frequently, girls in Panipaadu are married into families who live in nearby villages within a 20 km radius, rather than in the village per se.

Consanguineous marriage—for a woman with her mother's brother or a cross-cousin, either the mother's brother's son or father's sister's son—is preferred and very prevalent. Nearly 50 per cent of all marriages in the households I surveyed, are consanguineous. Consanguinity is widespread in some caste communities in Andhra Pradesh (Reddy 2005). The kinship term *atta* or *attamma* is the same for one's father's sister, mother's brother's wife and mother-in-law, as the former two are a woman's prospective mother-in-law. So also the same term *maama*, which is used for one's father's sister's husband, mother's brother and father-in-law. The prefix *mena*, as in *mena atta* (aunt) and *mena maama* (uncle), is a referent for normative consanguineous connections, which are called *menarikalu*. Rao (2004) suggests that mena is derived from *menu* which means body. Mena refers to a specific category of affines whom it is alright to marry. A daughter-in-law connected by such an affinal relationship is referred to as a *mena kodalu*. Such a woman is considered a daughter-in-law who is *degara* or close and *sontam* or one's own, related. Daughters-in-law who are not consanguineous are variously referred to as *durum* or distant; *mandi*, meaning of the people or masses or 'public'; or *paraya ammai*, outsider-girl. Consanguinity is customarily interpreted as a way to stay connected to daughters after their marriage and to maintain affinal relationships across generations.

In practical consciousness, consanguineous marriages are arranged for many reasons in Panipaadu. To help out kin, especially siblings who have too many daughters, consanguineous marriages forgo dowry. The expectation that daughters-in-law, who are kin will stay committed to the joint household is another reason to opt for a consanguineous alliance. So is the hope that consanguineous daughters or sons-in-law will take good care of their in-laws when they become old. Parents of daughters expect that marrying a girl into an affinal home will ensure that her in-laws *aasha istaru* (will love her) and *saaktaru* (nurture her), because the girl and her mother-in-law 'share a place of birth'. Consanguineous marriages are also a way that prospective sons-in-law and their parents may stake a claim to property, especially land, which belongs to affines.

Village and caste endogamy and consanguinity, common in Panipaadu, are identified in the sociological literature on marriage as characteristics of the 'Southern' or Dravidian kinship system (Karve 1953; Dumont 1953; Trautmann 1981). Debate in the 1980s turned on the issue of whether these 'cultural' factors explained the lower sex ratios in the south of India relative to the north or 'economic' factors, like women's higher labour participation rates and visibility, did (Miller 1981; Dyson and Moore 1983). In recent years, economists have been revisiting this debate to argue that village endogamy and consanguinity in South India are no longer so predictable or systematic. Changes—decrease in village and caste endogamy and in consanguinity, for instance—are explained as the rational economic behaviour of households to spread ecological risk, access sub-caste credit networks, smoothen consumption and so on (Rosenzweig and Stark 1989; Rahman and Rao 2004; Munshi and Rosenzweig 2007). These arguments, which are committed to understanding female disadvantage, are evocative but by not studying the empirical relationships between the household as an economic unit and kinship ideologies, family building strategies and class, they fall short.

The case for research that does so and considers the joint household as an ideological construct, a set of material arrangements and an emotional space, where not just the conjugal but a whole range of gendered relationships unfold, is made by sociologists like Shah (1998), Uberoi (2003) and Kannabiran (2006). The pay-offs are evident in rich ethnographies of marriage and the family which draw attention, for example, to the invisibilisation of daughter's labour in natal homes post marriage in Rajasthan (Palriwala 1991), the lack of fall-back options for daughter's who have had love marriages in Delhi slums (Grover 2009) and the multiple factors, including proximity and access to property, that mediate how mothers-in-law treat consanguineous daughters-in-law and daughters in Chennai slums (Vera-Sanso 1999). Taking my cues from these studies, I discuss three changing, emergent patterns of marriage and kinship in the context of smallholder capitalism in Panipaadu. I do so with a focus on labour circulation to pay ethnographic attention to the household as an economic unit, a zone of contestation, and a site where structures of feeling texture everyday life under global capitalism.

Pre-Marriage Patterns and Labour Circulation

A significant new phenomenon with multiple repercussions is the pre-marriage circulation of girls for floral sex work. The phenomenon, called *seed-suggilu*, started with girls migrating to work for large farmers but, since the early 2000s, entails children working for smallholders too. As in the case of large landholders, the labour of seed children is tied to an individual smallholder for the entire crossing (manual cross-pollination) season through 'advances' or loans of a bag of rice or INR 3000 to 4000 to their parents. They are required to work for the farmer continuously till the debt is cleared, which is usually by the end of the season. (This contrasts to daily wage labour, which is casual and intermittent.) Most seed children live in the smallholder seed farmer's house for the three-month crossing period. The advances and their earnings go directly to their parents and are mostly used for household consumption. Since seed children are neither 'free' to seek other work nor 'free' to move their labour, this is a form of unfree labour (Venkateswarlu and Da Corta 2001; Ramamurthy 2004).

Many seed children who work for smallholders are kin, the children of siblings, cousins, even young in-laws. The labour of kin is being commodified: even though they are relatives, parents are given an advance and the children are paid wages. Jayaraj, for instance, hired his elder sister's children—two girls and two boys—in 2006. These nephews and nieces 'learnt so well' that they returned to their parent's home and planted the same variety of cottonseed on their own land in 2007; they, in turn, hired other children as waged coolies for the crossing work that year. In 2007, Jayaraj hired his elder brother's daughter and two other unrelated girls. Jayaraj gave his brother an advance of INR 4000, and his niece a wage of INR 30 a day, on the same terms as the other two seed children. The hiring of seed children by adults who used to be seed children themselves as many smallholders are, is still exploitative, in terms of the wage relationship, but the new ideology of work in these households is generalised to treat seed children, both kin and non-kin 'like kin', in particular as daughters, i.e. as *inti-pillalu*, or *sontam pillalu* (literally, girls of the house and our own girls). This expression of kinship connectedness is not just discursive; it is put into practice as affect when seed children are induced to labour with *ubbinchidam*, *bonki ichadam* and *aasha chupiyadam* (encouragement, affection and love); i.e. with care, not beatings and abuse.

Seed children, whether kin or not, are taught modern, near-industrial work habits including the keeping of interminably long hours, time-bound work and regularity. These disciplinary practices include giving floral sex workers soap for daily baths and oil to comb their hair before they come to work each day. They are expected to be timely and are usually given a fixed number of rows to cross-pollinate by the end of the morning. Small gifts like ribbons, bindis, sweets and an occasional trip to the cinema double as incentives for productivity and demonstrations of care. Kinship is the rationale offered for feeding seed children as well as one's own *inti-pillalu* (children of the family). But smallholders themselves also reason, in starkly functionalist terms, that 'unless seed children are fed well, they will not have the strength to work long hours well'. The fact that seed children are fed three meals a day is noteworthy: they are being made responsible for meeting the daily costs of the reproduction of their own labour power even before they become adults. The idiom of kinship in this instance validates, ideologically and morally, the incitement to produce and expropriate labour surpluses.

The migration of unaccompanied, unmarried girls for agricultural field work was not common in Panipaadu and its environs before the introduction of cottonseed cultivation. With large-scale employment of unmarried girls in cottonseed fields as migrant labourers, older norms regarding the control of a girl's sexuality before her marriage come into conflict with capitalist work regimes. For instance, at the height of the crossing season in 2006, one young girl, Hanumakka, started menstruating for the first time. Puberty is usually marked by making a girl 'sit' at home for five days, followed by a ceremony at which her becoming a *peddamanshi* (big person) is celebrated. Rituals are performed to ensure her fertility. The occasion publically announces her suitability for marriage. Hanumakka's parents were sent for by her employer, a smallholder, and negotiations between them continued for the next two days. The smallholder, who was not kin, tried to convince the parents that he would take care of Hanumakka 'as if she were his own daughter', 'make her sit', and pay for all the rituals associated with her becoming a peddamanshi after the crossing season. When her parents dithered, asking 'What will be the point of that?', the smallholder's wife asked sarcastically, 'Will you announce with a tom-tom around the village that she's matured now?' Her husband then demanded that the advance he paid Hanumakka's parents be returned before he released their daughter from her obligation to stay for the entire crossing season. They somehow did so and took the girl back home, worrying: 'What will *mandi* (the people around) say if we leave her?' Their fear was of the public opprobrium if they failed to perform the puberty ceremony to mark her readiness for marriage; but, as much, it was a fear of sexual abuse if they left her, someone now liable to become pregnant, in a non-kin's house. Patriarchy trumped capital's needs, at least, temporarily. The smallholder was left scrambling without a crucial and efficient worker. He had already pulled his own three daughters out of school to do floral sex work and was unable to find a replacement. Each day, despite draconian work days by the floral sex workers who remained, the heap of self-pollinated cotton flowers grew (they have to be discarded or will contaminate the batch of hybrid seeds leading to an unacceptably low purity percentage come quality control time).

Marriage Arrangements and Labour Circulation

The pre-marriage circulation of girls for floral sex work, discussed in the previous section, is changing marriage itself as a social institution and a form of labour circulation. As I discuss in this section, transformations in the criteria for selecting daughters-in-law, in dowry negotiations and in contradictory readings of the benefits of consanguineous marriages are underway. The disjuncture between what parents' desire for their daughters and what they desire in daughters-in-law points to the contradictions of smallholder capitalism.

Just two days before Anand's return from Hyderabad (discussed in the opening account), the wedding of his younger brother Moshay, Jayaraj's second son, had been celebrated. Uneducated and the mainstay of his family's farming activities, Moshay's marriage had been arranged with Rahelamma from a village across the river by his *mama*, a cousin on his mother's side. Jayaraj and the uncle, I was told, had first asked the girl's parents for a *katnam* (dowry) of INR 50,000. But the girl's parents argued, 'She does *moggalu panni* (cross-pollination). How can you demand a large dowry when she does cross-pollination work?' 'So we agreed to a dowry of INR 5001.' Fourteen or fifteen years old, only just past puberty, Rahelamma was given 3 *tola*s (one tola is 11.66 grams) of gold by her parents. The church wedding cost them INR 90,000, and Jayaraj and Satyamma (Moshay's parents) gave her INR 10,000 to buy a grand wedding sari. A neighbour commented, 'They got her married so early because parents just don't want to keep a girl after she becomes a *peddamanshi*. Just see what happened with Anand ...'

In contrast to Anand's 'love' marriage, Moshay's was a typical arranged marriage. In the neighbour's account, Rahelamma's young age is reasonable because it concludes her parents' responsibility towards ensuring their daughter's sexual purity. Anand's misbehaviour serves as the cautionary tale that justifies their haste. (In the process, Sandhya's sexual agency and her role in running away are illegible.) The value now attached to prospective daughters-in-law 'knowing cross-pollination work' and the difference it makes in dowry negotiations is a more widespread phenomenon in smallholder households. The English word 'service' is routinely used to describe the number of years of experience as a floral sex worker a prospective daughter-in-law has. These new forms of bodiliness—the experience and the capacity to do floral sex work fast—have become criteria in the search for a 'good' daughter-in-law. They are simultaneously the attributes necessary for her to become a 'good worker', i.e. a surplus producing one, and co-exist with older ideals like *intithanam* (homeliness) and familialism, a commitment to the joint household and the capacity to look after in-laws when they are old.

Down a couple of fields from Jayaraj and Satyamma's is Maniamma's field. She's a feisty and capable widow who has single-handedly bought land, trained her sons to be expert farmers and lives with them and their wives in a joint household. In 2007, when I interviewed her, Maniamma had articulated a clear mandate for her third son, Pratap. 'I want a daughter-in-law who does cross-pollination work condition-*ga*', she'd said, using the English word 'condition' to express productivity. A year later, in 2008, Pratap had married Sukanya, and in 2009 when I visited, she was in the household's fields seven months pregnant and working away at cross-pollination. 'In their eagerness to get her out the door, her parents lied to us that she knows how to do crossing-work', Pratap complained. Then Maniamma filled in, 'She came with a dowry of INR 1 lakh and 3 tolas gold. She's an only daughter. The father grows peanuts. They have land under the Jurala canal, lots of water. She's her parents' only daughter. They nurtured her like a [baby] donkey' (meaning used to being well-fed and made to do no work). As we spoke, as if on cue, Pratap's cell phone rang and it was Sukanya's parents making sure he would bring her the next day to the private clinic in the nearest town, where she was receiving pre-natal care and would have the baby at their expense. In Maniamma's reckoning, the ability of a future daughter-in-law to do floral sex work was an important part of Pratap's marriage considerations. In actual day-to-day practice, Sukanya's inability to labour well enough to satisfy her husband and in-laws is linked to her privileged status as a daughter, an only daughter in her natal home and one on which she can fall-back for nurture and care.

The contradiction between parents, like Sukanya's, nurturing their daughters and having a different set of expectations for their daughters-in-law is apparent in the discourse around consanguineous alliances as well. Sukanya is a *duram* or *mandi pilla*, a girl who is unrelated. The conscious decision to not arrange a consanguineous marriage for Pratap was Maniamma's. She explained, 'All our girls in my mother's house have studied. If a man has a job, he can make his wife sit at home (i.e. not do field labour). But my sons are farmers. If an educated girl was married into this house she wouldn't be able to do cross-pollination work, would she? My elder brother came [to ask for Pratap to marry his daughter]. [I thought] I've been suffering ever since the ritual rice fell on my head [at my wedding]. Let it end with me. I told my brother, "Go look for someone else for my niece". Why should I witness what happens [if she were to marry my son]? If she—someone from my *puttina illu* (natal house, the house one is born in)—were to cry, I would be pained. If she didn't do the work, I'd hear complaints from the other daughters-in-law. That girl would say, "This is the kind of house my father gave me in marriage to?"

"Set fire to this mother-in-law's house", she'd curse and say.' In her account, Maniamma chose to not antagonise her brother on whom she depends for prestations and, on occasion, the sharing of expenses and the performance of rituals, by agreeing to his daughter marrying her son. It is quite possible that the dowry from a non-kin daughter-in-law was a factor in Maniamma's calculations as well. In fact, her behaviour contradicts the widespread practice in Panipaadu, also borne out in the literature, that marriages are arranged with the children of siblings so as not to antagonise them.

In other smallholder households, consanguineous marriages are a way to consolidate the pre-marriage circulation of kin for floral sex work or to bring in a daughter-in-law who is known to be a good floral sex worker. In one household, a girl lived and worked for her aunt for three years from the age of eight to eleven doing crossing work, before returning to her parent's home at menarche only to come back permanently two years later as a daughter-in-law. In another, a mother-in-law explained, 'We got a daughter-in-law from the house I was born in. [I knew she was a very fast worker.] How won't I know? She's my brother's child.' At the height of the crossing-season in 2006, Padmamma, the daughter-in-law, was away at her parent's for the birth of her second child and many attempts were made to re-call her before the normative three-month break. Her father resisted for a while telling Govindamma, his sister, to wait. She grumbled that every day Padmamma was away, a daily wage labourer was being hired at the cost of INR 50 a day. (In fact, Govindamma herself, a self-confessed 'very slow' floral sex worker, was pressed into service by her sons in the absence of her daughter-in-law and consequently, she didn't get the daily coolie wage she usually earned. Her neighbour contended that her grumbling was because she was missing the daily bottle of country liquor her wage made possible.) Eventually, Padmamma did return after two, not three, months. Although she was not the only daughter-in-law, Padmamma's status as a niece gave her some respite.

Recalcitrance against the new labour regime colours the narratives of some parents who are now being mindful of whether the family their daughter will marry into plants cottonseed. They expressed a willingness to pay higher katnam in the hope that their daughter will not be drawn into cottonseed's harsh work schedules. Others complain that they paid large dowries of INR 1 lakh, but their daughters have got no *sukham* (happiness). Inevitably, the explanation for why this is the case is that the woman's mother-in-law is a *duram manshi* (not related). Or, despite being related, the mother-in-law is uncaring. For Ratnamma, like Maniamma, the decision to not marry her son to a niece is a pro-active one that rests on the boundary between daughters and daughters-in-law being clearly maintained, 'What work will get done if I go for a close relation for my son? I need a girl who will listen to me. I have only one son.' The contradiction between parents wanting better futures for their daughters, which are free from field work, but daughters-in-law who are good floral sex workers plays out in joint households, as well, as discussed in the next section.

Joint Households and Labour Circulation

'*Yedigalu poyinam*' ('We've gone our own ways') was the very first thing Thimakka said to me on my visit to her family's fields in 2007. I was surprised that her joint household had split. Just the last year her mother-in-law, Sarojamma, had told me how theirs was a family in which everyone—all three sons, their wives and children, she and her husband—all *kallisi mellisi untamu* (get along really well). 'My daughters-in-law are so close they take a crying child to their breast without caring whose child it is.'

The majority of cottonseed smallholders I interviewed live in joint households, like Sarojamma's; units of more than one married couple and their children characterised by patrilocal co-residence and commensality. Smallholders now reason that unless everyone in the joint household—men, women and children—labour on the family cottonseed plots, their 'coolie' will not remain. This refers to the loss of their wages had they gone for daily wage work instead. In practice, cottonseed farming often pays less than daily wage or tied labour. Time and again, despite the hopefulness that cottonseed cultivation would lead to a change in class-status, no positive returns were reported at the end of the season. Many smallholders just about broke even and some even accumulated a debt, according to the calculations of the seed company. This was true for Sarojamma's household. The cost of the labour of smallholders is reduced to zero in these cases.

The risk of zero returns is countered by supplemental forms of labour circulation for which the joint household provides a large and flexible pool of labour. Own account cottonseed labour is interspersed with seasonal, circular and sometimes permanent migration. Most often, the youngest, unmarried sons or one or more married couples in the joint household migrate every year for construction work in the cities and for transplanting and harvesting rice in irrigated areas. These migration cycles match the lulls in the cottonseed cycle when floral sex labour demands are lower. Pooling migration earnings from several members of the joint household diversifies income flows, smoothens foodgrain consumption and subsidises the costs of reproduction of smallholder families. On occasion, capital accumulation for tube wells, water pumps, land levelling or other bulky production and reproduction expenses, like weddings and medical care, is possible from these earnings (Deshingkar and Farrington 2006).

With the shift to cottonseed, as the value of the joint family has increased, the textures of a whole range of gendered relations are being transformed. The pressures to form and preserve the joint household are felt most acutely by mothers-in-law who employ multiple strategies to keep daughters-in-law in the joint household. Ideologies of motherhood continue to serve as the glue that keeps daughters-in-law together, as we heard in Sarojamma's pride that her daughters-in-law breast-feed any hungry child in the family regardless of whether it is their child or not. She went on to explain, 'Becoming a mother is what binds daughters-in-law of the house together in relationships.' The metaphor of the joint household as a womb is expressed in the common understanding that, 'Brothers don't fight, they don't split households because they have shared a womb; they've been born of the same mother.' The motherhood discourse presses women's reproductive bodies into the service of the patrilocal joint household. The metaphor of the womb, which daughters-in-law can never share, prepares the grounds to blame daughters-in-law, not sons, for the dissolution of the joint family.

Older ideologies of familialism are now more difficult to sustain. In 2006, Sarojamma had explained how she managed 'her world, her joint household, with a lot of care':

> If my daughters-in-law have big expenses, for weddings in their natal homes, I give them money for ritual gifts ... as if they were living on their own. My mother-in-law troubled me. I don't want my daughters-in-law to experience that. I had seven brothers. I was the only girl. My brothers still buy me all my clothes.

Here, Sarojamma acknowledges the importance of daughters having good relations with their natal homes in terms of the prestations she still receives from her own brothers. She hopes that by sending her daughters-in-law to their natal homes for a bit of respite, and letting them spend on prestations 'as if they were living on their own', she will keep them committed to the joint household.

A newer strategy to keep households joint is to fulfill daughters-in-law's desires for modernity. Sarojamma explained, 'When my daughters-in-law go to their natal homes, I buy saris for them before they go home and only then send them. My daughters-in-law tell me what "design" to get, and I get it from the market.' This new form of caring is also expressed in her giving them money for '*shyampoolu, powderlu, creamlu*' (shampoo, powder, cream). Sarojamma contrasts this to the oppression her own mother-in-law, even though she was her aunt, subjected her to. She remembers, 'From the moment my wedding ceremonies took place, she didn't even let me comb my hair.' In other words, Sarojamma had been denied sensuality, even within the bounds of proprietary heteronormative sexuality. So while the consumer product multinationals

Proctor & Gamble and Hindustan Lever may benefit from the sale of packets of INR 5 Clinic shampoo and Fair and Lovely whitening cream to rural women, what makes buying these commodities meaningful to Sarojamma is that she is more loving, caring and modern than her own mother-in-law. Of course, the tying of a daughter-in-law's labour through new commodity relations simultaneously conjoins love, care and desire to the labour demands of smallholder capitalism.

The following year, Sarojamma explained why, despite her every effort, her joint household had split up:

> I used to give my daughters-in-law money for hair oil, body care products and clothes. Where do daughters-in-law give back these days? And they go on "sons, sons ..." when all they bring in are daughters-in-law who don't labour hard; they wither like flowers. We'd get paid one rupee to pound one kilo of chillies. We'd do 20 kg a day to earn money. Now they're like jasmine, wither and die at the slightest work. They're *aiybridu soppa manshi* [like stalks of hybrid Jowar]. We used to be scared of our in-laws. They can't work like we did. As soon as the rice blessings fall on their heads [at the wedding ceremonies] they want to separate. Only if we have a "balance" [i.e. bank balance], *paula bidda unte* [if we have a quarter], will they come close to us these days. We'd hide and talk to our mothers-in-law. Now, daughters-in-law tell us to our faces that they're going to split. They ask, "Should only we feed you? Did you not give birth to other sons? Go to them and eat".

Sarojamma distinguishes between old times when fear was the main emotion daughters-in-law had for their in-laws and their complete lack of fear today. Critiquing the commodification of kinship, Sarojamma regrets that her daughters-in-law have reduced familialism to a monetary transaction by their unwillingness to care for in-laws unless 'they have a balance'. Ironically, she herself is disappointed that they have not kept the transactional bargain she set up between modern purchased products of care and their labour. She went on to philosophise, 'The world, mankind, society has become like that. They see cinemas and have learnt from them. Aren't those representations, and this life? No one thinks about the difference. There's no thought to care for their in-laws. Even if they don't listen, we have some *akkara* [affection] for them. However much we earn we won't take it with us. Can neither take it nor eat it. Only one's goodness and badness are left when someone dies.' Putting thought to action, Sarojamma continues to babysit her grandchildren whenever she can.

Sarojamma's criticism of the value of having sons being over-rated is linked in her narrative to the capacity of their wives to labour. She contrasts the heavy labour she did when she was young with the wimpyness of young women today, who she likens to 'stalks of hybrid jowar.' Maniamma, as well, complains that her daughters-in-law have no *shakti* (strength), no *ghetti-thana* (fortitude) in comparison to herself. Her indomitable capacity to work—'like a donkey'—comes from her ability to do *kashtam*, the Telugu word for labour, and face *kashtam*, which is also the Telugu word for adversity. 'Till there's shakti in these arms', Maniamma predicts, taking a rare, if momentary break from floral sex work to flex her arms, 'my daughters-in-law will feed me'. In the new cottonseed economy, her only social security, it appears, is her own shakti for interminable floral sex work.

Inevitably, the rupture of the joint household, usually precipitated by an unequal division of labour, is represented as a failure of co-resident daughters-in-law 'to get along'. Thimakka explained, 'Kamlamamma [the younger daughter-in-law and niece] got up late and took an inordinate amount of time to finish bathing the kids and coming to the field. I would get up at four in the morning, cook two *seers* (1 seer = approx. 1 kg) of rice and come to the field early, only to hear complaints of "What took you so long?" Now that we've split up, she's there in her own field working from sun up to sun down. If only she'd shown this *hecherika* [mindfulness] then, it would have been good for us all ... We'd have no outstanding loans to clear had she worked like she is doing now.' Her comment is illustrative, on the one hand, of the difficulties of distributing reproductive work and field work between co-resident daughters-in-law in an equitable manner. On the other, it illustrates how workers themselves consent not just to labour in the new capitalist landscape, but to value the attributes necessary to be productive workers and to conduct themselves in a like manner. The desire to escape paid labour, expressed in the smallholder's pride that 'one's labour is one's own', seductively leads to the disciplining of one's kin and self-disciplining.

In particular, consanguineous daughters-in-law are faulted for the break-up of joint households. Kamlamma reckoned this is inevitable, 'I'm the *mena kodalu* [consanguineous daughter-in-law], *sontham kodalu* [one who is their own], so I'll be blamed. They'll say, "Are you *mandi* [unrelated]?" If Thimakka doesn't look after them no one will blame her but if I don't get along with them, they'll say, "Aren't you the *mena kodalu*? You should look after them [as a daughter would]".' Kamlamma experiences the contradiction of trying to be a good daughter-in-law and simultaneously daughter-like as an impossible condition.

While some parents try to protect unmarried daughters from the rigours of cottonseed farming with bigger dowries, as mentioned in the last section, married daughters are often being called back by their natal families to partake in it. Sarojamma's daughter, 'who plants no cottonseed herself', did floral sex work for the joint family in 2006 and for her younger brother after the split, for a daily wage. Maniamma's daughter, 'who is very poor because her husband is a drunkard', is leased one acre of the family's land to grow cottonseed and is given a share of water from the family well. She is gifted a bag of rice as well. Maniamma helps her daughter out with her own labour but only after the work on the joint fields she shares with her sons is done, as otherwise, 'Will my daughters-in-law be quiet?' On the one hand, this is further proof of the commodification of kinship. On the other, kinship constrains untrammelled commodification even as it encodes commodity exchanges in respectability by embedding them in kinship ties and values. Sarojamma's daughter, for example, is careful to not overstay her welcome, which is necessary to continue to keep on good terms with her brothers and sisters-in-law. Sanjamma too is careful not to antagonise her daughters-in-law by diverting too much of her labour to her daughter's cottonseed fields.

Conclusion: Reframing the Marriage Question

This essay's focus on agrarian India as a globalising context brings the discussion of continuities and changes in marriage and kinship to a sector which is not usually considered globalising. This is still the sector on which the majority of India's population depends. As I have argued, smallholder cultivation is a thoroughly globalised livelihood when foreign and Indian capital have large investments and reap huge returns from it. This is only likely to deepen over time. A lot more empirical research on marriage and kinship in different agricultural regions of the country and the world that are undergoing similar processes of globalisation is called for.

Second, in the essay I examined marriage and kinship in the context of smallholder capitalism. This is the model of a new global development discourse on agriculture. Emanating from the World Bank and other influential institutions, the 'gene revolution' is being promoted as the second Green Revolution, a way to increase agricultural productivity (World Bank 2007). To spread the benefits equitably, the new development strategy is based on increasing smallholder production through contract farming. As I have shown, gender ideologies are at the heart of protecting intellectual property rights in genes and constitutive of the new labour regimes aimed at raising agricultural productivity. Developing a framework to understand how this model is playing out in the field is, therefore, of critical significance not just in India but globally.

The essay's main contribution is to demonstrate that marriage ideologies and practices are changing in relation to forms of labour circulation to enable the social reproduction of labour in smallholder households which are now enmeshed in global market relations and advance capital accumulation on a global scale. The relationship between marriage and smallholder capitalism cannot be reduced to the economic functionality of cultural practices of marriage. Rather, preferential marriage practices are being subtly transformed and, in the process, they sometimes enable labour circulation in the service of capital and, at others, frustrate it. So, for instance, now that girls are moving out of their natal homes before marriage, kinship ideologies legitimate their treatment by emphasising the affective care of employers even as their labour is commodified and disciplined and they are being made responsible for their own reproduction. Sometimes, however, the need to control the pre-marital sexuality of girls leads to the contestation of capital logics by patriarchy. Given these divergent possibilities, a derivative relationship between marriage and smallholder agricultural production, as suggested by the economic literature on marriage, cannot be sustained. Instead, careful empirical research which studies the interplay between material and familial relations is called for.

The essay revisits the 'southern' pattern of marriage, characterised by village and caste endogamy, and demonstrates that while they are still preferred, considerations of dowry, experience, skill and the productivity of daughters-in-law in the new labour regime are weighty concerns, negotiable and contested. Similarly, another feature of the southern pattern, consanguinity, while still prevalent in this region of the south, is shown to be subject to multiple purposes and interpretations. Whether or not to arrange a consanguineous alliance is a struggle which reflects the demands on daughters-in-law in the new labour regime. A consanguineous alliance is now sometimes arranged to access a daughter-in-law who is known to be a good worker with specialised skills. On the other hand, a consanguineous alliance is not pursued if a woman does not want to risk antagonising her natal family by working a consanguineous daughter-in-law too hard. Nor do mothers-in-law want to risk antagonising other co-resident daughters-in-law in a joint household by allowing a niece to work less. The forgoing of a dowry in consanguineous alliances further complicates the stakes, especially when dowries can be used for investments in irrigation, land levelling and inputs which are all essential to smallholders now engaged in highly capital-intensive agriculture.

Several contradictions of smallholder capitalism in the context of contemporary agrarian change are underscored in the essay: the continued reliance of capitalism on various forms of unpaid and unfree labour, the need for smallholders to self-discipline in the pursuit of autonomous cultivation and the freedom to quit wage labour so as to labour for one's self only to be trapped in the unfreedom of the contract. The essay shows how these contradictions are indexed in the contestations over the commodification of kinship and the contradictions in what parents' desire for their daughters and in their daughters-in-law. The sociological literature has long pointed out these conflicts in the normative kinship system; this essay also does so, not only by demonstrating the importance of kinship and marriage as moral and ideological validation for the expropriation of labour at specific times in the current context, but by tracking the dynamics and tensions of kin and family relations over time. By relating changing marriage and kinship patterns to structures of feeling, the affective centrality of relationships are linked to contradictions and patterns of differentiation. The experience of family life under capitalism and how it is experienced are thus discernable in the marriage of affect and exploitation.

Notes

[1] Panipaadu and the names of all the people quoted are pseudonyms.

[2] Cottonseed is the seed that is sown to grow cotton for fibre. This essay is about cottonseed cultivators.

[3] See also Grover (2009).

[4] On labour circulation see Standing (1985).

[5] Contract farming entails individual farmers agreeing to produce exclusively for corporations at a pre-fixed price and quality in exchange for proprietary seed and credit.

[6] Bt refers to *Bacillus thuringiensis*, a soil bacterium from which a gene is inserted into cottonseeds to make cotton plants produce a protein toxic to the American bollworm.

[7] The designation of plants by sex is common to Telugu and scientific English.

[8] For more on Kammas see Upadhya (1988) and Ramamurthy (2011).

[9] This was equal to five-and-a-half years of daily male wages at INR 50 per day in 2006. In comparison, adult females were paid INR 30 and children INR 25. Wages went up by 20 per cent in 2007, due to the National Rural Employment Guarantee Scheme, and even further in 2009 when adult males were paid INR 150, adult females INR 100 and children INR 50 for daily wage labour.

[10] The median age of marriage in Andhra Pradesh is 17.5 years, one of the lowest in India. The reproductive span of rural women was only 5 years in 1990, between the age of 15 and 20, due to an aggressive state-sponsored family planning programme and the widespread acceptance of female sterilisation as contraception (Padmadas et al. 2004).

References

Deshingkar, Priya, and John Farrington. 2006. *Rural Labor Markets and Migration in South Asia: Evidence from India and Bangladesh*. Background paper for the World Development Report, 2008. Available at: http://siteresources.worldbank.org/INTWDR2008/Resources/2795087-191427986785/Rural_Labour_Markets.pdf. Accessed on: 12 December 2007.

Dumont, Louis. 1953. 'The Dravidian Kinship Terminology as an Expression of Marriage'. *Man* 54:34–39.

Dyson, Tim, and Mick Moore. 1983. 'On Kinship Structure, Female Autonomy and Demographic Behaviour in India'. *Population and Development Review* 9 (1): 35–60.

Grover, Shalini. 2009. 'Lived Experiences: Marriage, Notions of Love and Kinship Support Amongst Poor Women in Delhi'. *Contributions to Indian Sociology* 43 (1): 1–33.

Kannabiran, Kalpana. 2006. 'Three-Dimensional Family: Remapping a Multi-disciplinary Approach to Family Studies'. *Economic and Political Weekly* 41 (42): 4427–33.

Karve, Iravati. 1953. *Kinship Organization in India*. Bombay: Asia Publishing House.

Miller, Barbara D. 1981. *The Endangered Sex: Neglect of Female Children in Rural North India*. Ithaca: Cornell University Press.

Monsanto. 2007. *Presentation by Brett Bergmann, Executive Vice President, Global Commercial, at the Credit Suisse 16th Annual Chemical Conference*. Available at: http://www.monsanto.com/pdf/investors/2007/09-26-07.pdf. Accessed on: 1 May 2008.

Munshi, Kaivan, and Mark Rosenzweig. 2007. 'Why is Mobility in India so Low? Social Insurance, Inequality, and Growth'. *NBER Working Paper*.

Padmadas Sabu S., Inge Hutter, and Frans Willekens. 2004. 'Compression of Women's Reproductive Spans in Andhra Pradesh, India'. *International Family Planning Perspectives* 30 (1): 12–19.

Palriwala, Rajni. 1991. 'Transitory Residence and Invisible Work: A Case Study of a Rajasthani Village'. *Economic and Political Weekly* 26 (48): 2763–77.

Rahman, Lupin, and Vijayendra Rao. 2004. 'The Determinants of Gender Equity in India: Examining Dyson and Moore's Thesis with New Data'. *Population and Development Review* 30 (2): 239–68.

Ramamurthy, Priti. 2011. 'Rearticulating Caste: The Global Cottonseed Commodity Chain and The Paradox of Smallholder Capitalism in South India'. *Environment and Planning A* 43:1035–56.

———. 2010. 'Why are Men Doing Floral Sex Work? Gender, Cultural Reproduction, and the Feminization of Agriculture'. *Signs* 35 (2): 387–424.

———. 2004. 'Why is Buying a "Madras" Cotton Shirt a Political Act? A Feminist Commodity Chain Analysis'. *Feminist Studies* 30 (3): 734–79.

———. 2003. 'Material Consumers, Fabricating Subjects: Perplexity, Global Discourses, and Transnational Feminist Research Practices'. *Cultural Anthropology* 18 (4): 524–50.

———. 2000. 'The Cotton Commodity Chain, Women, Work, and Agency in India and Japan: The Case for Feminist Agro-food Systems Research'. *World Development* 28 (3): 551–78.

Rao, N. Sudhakar. 2004. 'Yanadi Kinship Terminology and the Expression of Affinity'. *Contributions to Indian Sociology* 38 (3): 351–75.

Reddy, K. Rajasekhara. 2005. 'Fertility and Mortality Among the Scheduled Caste Madigas of Andhra Pradesh, India'. *Current Science* 88 (10): 1664–68.

Rosenzweig, Mark R., and Oded Stark. 1989. 'Consumption Smoothing, Migration, and Marriage: Evidence from Rural India'. *The Journal of Political Economy* 97 (4): 905–26.

Shah, A. M. 1998. *The Family in India: Critical Essays*. Hyderabad: Orient Longman.

Standing, Guy. 1985. 'Circulation and the Labour Process'. In *Labour Circulation and the Labour Process*, ed. Guy Standing. London: Croom Helm.

Trautmann, Thomas R. 1981. *Dravidian Kinship*. Cambridge: Cambridge University Press.

Uberoi, Patricia. 2003. 'The Family in India: Beyond the Nuclear versus Joint Debate'. In *The Oxford India Companion to Sociology and Social Anthropology* 2:1061–03, ed. Veena Das. New Delhi: Oxford University Press.

Upadhya, Carol B. 1988. 'The Farmer-Capitalists of Coastal Andhra Pradesh'. *Economic and Political Weekly* 23 (28): 1433–42.

Venkateswarlu, Davaluri, and Lucia Da Corta. 2001. 'Transformations in the Age and Gender of Unfree Workers on Hybrid Cotton Seed Farms in Andhra Pradesh'. *Journal of Peasant Studies* 28 (3): 1–36.

Vera-Sanso, Penny. 1999. 'Dominant Daughters-in-Law and Submissive Mothers-in-Law? Co-operation and Conflict in South India'. *Journal of Royal Anthropological Institute* 5 (4): 577–93.

Williams, Raymond. 1977. *Marxism and Literature*. Oxford, England: Oxford University Press.

World Bank. 2007. *Agriculture for Development*. World Development Report, 2008. Washington: The World Bank.

Marriage, Women's Economic Participation and Patterns of Support in Urban Karachi

Anwar Shaheen

Introduction

This essay deals with two major dimensions of women's lives in Pakistan: marriage and paid work. It is based on data collected from urban women of lower and middle strata of the middle class of Karachi, who are engaged in wage work outside the home. Traditionally, these women have been largely dependent upon wages of male breadwinners while they contributed to the household economy through unpaid housework, making items of daily use, and working as unpaid helpers in agriculture and family enterprises. With capitalist economic development women's waged work increased. While for some women entry into waged work was for personal satisfaction and for others it was to achieve better living standards, yet for most work outside the home was due to economic exigency and necessity. Changes in economic policies such as recent neoliberal reforms have affected the availability of work for men—the traditional breadwinners—making families more vulnerable and driving women into paid work. Due to rapid economic changes, families are also migrating, relocating and trying to diversify their economic portfolios. In the process some traditional cultural values are defied, particularly those circumscribing women's roles. As a result, some socio-cultural barriers to women's entry in the workforce are, perforce, breaking down.

Cultural norms in Pakistan have defined marriage as being compulsory, natural and the preferred mode of adult life for women; this ideological primacy given to marriage and domestic life has critical implications for women's work. This essay argues that women's efforts to combine marriage and wage work are negotiated by two sets of actions embedded in the culture-gender structure of the society and these actions/arrangements determine the nature of women's economic participation before and after marriage, as also their control over income earned through paid work. I have labelled these sets of actions as 'patterns of facilitation' and 'patterns of support' corresponding to two stages of a woman's life—before and after marriage. The importance of the study emerges from the fact that both work and marriage have crucial effects on the physical, social, psychological and economic well-being of earning women as well as on their families, especially as women's entry into wage work continues to rise.

The essay is based on the findings of a survey conducted with 240 women engaged in paid work outside the home. A model based on the findings, illustrating the role of supporting and facilitating factors through women's working lives is presented towards the end of the essay.

Women's Work and Gendered Roles

There is a long and rich discussion regarding the material and ideological dimensions of the relationship between women's paid and unpaid work, family structures and gendered inequalities (Engels 1972; Boserup 1970; Mies 1982; Agarwal 1994; Standing 1991). While women's reproductive labour is generally given recognition in some form or the other in every social system, women's productive labour is often made invisible and remains unacknowledged. The labour of women working in family enterprises is taken to be an extension of their domestic tasks; home-based work may suffer the same fate. Even when women's work is paid for, their earnings may be appropriated by other members of the family. Thus the relationship between women's work and their autonomy is not straightforward. As Standing remarks, women's 'access to paid work is constrained by historically and culturally specific concepts of familial dependency and what are considered appropriate behaviours and occupations for women.' (1991: 142–43) Thus, males have greater access to capital and to a variety of earning opportunities, while domesticity is prescribed for women who are viewed as suited to the role of 'carer' and homemaker. The latters' roles are given less value than the men's roles of breadwinners and supporters. As Kabeer (1996: 283) says, 'Women's unpaid—and frequently unacknowledged—domestic responsibilities also represent a prior set of demands on their labour time. ... their ability to participate in other, more remunerative forms of production is likely to be conditioned by the degree of flexibility in their domestic labour as well as by the norms and values which govern access to extra-domestic institutions.'[1]

Given the various inequalities that structure women's status in Pakistani society (and elsewhere), this essay examines the impact of increased female labour force participation on gender relations within the family. It analyses the consequences for cultural notions of women's roles, intra-household relations and marriage. The traditional ideologies of domesticity for women and breadwinning for men are analysed in the context of changed conditions. Working women's perceptions of managing paid work, marriage and family responsibilities simultaneously are explored, as also their views on factors that enable their choice of work and those that impede their work or careers. Finally, it examines whether women's paid work leads to any restructuring of patriarchal gender structures. The survey questions were centred around the impact of women's wage work on their economic condition, psychological and physical well-being, the care and education of children, family life, intra-household relations, and the marital prospects of unmarried earning women.

Women in Pakistan's Labour Force

In mid-2011, the total population of Pakistan was estimated to be 177.1 million. Of these, an estimated number of 87.82 million are women.[2] The urban population was estimated to be 65.3 million in 2011. Urban women of all ages accounted for 48.06 per cent of the total urban population. Distribution of urban women regarding marital status is slightly different from the national data. The distribution shows 56.73 per cent of the 65.3 million as never married, 38.52 per cent as married, 4.5 per cent as widowed and 0.25 per cent as divorced urban women in all ages (Government of Pakistan 2011a). The singulate mean age at marriage for women in Pakistan has been steadily rising. It was 16.9 years in 1951, 20.2 years in 1981 and 21.7 years in 1998 (Sathar 2001).

According to the Labour Force Survey 2009–10, the overall number of people in the labour force is rising; the same being true for the female labour force. However, while there was an increase in the provinces of Punjab and Sindh, in Khyber Pakhtunkhwa and Balochistan there was a decline in the proportion of women in the work force. In the total labour force of 54.92 million, there are estimated to be 12.48 million women working. For the urban areas, these estimates are of 2.08 million women out of a total 16.75 million work force. According to the employment status of women in 2009–10, at the national level their distribution is: employed 0.1 per cent, self-employed 13.6 per cent, unpaid family helpers 66.3 per cent and employees 20 per cent (Government of Pakistan 2011b: 160). Of the women working in the informal sector 49.1 per cent are employees, 28.9 per cent are own-account workers, 21.7 per cent are unpaid family helpers and 0.3 per cent are employers. Their distribution in the urban formal and informal sectors is 30.9 and 69.9 per cent respectively. In urban Sindh, there are an estimated 0.45 million women in the total labour force of 5.72 million (ibid.: 159). This study is based on a sample of urban women from Karachi, a megapolis different from other cities of Sindh province. Hence, the picture that emerges needs to be applied very cautiously to other urban women of Sindh province or Pakistan.

The age-specific activity rate shows that 9.2 and 16.9 per cent females of ages 10–14 and 15–19 respectively, are currently in the labour force. Women above the age of 60 years constitute a substantial proportion, at 14.7 per cent, among them. The highest rate is recorded for women in the ages of 45–49 years. Generally, women workers are under-reported in economic surveys and censuses; feminists in Pakistan have been trying to highlight women's contributions to productive activities in the major economic sectors, including agriculture and services, as well as in unpaid housework. 'The contribution of rural women is recorded to be improving faster as compared with that of urban women in official estimates' (ibid.: 159).

Norms Governing Gender Roles in Pakistani Society

Muslims constitute the majority community at 96.28 per cent according to the 1998 census and hence, Islamic religious values and cultural practices have implications for gender roles and for women's work. As Bano (1997) argues, for Pakistani women conjugal and parenting roles take precedence over other kinds of roles. The ideological primacy of the universal, compulsory marriage prevalent in South Asia is found here as well. No respondent mentioned that women could live alone while being unmarried and self-reliant, with the acceptance of society. Women are expected to stay at home, do housework, bear children and observe purdah.[3] Bano (ibid.: 192) emphasises that in a predominantly agrarian economy with a feudal setup, religious ideology has been deployed to shore up patriarchy and enforce traditional roles for women. Women are expected to confine themselves to the household for protection because of perceived threats to their chastity and morality. Even though the balance of power in marriage depends a lot on the mutual understanding between the couple, generally, husbands take control of financial matters, and women, in keeping with predominant cultural norms, take charge of bringing up children, and maintaining home and social relations (Babar 1992; Farooqui 1992). Although a Muslim woman reserves the right to paid work and has control over her income (The Quran 4:32), women generally defer to male or senior members of the family over the use of their income.

Liberalisation policies have driven out women from low-income households to enter the labour market to meeting survival and other needs of the family. Many women are forced to step out and become earners to support the family. The obligation to protect women and preserve the honour of the family is put to a severe test under these circumstances. As women are unable to live up to culturally and religiously defined ideals, the society accepts their joining the workforce. Lower-class women are allowed freedom of mobility and work, because their very survival depends on being able to earn their living; middle-class families on the other hand, allow women to take up certain kinds of work under pressure of maintaining a higher standard of living. Thus, despite the ideology of domesticity (Standing 1991) the lower class allows greater freedom of mobility to women as their survival is at stake, while middle-class families face the challenge of maintaining both family honour and a high standard of living. While purdah norms may be relaxed due to necessity, and limited mobility may be allowed for education, training and jobs, the sexuality and chastity of women is kept under surveillance at all times, in all possible ways. A survey in Karachi shows that the ethnic groups that most disapprove women working outside the home include Sindhis, Balochis and Pathans, while Punjabis and Urdu-speaking households are more liberal in their attitude (Kazi and Raza 1989).

Due to purdah and restrictions on mobility, a large number of women resort to home-based work which may entail severe exploitation at the hands of middlemen (Sayeed 2001; Shaheen 2012). It is true that self-employed women enjoy a better work environment than subcontracted women, but lack of capital, training and access to market limits their possibilities to earn (Ayub 1994). Both home-based and self-employed women are in a better position to manage their household duties along with waged work than women employed outside, but this may not always be possible. The paid work may be disturbed frequently and women may have less time available for the paid work than needed.

Impact of Paid Work on Women's Lives: Some Findings from the Literature

Studies on the impact of paid work on various aspects of women's lives and on marital and family relations reveal diverse findings. The empowering effect of earning an income on women's status is found to be largely positive (Shaheen 2012; Mirza 2002; Sathar and Kazi 1988). Some studies, however, such as Khattak and Sayeed (2006), show that for lower income groups, traditional cultural limitations and roles determine women's status and women's earnings do not bring any improvement in it. Khattak (2001) asserts that there is no automatic link between women's economic earning and their empowerment or weakening of the patriarchal hold on women. A survey of factory women in Korangi Industrial Area, Karachi, reveals that 'these women are subjugated not by men but by circumstances no matter what their marital status—single, married or divorced ... poverty being their biggest enemy.' (Muzaffar 2008)

Sathar and Kiani (1998) found that working women marry later than non-working women. Young women work to collect their own dowries. Earning by both men and women has become a necessity for an economically secure marriage as a woman's earnings can also assure a strong financial base for the couple before entering into marriage.

Hashmi, Khurshid and Hassan (2007) argued that there was a negative relationship between paid work, marital adjustment and depression. They found that working married women could not pay proper attention to their household duties. Women also faced trouble with the bosses and the work environment. However, non-working married women were no better adjusted in marriage than working married women; both groups had to face depression in their life. Thus, work is not necessarily the cause of stress in a married woman's life.

Findings from a study (Shaheen 2012) with 250 women of five low-income localities of Karachi confirm most of the trends found in other surveys on urban women of Karachi. Forty per cent of these women saved their income and spent it on marriage and dowry after other urgent needs were fulfilled. According to respondents, the other major outcomes of women's job and income, in decreasing order of importance were: economic problems reduced (79.6 per cent), women got control over spending own income (74.4 per cent), personal contentment (70.8 per cent), respect enhanced in the family and the community (58.4 per cent), collected large dowry (54.4 per cent), got awareness of women's rights (52.8 per cent), developed a sense of freedom (50.8 per cent), increased educational level of children (48 per cent), and helped good upbringing of children (47.6 per cent). Women's own feelings about their waged work included: 'women must work to be free of dependence' (82.8 per cent), 'life is successful and useful' (69.6 per cent), 'family life standard improves' (65.2 per cent), 'I am happy as my job helps others' (54.8 per cent), 'I can become a good mother/wife along with being a good worker' (51.2 per cent), 'if circumstances get better I'll leave my job' (46.4 per cent), and 'I'll continue to work under all conditions' (41.2 per cent). Most women in the lowest income bracket were ready to quit work, but those in the better income groups wanted to continue working even if the extra income was no longer needed.

Setting and Methodology of the Present Survey

This survey was conducted in Karachi, the largest metropolis of Pakistan, with a population of 9.2 million in 1998 and growing at 3.4 per cent per annum (inter-censal rate 1981–98) (Government of Pakistan 2004).[4] According to this census, marriage profile of the city showed the following statistics: married (male 53.34 per cent, females 59.13 per cent), never married (male 44.28 per cent, female 32.46 per cent), widowed (male 2.17 per cent, females 7.87 per cent), and divorced (male 0.21 per cent, female 0.54 per cent). Average household size was 6.8 persons. Karachi is a highly multi-ethnic and cosmopolitan city. The Government of Pakistan reports that the literate population stood at 68.69 per cent of the total population in 1998; literate females were 64.45 per cent against 72.2 per cent literate males (ibid.: 15, 18, 21, 23, 24). It has a vibrant informal sector alongside the modernising formal sectors of economy.

Industrial, commercial and port activities provide a highly diverse employment market in Karachi. One quarter of the city population was economically active in 1998. Here, the employed women included private sector employees (36.8 per cent), government employees (27.07 per cent), self-employed (14.77 per cent), unpaid family helpers (13.93 per cent), and employers (2.55 per cent). Women were mostly employed in community, social and personal services (53.44 per cent), and manufacturing (19.26 per cent) (Government of Pakistan 2004: 36).

This highly stratified city has localities easily classifiable according to socio-economic criteria, but within any locality there is considerable variation. This sample included higher-income, middle-income and low-income areas. Some areas are dominated by one or two ethnic communities, those selected in the sample (listed in Appendix) are mostly diverse, so the major ethnic groups are represented.

The survey population was restricted to women who earn a regular income, in the formal or informal sectors, and leave their home for at least four hours a day. Mothers with young children were specially included to highlight their conditions. Occupational variety was maintained, which also served the purpose of selecting women with a range of education.

Survey Findings and Interpretation

The respondents were mostly concentrated in the age bracket of 26–45 years, with the mean age being 36.6 years. Of these, 16.9 per cent were illiterate or educated to different levels up to matriculation, 14.2 per cent had passed the higher secondary exam, 37.5 per cent were graduates, 23.7 per cent were postgraduates while 5.4 per cent had a medical degree. Among lower middle-income families in the sample, higher education of daughters has become a norm because it ensures jobs with a good income and good proposals for marriage. Fifty-five per cent of the respondents lived in nuclear households and 45 per cent in joint households. In a majority of the cases, the surveyed women spent six to eight hours outside home (the mean being 7.1 hours), which is a fairly long time considering the needs of child care.

An overwhelming number (89.2 per cent) responded that women should work if they are educated, but the ratio favouring paid work after marriage dropped to 75.8 per cent. The reasons given as to why paid work before marriage should be encouraged included: utility of education and job, relieving the economic burden of parents and family, contributing to national development, and gaining confidence, a sense of responsibility and maturity. Work was also seen to enhance the ability to exercise judgement, self-actualisation, self-reliance, gaining experience that may help in post-marriage crises, and raising social status along with accumulation of dowry. The reported negative aspect of paid work before marriage was the dependence of the natal family on a daughter's income, thereby causing a delay in her marriage. Unmarried girls were, instead, advised to learn household skills.

Reasons for favouring paid work after marriage referred to a wife supporting and sharing her husband's load, ensuring a better standard of living, better upbringing and education of children, better ability to meet children's demands, and becoming free of the sense of inferiority. Other possible results reported were an active and contented life, improvement in health, self-reliance, and pocket money. It was also believed that a single earner was not sufficient, while economic relief could make life happy and reduce conflict. People who did not favour outside paid work after marriage mentioned factors like the increase in responsibilities, causing neglect of children as well as social disapproval. They suggested that women could earn through home-based work. A notable feature was that the positive responses were tied to various conditions if women were to work: 'permission from the husband and his family', 'children and family life should not be affected', 'if joint family takes care of children', 'out of necessity', 'if she has time', and 'only if she is a professional'.

These responses overwhelmingly endorse the traditional ideologies of patriarchal control, in-laws' control and domesticity. The benefits of paid work are accepted only under economic pressures even though the advantages of dual/multiple earning have been accepted widely, as shown by the data given in Table 8.2. Women are expected to support their families both before and after marriage. Thus women's participation in the workforce is clearly in contradiction with ideologically privileged patriarchal and religious societal norms, making its acceptance difficult, and increasing the challenges women face in pursuing career goals or supporting families. Women's workforce participation is accommodated by maintaining surveillance over their freedom and, wherever possible, prescribing the type of work considered more suitable for women, work that is congruent with their domestic roles.

Findings from the Survey

The sections below present findings from the survey and interpret women's responses. Child care is one of the most pressing and unattended problems that working mothers face. Table 8.1 identifies those who take responsibility for the children when the mother is away at work. The statistics reveal the network of care that women need to nurture in order to go out to work. Kinship and family links remain the most important while servants and day care centres are far behind. In poor families, the children may be left to fend for themselves or in the care of older siblings. Patrilocal residence norms ensure that mostly paternal relatives are in-charge, followed by maternal relatives.

Table 8.1: Substitute Caretaker of Children in Mother's Absence

Relation to the child	*Frequency*	*Percentage*
Paternal grandparents	56	23.3
Father's sister/sister-in-law	31	12.9
Father	15	6.3
Maternal grandparents	33	13.8
Mother's sister	17	7.1
Mother's brother/brother's wife	5	2.1
Children's elder sister	7	2.9
Neighbour woman	14	5.8
Servant woman	14	5.8
Day care centres	3	1.2
No one cares	34	14.2
Children are grown-up	14	5.8
No children	27	11.3
No response	1	0.4

Note: Multiple responses.
N = 240.

Thirty-six per cent of the women relied on their in-laws for child care, and only 6.25 per cent on husbands. Fathers rarely cared for children (6.25 per cent) and that too only when they happened to be at home. Mostly such fathers have shift jobs and hence can be at home when the mother is away. The women's natal family were the other main carers, in 23 per cent cases, and servants and day care were resorted to in only seven per cent of the cases. Neighbours were asked to oversee children in only four of the families, given the lack of networks of reciprocity among urban residents. The children in these families were older and hence did not require much supervision. A large 14.2 per cent of families left children in the care of their siblings—themselves young in age—because of a lack of substitute care.

TABLE 8.2: Perceptions of Impact of Women's Waged Work in the Households of Married Women

Nature of impact	*Degree of impact*		
	Yes	*Somewhat*	*No*
Economic Effect			
Increase in household income and reduction in economic problems	162 (67.5)	62 (25.8)	14 (5.8)
Raising standard of living of the household	166 (69.2)	54 (22.5)	19 (7.9)
Psychological/Physical Effects for Women			
Women feel they are leading a productive and successful life	135 (56.3)	77 (32.1)	24 (10.0)
Feel secure in case of crisis	138 (57.7)	66 (27.6)	24 (10.0)
Freedom from sense of dependence	123 (51.3)	84 (35.0)	30 (1.3)
Negative impact on women's health and housework	84 (35.0)	93 (38.8)	62 (25.8)
Patriarchal Control			
Women meeting their personal needs easily	186 (77.5)	43 (17.9)	9 (3.8)
Women's control in household enhanced	89 (37.1)	100 (41.7)	48 (20.0)
Men sharing housework	63 (26.4)	89 (37.2)	87 (36.4)
Men feeling inferior	55 (22.9)	48 (20.2)	134 (55.8)
Men perturbed at wife's economic independence	39 (16.3)	36 (15.0)	162 (67.5)
Men's household duties reduced	113 (47.3)	91 (38.1)	31 (13.0)

(Contd.)

(Table 8.2 Contd.)

Nature of impact	*Degree of impact*		
	Yes	*Somewhat*	*No*
Child Care, Training and Education			
Negative impact on children's education	46 (19.2)	73 (30.4)	111 (46.3)
Children become more disciplined and responsible	129 (53.8)	63 (26.3)	30 (12.5)
Children feel ignored and show disobedience	49 (20.5)	59 (24.7)	113 (47.3)
Family Life			
Family life becomes more disciplined/ punctual	172 (71.7)	39 (16.3)	27 (11.3)
Women lead a more purposeful life	174 (72.5)	41 (17.1)	21 (8.8)
Women become more confident thus life become easy	178 (74.2)	45 (18.8)	13 (5.4)
Intra-household Relations			
Other women show jealousy and create problems	63 (26.3)	64 (26.7)	108 (45.0)
Women face allegations from the in-laws about their character	52 (21.7)	61 (25.4)	114 (47.5)
Employed women take little part in quarrels with mother-in-law	130 (54.6)	59 (24.8)	29 (12.2)
Marriage of Women			
Problems emerge in arranging marriage of employed girls	67 (27.9)	84 (35.0)	82 (34.2)

Note: The missing numbers account for 'no response'
Percentage in parentheses.
N = 240.

Data presented in Table 8.2 show the impact of women's income on different aspects of their lives. The explanations given by respondents for their answers are outlined below.

Economic Effects

The greatest advantage accruing from women's earnings is an increase in household income and alleviation of the economic problems of the household (93 per cent). Those who did not feel a positive impact mostly belonged to the lower-income bracket, or female-headed households. Some respondents were dissatisfied due to high inflation, economic difficulties or their own inadequate wage. Two respondents referred to the traditional notion of *barkat* (meaning, women's income cannot bring prosperity and divine blessing). On the whole, the impression was of satisfaction with women's income and that, 'if I had not been earning, there would have been a plethora of problems'. The satisfaction was also explained in terms of the easier provision of women's own personal needs, children's educational expenses and favourite games, or entertainment. Only three women reported a higher level of savings and one mentioned meeting beauty parlour bills with her own income.

Regarding improvement in standard of living, the response was overwhelmingly positive (91.7 per cent) showing a direct link between women's contribution to the family income resulting in a higher standard of living. Respondents who were dissatisfied were largely complaining about high prices and low incomes, high cost of education, and increase in desires they wished to fulfill.

Psychological and Physical Effects on Women

The most positive effect reported was freedom from dependence on men (86.3 per cent). Women also felt that they were leading a useful and fruitful life (88.4 per cent), and felt assured of economic security in case of any crisis (85.3 per cent cases). In three-fourths (73.8 per cent) of the cases, the women did report some negative health consequences, while one-quarter of the women did not. The latter mentioned the following factors as contributing to lack of health problems: small family size, sharing of housework, good management, availability of domestic help, easy nature of work, and family members being considerate. Severe problems in health were reported mostly by domestic helpers and factory labourers. These arise due to the excess burden of work once waged work and housework had to be combined: long working hours, less sleep, demands of caring for small children, and looking after older family members. Among those with lower income, women's multiple health problems were a regular feature due to overwork, malnutrition, and lack of health care.

Patriarchal Control

Answers to questions exploring aspects of patriarchal control generally showed that, though women were enabled to meet their personal needs easily due to personal income and men's household responsibilities were reduced by a large amount (85.4 per cent of cases), increase in women's decision-making in household matters did not take place in the same proportion. In 31 per cent of the cases men felt somewhat disturbed, and in 42 per cent of the cases men felt frustrated due to the waged work of women. Only in

16.3 per cent cases were men reported to be happy; these men, wanting to see women progress and empowered, helped their women keep their jobs. This group included men who preferred working women as marriage partners. The majority of respondents expressed their belief that earning made women confident, assertive and free from men's dominance. Responses indicated that husbands who had an open and progressive mind and trusted their wives were not threatened by women's economic independence, while those who believed in male superiority found it harder to accept working wives. Some men had contradictory feelings as they were happy that family income was enhanced, but were jealous and felt insecure about their wives going out to work. In many cases, they were unable to conceal their frustration. In one case, a non-earning husband would chase and keep a watch on his wife whenever she went to work as a domestic helper.

Men have largely accepted women's going-out to work, but have not started sharing housework, as reported in more than half (55 per cent) of the cases. Only 22.9 per cent were sharing it wholeheartedly. The other 20.2 per cent shared to some extent, which meant they shared whatever and whenever they wished to—mostly preferring to do less demanding or outdoor work related to home management. More helpful men were usually those who worked in the absence or illness of the wife, but even they would do only a few necessary things. They may already have been doing light tasks like preparing tea or helping a bit in the kitchen. This clearly shows that gender ideology related to housework has not changed significantly. Men's household responsibilities outside the home are in fact lessened due to women's increased mobility, confidence and personal income.

Children

Generally positive effects were reported, though it was reported that children's education and upbringing was affected to some extent. Children were largely reported as being more disciplined due to the mother's work outside home. However, many children felt ignored, and bad behaviour was reported by 45.2 per cent. Yet, the mother's absence is not the single decisive factor for bad behaviour; several factors such as the amount of time spent with children, the attitude of the rest of the family members, and proper upbringing also shape their behaviour.

Family Life

It was generally reported that daily life was better organised when women did things quickly and went out regularly. They felt that they had developed a sense of leading a purposeful and fruitful life, and could solve problems due to the confidence gained through working outside home.

Intra-household Relations

Relations within the household were also not affected negatively due to women's jobs in the majority of the cases, as women's paid work is becoming an accepted norm. It is widely accepted that working women find little time to engage in quarrels with the in-laws whose help they seek in child care and household chores.

To ensure that women continue to perform their domestic roles properly, they are provided support by the family, while leaving patriarchal ideologies and women's dependency intact. Economic earning does give women some role in decision-making regarding their own lives and the family they support, but even this limited role is reduced in case the support is provided by kin/her natal family, the joint family or any other relative. In fact, women's autonomy in decision-making is greater if they do not have to depend on kin and family for support.

Marriage of Women

Many now feel that an unmarried woman's paid work improves her prospects in the marriage market, but this is not the case for a good number of households that still follow a traditional ideology. A broad range of attitudes prevails, from very conservative to very liberal, but the basic fact remains that traditional people do not like women to work.[5] Interestingly, in-laws use the right to decide whether the bride will work after marriage or not as a bargaining chip in pre-marriage negotiations. A woman's paid work may actually be needed to support the family income in a majority of the cases, but in-laws show resistance to allowing her to work after marriage in order to retain control over her. They impose conditions such as 'she will have to give up her job if we wish so', 'she has to give her money to the husband or mother-in-law', or 'she cannot give money to her parents', etc. The in-laws fear that a woman may not be able to adequately perform her role as wife, daughter-in-law or mother due to the timing and nature of a job or her long absence from home. There are also worries about women mixing with males at the workplace (in factories, banks and health facilities), developing independent behaviour, assertiveness or a non-compromising attitude or ignoring the family due to work responsibilities, which may take priority. Greed is shown by the groom's side when they demand a larger dowry. Earning women are also preferred for marriage in families in which men tend to evade the responsibility of earning.

Table 8.3 reflects the perception of respondents showing flexibility in the notion of only men being responsible for breadwinning, and it is further confirmed by acceptance of women's waged work though it is taken as a solution

TABLE 8.3: Opinion about the Need for Women's Paid Work and the Ideology of Breadwinning

Statement	*Yes*	*Somewhat*	*No*	*Total*
Only men should be responsible for providing financial resources in the household	67 (28.0)	53 (22.2)	119 (49.8)	239 (100.0)
Women should not raise the issue of job in marriage arrangements	111 (46.4)	41 (17.2)	87 (36.4)	239 (100.0)
Women should not go for waged work in early years of marriage	114 (47.9)	44 (18.5)	80 (33.6)	238 (100.0)
Unless children become mature, women should not go for waged work	96 (40.3)	74 (31.4)	66 (28.0)	236 (100.0)
After marriage job should be taken up only in case of sheer necessity	139 (58.2)	31 (13.0)	69 (28.9)	239 (100.0)
Economic stringency has made women's work acceptable, otherwise it is not proper for them to work outside the home	148 (61.9)	55 (23.0)	36 (15.1)	239 (100.0)
If job is easy and does not disturb the household responsibilities, it is okay	202 (84.2)	29 (12.1)	9 (3.8)	240 (100.0)
Employed women fare better in joint family	121 (50.6)	60 (25.1)	58 (24.3)	239 (100.0)
Employed women fare better in nuclear family	86 (36.1)	55 (23.1)	97 (40.8)	238 (100.0)
Men are impressed by an earning wife	56 (23.8)	85 (36.2)	94 (40.0)	235 (100.0)
Men are ashamed of an earning wife	26 (10.9)	55 (23.0)	158 (66.1)	239 (100.0)
Relations between spouses become more equal and male control is lessened	49 (20.6)	75 (31.5)	114 (47.9)	238 (100.0)
An employed woman keeps her home tidy	102 (42.7)	106 (44.4)	31 (13.0)	238 (100.0)

Note: N varies.
Percentage in parentheses.

to economic hardships caused by poor economic conditions. About two-thirds of the respondents agreed to the statement that women should not bring up the issue of working in marriage negotiations, thus indicating priority of marriage over paid work for females. Again, two-thirds of the responses (66.4 per cent) also supported the idea that women should avoid waged work in early years of marriage, but the number of responses favouring work outside the home once children have grown up was slightly higher (71.7 per cent). About 85 per cent of the responses showed acceptance of women's paid work in the face of economic problems. The most striking is the 96 per cent favourable response for a woman's job if it is easy and does not conflict with her household or child care responsibilities. This explains why teaching is very popular with women, apart from being taken as a natural extension of the feminine role of motherhood. Joint-family living is declared to be comparatively more suitable for working women (75.7 per cent) as compared to the nuclear family (59.2 per cent), as help of family members is needed to take care of household chores that the working woman cannot perform. About one-fifth of the respondents confirmed with 'Yes', another 31.5 per cent expressed 'Somewhat' impact, but 47.9 per cent respondents rejected outright the conclusion that female independence due to waged work leads to lessening of male control and greater equality in marriage. Both sets of responses to the statements about husbands' feeling about wives' jobs confirm widespread acceptance and largely no negative feeling of being ashamed (66.1 per cent), while there was a slightly better response (23.8 per cent) to being impressed, which may be encouraging for women. Women explained that their jobs did not threaten or damage male dominance, which is quite resilient due to socio-cultural norms and political-economic power. Efficiency of working women regarding housework and keeping their homes tidy is found negatively affected in only 13 per cent of the cases and somewhat affected in 44.4 per cent of the cases. This is explained as a result of time constraint or the natural disposition of women whether or not they work outside. Since women undertake a double burden and try to justify their jobs by not ignoring the household, their responses show the same views.

Discussion

The findings of the study show a clear shift in women taking up waged work in greater numbers even as the ideology of the male breadwinner remains intact. Men and families are seen to adjust to women's paid work outside the household as the latter's income allows families to either stay afloat or improve their economic circumstances. Women, however, may have multiple reasons for taking up paid work, of which contributing towards family well-being is primary. Women also feel more in control of their households and their lives, and enjoy the benefits of personal income. While they may also enjoy independence derived from earning an income and being able to do things on their own and may feel 'modern', their economic independence does not necessarily or automatically translate into greater gender equality. It also means that the feeling of gaining more equal and egalitarian status within the family is felt and appreciated mostly by women, while men are still not supportive of the ideology of women's equality. One reason for this is their superior position in the overall structures of power, within the family, community, economy, religion and state. Collectively, men are perceived to be welcoming of changes brought about by women's earnings since it partially relieves the burden on them, improves living standards while they do not have to pay any significant costs for it. This is obvious from their nominal sharing of housework and other duties, which largely remain an obligation of women, and which men may undertake only under duress—such as when a wife or child is sick. Therefore, the change in gender ideology based on the sexual division of labour seems far slower than the pace of acceptance of women's paid work outside the home.

The effect on family relations is also critical in the sense that women feel more secure in a joint family when they have to go out and children need substitute care. A nuclear family in that case poses more problems. On the other hand, the feeling of jealousy and allegations of immorality are directed more towards working women by women of the joint family. However, such attitudes seem to be gradually weakening.

Patterns of Support and Facilitation for Women's Wage Work: A Model

Based on major findings of the study quoted above as well as of those mentioned in the section on review, a diagram is presented in Figure 8.1.

The diagram presents various stages in a woman's life regarding paid work and support. The decision made in the private domain is affected by both push and pull factors. Push factors include insufficient income, absence or illness of a male breadwinner, and higher aspirations.

Pre-Marriage Stage

At the pre-marriage stage, a needy natal family grants a woman permission to work and facilitates this by helping her in case she faces a problem in commuting, attaining competence, performing well, or a dispute at the work place. The support and facilitation provided by the family affects her own claim over her income according to the needs and preferences of the family, lessening her own control over her earnings. A mother remarked in a derogatory manner, 'If we do not use their income, what are these daughters good for? Where would they take this money? From where would we feed them?' Furthermore, Islam prescribes rules for spending men's income, making it obligatory to give first preference to the family, while there is no such rule for women. Therefore, it is automatically assumed that when women go out to earn out of sheer necessity,

FIGURE 8.1: Patterns of Support and Facilitation for Women's Wage Work

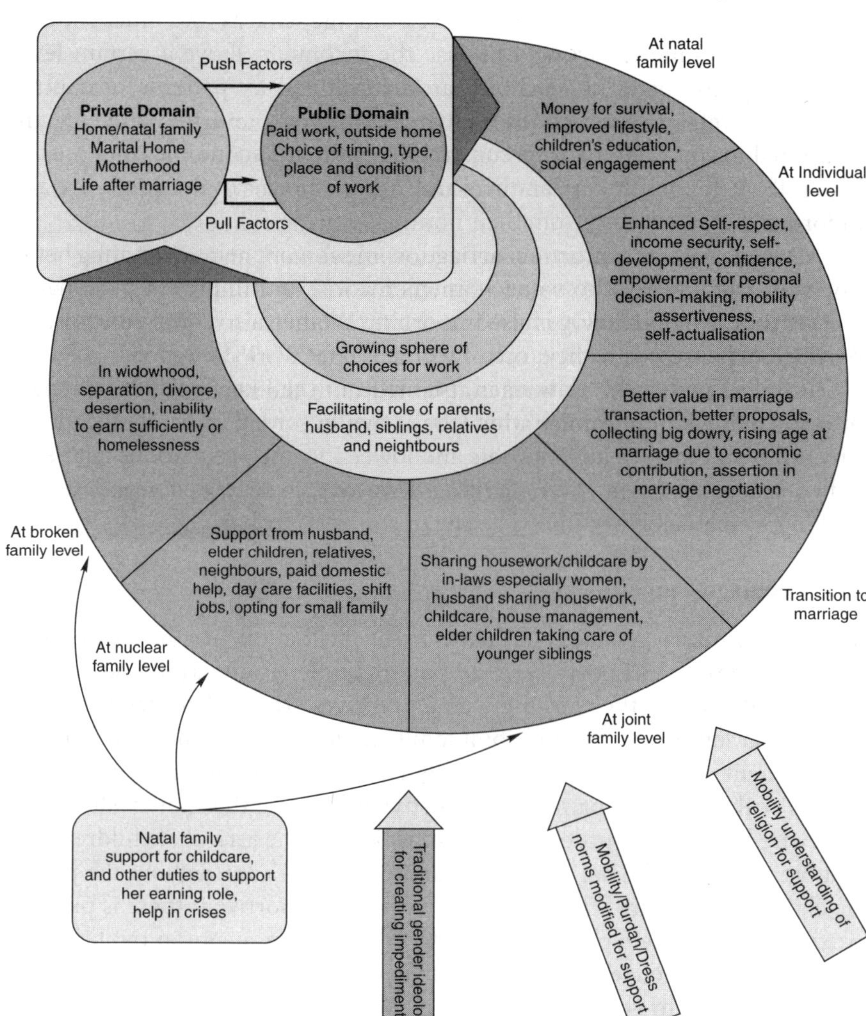

Source: Drawn by author

they are taking up men's role, so their income should be treated in the same way as men's income is.

The pull factors which attract a woman to paid labour include the benefits of extra income such as personal grooming, self-development, enhanced confidence, independence in terms of personal and family affairs, betterment of lifestyle, improved standard of living, income security, savings, better education, recreation for the siblings, support to parents, and better self-image due to respect granted by paid work. Even old-age security and independence from men's income is expected in case the income is above a certain level. For women, the patterns of choice are determined by patterns of control. The former refer to the actions allowing paid work, and the latter are the traditional norms and practices constraining women's economic roles outside the family. Religious understandings and cultural norms of the family are also important.

At the stage of transition to marriage, women's work helps in inviting better proposals from those who value women's income and improved personality, while expecting good dowry is also important. Women also contribute towards marriage expenses with their own income. Hafeez (1981), reporting on the conditions of metropolitan women, pointed out the likely delay in marriage for women in public administration jobs as they accorded more significance to careers; also women in high, middle and lower-income occupations felt better and confident while they were earning. However, in marriage negotiations a working woman's job becomes an issue of control over her.

Post-Marriage Stage

At the post-marriage stage, the patterns of facilitation become patterns of support; the pre- and post-marriage patterns differ in the kind and amount of practical support the working woman receives. These also vary with joint and nuclear family set-ups. In a joint family, a wife's duty of housework, house management and child care is partially shared by the husband and female in-laws if they are sympathetic, supportive and value the money she earns; otherwise her double burden turns into triple with the arrival of children. The support of joint and natal families facilitates her work throughout the period the children need care. The natal family can be supportive if there is physical proximity and someone can visit or stay regularly for a substantial length of time. Mostly, women leave their children at the home of parents or brothers or sisters to be able to go to work. If this is not the regular pattern, natal family support is extended in times of crisis, extra engagements, sickness or long absence. Women's going to their parental home at childbirth is a traditional practice, but this is now deployed towards facilitating their economic role. This is usually done in addition to support from in-laws.

In the case of a nuclear family, women are facilitated by husbands and older kids. When this is not possible, they seek paid domestic help or day care facilities, if these are affordable. Women seek help when living in a nuclear set-up, because the needs of childbearing and child caring go on for many years. Even the children's school timings vary and the chores of picking and dropping may clash with the mother's working hours. Office or factory work and professional jobs like doctors, lawyers, nurses, bankers and engineers, pose problems for which the family has to again facilitate them. Undoubtedly, better income enables them to afford a babysitter or day care, but again children's supervision and study is at stake. In this sense, the joint family is preferred by working women with small children. Jobs which create the least conflict with domestic duties are therefore preferred.

Co-existing with the patterns of support are patterns of impediments or obstacles which generate conflict and tension. These emanate from traditional patriarchal ideologies, women's modesty, and honour and motherhood. Two other situations of conflict are when the husband tries to grab the wife's income on various pretexts and the jealousy of other women in the family, because they do not earn or have less satisfying lives due to financial reasons. The usual patterns include moral allegations, discord, violence, demand for more children or specifically more sons, and not allowing her to seek the services of a servant or request help from the natal family. Control on her mobility, sexuality and independence is asserted to discourage her from remaining in paid work. Patterns of impediment in life-after-marriage correspond to patterns of control in life-before-marriage. Though the control itself continues after marriage it assumes more the form of denial of practical support than psychological and verbal forms.

If a woman's marriage breaks down, she is supported by the natal family and sometimes other relatives, to earn for herself and her children and sometimes for the in-laws as well.

In this way, at all stages of life women's economic pursuit is tacitly supported by families. The ideology of domesticity is perhaps the one more in need of drastic change than the ideology of breadwinner, since the latter has been gradually shifting in favour of accepting women's income from (non-family) public spheres. The institution of marriage is slowly adapting to women's paid work, but women's domestic and reproductive roles still pose a great challenge to gender equality especially in the absence of facilities to support their mothering role. Such structural conditions perpetuate control over women's lives even if support is offered. Laws for providing day care are rarely implemented. Amendments in laws are being demanded in Pakistan to abolish the condition of maximum age for employment of women and to ensure maternity benefits in private sector jobs, but so far no success has been achieved. Many structural and cultural biases prevail against married women's participation in economic activities and this issue still needs to be addressed.

Conclusion

Four major conclusions can be drawn from this study. First, the asymmetry of relationship between the husband and wife will continue in the foreseeable future, because the conditions which support this asymmetry—specified by the culture-gender system—are not being challenged. Second, it is generally due to economic pressure and aspirations of women that their role in employment is increasing. Third, the ideology of domesticity is weakening much too slowly. It is, in fact, the dynamics of economic relations within the family, which, if handled properly, can make some alteration, since the acceptance of authority based on earning power is visible. Fourth, women have been assuming more power at least over their personal lives and in contributing to household income; however, this is not generally perceived as a threat to traditional patriarchal control. Rather a neo-patriarchal set-up is emerging, because the support women get from their natal and conjugal families to cope with the pressures of double and triple roles, and to overcome role conflict prevents any serious challenge being posed to existing male dominance and the gendered division of labour.

Appendix

Background Information about the Respondents and Survey Data

Survey Localities

These included Defence Housing Society, Gulshan-e-Iqbal, North Nazimabad, Gulistan-e-Jauhar, PIB Colony, Gulzar-e-Hijri, Federal B. Area, Nazimabad, Tariq Bin Zayad Society, Pak Kausar Town, Shah Faisal Colony, Rehmanabad, Shadman Town, Nagan Chorangi, Korangi, Saddar, Jamshed Town, Metroville SITE, Saeedabad, Indus Mehran, Model Colony, Saudabad, Malir, Alfalah Society, and Sir Syed Town, North Karachi, Landhi, Sohrab Goth, New Karachi, Nai Abadi, Orangi Town, Sher Shah, Khokhrapar, Agra Taj and Surjani Town. In this way different areas of city were fairly represented.

Table 8A.1: Respondents by Age

Age (years)	*Frequency*	*Percentage*
19–25	11	4.6
26–35	113	47.1
36–45	89	37.1
46–55	25	10.4
56 and above	2	0.8
Total	240	100.0

Note: Median 35; mode 30; variance 56.5.

TABLE 8A.2: Respondents by Educational Qualification

Education	*Frequency*	*Percentage*
Illiterate	8	3.3
Primary/Quran literate	3	1.3
Middle	9	3.7
Secondary	23	9.6
Intermediate	34	14.2
BA	90	37.5
MBBS	13	5.4
MA	56	23.3
M.Phil.	1	0.4
Diploma in Nursing	3	1.3
Total	240	100.0

Note: Median at Graduation; Variance at 1.66.

TABLE 8A.3: Respondents by Marital Status

Marital status	*Frequency*	*Percentage*
Married	226	94.2
Widowed	8	3.3
Divorced	1	0.4
Separated/Deserted	5	2.1
Total	240	100.0

TABLE 8A.4: Respondents by Present Occupation

Occupation	*Frequency*	*Percentage*
Teaching	117	48.8
Factory worker	34	14.2
Medical doctor	20	8.3
Beautician	15	6.2
Office work/management	11	4.6
Nursing	11	4.6

(Contd.)

(Table 8A.4 Contd.)

Occupation	*Frequency*	*Percentage*
Domestic service	9	3.7
Banker	9	3.7
Customer service	3	1.3
Miscellaneous	11	4.6
Total	240	100.0

Note: Respondent women are largely concentrated in the services sector which constitutes the major employer in urban areas. The variety of selected occupations is much larger. Respondents were mostly employed by others, except a few tutors, doctors and beauticians who were self-employed.

TABLE 8A.5: Working Women's Hours Spent Outside Home

Hours	*Frequency*	*Percentage*
Up to 5	47	19.6
6–8	137	57.1
9–11	43	17.9
12 and more	13	5.4
Total	240	100.0

TABLE 8A.6: Respondents by Reported Household Monthly Income

Monthly income (PKR)	*Frequency*	*Percentage*
Up to 10,000	62	25.8
11,000–20,000	83	34.6
21,000–30,000	57	23.8
31,000–50,000	26	10.8
51,000–75,000	5	2.1
76,000–1,00,000	3	1.3
Above 1,00,000	4	1.6
Total	240	100.0

Note: The household monthly income was to a large extent under-reported, and in many cases only personal income was reported as household income. Better reporting is seen in the income bracket above PKR 30,000. Mean income lay between PKR 31,000–50,000, indicating a lower-middle-class income.

TABLE 8A.7: Respondents by Size of Household

Size	*Frequency*	*Percentage*
1–3	37	15.5
4–6	111	46.3
7–9	58	24.2
10–12	19	8.0
More than 12	15	6.0
Total	240	100.0

Note: Mean household size was 6.47 persons.

TABLE 8A.8: Respondents by Composition of Their Family

Number	*Males*		*Females*		*Children*	
	No.	*Per cent*	*No.*	*Per cent*	*No.*	*Per cent*
1	129	54.9	111	46.3	38	17.8
2–3	80	34.1	87	36.2	123	57.7
4–5	23	9.8	39	16.3	42	19.8
6–8	3	1.2	3	1.2	10	4.7
Total	235	100.0	240	100.0	213	100.0

Note: In the sample households, five households had no males and 27 had no children under the age of 15 years.

NOTES

[1] Also see Kabeer (1996: 95–135, 264–306) for discussion on household economics, institutional hierarchy, power and control.

[2] Women comprised 49.59 per cent of the total population in the 1998 census. This proportion is assumed here for the purpose of this chapter due to the absence of fresh census data.

[3] Purdah may be viewed as a set of rules aimed at segregating women physically from men, hiding their body and identity when they are in public places, ensuring women's behaviour such as to maintain distance, and show disinterest and disregard for the male world even if they earn their living in that world. The main purpose of purdah is to control a woman's sexuality, and safeguard her chastity and the honour of male kin.

[4] Data provided in this introduction of Karachi is rather old for being based on the 1998 census (Government of Pakistan 2004: 15–16) figures. The next census of 2011 is underway.

[5] According to the survey findings and author's own extensive observation, such people refer to women's mixing with unknown men and women's earning as threats to family honour. Moreover, there are people who justify restricting women's mobility and paid work in the name of religious norms.

References

Agarwal, Bina. 1994. *A Field of One's Own: Gender and Land Rights in South Asia*, Cambridge: Cambridge University Press.

Ayub, Nasreen. 1994. *Self-employed Women in Karachi*. Karachi: Pakistan Association of Women Studies.

Babar, Najma. 1992. 'Balance of Power in Marriage'. *Dawn, Tuesday Review*. 23–30 June, 6–7.

Bano, Sabra. 1997. 'Women, Class and Islam in Karachi'. In *Family and Gender in Pakistan: Domestic Organization in a Muslim Society*, eds. Hasting Donnan and Frits Selier, 189–207, New Delhi: Hindustan Publishing Corporation.

Boserup, Ester. 1970. *Women's Role in Economic Development*. New York: St Martin's Press.

Engels, Friedrich. 1972 Reprint. First published in 1884. *The Origin of the Family, Private Property and the State*. London: Lawrence and Wishart.

Farooqui, Bushra. 1992. 'Who is at the Helm of Affairs?' *Dawn, Tuesday Review*, 23–30 June, 9.

Government of Pakistan. 2011a. *Labour Force Survey 2010–11*. Islamabad: Statistics Division, Federal Bureau of Statistics.

_______. 2011b. *Pakistan Economic Survey 2010–11*. Islamabad: Finance Division, Economic Adviser's Wing.

_______. 2004. *City Report, Karachi City, Population and Housing Census 1998*. Islamabad: Statistics Division, Population Census Organization.

Hafeez, Sabeeha. 1981. *Metropolitan Women in Pakistan*. Karachi: Royal Books.

Hashmi, H. A., M. Khurshid, and I. Hassan. 2007. 'Marital Adjustment, Stress, and Depression among Working and Non-Working Married Women'. *Internet Journal of Medical Update* 2 (1): 19–26, January–June. Available at: http://www.geocities.com/agnihotrimed. Accessed on: 11 November 2011.

Kabeer, Naila. 1996. *Reversed Realities, Gender Hierarchies in Development Thoughts*. Karachi: Oxford University Press.

Kazi, Shahnaz, and Bilquees Raza. 1989. 'Women in the Informal Sector: Home-based Workers in Karachi'. *Pakistan Development Review* 28 (4): 777–88. Available at: http://www.pide.org.pk/pdf/PDR/1989/Volume4/777-788.pdf. Accessed on: 8 November 2012.

Khattak, Saba Gul. 2001. *Women, Work and Empowerment*. Karachi: Pakistan Institute of Labour Education and Research.

Khattak, Saba Gul, and Asad Sayeed. 2006. *Pakistan ki Karkun Khawateen*. Karachi: World Social Forum.

Mies, Maria. 1982. *The Lace Makers of Narsapur: Indian Housewives Produce for the World Market*. London: Zed Press.

Mirza, Jasmin. 2002. *Between Chaddor and the Market Female Office Workers in Lahore*. Karachi: Oxford University Press.

Muzaffar, Iram Noor. 2008. 'Tales of Sorrow'. *The News* 19 (11): 1.

Sathar, Zeba A. 2001. 'Fertility in Pakistan: Past, Present and Future'. *Workshop on Prospects for Fertility Decline in High Fertility Countries*. New York: Population Division, Department of Economic Affairs, United Nations Secretariat.

Sathar, Zeba A., and M. Framurz Kiani. 1998. 'Some Consequences of Rising Age at Marriage in Pakistan'. *The Pakistan Development Review* 37, II (4): 548.

Sathar, Zeba A., and Shahnaz Kazi. 1988. *Productive and Reproductive Choices of Metropolitan Women in Karachi*. Islamabad: Pakistan Institute of Development Economics.

Sayeed, Asad. 2001. *Structural Adjustment and its Impact on Women*. Karachi: Pakistan Institute of Labour Education and Research.

Shaheen, Anwar. 2012. 'Urban Women, Alternative Earning Strategies and the Exigencies of Globalization: A Study of Karachi'. In *The Future of Asian Feminism: Confronting Fundamentalisms, Conflicts and Neoliberalism*, ed. S. Seweieringa and N. Katjasungkana, 155–81, Newcastle: Cambridge Scholars Publishing.

Standing, Hillary. 1991. *Dependence and Autonomy: Women's Employment and Family Life in Calcutta*. London: Routledge.

Why Marry A Cousin?

Insights from Bangladesh

Shareen Joshi, Sriya Iyer and Quy Toan Do

Introduction

The practice of consanguineous marriage, or marriage between close biological relatives, shows significant heterogeneity across the world (Bittles 1994; Hussain and Bittles 2000).[1] In the Western world, only 1 per cent of marriages are consanguineous. Estimates elsewhere, however, range from 30 per cent to 50 per cent in Middle Eastern countries, 20 per cent to 40 per cent in North Africa and 10 per cent to 20 per cent in South Asia (Kapadia 1958: 117–37; Naderi 1979; Maian and Mushtaq 1994; Bittles 1994; Bittles 2001).

Most of the research on consanguinity falls into two categories. The first focuses on biological aspects showing that consanguinity leads to higher risks of congenital malformations in offspring and as a result higher levels of infant and child mortality (Schull 1959; Bittles 1994). Consanguineous marriage has also been linked to distinctive reproductive behaviour: lower ages at first marriage, lower ages at first birth and higher levels of fertility are the parameters often discussed (Bittles 1998 and 2001; Iyer 2002).

The second branch of the literature is best described as anthropological or sociological in nature. It explores the social, cultural and religious aspects of this form of marriage. This literature provided rich insights into some of the advantages of such marriage arrangements for families: the preservation of tradition, the consolidation of family structure and property, the strengthening of family ties and avoidance of dowry or bridewealth payments (Bittles 1994; Hussain 1999).

In recent years, economists have increasingly studied marriage practices and marriage markets. Central to these models is the recognition that marriage decisions typically involve tradeoffs between costs and benefits for families (Anderson 2007; Becker 1973, 1981; Bloch and Rao 2002; Jacoby and Mansuri 2006; Rao 1993; Zhang and Chan 1999). Economists argue that many aspects of marriage decisions—marriage timing, partner characteristics, marriage payments, divorce decisions and even the risks of violence in marriage—involve such tradeoffs. This research also shows that marriage decisions are affected by the characteristics of marriage markets. For example, when markets are 'incomplete', i.e. two families cannot credibly commit to some type of future behaviour (such as ensuring no violence towards a bride), certain types of marriages, such as *watta satta* marriages or the exchange of sisters between families, become more likely than others (Jacoby and Mansuri 2006). In particular, a recent essay by Do, Iyer and Joshi (2006) shows how market incompleteness can also lead to consanguinity. We argue that where marriage payments such as dowry are customary, consanguinity may be chosen when a family can neither afford a dowry nor credibly commit to paying a dowry in the future. Instead, by marrying a relative, a family can leverage the trust in kinship ties to promise future transfers in the form of inheritances.

This essay reviews existing explanations of consanguinity in light of empirical evidence from Bangladesh. In our data, we find evidence for higher rates of infant mortality in consanguineous marriages, confirming the insights of the biological literature. We also find some evidence of the role of socio-economic considerations.

The essay is organised as follows: The first section discusses existing explanations for consanguinity. The second section presents a case study of cousin marriage from Bangladesh and the third section concludes.

Existing Explanations of Consanguineous Marriage

The existence of consanguinity between spouses can be attributed to many causes: religious, social or economic (Bittles 1994: 561–84) all of which are reviewed below.

Religion

Religions of the world vary in the extent to which they permit consanguineous marriages. Protestant denominations permit first-cousin marriage, while the Roman Catholic Church requires permission from a diocese to allow them. Judaism permits consanguineous marriage in certain situations, such as for example, uncle-niece unions. Islam has also permitted some types of consanguineous marriages. A Muslim man is prohibited from marrying his mother or grandmother, daughter or granddaughter, sister, niece or great niece, aunt or great aunt, and is also prohibited from marrying two wives who are related to each other (Azim 1997: 169). However, it is often cited that the Prophet Mohammad married his daughter Fatima to Ali, his paternal first cousin which has led researchers to argue that for Muslims first-cousin marriage might be permitted in practice (Bittles 2001: 91; Hussain 1999).

Within Hinduism, practices vary between the North and the South of India. In the Aryan Hindu tradition of North India, marriage between relatives is usually prohibited (Kapadia 1958: 117–37). For example, early Indian economic historiography describes marriage within the Hindu caste system in North India as one in which a man is obliged to marry outside his family, but within the caste and usually within the sub-caste to which his family belongs. A family consists of persons reputed to be descended from a common ancestor and between whom marriage is prohibited (Anstey 1952: 48). This tradition prohibits marriage to relatives for seven generations on the male side and for five generations on the female side (Balasubramaniam 2002). The south Indian or Dravidian, Hindu tradition, however, permits consanguineous marriages (Balasubramaniam 2002; Epstein 1973; Reddy 1993; Vatuk 1982).

Overall, we believe religion may contribute to the prevalence of consanguinity in some parts of the world, but it is not the primary driver of this practice. The religious sanctions and prohibitions around this practice are also quite diverse and have changed over time.

Social Capital

Consanguinity is often regarded as a valuable tool to strengthen economic, political and social ties between members of a single family. In other words, consanguinity builds 'social capital' within a family.[2] Two types of social capital are relevant to the interested researcher of consanguinity—'bridging' social capital and 'bonding' social capital. The former is also termed cross-cutting social ties between disparate groups (Granovetter 1973), while the latter is similar to horizontal associations, which links sameness and enables cooperation between groups, for example, networks and clubs. A feature of bonding social capital is that the bigger the group that sustains it the more powerful bonding social capital is.

It is easy to see how consanguineous marriage is both bridging social capital and bonding social capital. By uniting different descent groups under patrilineal kinship rules, it strengthens ties between family members, lowers the possibility for conflict and consolidates both assets and power.[3] It also encourages cooperation about matters relating to production, household decisions, property, market work and interactions with the community.

Consanguineous marriages have additional advantages when families are separated by great distance, as wider kinship networks also provide an important source of economic assistance and cooperation. The importance of such networks has been documented across the Middle East and they are believed to have contributed to the establishment of strong trading networks in the Middle Ages (Kuran 2002).

Marriage Costs

In some cultures, marriage payments such as dowry and brideprice are customary. Recent estimates suggest that such transfers together with the costs of marriages themselves amount to approximately six times the annual household income in South Asia (Rao 1993) and four times in sub-Saharan Africa (Dekker and Hoogeveen 2002). In the Middle East, inflows of oil wealth are believed to increase brideprices significantly (Casterline, Mensch and Singh 2005). In South Asia, where dowries are very common if not almost universal, dowry payments are well-known to influence marriage decisions (Anderson 2007; Caldwell, Reddy and Caldwell 1983; Rao 1993). This is particularly because dowries have escalated over time.[4] In situations where parents feel that they are unable to afford the costs of a wedding (especially if there is more than one daughter to be married), marriage for the daughter may be delayed (Epstein 1973: 193). In communities where it is permitted, marriage to a relative may be desirable; anecdotal evidence and evidence we provide later in this essay suggest that in a consanguineous marriage dowry payments may be reduced or rendered non-obligatory.

Considerations of Inheritance

The practice of consanguinity by royalty and major landowning families has often been cited as a clear indication that it is motivated by considerations of inheritance and desire to maintain control over asset holdings (Bittles 1994: 563). This argument is further bolstered because, in patrilineal systems most consanguineous marriages occur between cross-cousins and not parallel-cousins. By bringing individuals from outside the patriline into its fold, a family ensures that its assets are consolidated. This motivation for consanguineous marriage is particularly powerful in cases where women can inherit property and where land is a significant determinant of political and economic power. Using data from India, Agarwal (1994) argues that in south Asian communities which recognised women's rights in landed property, land was kept within members of the extended family by means of strict rules on land alienation, post-marital residence in the village taking the form of uxorilocality or matrilocality and close-kin marriages. Similarly, in the Islamic world, arranged marriages to individuals within the kinship network have helped families circumvent mandatory Islamic sharing rules for inheritances for several hundred years (Kuran 2002; Meriwether 1999).

Agency Models of Marriage

An alternative view of consanguinity—one that integrates many of these ideas and acknowledges the costs as well as benefits of this form of marriage—is provided by Do, Iyer and Joshi (2006). It relies on several assumptions: (i) marriage requires two families to make a long-term commitment to support their offspring through gifts, bequests, transfers of movable and immovable capital, etc.; (ii) divorce is very costly and once marriages are fixed, the relationship is difficult to sever; (iii) marriages to non-relatives have important advantages (diversification of networks and, more importantly, genes); (iv) the greater the social distance between families the harder it is to commit future bequests and gifts or make promises, since the two families do not have a familiarity with each other. This imposes pressure to make any requisite transfers prior to marriage or at the time of the marriage; and finally, (v) it is difficult and expensive to borrow funds to make marriage payments.

Taken together, these assumptions lead to the conclusion that a marriage to a cousin occurs when individuals are too poor and credit-constrained to afford a high-quality socially-distant match, since this would require high levels of marriage payments. Instead of making such payments, such individuals are able to leverage the trust within kinship bonds to promise transfers and bequests later on in life. In other words, cousin marriage emerges when marriage payments such as dowry and brideprice are customary and high.

In South Asia, where marriage is characterised by patrilocal exogamy, consanguineous marriage is related to the practice of dowry. The precise intuition behind this is as follows. Since the bride moves away from her natal home and into the home of her husband (and his family) at the time of marriage, her parents do not directly benefit from investments made in her household in the form of movable and immovable assets, rights to property, etc. Such investments are more valued by the groom's family, since they generally reside with the couple and depend on them for participation in income-generating opportunities, old-age support, etc. As a result of this asymmetry, the bride's parents have less incentive (than the groom's parents) to invest in their child's marriage after it has occurred. Since it is not possible to write an enforceable contract that requires both families to make binding commitments after marriage, the marriage contract is 'incomplete'. The incompleteness is typically addressed by dowry payments: the groom's family requires the bride's family to make these payments prior to marriage. In other words, the dowry transfers investments to those who have the highest incentives to invest in the marriage after it occurs.

When the families of the bride and groom are socially distant, they are likely to benefit from the diversification of genes and socio-economic networks, but the lack of familiarity or trust between the families means that there is little flexibility on the dowry payment; it must be paid in full at the time of marriage. Moreover, larger dowries may be necessary to mitigate any uncertainty about the timing and size of future transfers from the bride's family. When two families are related (as is the case when cousins marry), however, ex-ante commitments are more credible arguably because informal contracts are easier to enforce within the extended family. In this case, a bride's family can easily promise to make transfers later. They will be more likely to uphold their promise to their own family members.

Insights from Bangladesh

In this section, we use data from Bangladesh to examine the prevalence of consanguinity in rural South Asia and also test some of the theories of consanguinity that have been discussed in this essay. The data are drawn from the 1996 Matlab Health and Socioeconomic Survey (MHSS).[5] We also supplement these data with that of climate data on annual rainfall levels in the Matlab area for the period 1950–96.[6]

The 1996 MHSS contains information on 4364 households clustered in 2687 *baris* (homestead) in 141 villages.[7] Matlab is a sub-district of Chandpur district, which is about 50 miles south of Dhaka, the capital of Bangladesh. Eighty-five per cent or more of the people in Matlab are Muslims and the remaining are Hindus. Agriculture is the main occupation, though 30 per cent of households are landless. The area has been relatively isolated and inaccessible to communication and transportation and remains largely undeveloped and traditional (Fauveau 1994).

Our analysis relies on the section of the survey that asked men and women retrospective information about marriage. The sample includes 5083 married men and 6068 married women. We restrict our attention to first marriages.[8] For the purpose of our empirical tests, however, we restrict our attention to a sub-sample of 4087 married women and 3357 married men, who provided complete information on age and education, marriage (including age at marriage, relationships to their spouses and payments of dowry), parental characteristics, parental assets, inheritances and inherited assets, and numbers of brothers and sisters (as well as their ages). Descriptive summary statistics are provided in Table 9.1.

TABLE 9.1: Summary Statistics for Key Variables used in Regression Analysis

Variable name	Description	Female Sample		Male Sample	
		Mean	Std. dev.	Mean	Std. dev.
Married a Cousin	Married a first-cousin	0.1065	0.3085	0.1072	0.3094
Married a Relative	Married a relative other than a first-cousin	0.0786	0.2692	0.0813	0.2733
Married a non-relative in village	Married a non-relative within village	0.1429	0.35	0.14	0.347
Dowry	Dowry (in thousands of taka)	0.3663	0.4819	0.14	0.347
Log of dowry	Log of dowry value	–1.6938	1.025	-2.0152	0.7589
Age at first birth	Age at first birth (in years)	22.937	5.102		
Live births	Number of live births	4.987	2.902		
Total children died	Number of children who died	1.054	1.393		
Children died, boys	Total number of boys who died	0.519	0.884		
Children died, girls	Total number of girls who died	0.534	0.851		
Any inheritance	Inherited anything from parents	0.0967	0.2956	0.6942	0.4608
Inherited farmland	Inherited farmland from parents	0.0554	0.2289	0.5625	0.4961
Inherited homestead	Inherited homestead land from parents	0.0276	0.1638	0.6593	0.474
Inherited money	Inherited money from parents	0.0107	0.1031	0.0113	0.1058
Advisor	Advisor to anyone in community	0.367	0.482		
OutBariOnceWeek	Go out of the bari at least once a week	0.366	0.482		
RelVisitOnceWeek	Visited by relatives at least once a week	0.368	0.482		

(Contd.)

(Table 9.1 Contd.)

Variable name	Description	Female Sample		Male Sample	
		Mean	Std. dev.	Mean	Std. dev.
PartHhdDecisions	Participate in household decisions	0.767	0.423		
Burqa	Wear a burqa outside the home	0.759	0.428		
Assault	Ever a victim of assault at home	0.186	0.389		
GrMember	Member of any kind of organisation/group	0.14	0.347		
Age	Age (in years)	36.652	10.135	47.4824	14.0885
Muslim	Muslim	0.8877	0.3158	0.8916	0.3109
Years of schooling	Years of schooling (in years)	2.2039	3.0021	3.3556	3.887
Birth order	Birth order	2.9201	1.8008	2.5116	1.5659
Mother alive at marriage	Mother alive at time of first marriage	0.9326	0.2507	0.8615	0.3454
Father alive at marriage	Father alive at time of first marriage	0.8415	0.3652	0.656	0.4751
Brothers at marriage	Brothers alive at time of marriage	2.2107	1.4692	1.6998	1.3904
Sisters at marriage	Sisters alive at time of marriage	1.9043	1.3681	1.7433	1.3379
Parents land	Log of parents farmland (log of 10^3, in decimals)	0.8535	5.0853	1.4366	4.7823
Rainfall dev when aged 11	Rainfall deviations when aged 11 (in millimeter)	2.0792	0.3847		
Household land value	Household land value (%10^5 taka)	1.533	3.315	1.533	3.315
Agricultural assets	Agricultural assets (10^5 taka)	0.657	1.333	0.657	1.333
Non-Agricultural assets	Non-Agricultural assets (10^5 taka)	1.093	3.002	1.093	3.002

Notes: i. The variable *Married a Cousin* includes marriages to first-cousins.
ii. The variable *Married a Relative* includes marriages to all relatives other than first-cousins.

Source: 1996 Matlab Health and Socioeconomic Survey (MHSS); Author's own data.

It is interesting to note that of all the female respondents in our sample, 10 per cent married a first cousin, 8 per cent had married a relative other than a first cousin and 14 per cent had married a non-relative in the same village. Thirty-six per cent of women and only 18 per cent of men report the payment of a dowry at the time of marriage. We believe the difference is in psychological biases in the interpretation of gifts and transfers as 'dowries' between the giver (the bride) and the receiver (the groom); since women want their dowries to improve their status and acceptance in their new home, they will have a tendency to interpret all gifts given at marriage as dowry. Men, on the other hand, do not want to interpret all gifts as dowry since doing so would reduce their bargaining position with the new bride. For the remainder of this essay, we use the female sample to carry out our analysis and, thus, include in our definition of dowry all transfers that were paid at the time of marriage.[9]

Biological Impacts of Consanguinity

The first step of our analysis is to examine the effect of consanguinity on fertility and child mortality. We analyse this issue in Bangladesh by considering five key variables: a woman's age at marriage, her age at first birth, her total number of births, the total number of child deaths and the number of deaths by gender. We look at these variables across three types of marriages: first-cousin marriages (henceforth just referred to as cousin marriages), marriages to relatives other than first cousins and marriages to non-relatives within a village. Dummy variables corresponding to these three types of marriages are constructed and labelled as *Married a Cousin*, *Married a Relative* and *Married a Non-Relative in Village* respectively. Since these three types of marriages are in decreasing order of genetic and familial closeness, but occurring within a family's social network, the comparison allows us to distinguish between genetic and social distance.

To examine reproductive behaviour across these three groups, we regress the variable of interest on the three types of marriage variables as well as a set of socio-economic controls that include a woman's age, her years of schooling, her husband's age, her husband's years of schooling, her religion (a dummy that indicates whether or not she is Muslim), her birth order, the number of her brothers and sisters, and the value of her household's land and agricultural and non-agricultural assets. A summary of all variables involved is presented in Table 9.1. The results of our regressions are presented in Table 9.2. Note that marriage to a cousin or a relative is associated with a higher number of live births, though the result is statistically significant only in the case of marriage to relatives other than cousins. Marriage to cousins is clearly associated with a higher likelihood of experiencing the death of a child. This is presumably due to birth defects or the greater likelihood of inheriting a recessive gene, and

TABLE 9.2: Consanguinity, Fertility and Mortality

	Age at marriage	*Age at first birth*	*Number of live births*	*Total*	*Child deaths*	
					Boys	*Girls*
	(1)	*(2)*	*(3)*	*(4)*	*(5)*	*(6)*
Married a Cousin	–0.8629***	–0.3955	0.0633	0.0924*	0.0372	0.0552*
	(0.1860)	(0.2493)	(0.1039)	(0.0509)	(0.0316)	(0.0336)
Married a Relative	0.7647	–0.4477*	0.1064	0.0312	0.0314	–0.0002
	(0.5294)	(0.2653)	(0.1158)	(0.0518)	(0.0368)	(0.0350)
Married a non-relative in village	–0.2494*	–1.0529***	0.0221	–0.0210	0.0162	–0.0372
	(0.1514)	(0.2665)	(0.0871)	(0.0427)	(0.0296)	(0.0249)
Age	0.0179	–0.0593**	0.2122***	0.0204***	0.0091***	0.0113***
	(0.0160)	(0.0239)	(0.0079)	(0.0033)	(0.0023)	(0.0021)
Spouse age	–0.0945***	–0.1235***	–0.0111*	0.0016	0.0017	–0.0001
	(0.0138)	(0.0199)	(0.0066)	(0.0027)	(0.0018)	(0.0017)
Years of schooling	0.1906***	0.0794**	–0.0782***	–0.0165***	–0.0065*	–0.0100***
	(0.0268)	(0.0369)	(0.0117)	(0.0052)	(0.0036)	(0.0033)
Spouse years of schooling	–0.0060	0.0111	–0.0085	–0.0038	–0.0017	–0.0021
	(0.0195)	(0.0256)	(0.0097)	(0.0041)	(0.0028)	(0.0027)
Muslim	–1.0513***	–0.3378	0.5313***	–0.0132	–0.0207	0.0076
	(0.2483)	(0.2449)	(0.0840)	(0.0441)	(0.0310)	(0.0267)
Birth order	0.0777**	0.0489	–0.0279	–0.0059	–0.0073	0.0014
	(0.0390)	(0.0450)	(0.0176)	(0.0074)	(0.0050)	(0.0049)

(Contd.)

(Table 9.2 Contd.)

	Age at marriage	*Age at first birth*	*Number of live births*	*Total*	*Child deaths*	
					Boys	*Girls*
	(1)	*(2)*	*(3)*	*(4)*	*(5)*	*(6)*
Number of brothers	–0.0718*	–0.0080	0.0439**	–0.0051	–0.0004	–0.0047
	(0.0412)	(0.0521)	(0.0208)	(0.0103)	(0.0068)	(0.0066)
Number of sisters	–0.0063	0.0832	0.0017	–0.0132	–0.0050	–0.0082
	(0.0451)	(0.0566)	(0.0214)	(0.0106)	(0.0073)	(0.0066)
Father years of schooling	–0.0312	–0.0052	0.0109	0.0033	–0.0007	0.0040
	(0.0193)	(0.0242)	(0.0091)	(0.0042)	(0.0029)	(0.0029)
Land value	0.0715	0.1364	0.0405	–0.0290	–0.0193	–0.0098
	(0.1358)	(0.1431)	(0.0561)	(0.0227)	(0.0174)	(0.0147)
Value of agricultural assets	–0.0853	–0.1523	–0.0281	0.0162	0.0146	0.0016
	(0.1253)	(0.1300)	(0.0529)	(0.0206)	(0.0153)	(0.0136)
Value of non-agricultural assets	–0.0318	–0.1326	–0.0359	0.0248	0.0167	0.0081
	(0.1187)	(0.1347)	(0.0514)	(0.0218)	(0.0165)	(0.0142)
R-squared	0.0965	0.1898	0.5901	0.0854	0.0484	0.0528
N	3326	3177	3324	3218	3218	3218

Notes: Standard errors (shown in parentheses) are clustered at the bari level.
* significance at 10 per cent level.
** significance at 5 per cent level.
*** significance at 1 per cent level.
Source: Constructed by authors from MHSS data.

confirms what many have already documented about the biological disadvantages of consanguineous marriages. We view this as evidence in support of the existing evidence on the effects of consanguinity on reproductive behaviour as well as reproductive outcomes. In the sections ahead, we examine the rationale for such marriages, keeping in mind that this form of marriage can often have negative effects on child survival.

Credit Constraints and Consanguinity

In recent years, dowry payments have become common in Bangladesh. We thus examine whether credit constraints may affect an individual's decision to enter a consanguineous union. We again consider the three types of marriages outlined earlier. Our set of independent variables includes socioeconomic controls such as age, education, birth order, religion and parental socio-economic status. Since credit constraints in agricultural societies can collectively vary across households in a region, we also condition on year-of-marriage fixed effects and deviations of rainfall from average values when the woman was of marriageable age.[10]

The results of the regressions are presented in Table 9.3. Note also that cousin marriages are negatively associated with age, years of schooling and birth order. In other words, marriages to a cousin are likely to occur when a girl is younger, less educated and higher-up in birth order, than in cases where marriages are to non-relatives. This is consistent with the possibility of credit constraints: poorer families are less likely to have assets to draw on to pay high dowries and/or marriage expenses for later-born children. Further evidence of credit constraints comes from the negative and statistically significant coefficient of the variables that measure the number of brothers that a girl had at the time of marriage[11], and her parents' farmland value.[12]

Another important finding from Table 9.3 is that the socio-economic factors that drive marriages between relatives and/or non-relatives within a village are different from those that drive cousin marriages. Birth order, for example, is positively associated with marriage between relatives and does not have a statistically significant effect on marriages to non-relatives within a village. Having more brothers at the time of marriage has a positive effect on the probability of marrying non-relatives within the village.

Finally, note that all three forms of marriage—to cousins, relatives other than cousins and non-relatives within a village—are more common among Muslims than Hindus. We conclude that while religion (being Muslim) does play a role, there is also evidence that families who contract consanguineous marriages for their children may be poorer and credit-constrained. This is consistent with two of the theories of marriage presented earlier. Both the theory of marriage costs and the agency theory of cousin marriage would

Table 9.3: Determinants of Social Distance in Marriages

	Married cousin			*Married a relative*			*Married a non-relative In village*		
	(1)	*(2)*	*(3)*	*(4)*	*(5)*	*(6)*	*(7)*	*(8)*	*(9)*
Age	–0.0029 (0.0037)	–0.0016 (0.0037)	–0.0156** (0.0067)	0.0055** (0.0027)	0.0059** (0.0028)	0.0107* (0.0061)	–0.0082* (0.0042)	–0.0081* (0.0042)	–0.0269*** (0.0074)
Age squared	0.0002 (0.0005)	0.0000 (0.0005)	0.0013 (0.0009)	–0.0007* (0.0004)	–0.0007* (0.0004)	–0.0009 (0.0008)	0.0011* (0.0006)	0.0011** (0.0006)	0.0035*** (0.0010)
Years of schooling	–0.0044*** (0.0016)	–0.0025 (0.0019)	–0.0016 (0.0019)	–0.0005 (0.0014)	–0.0001 (0.0016)	–0.0007 (0.0017)	–0.0070*** (0.0018)	–0.0052** (0.0021)	–0.0046** (0.0021)
Muslim	0.1201*** (0.0060)	0.1245*** (0.0068)	0.1205*** (0.0069)	0.0479*** (0.0100)	0.0520*** (0.0103)	0.0558*** (0.0103)	–0.0582*** (0.0218)	–0.0598*** (0.0220)	–0.0624*** (0.0219)
Birth order	–0.0093*** (0.0026)	–0.0049 (0.0031)	–0.0049 (0.0031)	0.0046** (0.0024)	0.0057** (0.0027)	0.0061** (0.0027)	0.0000 (0.0032)	–0.0034 (0.0038)	–0.0031 (0.0038)
Father alive at marriage		–0.0168 (0.0142)	–0.0222 (0.0142)		–0.0019 (0.0120)	0.0003 (0.0121)		–0.0028 (0.0159)	–0.0029 (0.0160)
Father years of schooling		–0.0008 (0.0015)	–0.0008 (0.0015)		0.0003 (0.0014)	0.0004 (0.0014)		–0.0029* (0.0015)	–0.0029* (0.0015)
Brothers at marriage		–0.0104*** (0.0038)	–0.0097** (0.0038)		0.0007 (0.0034)	–0.0002 (0.0034)		0.0123*** (0.0043)	0.0121*** (0.0043)
Sisters at marriage		–0.0055 (0.0040)	–0.0045 (0.0040)		–0.0047 (0.0033)	–0.0055 (0.0034)		–0.0003 (0.0043)	–0.0005 (0.0044)

(Contd.)

(Table 9.3 Contd.)

	Married cousin			*Married a relative*			*Married a non-relative In village*		
	(1)	*(2)*	*(3)*	*(4)*	*(5)*	*(6)*	*(7)*	*(8)*	*(9)*
Log of parents farmland		0.0010 (0.0012)	0.0009 (0.0012)		–0.0009 (0.0010)	–0.0008 (0.0010)		0.0005 (0.0014)	0.0005 (0.0014)
Log of parents farmland squared		–0.0013*** (0.0005)	–0.0013*** (0.0005)		–0.0002 (0.0004)	–0.0002 (0.0004)		–0.0006 (0.0006)	–0.0007 (0.0006)
R-squared	0.0196	0.0245	0.0314	0.0051	0.0062	0.0084	0.0074	0.0106	0.0134
N	4069	4069	4069	4069	4069	4069	4089	4089	4089

Notes: Standard errors (shown in parentheses) are clustered at the bari level.
* significance at 10 per cent level.
** significance at 5 per cent level.
*** significance at 1 per cent level.
Source: Constructed by authors from MHSS data.

predict that poorer individuals prefer consanguineous marriage, since it would avoid the immediate requirement of marriage payments. Later in this section, we test this hypothesis directly, by examining the relationship between consanguinity and dowry.

Social Capital

As seen earlier, many commonly regarded explanations of consanguinity are built on the idea that consanguinity builds 'social capital'. To examine whether consanguineous and 'close' marriages lead to higher levels of social capital, we consider a variety of variables that describe an individual's social network and social capital. We consider several aspects of a woman's well-being: whether or not she acts as an advisor (formally or informally) to anyone in her family or village (labelled here as *Advisor*), whether or not she leaves her bari more than once a week (*OutBariOnceWeek*), whether or not relatives visit her bari more than once a week (*RelVisitOnceWeek*), whether or not she participates in household decisions (*PartHhdDecisions*), whether or not she wears a burqa or traditional veil (*Burqa*), whether or not she has ever been assaulted or abused (*Assault*) and, finally, whether or not she participates in any kind of group in the village (*GrMember*) that includes savings groups, credit groups, social groups or religious groups.[13]

To determine whether women in consanguineous relationships have different levels of autonomy, decision-making capability, social interaction and/or community participation, we regressed these variables on the three measures of social distance considered previously and a variety of controls that were featured in previous regressions. To the list of controls, we add contemporaneous measures of wealth—the value of land, agricultural assets and also non-agricultural assets—since these may have independent effects on these variables. The results are presented in Table 9.6. Note that there is almost no evidence in support of the fact that women in consanguineous marriages enjoy any overall significant advantage or disadvantage with respect to these variables. In results not shown here, we found this to be true in all the measures of social networks that we considered in our analysis.

While this is by no means sufficient evidence to rule out the idea that consanguineous marriages build stronger families and preserve traditions in families, we interpret this as evidence that a woman who marries her cousin does not appear to have significantly greater autonomy, greater decision-making authority, or greater participation in community matters. Though we found similar (non)effects in every social network variable we examined, we nevertheless acknowledge that she and the entire family may benefit in ways that are not examined here. We turn now to a closer look at the relationship between consanguinity and two other variables: marriage payments and inheritances.

TABLE 9.4: Relationship between Consanguinity and Social Networks

	Advisor	*OutBariOnceWeek*	*RelVisitOnceWeek*	*PartHhdDecisions*	*Burqa*	*Assault*	*Gr member*
	(1)	*(2)*	*(3)*	*(4)*	*(5)*	*(6)*	*(7)*
Married a Cousin	0.0333	0.0392	0.0146	0.0217	0.0026	–0.0278	0.0037
	(0.0255)	(0.0250)	(0.0249)	(0.0174)	(0.0184)	(0.0207)	(0.0196)
Married a Relative	0.0773***	–0.0154	0.0807***	0.0272	0.0083	–0.0204	0.0231
	(0.0292)	(0.0278)	(0.0292)	(0.0190)	(0.0205)	(0.0235)	(0.0227)
Married a non-relative in village	0.0208	0.0453**	0.0342	–0.0248	0.0082	–0.0059	0.0487***
	(0.0218)	(0.0217)	(0.0221)	(0.0165)	(0.0165)	(0.0184)	(0.0186)
Age	0.0128	–0.0003	0.0095	–0.0159	0.0082	–0.0001	0.0025
	(0.0106)	(0.0098)	(0.0114)	(0.0121)	(0.0068)	(0.0087)	(0.0110)
Years of schooling	0.0204***	–0.0094***	–0.0026	0.0038*	–0.0025	–0.0180***	0.0028
	(0.0030)	(0.0031)	(0.0031)	(0.0022)	(0.0025)	(0.0023)	(0.0025)
Muslim	–0.0071	–0.0328	0.0026	0.0211	0.1754***	0.0684***	–0.0518**
	(0.0245)	(0.0248)	(0.0245)	(0.0203)	(0.0235)	(0.0197)	(0.0233)
Birth order	–0.0023	–0.0021	0.0007	0.0007	–0.0051	–0.0058	0.0017
	(0.0046)	(0.0045)	(0.0046)	(0.0033)	(0.0035)	(0.0037)	(0.0038)
Years of marriage	–0.0019	0.0028	–0.0081	0.0229*	–0.0073	–0.0019	–0.0033
	(0.0105)	(0.0098)	(0.0114)	(0.0120)	(0.0068)	(0.0086)	(0.0110)
Age at marriage	–0.0047	0.0034	–0.0106	0.0194	–0.0057	–0.0018	–0.0065
	(0.0103)	(0.0096)	(0.0112)	(0.0119)	(0.0068)	(0.0085)	(0.0109)

(Contd.)

(Table 9.4 Contd.)

	Advisor	*OutBariOnceWeek*	*RelVisitOnceWeek*	*PartHhdDecisions*	*Burqa*	*Assault*	*Gr member*
	(1)	*(2)*	*(3)*	*(4)*	*(5)*	*(6)*	*(7)*
Number of brothers	0.0128**	–0.0032	0.0027	0.0067*	0.0041	–0.0040	0.0021
	(0.0054)	(0.0052)	(0.0053)	(0.0037)	(0.0041)	(0.0044)	(0.0042)
Number of sisters	0.0057	0.0003	0.0099*	0.0010	0.0072*	–0.0045	0.0108**
	(0.0055)	(0.0054)	(0.0054)	(0.0040)	(0.0040)	(0.0046)	(0.0046)
Father years of schooling	0.0045*	–0.0027	–0.0000	0.0055***	0.0023	–0.0023	0.0022
	(0.0024)	(0.0023)	(0.0024)	(0.0016)	(0.0017)	(0.0019)	(0.0019)
Value of land	–0.0179	–0.0021	0.0148	–0.0215***	0.0171*	0.0003	–0.0195*
	(0.0122)	(0.0128)	(0.0120)	(0.0072)	(0.0095)	(0.0073)	(0.0104)
Agricultural assets	0.0196*	–0.0133	–0.0094	0.0101	0.0018	–0.0109	0.0079
	(0.0113)	(0.0118)	(0.0115)	(0.0069)	(0.0085)	(0.0067)	(0.0101)
Non-Agricultural assets	0.0168	0.0048	–0.0141	0.0142**	–0.0160*	–0.0023	0.0115
	(0.0121)	(0.0124)	(0.0112)	(0.0066)	(0.0097)	(0.0068)	(0.0099)
R-squared	0.0598	0.0157	0.0056	0.0513	0.0316	0.0279	0.0121
N	4061	4046	4054	4028	4061	4038	4056

Notes: Standard errors (shown in parentheses) are clustered at the bari level.
* significance at 10 per cent level.
** significance at 5 per cent level.
*** significance at 1 per cent level.
Source: Constructed by authors from MHSS data.

TABLE 9.5: Relationship between Dowry and Social Distance

	Dowry			*Log of dowry value*		
	(1)	*(2)*	*(3)*	*(4)*	*(5)*	*(6)*
Married a Cousin	–0.0845*** (0.0239)	–0.0690*** (0.0199)	–0.0609*** (0.0197)	–0.1533*** (0.0489)	–0.0957** (0.0410)	–0.0730* (0.0410)
Married a Relative	–0.0705** (0.0277)	–0.0414* (0.0239)	–0.0418* (0.0233)	–0.1572*** (0.0581)	–0.0764 (0.0492)	–0.0805* (0.0482)
Married a non-relative in village	–0.0272 (0.0222)	–0.0379** (0.0186)	–0.0346* (0.0184)	–0.0789* (0.0462)	–0.0868** (0.0381)	–0.0731* (0.0378)
Controls	Yes	Yes	Yes	Yes	Yes	Yes
R-squared	0.0039	0.3226	0.3443	0.0036	0.3243	0.3375
N	4056	4056	4056	4056	4056	4056

Notes: The variable *Log of Dowry Value* assumes a dowry value of Tk. 1 if no dowry was paid.
Standard errors (shown in parentheses) are clustered at the bari level.
* significance at 10 per cent level.
** significance at 5 per cent level.
*** significance at 1 per cent level.
Source: Constructed by authors from MHSS data.

TABLE 9.6: Relationship between Consanguinity and Inheritance

	Female sample				*Male sample*			
	Any inheritance	*Type of inheritance*			*Any inheritance*	*Type of inheritance*		
		Farmland	*Home*	*Money*		*Farmland*	*Home*	*Money*
	(1)	*(2)*	*(3)*	*(4)*	*(5)*	*(6)*	*(7)*	*(8)*
Married a cousin	0.0429***	0.0341***	0.0160*	0.0098*	–0.0200	–0.0392*	–0.0193	–0.0105*
	(0.0145)	(0.0116)	(0.0083)	(0.0053)	(0.0225)	(0.0221)	(0.0238)	(0.0063)
Married a relative	0.0419**	0.0299**	0.0237**	0.0076	0.0191	–0.0057	0.0057	–0.0101
	(0.0168)	(0.0134)	(0.0096)	(0.0062)	(0.0249)	(0.0245)	(0.0264)	(0.0069)
Married a non-relative in village	0.0374***	0.0291***	0.0107	0.0038	–0.0347*	–0.0280	–0.0443**	0.0114**
	(0.0128)	(0.0102)	(0.0073)	(0.0047)	(0.0197)	(0.0193)	(0.0208)	(0.0055)
Controls	Yes	Yes	Yes	Yes	Yes	Yes		
R-squared	0.0913	0.0670	0.0422	0.0162	0.2914	0.4305	0.2565	0.0397
N	4795	4795	4795	4795	3242	3242	3242	3242

Notes: Standard errors (shown in parentheses) are clustered at the bari level.
* significance at 10 per cent level.
** significance at 5 per cent level.
*** significance at 1 per cent level.
Source: Constructed by authors from MHSS data.

Dowry and Consanguinity

To examine the relationship between consanguinity and dowry, we regress the dummy variable *Dowry* on the three types of marriage variables considered previously and include a set of socio-economic controls. The results are in Table 9.4. Since a similar set of results has already been presented and discussed in Do, Iyer and Joshi (2006), we present here only the main coefficients and omit the other variables. Estimates in the first three columns indicate that compared to women who marry non-relatives, women who marry their first cousins are 5 per cent less likely to bring a dowry and this effect remains even after we control for individual characteristics (age, years of schooling, religion and birth order), family characteristics (mother and father were alive at the time of marriage, number of brothers and sisters at the time of marriage and father's landholdings) and rainfall at the time that a woman was of marriageable age. Considering that in this population, about 35 per cent of all women report the payment of a dowry at the time of marriage, this is a substantial and important difference.

The results are similar if we expand the definition of consanguinity to include marriages between second cousins and other types of marriages between relatives (Table 9.4, Panels B and C, Columns 1–3). It is interesting to note that marriages to other kin as well as marriages to non-kin within a village are also associated with a lower likelihood of dowry payment. This suggests that other forms of social capital may also play a role in enforcing marriage contracts. Note, however, the smaller magnitude of the coefficients in Panels B and C of Table 9.4 (Columns 1–3). The relationship between dowry and social distance is strongest in the case of cousins.

To check the robustness of the finding, we also use the logarithm of the dowry values as a dependent variable, and obtain similar qualitative results for marriages between relatives (Table 9.4, Columns 4–6). After controlling for individual, household characteristics and year of marriage fixed-effects, the results show 7–8 per cent lower dowry values when the two spouses are relatives to each other.

The negative relationship between consanguinity and dowry is consistent with two theories of consanguinity discussed earlier. The theory of marriage costs simply regards consanguinity as a method of avoiding high dowry and/or other marriage payments. The agency theory, however, argues that low levels of dowry in consanguineous marriages involve lower marriage payments, but higher inheritances in the long run and, thus, it is the timing of payments that is the key and not magnitude. To distinguish between these two explanations of consanguinity, we turn to an examination of inheritances.

Inheritances

To analyse the relationship between inheritances and consanguinity, we consider several measures of inheritance levels on the three measures of social distance used in previous regressions. In particular, we define dummy variables that take a value of 1 if an individual has inherited or expects to inherit a particular type of asset from their parents. Table 9.5 (Columns 1–4) reports the results of the regressions of the inheritance measures on the three measures of social distance as well as a list of controls. Again, since the full set of results has been presented and discussed in Do, Iyer and Joshi (2006), we present only the main coefficients here and refer readers to that paper for complete results.

As before, the regressions are first performed on the female sample. The positive and significant estimates for the variable *Married a Cousin* are consistent with the hypothesis that women in consanguineous unions are more likely to receive or expect to receive transfers from their parents. The level of bequests received by women who marry other relatives or non-relatives in the same village is not always statistically significant. This suggests that the commitment to bequeath their assets to their daughters is likely to be weaker when she marries more distant relatives or non-kin in a village, since the costs or consequences of non-payment are likely to be smaller in such relationships.

It is interesting that when we focus on the male sample (Table 9.5, Columns 5–8), the coefficients for the variable *Married a Cousin* are negative, although the coefficients are rarely statistically significant. Our explanation of this is that men inherit from their parents, regardless of whether or not they marry a cousin. The effect is likely to be significant only for women, because cousin-marriages (and to a lesser extent, other types of kin-marriage) are the only means through which they are able to inherit property from their parents.

The strength of the findings on consanguinity and inheritance lend support to an agency view of consanguineous marriages. They also lead us to dismiss the idea that consanguinity is chosen simply to minimise the outflow of wealth in the form of marriage payments. If that 'alone' was the driver of consanguineous marriage, we ought to see it in 'all' segments of society and particularly among the wealthy, since they have the most to gain by keeping assets within a single family. The agency theory of marriage is the only explanation of consanguinity that can reconcile the three facts observed so far: credit constraints among families that choose it, lower levels of dowry and higher levels of inheritances in consanguineous marriages.

Overall, the data from Bangladesh leads us to five conclusions:

1. The levels of fertility and infant mortality are higher in consanguineous marriages than in marriages between non-kin.
2. Credit-constrained families are more likely to choose consanguineous marriages over non-kin marriages.
3. Women who marry their cousins are no different than those who marry non-kin when it comes to measures of female autonomy and social capital.
4. Dowry levels are lower in consanguineous marriages than in marriages between non-kin.
5. Inheritance levels are higher in consanguineous marriages than in marriages between non-kin.

Taken together, this evidence supports the agency theory of consanguinity, i.e. individuals marry their cousins when they cannot afford expensive marriage payments and they choose, instead, to make these transfers later on in life, in the form of bequests/inheritances instead. All other theories, with their emphasis on a single or else limited number of variables—religion, credit constraints, marriage payments and social capital—explain, at best, only some of these facts.

Conclusion

Despite significant awareness of the disadvantages of this practice, consanguineous marriage remains popular in many parts of the developing world. Explanations for this are often based on arguments about religious sanction, culture, preferences to keep wealth within a single family and the need to build alliances. Our explanation synthesises some of these ideas. We argue that consanguinity is related to the practice of dowry and both emerge from incomplete marriage contracts. By assuming that the families of the bride and groom must both invest continually in a marriage, patrilocal residence creates an incentive for the bride's family to free-ride on the investments of their in-laws after the marriage is contracted. Dowry can alleviate this by transferring control rights over assets to the family with the highest incentives to invest at the time of marriage. Where dowries are unaffordable, consanguinity emerges as an alternative. A bride's family relies on trust among kin rather than on upfront payments, in order to make credible commitments to future transfers to their daughter's household. Evidence from Bangladesh confirms these findings.

Overall, the main contribution of this analysis is to demonstrate that economic factors such as credit constraints and high marriage costs may be a significant driver of the decision to marry a relative. Other oft-cited factors—religion, culture, social norms and the desire to build alliances may be important as well, but these do not explain why some individuals in a community or religious group make the choice to marry a relative while others do not. By presenting the choice of marriage to a relative as a trade-off between expanding a gene pool and social networks, on one hand, and raising capital on the other, we are able to explain the diversity of choices in a community that shares similar religious and social values. This research highlights the importance of analysing marriage markets and marriage traditions through a prism that includes not only a deep understanding of culture and context, but equally a more precise focus on the main economic mechanisms.

Notes

[1] In the field of clinical genetics, a consanguineous marriage is defined as 'a union between a couple related as second cousins or closer, equivalent to a coefficient of inbreeding in their progeny of F≥0.0156' (Bittles 2001). This is the probability that two homologous alleles in an individual are identical by descent from a recent common ancestor.

[2] Putnam (1995) describes social capital as a set of horizontal associations between people networks and associated norms which have an effect on the productivity of a community and which can be either positive or negative.

[3] In a patrilineal system, parallel-cousins are part of an individual's unilineage, whereas cross-cousins are not. If every man in a patrilineal society married his mother's brother's daughter, every man would be marrying someone from a different lineal group. This would unite members of the same family and build stronger relationships between them.

[4] Rao (1993), for example, shows that real dowry increased 15 per cent annually between 1921 and 1981 in India and this increase was robust to controlling for characteristics of the bride and groom, the wealth of both families, and the imposition of a real price index. Despite the passage of the Dowry Prohibition Act in 1961 that outlaws the practice, dowry inflation has persisted unabated in this region. The custom of giving dowries has also spread from India to neighbouring Pakistan and Bangladesh (Anderson 2007).

[5] This survey is a collaborative effort of RAND, the Harvard School of Public Health, the University of Pennsylvania, the University of Colorado at Boulder, Brown University, Mitra and Associates, and the International Centre for Diarrhoeal Disease Research, Bangladesh (ICDDRB).

[6] These data—the University of Delaware Air and Temperature Precipitation Data—are provided by the NOAA-CIRES Climate Diagnostics Center, Boulder, Colorado, USA, from their website at http://www.cdc.noaa.gov/ (accessed: 8 August 2013).

[7] *Bari* is the basic unit of social organisation in Matlab (Fauveau 1994). Bari literally means 'homestead', but commonly refers to a cluster of households in close physical proximity that share common resources.

[8] Fifteen per cent of men and about 7 per cent of women reported that they have had more than one marriage.

[9] Dowry was assessed in two ways. First, respondents were asked whether or not they paid a dowry at the time of marriage (this is a binary variable) and whether this took the form of bridewealth or gifts and transfers to the woman's in-laws. Respondents were also asked to provide an estimate of the dowry's value. In the analysis ahead, we use both the binary indicators as the logarithm of the dowry values. In constructing the series of the logarithm of the dowry value, we assign a value of Tk. 1 in cases where no dowry transfer is reported.

[10] Since age at marriage and year of marriage are often not remembered with great precision, we define fixed effects over 5-year windows. This allows us to control for local marriage market conditions (e.g. market squeeze).

[11] Since brothers are recipients of dowries, having more brothers is a measure of future wealth inflows.

[12] Since MHSS is a cross-sectional survey, there is limited information on parents' pre-marital wealth. We hence rely on proxies such as parental education and value of landholdings.

[13] The MHSS contained information on a wide variety of social indicators. We chose these because they were most representative of all the indicators in the survey. In results not shown here, we use each and every indicator that is included in the MHSS and confirm that the results presented here are not anomalous in any way.

References

Agarwal, B. 1994. *A Field of One's Own: Gender and Land Rights in South Asia*. Cambridge: Cambridge University Press.

Anderson, S. 2007. 'The Economics of Dowry and Brideprice'. *Journal of Economic Perspectives* 21 (4): 151–74.

Anstey, V. 1952. *The Economic Development of India*. Fourth Edition. London: Longmans, Green and Company.

Appaji Rao, N., H. S. Savithri, and A. H. Bittles. 2002. 'A Genetic Perspective on the South Indian Tradition of Consanguineous Marriage'. In *Austral-Asian Encounters*, eds. C. Vanden and S. Nandan. New Delhi: Prestige Books.

Azim, S. 1997. *Muslim Women: Emerging Identity*. New Delhi: Rawat Publications.

Balasubramaniam, D. 2002. 'Matchmaking within community or in cyberspace?'. *The Hindu*. 24 October.

Becker, G. 1981. *A Treatise on the Family*. Cambridge, MA: Harvard University Press.

———. 1973. 'A Theory of Marriage: Part I'. *Journal of Political Economy* 81 (4): 813–46.

Bittles, A. H. 2003. 'Endogamy, Consanguinity and Community Genetics'. Centre for Human Genetics. Working Paper. Perth: Edith Cowan University.

———. 2001. 'Consanguinity and its Relevance to Clinical Genetics'. *Clinical Genetics* 60:89–98.

———. 1994. 'The Role and Significance of Consanguinity as a Demographic Variable'. *Population and Development Review* 20 (3): 561–84.

Bittles, A. H., J. M. Cobles, and N. Appaji Rao. 1993. 'Trends in Consanguineous Marriage in Karnataka, South India, 1980–1989'. *Journal of Biosocial Science* 25 (1): 111–16.

Bittles, A. H., W. M. Mason, J. Greene, and N. Appaji Rao. 1993. 'Reproductive Behavior and Health in Consanguineous Marriages'. *Science New Series* 252 (5007): 789–94.

Bloch, F., and V. Rao. 2002. 'Terror as a Bargaining Instrument: A Case Study of Dowry Violence in Rural India'. *The American Economic Review* 92 (4): 1029–43.

Botticini, M., and A. Siow. 2003. 'Why Dowries?' *American Economic Review* 93 (4): 1385–98.

Caldwell, J. C., P. H. Reddy, and P. Caldwell. 1983. 'The Causes of Marriage Change in South India'. *Population Studies* 37 (3): 343–61.

Casterline, J. B., B. S. Mensch, and S. Singh. 2005. 'Trends in the Timing of First Marriage Among Men and Women in the Developing World'. Population Council Working Paper 202.

Dekker, Marleen, and Hans Hoogeveen. 2002. 'Bridewealth and Household Security in Rural Zimbabwe.' *Journal of African Economies* 11 (1): 114–45.

Do, Q. T., S. Iyer, and S. Joshi. 2006. 'The Economics of Consanguineous Marriages'. *Policy Working Paper Research Series* 4085. The World Bank.

Epstein, T. S. 1973. *South India: Yesterday, Today and Tomorrow*. London: Macmillan.

Fauveau, V. 1994. Ed. 'Matlab: Women, Children and Health'. Bangladesh: International Center for Diarrhoeal Disease Research.

Granovetter, M. S. 1973. 'The Strength of Weak Ties'. *American Journal of Sociology* 78:1360–80.

Griffin, Keith, Azizur Rahman Khan, and Amy Ickowitz. 2002. 'Poverty and the Distribution of Land'. *Journal of Agrarian Change* 2 (3): 279–330.

Hussain, R. 1999. 'Community Perceptions of Reasons for Preference for Consanguineous Marriages in Pakistan'. *Journal of Biosocial Science* 31:449–61.

Hussain, R., and A. H. Bittles. 2000. 'Socio-Demographic Correlates of Consanguineous Marriage in the Muslim Population of India'. *Journal of Biosocial Science* 32:433–42.

Iyer, S. 2002. *Demography and Religion in India*. New Delhi: Oxford University Press.

Jacoby, H., and G. Mansuri. 2006. 'Watta Satta: Exchange Marriage and Women's Welfare in Rural Pakistan'. Manuscript. The World Bank.

Kapadia, K. M. 1958. *Marriage and Family in India*. Second Edition. Calcutta: Oxford University Press.

Kuran, T. 2002. 'The Islamic Commercial Crisis: Institutional Roots of Economic Underdevelopment in the Middle East'. USC Center for Law, Economics, and Organization. Research Paper Number C01-12.

Maian, A., and R. Mushtaq. 1994. 'Consanguinity in Population of Quetta (Pakistan): A Preliminary Study'. *Journal of Human Ecology* 5:49–53.

McCullough, J. M., and D. H. O'Rourke. 1986. 'Geographic Distribution of Consanguinity in Europe'. *Annals of Human Biology* 13:359–68.

Meriwether, M. L. 1999. *The Kin Who Count: Family and Society in Ottoman Aleppo, 1770–1840*. Austin: University of Texas Press.

Naderi, S. 1979. 'Congenital Abnormalities in Newborns of Consanguineous and Non-consanguineous Parents'. *Obstetric Gynaecology* 53:195–99.
Ottenheimer, M. 1996. *Forbidden Relatives: The American Myth of Cousin Marriage.* Chicago: University of Illinois Press.
Putnam, R. 2000. *Bowling Alone: The Collapse and Renewal of American Community.* Connecticut New York: Simon and Schuster.
———. 1995. 'Bowling Alone: America's Declining Social Capital'. *Journal of Democracy* 6:65–78.
Rao, V. 1993. 'The Rising Price of Husbands: A Hedonic Analysis of Dowry Increase in Rural India'. *Journal of Political Economy* 101 (3): 666–77.
Rao, P. S. S., and S. G. Inbaraj. 1977. 'Inbreeding in Tamil Nadu, South India'. *Social Biology* 24:281–88.
Reddy, P. G. 1993. *Marriage Practices in South India*. Madras: University of Madras.
Rosenzweig, M., and O. Stark. 'Consumption Smoothing, Migration, and Marriage: Evidence from Rural India'. *Journal of Political Economy* 97 (4): 905–26.
Schull, W. J. 1959. 'Inbreeding Effects on Man'. *Eugenics Quarterly* 6:102–09.
Vatuk, S. 1982. 'Purdah Revisited: A Comparison of Hindu and Muslim Interpretations of the Cultural Meaning of Purdah in South Asia'. In *Separate Worlds: Studies of Purdah in South Asia*, eds. Hanna Papanek and Gail Minault. Delhi: Chanakya Publications.
Walker, T. S., and J. G. Ryan. 1990. *Village and Household Economies in India's Semi-arid Tropics*. Baltimore: Johns Hopkins University Press.
Zhang, J., and W. Chan. 1999. 'Dowry and Wife's Welfare: A Theoretical and Empirical Analysis'. *Journal of Political Economy* 107 (4): 786–808.

10

'LOVE' IN THE SHADOW OF THE SEWING MACHINE*

A Study of Marriage in the Garment Industry of Chennai, South India

JOHANNA LESSINGER

INTRODUCTION

When the export garment industry first came to Chennai (formerly Madras city, the capital of the south Indian state of Tamil Nadu) in the 1970s (Kalpagam 1994), it created a series of minor earthquakes in the lives of the young, working-class women who flocked to new factories to work as sewing-machine operators, pressers, packers, thread trimmers and button-hole makers. Hundreds of small and medium-sized garment export manufacturers dotted round the city began to offer women and girls from poor Chennai families something new: a chance to earn a weekly wage. However low the pay rates, garment work marked a major change for working-class women in a city where, for lack of jobs, women's labour-force participation is historically far lower than men's and in fact lower than that of rural women in Tamil

* The research on which this work is based was carried out in 1991–92 under an American Institute of Indian Studies (AIIS) grant. I am immensely grateful to the staff of AIIS and to supportive colleagues at the Department of Anthropology, University of Madras. Follow-up work was done in 2002. My greatest debt is to my assistants, Ms Suchitra Rao and Mr M. Thavamani, whose sensitivity to the nuances of language and behaviour greatly enlarged my own understanding.

Nadu (Sundari 2007: 110–11). Tamil Nadu was slower than North India in the development of an export garment industry (Banerjee 1991) but many of the social issues created by female employment are similar. Nor is India alone in experiencing the impact of export-oriented factory production on the roles of women workers. Elsewhere in South Asia, Pakistan, Sri Lanka and Bangladesh have also developed large female work forces tied to expanding garment industries over the last decades (Kabeer 2000; Dannecker 2002; Hewamanne 2006; Lynch 2007; Gunewardena 2007).[1]

By the 1990s, the labour force of these Chennai garment factories was overwhelmingly female and young; factory owners were determined to keep it that way, delighted with the apparently endless supply of docile, low-wage workers a modernising city offered. A man who had once worked in such factories as a supervisor and sample maker, in the earlier period when male tailors predominated, sighed and remarked, 'Today, garments means woman.'

Social scientists have identified major dislocations—in gender roles and family structures, in moral codes and local customs, in communities and social classes—which follow wherever and whenever globalising capitalism sweeps through once-traditional societies. At the same time a body of feminist scholarship since the 1970s has argued whether paid jobs and income for women create female autonomy in patriarchal societies or not, or if patriarchy is simply reproduced in the workplace (see among many, Fernandez 1997; Standing 1991; Caraway 2007; Gunewardena 2007; Kabeer 2000).

Those who 'go to garments' in Chennai certainly experience shifts in familial status as working-class households, governed by gender and age hierarchies favouring men and older people, confront the reality of wage-earning young women. The factory job makes a young, unmarried girl—once the most disregarded member of her household—the major breadwinner. This does not necessarily give her power and autonomy within her family, but does confront her with heavy financial and moral responsibilities to support her household—responsibilities once borne by fathers, brothers and husbands. Meanwhile, the long hours of work on the factory floor, the strenuous daily commute and the friendships with fellow workers take young women beyond the customary seclusion of home and the protective circle of kin and neighbours, and into a wider world of choices and potential dangers, including those involved in choosing a mate.

Some Chennai garment workers (and their mothers) are acutely conscious of the changes occurring. Jyothi, eldest child of a recently widowed mother and major household breadwinner, noted the growth in her own self-confidence and maturity after becoming a sewing-machine operator, then added, 'We must become ... what is it that [the nationalist Tamil poet Subramania] Bharati said? "New women." Yes, we become new.'

This essay focuses on one aspect of female newness related to marriage, in particular the kind of self-arranged marriage that garment workers call (in English) 'love marriage', to distinguish it from the older forms of arranged marriage. These new unions embody a series of factors—earned money, women's autonomous action, individual desire versus family decision-making, and modernising ideas about 'love'—which are precisely the fruits of globalisation. The shift is a crucial one, since marriage is the most critical institution shaping every Indian woman's life. Marriage is equally critical for entire families obligated by religion and custom to marry their daughters, although the circumstances of urban poverty make it ever harder to do so. Scholars now focus on the reworking of love, intimacy and marriage under the impact of globalisation (Rebhun 2007; Grover 2009). This essay's case studies, collected in Chennai in 1991–92 and 2002, suggest what love and marriage mean to female workers and their families. There appears no single, straight-line evolution from 'traditional' to 'modern' marriage, or from 'arrangement' to 'love'. As Grover (2009), Chowdhry (2004) and Donner (2002) make clear, love marriages are a growing phenomenon all over India, although they are also still vigorously contested at every social level. This material also suggests that 'love' has a variety of meanings to those who invoke it.

Almost half my sample of 55 female garment workers had, by 1992, contracted what they termed (in English) 'love marriages', usually in the face of family opposition, with men they had chosen themselves. A few, like young Jyothi herself, did not wish to marry at all. Many others were quietly bypassing their families and the financial role of elders in order to accumulate their own dowries, hoping to improve their chances in the arranged marriage market. And every one of these women had, in the workplace, avidly discussed at length the issues of love and love marriage as depicted in the enormously popular TV shows and films everyone in Chennai watches. Popular entertainment harps on the issue of love incessantly, both as a marker of modernity and 'modern' behaviour and because, as everywhere, the hint of sex sells. Whatever their thoughts about love marriage (and not all young women desire it), the modernising concepts of love and individual choice of partner are now firmly linked to any local discourse about male-female relationships, in contrast to the concepts underlying the system of arranged marriage.

The Dangers of Women's Work

In Chennai's working-class communities of the past, a household that sent its women out to work was confessing poverty and the incapacity of its male members (Vera-Sanso 1999), as well as flouting traditional norms of female modesty and seclusion (Lessinger 1990). This is true, despite Tamil Nadu's history of female agricultural work, particularly in rice-growing areas. Women are not demeaned by agricultural work on family land, amid relatives, but lose status if their labour is paid for and controlled, by others. In Chennai, these ideas change less quickly than the economic reality of available factory work and the growing need of poor households for women's earnings. Most working-class households with employed women still find it necessary to excuse themselves on the grounds of economic necessity, pointing to rising prices and, more obliquely, to male un- or under-employment. Additionally some adolescent girls added that they want to work because they are 'bored' (using the English term, suggesting a modern restlessness under the constraints of traditional house-bound girlhood.)

Working-class conservatives in Chennai, male and female, still denounce female employment, and garment factories in particular, as undermining female chastity and obedience and exposing young women to dangerous outsiders. 'Love', involving loss of reputation and rejection of parental authority, is spoken of as the first danger a young garment worker faces in the factory, rather than the exhaustion, ill health, contemptuous treatment, mulcted pay or sexual harassment she is sure to encounter at work. This fear of women factory workers' unconstrained sexuality is, of course, part of the long, gendered history of industrial capitalism. Female factory workers, particularly when they are new in the public eye, have always been accused of sexual laxity (Walkowitz 1992; Yelvington 1996; Hewamanne 2006; Lynch 2007) and have, in fact, used their relative freedom to push against old constraints. In India the conflict in moral norms is heightened because of an intense, pre-existing preoccupation with female chastity and sexual reputation as markers of family honour.

In Chennai, conservatives' forebodings linking garment work to 'love' have a certain grounding in fact: many workers do indeed use their work-related travels and their widened social experience, as well as their earning power, to contract dowry-less (and often inter-caste) matches. For the young people involved, the most salient aspect of love marriage is individual choice and desire. For parents, lack of dowry, flouting of parental authority, threat to family honour and status, and loss of possibly advantageous marriage alliances are at issue, but the risk to daughters' future wellbeing is also acknowledged.

Because the Chennai public recognises garment factories as sites where dangerous mixing of the sexes and love are likely to occur, factory managers and owners work strenuously to thwart it and to preserve their company's reputation, if only to retain a steady supply of local female workers. Monitoring workers closely, physically separating the sexes into different work sections or refusing to hire any men except supervisors are rarely wholly successful tactics. Shanti, a sample maker and union activist, said that after an elopement at her factory, 'The parents came and shouted in the factory. Now our management is very strict.' Daniyammal was upset enough to quit her job after finding a female supervisor and a stock boy embracing in a storage room. Yet, despite the vigilance of supervisors, families and tattling neighbours, love happens.

For most families these unsanctioned unions are a source of shame, anger and ostracism. None in my sample led to murder, police cases or prosecutions, unlike the law suits Chowdhry (2004) records. Instead, at their most extreme, families declared the erring young people dead. Sometimes a gradual, partial reconciliation occurred with the arrival of grandchildren. In virtually all cases, however, the young couple was initially very much on its own as a nuclear unit, deprived of the family advice, companionship and financial help so crucial to the newly married. In such cases, it is often the young wife's continued employment in a garment factory which makes possible an eloping couple's struggle to pay for food, rent and bus fare.

'They Watch Too Many Films...'

The role of the media—primarily television and films—in promoting or encouraging concepts of love and the practice of love marriage for garment workers is complex. In a movie-mad city like Chennai (Dickey 1993), garment workers are avid media consumers. A factory manager joked that Sunday evening was the one time it was impossible to impose overtime work, because an entire Tamil movie was broadcast on television and it was watched in virtually every city household. 'If they [workers] cannot get home in time to see that movie, I would have a riot in my hand.'

Although Madrasis often blame the cinema for propagating immoral ideas about love, it is probably best to look at the films and TV dramas, watched so raptly by so many, as what Mankekar labels 'discursive space' (1999: 125), an arena in which discourses about modernity and tradition, gender and family are offered for debate. Much of India's on-going discussion about tradition and social change is embedded in Tamil and Bollywood plots featuring love and love marriage—behaviours which are shown as good, bad, risky, undutiful, romantic, heart-breaking, futile, modern, immoral, noble, destructive. Collectively these filmic depictions of love are ambiguous and contradictory. What is important is that the theme of love is constantly re-invoked and ever-present, and interpreted personally by each viewer. Young workers frame discussions around film plot lines as a way to talk about their own home lives obliquely, to solicit the opinions of age-mates, and to test out new ideas without seeming to betray family confidences or voice disloyalty before outsiders. One woman reported that after an animated film discussion, 'some girls declare, "I'll marry whom I love. Otherwise, I won't marry at all."'

The Burden of Arranging Marriages

A tart-tongued Chennai matron, a working-class critic of both women's employment and love marriages, suggested the burden of parental responsibility placed on families morally obligated to marry their daughters, and the social disruption that looms if parents fail to carry out that duty: 'If you have a girl, you should be prepared to spend lavishly for her marriage, whether you have the money or borrow it. If you aren't going to spend, if you are going to be careless, it will be love marriage. She'll just get married anywhere, on the roadside, anywhere.'

Yet, increasing numbers of working class Chennai families are 'careless.' Unable to repudiate the concept of an arranged marriage, but too poor or disorganised to accomplish it, such families do nothing as their girls grow older; nor does the wider kin group. Parents continue to hope that some stroke of fortune will extricate them from difficulties and produce a dowry, or a groom who doesn't ask much. Or, as a professional woman in Chennai observing the slums around her neighbourhood remarked bitterly, a garment girl is, 'the goose laying the golden egg. The family won't let her go.'

Although young women frequently expressed fear of marriage itself (echoed by older women's gloomy reflections on the married state), most garment workers still unwed in their mid-twenties are also fearful of never marrying. A single 'girl' sees her close female friends vanish into marriages of their own, finds herself dependent on censorious kin, pitied by neighbours and employers, cut off from the adult status embodied in a husband and children. As time goes on, unmarried women are also vulnerable to men who would manoeuvre them into concubinage or prostitution, judging that their families are too negligent, too powerless or too greedy to offer them protection. What this suggests is the failure of tradition itself. Families are increasingly unable, through poverty and social dislocation, to do for their girls what tradition demands. Young wage earners feel exploited as their families refuse to forego their incomes by marrying them off. If they cannot force their families into arranging suitable marriages by accumulating some or all of their own dowries, they may take matters into their own hands, using their relative freedom as working women to decide their own futures.

A desperate daughter of a 'careless' family, reaching her late twenties, fearing she is becoming unmarriageable, sees a way out through love. With the collaboration of an equally impetuous and undutiful young man,[2] she elopes, getting married in a temple (some temples are famous for this), a registry office, or by simply declaring herself married. Some of these marriages survive, against the odds, because the man is genuinely devoted and the woman has a garment factory job.

In opting for love marriages, which throw most parents into paroxysms of rage, shouts and violence, young working-class people in Chennai are rejecting a very durable institution still widely considered the cultural ideal in Tamil Nadu. This is particularly so among a culturally conservative working class—doubly uneasy about status and honour in the context of rural-to-urban migration, social dislocation and impoverishment brought about by globalisation's economic restructuring. Families cling to concepts of caste endogamy and potential upward mobility through 'good' marriages. In contrast some of their daughters and sons seem to have abandoned such ideas.

Although feminists may shudder, for working-class Tamil women, there is still something to be said in favour of arranged marriage, if successfully executed, as Kishwar (1994) argues. Entire kin groups have a stake in an alliance which both creates and reinforces family prestige. Relatives' involvement in finding a groom, evaluating his family and arranging the necessary financial exchanges surrounds the new relationship with social supports which have, until recently, helped to keep marriages stable and to protect women and children from abandonment and abuse. In Chennai one of the most frequent arguments against love marriages, aside from the fact that they tend to be inter-caste, is that men who enter them are more likely to abandon their wives after a few years precisely because the kin group has no hold over them and no dowry has been exchanged.

'You Cannot Support the Family on One Salary...'

The breakdown of a family's ability to arrange marriages must be seen in the context of the deteriorating economic position of Chennai's urban working class, and particularly of its men—a deterioration to which female wage work, once socially undesirable, is one response. Safa (1995) has noted the Caribbean 'myth of the male breadwinner'. It persists in Chennai as well, where young women find themselves thrust into the work force and obliged to support parents and siblings—including unemployed or underemployed fathers and brothers—because working-class men can no longer find steady jobs. In Chennai, old factories are closing or making their workers 'temporary'. Public sector jobs have been slashed by neoliberal economic restructuring. The city's new high-tech industries have no room for the semi-literate and unskilled. Meanwhile economically marginalised men continue to claim the right to control female behaviour. Wives find themselves scraping for daily survival because husbands or sons cannot, or will not, work or have jobs that do not pay enough to feed and house a family. The household's last economic resource may be its adolescent daughters, and work in the new 'global assembly line'.

As soon as a garment factory opened at the edge of their slum neighbourhood, Saroja marched in and demanded jobs for her two adolescent girls, in an effort to keep a household of seven adults and two children afloat. The men were carpenters with only seasonal work. Unlike the numerous households whose parents and elders initially opposed a young woman's garment job, insisting that it was improper and that 'no lady in our house has ever gone out to work', Saroja recognised almost immediately the potential the new industry offered her girls and her household.

Sending women out to work nevertheless poses social and moral dilemma for conservative families. Older women with adolescent daughters articulated this dilemma. 'When I was a girl, I never set foot beyond my father's threshold', said Valliyammal about her village upbringing. 'Not until I got married and came away. Today in our Madras, things are different. If I had learned anything when I was young, I could have helped out now.' Over her husband's objections, Valliyammal has allowed her daughter to attend a tailoring class, and was currently trying to persuade him to let the girl enter a garment factory.

Valliyammal went on to make an important point, reiterated in virtually the same words by many other women, that the implied economic contract built into marriage is now different. 'You cannot run the house on one salary alone ... She [a daughter] has to be able to support herself even after she marries. If something happens, she needs to be able to support herself. Let her get the experience now. It's for her life. If her husband isn't good ...' Saying this, Valliyammal cast her eyes towards the bench where her unemployed and tipsy husband had sat grumbling and muttering through the first part of the interview.

To the economic upheavals of globalisation must be added physical dislocation from speculative real-estate development, which has had a severe impact on poor Chennai families, their kin networks and neighbourhoods. Entire working-class residential areas were pulled down in the late 1990s and replaced by glossy apartment blocks and shopping malls. Neighbourhoods present in the 1990s have vanished, scattering neighbours and relatives to distant perimeters of the city and vaporising whatever small capital a dwelling represented. Such a situation probably exacerbates family anxieties about status and honour, as the uprooting disrupts the moral communities which might have provided resources and social pressure to help stabilise family life. Households are left increasingly isolated to cope with poverty, stress and moral ambiguity.

Mayil, a single woman of 21, toughened by four years of singlehandedly supporting her mother and two non-working adult brothers, defended herself against the disapproval her mother's brother and his wife expressed when she went out to work, 'Only we will know our own difficulties, because we are suffering, but they aren't giving and helping. If we go to work our problems will be solved. So, thinking this, I went to work. Gradually they accepted it.' Mayil's problems included feeding and housing four adults on INR 520 a month. Her uncle and his wife lived in a distant part of the city and rarely visited; no doubt to avoid pressure to help.

Widespread alcoholism and domestic violence, exacerbated by male unemployment, have helped to disillusion young women with marriage itself. For instance, Jyothi, at 18, says she does not want to marry at all:

> **Jyothi:** Not interested in marriage! ... In this present time it's frightening to see men. You can't tell who's good and who's bad. In my [factory] section alone four have been abandoned by their husbands, poor things. If I see all this I feel it is better to be free, to be like this [single]. No interest in marriage at all!
> **Older married woman neighbour:** If a good alliance comes, they have to marry. Without getting married can we keep them like that?
> **Interviewer:** Why are you afraid of marriage?
> **Jyothi:** In this present day, who can you believe? If he abandons me too, that's the fear! And then if he's a drunkard, in this quiet and calm family! Will he pull me into the street, being drunk and making trouble and putting me to shame?

In another conversation that turned to women's economic helplessness after marriage and the current inability of men to support families, an older woman muttered anxiously under her breath, 'We mustn't say such things; it will discourage the young ones [from marrying].' The young one present simply laughed. Eventually most young women like Jyothi do marry. However, some may reason that their own choices, based on emotion and personal knowledge, cannot be any worse than the toxic marital relationships they see around them.

Family Dramas: Pure Romance

Some of the love marriages recounted to us seem sweetly, cinematically romantic. What is notable about the story of Stella Mary and Selvam, aside from their touching determination to wed, is that they were able to flee to Chennai and create a family largely because Stella Mary was, and is, a garment worker. Her income tided the young couple over in their early days, and now makes it possible for them to live in lower-middle-class comfort with little extended family support.

Stella Mary, beautiful even at 14, went to a wedding, where her 20-year-old father's sister's son, Selvam, saw her and fell instantly in love. As a cross-cousin, it was a wholly suitable match in the traditional view. Selvam begged his parents to arrange it, but they refused.

The young couple remained in touch, and at 16, when her mother died and her father remarried, Stella Mary left for Chennai, alone, to stay with her father's childless younger brother and his wife, who ran a small gold-covering (cheap jewellery) shop. Selvam, meanwhile, steadily refused various marriage offers.

Stella Mary quickly found work in the Chennai garment industry. Paying her aunt only for her food, she managed to save INR 10,000 and to buy some gold jewellery to constitute her own small dowry. After three years, Selvam shook free of his family and came to Chennai to marry her. He worked briefly in her uncle's shop and then found a job driving buses for the state transport company, and later as a long-distance truck driver.

Today, modestly prosperous and with two healthy boys, Stella Mary and Selvam say they are only on distant, formal terms with their natal families. The aunt and uncle, now very old, live with them as babysitters.

Ramakrishnan and Vasanthy are brisk, modern and self-confident. They fell in love as co-workers. Ramakrishnan assured me that neither set of parents had objected for long, perhaps because they were of the same caste and because he was a valued, long-term employee earning INR 1500–2000, a month. 'We loved each other. We informed the big people [factory managers], and we got married in a good way', thus avoiding getting fired. The handsome young pair, sitting surrounded by wedding gifts, explained their ambitious plans for future promotions, further savings and eventual children to be raised with the help of a hired ayah, since Vasanthy intends to go on working after she has children.

Valli and Vijay fell in love as neighbours working in different garment factories. Valli notes that her family could not have given her a dowry even if they had approved her choice since they had been using all her INR 600 monthly earnings to live on.

Their inter-caste match brought down the wrath of both sets of parents; they eloped, but now struggle to make ends meet. From a tiny budget Valli is also still trying to put together the equivalent of a dowry. She says that she began to save some of her salary surreptitiously to buy a bit of gold jewellery and some saris, 'when I knew that he was serious about wanting to marry me'. She specifies that she is still doing so because it is better for a woman to wed 'with something in your hand so that they [in-laws] will respect you.'

Vijay, rebel enough to marry against his parents' wishes, remains traditional in one respect: he still feels married women ought not to work. He says rather shame-facedly that he is 'still sending [his] wife out to work after marriage', but excuses himself on the grounds of his own low wages. When we visited them, Valli had been ill and Vijay hovered over her anxiously. It was a smiling neighbour who directed us to their door, telling us, 'You know, they loved and ran away together. See, he even stayed home today because she is sick.' This sympathy suggests that the aura of love and romance casts its glamour over observers, at least when their own families are not directly involved.

Family Dramas: Careless Families and Desperate Daughters

Mayil, 21, had earlier talked about her sense of struggle in carrying the family financial burden alone. She and her mother are discussing the impact of household poverty on her marriage chances. Mayil's unemployed older brother sleeps soundly beside us throughout. Another brother, also unemployed, has had the tact to remove himself. The interview is poignant for Mayil's bitterness, her mother's regrets, and the family's sense of isolation.

> **Mother:** You see here (gesturing to adult son deeply asleep on the floor) he is old enough to earn, he has skills [as a lathe operator] but he is sleeping ... And if we had kept this girl's [Mayil's] earnings by now we could have gotten her married.
>
> **Mayil:** Mmmmm. He is sleeping.
>
> **Mother:** If I say that this country has progressed at all, it is because now girls are earning in a good way, better than boys, and are taking care of the family.
>
> **Interviewer:** You haven't saved anything for her marriage?
>
> **Mother:** (Sadly) Nothing now.
>
> **Mayil:** (Bitterly) Not even a paisa.
>
> **Mother:** Not even a paisa.
>
> **Mayil:** I have completed four years of work. This is the fifth year. In those years I have earned a lot but I haven't put even a paisa for myself into the bank.
>
> **Mother:** Not in the bank and not in the house. If there were money she could get married tomorrow.

Usha, a plump, pretty Dalit woman now in her mid-twenties, is unusually articulate about her desperation to marry and the evolution of her decision—from resistance to pragmatic acceptance to 'love'—to elope with a less-than-ideal husband. She is the second wife of Aziz, a young Muslim tailor recently migrated to Chennai from a rural area near Pondicherry. By 1992, they had a daughter and Usha was pregnant again. She seemed content in a marriage she had initially evaded. Aziz's theatrical performance of romantic love, the urgings of workmates, plus her recognition of her natal family's financial and moral shortcomings, eventually moved Usha to accept Aziz; but she does not claim to have been swept away by romance initially and she still disapproves of love marriages in general.

With a sixth-standard education, Usha went to work at the age of 19 in a very small garment factory on a distant edge of the city. The factory, unusually, hired only male tailors to assemble entire garments, leaving the simpler jobs for women. On occasion, during the rush season, the entire factory worked through the night; workers could not get home until the first buses ran again at dawn.

For this, Usha brought in INR 280–350 a month to her natal household of eight. Her mother, a former domestic servant, was too anaemic to work. Her father, a truck loader, had been too weak (and perhaps too drunk) to work for several years past. Three brothers, a 12-year-old sister in school and a grandmother also had to be supported.

When Usha first went to work, 'only one of my brothers was working [as a lorry cleaner, or loader], so I worked ... I was earning and giving to my house. I wouldn't take any money for my own expenses. I gave it all to my mother. We used it for house difficulties ... We were in very great difficulties.'

Nevertheless, Usha's brothers objected to her employment from the first day on grounds of respectability, saying, 'We told her to stay home quietly. Why is she coming late? She is going in the morning, coming in the night-time' (suggesting sexual laxity). Her father protested, 'Why do you have to go so far away?' Only her mother defended her, saying, 'She alone is working. Sometimes the bus isn't available.'

At the factory Usha encountered Aziz, who soon began to woo her publicly. Interestingly, she still sees herself as a traditionalist on the subject of love marriage, 'Nobody chooses husbands according to their desire. Their family elders should choose for them.' However, it became clear to her eventually that her impoverished family was not going to choose for her.

> Because of my family difficulties, until now I would have been at home [i.e. unmarried] ... Near my house, girls who studied with me had gotten married and even younger girls have gotten married. I thought, "If I'm going to be like this, what is going to happen?" So I married him ... Because of their difficulties they [parents] were not in a position to marry me of. And I have two younger brothers who also have to get married. They are of that age. [A third brother had married but left the household, refusing to share the burden of supporting the others.]

Aziz's courtship of Usha conformed to the romantic stereotype. He took every occasion to talk to Usha, and quickly declared himself in love. When he persisted, she left to find work in another factory. However, her former supervisor, a woman, came to visit and reproached her, telling her how Aziz had gotten sick (those thwarted in love are thought to pine and grow thin) after she left and had grown a beard (a sign of romantic distress). 'At the company they were scolding me ... then I felt sorry for him.'

Her supervisor and a former co-worker strongly advised Usha to marry Aziz. Perhaps they sympathised with the romance, but they may also have recognised Usha's vulnerability, thanks to her voluptuous looks, the low-caste status, poverty and family neglect. Eventually, an older man would have bid for her as a mistress or 'second wife'. At least, Aziz offered affection, economic support and a publicly-acknowledged marriage.

When Aziz approached Usha's parents for permission, they were initially reluctant because he was a Muslim. However he claimed to be single, clearly had a job, and promised to accept a Hindu wedding. No other offers for the girl were in sight, and Aziz asked no dowry. They agreed, grudgingly.

'Then we came to know he was already married and had a wife. So they [parents] said, "No. We won't give her." I knew he was married, he had told me all about himself. He told me his wife ran away.' (Reliable informants say the first wife actually remains in Aziz's village, with his child and his parents.) A crowd of neighbours, led by Usha's brothers, gathered to beat up Aziz.

The opposition may actually have stiffened Usha's resolve. 'I thought, "Why should I marry a Muslim man? I waited so long. Why should I be a second wife?" Then after some more time I realised, "No caste, and no religion. If he provides me with food to eat without my crying for it, that's enough." Then I married him ... I loved him and I married him.'

The marriage was established as fact when Usha and Aziz ran away together to a distant village. When they returned, Usha was pregnant. Her parents took her home for the delivery of her first child, the couple settled in the same slum community, and Usha sees her mother, sister and beloved grandmother regularly, but no longer speaks to her brothers. Her concern now is to get her husband's permission to return to work, since they struggle on his earnings alone. He is resisting on grounds of respectability.

The Failure of Love

If Usha escaped from intolerable poverty, exploitation and potential spinsterhood with a man willing to love, marry and support her, Shanti found only lasting sorrow in a bigamous, abusive relationship. A lively, intelligent and headstrong girl when we met her in 1992, Shanti had braved paternal disapproval first to work, then in 1994 to fall in love with a boy in the neighbourhood whom she was forbidden to marry, and finally to elope with a married man in 1997. He, after she gave birth to his child, deserted her for another woman. This is every parent's nightmare about love marriage, where kin have no control over a man who arrives without credentials, proclaims 'love', then vanishes leaving a dependent, abandoned woman and child, now a source of acute social shame.

Although Shanti was certainly an active agent in her own tragedy, her tale also shows a lower-middle-class family exploiting a daughter's earning power, then neglecting her future in favour of other economic ends—in this case, education of a son and pursuit of social mobility. Declared dead by her natal family, Shanti's subsequent struggles illustrate the terrors of social isolation in the wake of failed love.

In 1992, Shanti's job disturbed her family because her Nadar caste is both uneasy about its status and highly conservative regarding female education and female employment. Yet, with five daughters (two still unmarried), and with only one incompetent son, Shanti's father had found himself struggling financially. He reluctantly obliged to let both girls work in garments.

The father had operated a provisions shop in a village south of the city, but had decided to relocate to Chennai to improve the family prospects. Intent on establishing a business in the big city, he had already married off three older daughters into the local Nadar shop-keeping community with the large dowries expected (20–25 sovereigns of gold for each girl, where roughly 8 grams make one sovereign).

At that time, Shanti had been working for two years. She told us proudly that her INR 500 salary helped pay the rent and living expenses for five people. Her mother admitted that she had saved INR 30,000 from the earnings of Shanti and her sister—a major contribution to the INR 40,000 promised as that sister's dowry.

Shanti's father wept as he explained,

> Because of family circumstances, we are sending them to work ... In our community there are around 200 people. Nobody has sent their daughters to work ... My son cannot do much because he won't study, can't learn English ... So I have many things churning around in my heart that nobody knows ... I myself told my relatives, "Nobody should send their girls to work", yet I'm doing so ... At least, whatever she is earning we are saving. We haven't touched a paisa. That much God has given me.

The father's account is equivocal. Shanti, her mother and sister made it clear: the girls' earnings had been essential to marriages allying the family in Chennai's Nadar commercial community. Status concerns also explain the ferocious reaction to Shanti's later rebellion.

We located Shanti again in 2002 with the help of a former workmate who knew some of her unhappy story. This time we met a thin, crushed and tear-stained woman in a bare little house in a desolate suburb far beyond the city limits. She cried intermittently throughout the interview, painfully reminded of her parents, whom she had not seen since they cast her out five years earlier, her lover's betrayal, and present anxieties about survival. 'Today you see me like this. It was my mistake. I loved him, I left my family ... He deserted me. He has done this to several women. How could I judge?'

Shanti's account mixes regret and self-justification with anger at her family. Her final act of romantic defiance and self-assertion seems inevitable.

In her mid-twenties, now the only girl left at home, Shanti fell in love with somebody she met on the way to work. Discovered, her irate family locked her up and beat her, although the man was a fellow Nadar. Several years later, after being allowed to return to work, she eloped with a second man. 'Near my house there was a Thompson TV factory. He was working there. I was talking with him. Just like that I was falling in love. He compelled me and eloped with me. I did not like that but he compelled me and brought me out [of my parents' house] ... He was already a married man. That's why I didn't want to marry him. But he compelled me and brought me to marry.'

After they moved to a tiny house on the city's edge, Shanti bore a son. When the child was less than a year old the man ran off with another girl, taking with him INR 10,000, he had just persuaded Shanti to borrow from a moneylender. Without social support or a marriage certificate, Shanti had no way to pursue the man, even if he could have been located. She now supports herself and her four-year-old on INR 1200–2000 a month, by way of her garment factory salary. She pays a weekly sum to her landlady, who has cared for the child since he was three-months old.

Shanti's parents, led by her father, remain estranged and hostile, denying that they have a younger daughter. Her brother, whom Shanti labels 'completely useless', tells visitors, 'I don't know her', or 'She died.' Shanti does get occasional surreptitious visits and donations from her older married sister. This woman, still working in garments, visits her disgraced sister without her own husband's knowledge, to avoid quarrels. She doesn't offer much emotional support. 'She too thinks my fate is like this', Shanti says.

Her mother sneaks her occasional money via the sister. 'Mother has love. I earned and gave one lakh to my mother. She thinks, "She earned so much, but we did not give anything, so we will at least give this money."' Shanti is currently negotiating to send her son to stay with her sister so that his grandmother can see him for the first time, but she is not optimistic about a reconciliation. 'What I did was wrong. I know. As punishment, if they were to beat me but then ask me to come home, I could go. But I don't have the courage ... My father says, "Don't come here." ... Sometimes I ask myself, "Who will give me shelter?"'

Shanti's account makes more explicit the sexual dangers a single woman faces, particularly if she is compromised by a failed love marriage. Her factory manager, whom she calls 'golden', is fortunately sympathetic rather than predatory. 'Since he knows my situation he keeps me on [amid layoffs and closures]. He knows my story.' She also relies on her landlord's family.

> Because of the landlord's support I am staying here ... If they were not here I would not be here.... Otherwise, in this [lonely, deserted] area I couldn't move around bravely. Many men have called me to go with them and wanted me to be their mistress. But I'm enduring it all bravely.... When

> they know my story they know my weakness so they take advantage. If she [landlady] were not here I would be on the street.

Shanti's difficult story suggests the risks of love marriage, the gamble that 'love' is sincere enough to produce a lasting relationship to compensate for isolation and family ostracism. When love marriage fails, young women become more vulnerable than ever (see also the discussion in Grover 2009). Shanti is clearly not the only victim in and around the Chennai garment industry. In interviewing we heard of other predatory suitors who took advantage of the 'love' model to acquire temporary sex partners and then disappeared, leaving women disgraced and abandoned, forced to seek abortions or to raise their children alone. Only Shanti poured out the sad details to us because we had known her in happier times. For such women, the ideology and practice of love marriage have not empowered them or given them autonomy, but simply left them very poor and profoundly alone.

Conclusion

This study suggests that 'love marriage' in Chennai's new, feminised working class is a complex phenomenon. On one hand it is an outgrowth of a major shift in women's employment opportunities, giving women new earning power, the right to move outside the home, a range of new social relationships and a sense of autonomy. It coincides with a global ideology of romance and individual choice, creating a behavioural model widely accessible through the media. On the other hand such marriages are an adaptive reaction to the impoverishment and social dislocation created by globalisation. Some young people reach for a vision of romantic love for fear of never achieving social adulthood as their worlds fall apart. For working-class women this adulthood is still achievable only through husband, children and a home of one's own. Even those fearful of the known pitfalls in contemporary Chennai marriage come to understand that to be young, poor, single and female is also to be a victim. Thus, globalisation presents the garment workers in this study with a new kind of dilemma: husbands remain necessary, but eligible ones are increasingly out of reach. Those who are lucky use the attractiveness of youth, and the small freedoms their jobs bring them to attract starry-eyed young men willing to fall in love, defy their families and enter a runaway marriage. Those who are unlucky find themselves cynically seduced and abandoned by their chosen partners. They join the ranks of deserted wives and mothers who form the female-headed households increasingly prevalent in working-class areas of Indian cities. An added element of misery is that the woman known to have brought her misfortune on herself, through that disreputable set of actions and emotions called 'love', may lose even moral support from family and community.

After the fact, do love marriages produce less patriarchal more 'modern' relationships or social arrangements? Certainly some couples have evolved relatively egalitarian patterns of interaction, reinforced by the absence of the extended family and the young pair's need to rely on each other almost exclusively in the struggle to form a new nuclear family. Without an older generation in the house, there is nobody to enforce the stricter forms of female subordination and male-female separation. The fact that so many young wives are financially obliged to continue work after marriage gives a woman an important voice in household decision-making, however her husband may resent the necessity.

It is important to note that those who embark on love marriages face a period of economic and social isolation, and thus, considerable hardship. A disobedient couple has no dowry or wedding gifts to fall back on; they are excluded from periodic ritual family exchanges of food, gifts and new clothes; the young man will not be asked to join a family business or inherit a father's job. A young woman cannot expect sympathy, child care and small presents from mother and sisters. Influential family social networks are no longer available to the young couple. The occasional support of work-mates or neighbours cannot replace what has been lost. It is in this context that one understands why women involved in love marriages spend time and hard-earned cash trying to put together small dowries for themselves: as markers of individual honour and self-respect vis-a-vis reluctant in-laws and as small savings accounts to hedge against the kind of financial disasters—job loss, house fire, illness, death—which haunt poor communities.

It is evident that love marriages are accelerating what is already an urban Indian trend towards nuclear households and weakened kinship ties. For Chennai garment workers it also increases the likelihood that a woman will remain in the workforce after marriage, at least as long as the garment plants continue to favour south Indian female workers. Furthermore, the frequency with which those marriages breach caste and religious boundaries suggests that many young people no longer care about such distinctions, finding common ground instead in their shared Chennai upbringing, in similar class positions and in shared industrial workplace experiences.

What appears in all of the case studies offered here is a growing degree of female self-assertion. A great many women refuse to be passive pawns in family survival strategies which hinge on the sacrifice of their futures. They insist on the validity of their own desires—actually, very traditional desires—for marriage, for children, for the right 'to live like others'. For those women who actually have the courage to elope, enduring the subsequent uproar and stigma to carve out homes for themselves and their husbands, that self-assertion is life-changing. 'Yes,' says young Jyothi, 'We become new.'

Notes

[1] Although work processes are very similar throughout South Asia, cultural and historical differences do produce varied outcomes. In particular, different living arrangements seem to have an impact on workers' ability to act autonomously. In contrast to Sri Lankan or Bangladeshi women, Chennai workers by and large live with their parents, and are under greater familial and community control, meaning that political activism, as well as love affairs, are strongly discouraged.

[2] The data missing from this study is the motivation of young men. Why do young men consent to defy their families to enter love marriages? Why do so many young men refuse to work, leaving their sisters to support the household? Are young men stirred by other discourses of modernity, wanting lives and careers—free of endless, exhausting manual labour, alcoholism and domestic abuse—which are just out of reach?

References

Banerjee, Nirmala. 1991a. 'Introduction'. In *Women in a Changing Industrial Scenario*, ed. N. Banerjee, 11–32. New Delhi: SAGE.

______. 1991b. 'The More It Changes The More It Is The Same: Women Workers in Export-oriented Industries'. In *Women in a Changing Industrial Scenario*, ed. N. Banerjee, 237–98. New Delhi: SAGE.

Caraway, Teri. 2007. *Assembling Women: The Feminization of Global Manufacturing*. Ithaca: ILR Press for Cornell University Press.

Chowdhry, Prem. 2004. 'Private Lives, State Intervention: Cases of Runaway Marriage in Rural North India'. *Modern Asian Studies* 38 (1): 55–84.

Dannecker, Petra. 2002. *Between Conformity and Resistance: Women Garment Workers in Bangladesh*. Dhaka: Dhaka University Press.

Dickey, Sara. 1993. *Cinema and the Urban Poor in South India*. Cambridge: Cambridge University Press.

Donner, Henrike. 2002. 'One's Own Marriage: Love Marriages in a Calcutta Neighbourhood'. *South Asia Research* 22 (1): 79–94.

Fernandez, Leela. 1997. *Producing Workers: The Politics of Gender, Class and Culture in the Calcutta Jute Mills*. Philadelphia: University of Pennsylvania Press.

Grover, Shalini. 2009. 'Lived Experience: Marriage, Notions of Love and Kinship Support Amongst Poor Women in Delhi'. *Contributions to Indian Sociology* 43 (1): 1–33.

Gunewardena, Nandini. 2007. 'Disrupting Subordination and Negotiating Belonging, Women Workers in the Transnational Production Sites of Sri Lanka'. In *The Gender of Globalization, Women Navigating Cultural and Economic Marginalities*, eds. N. Gudewardena and A. Kingsolver. Santa Fe: School for Advanced Research Press.

Hewamanne, Sandya. 2006. 'Pornographic Voice: Critical Feminist Practices Among Sri Lanka's Female Garment Workers'. *Feminist Studies* 32 (1): 125–54.

Kabeer, Naila. 2000. *Power To Choose: Bangladeshi Women and Labour Market Decisions in London and Dhaka*. London and New York: Verso Press.

Kalpagam, U. 1994. 'Labour in Small Industry: The Case of The Garment Export Industry in Madras'. In *Labour and Gender, Survival in Urban India*, ed. U. Kalpagam. New Delhi: SAGE.

Kishwar, Madhu. 1994. 'Love and Marriage'. *Manushi* 80:11–19.

Lessinger, Johanna. 1990. 'Work and Modesty: The Dilemma of Women Market Traders in South India'. In *Structures and Strategies, Women, Work and Family*, eds. L. Dube and R. Palriwala, New Delhi: SAGE.

Lynch, Caitrin. 2007. *Juki Girls, Good Girls, Gender and Cultural Politics in Sri Lanka's Global Garment Industry*. Ithaca: ILR Press of Cornell University Press.

Mankekar, Purnima. 1999. *Screening Culture, Viewing Politics: An Ethnography of Television, Womanhood, and Nation in Postcolonial India*. Durham, N. C.: Duke University Press.

Rebhun, Linda Ann. 2007. 'The Strange Marriage of Love and Interest, Economic Change and Emotional Intimacy in Northeast Brazil, Public and Private'. In *Love and Globalization, Transformations of Intimacy in the Contemporary World*, eds. M. Padilla, J. Hirsch, M. Munoz-Laboy, R. Sember, and R. Parker. Nashville: Vanderbilt University Press.

Safa, Helen. 1995. *Myth of the Male Breadwinner: Women and Industrialization in the Caribbean*. Boulder, CO: Westview Press.

Standing, Hillary. 1991. *Dependence and Autonomy: Women's Employment and The Family in Calcutta*. London: Routledge.

Sundari, S. 2007. *Migrant Women and Urban Labour Market: Concepts and Case Studies of Problems, Gains and Losses*. New Delhi: Deep and Deep Publications.

Vera-Sanso, Penny. 1999. 'Dominant Daughters-in-Law and Submissive Mothers-in-Law? Cooperation and Conflict in South India'. *Journal of the Royal Anthropological Institute* 5 (4): 577–99.

Walkowitz, Judith. 1992. *City of Dreadful Delight: Narratives of Sexual Danger in Late-Victorian London*. Chicago: University of Chicago Press.

Yelvington, Kevin. 1996. 'Flirting in the Factory'. *Journal of the Royal Anthropological Institute* 2 (2): 313–33.

Transnational Marriages

Documents, Wedding Albums, Photographers and Jaffna Tamil Marriages

Sidharthan Maunaguru

Introduction

The past three decades of political violence in Sri Lanka have devastated the social and economic landscape of the Tamil communities, disrupting their relationships. Consequently, Jaffna Tamils are now widely dispersed across other parts of Sri Lanka and throughout the world—predominantly in India, Canada, England and continental Europe (Fuglerud 1999; Daniel 1996). Moreover, due to the armed hostilities, mass internal and external displacement has occurred over the course of the last two decades. This has resulted in a large Tamil diaspora comprising over 7,00,000 people (Fuglerud 1999). This situation has resulted in a breakdown of personal networks as families have dispersed and suffered internal division, both within and across spaces (Lawrence 2000; Perera 1999). Many scholars have studied the devastation that the political conflict has wreaked on the families, lives and personal networks of the Tamil and Sinhala communities (Lawrence 2000; Perera 1999; Daniel 1996; Fuglerud 1999). However, no attempt has been made to study how these communities have attempted to rebuild their lives, within Sri Lanka and across the globe.

A key way in which the rebuilding of Tamil communities has been taking place is through the institution of marriage across (often, transnational) borders. The institution of marriage has emerged as a means of building alliances between dispersed members of Tamil communities, allowing them to reunite communities that have been fragmented. While transnational marriages among Tamils may be seen as a by-product of the war and displacement in Sri Lanka—and in that sense a fairly new phenomenon—they are still strongly linked to earlier forms of marriage and marriage negotiations within the Tamil communities.

Of particular significance within the phenomenon of transnational marriages is the reunion of bride and groom in the migrant spouse's 'adoptive' country, post the marriage ceremony. Many Tamil men and women, who have achieved either formal or informal refugee status in their adoptive countries, seek a prospective spouse from Sri Lanka. The spouse, who has to migrate in order to be reunited with a husband/wife, has to first navigate through embassies and the immigration laws and practices of different states. Aspiring immigrants are required to produce a number of documents at the embassies. The visa officers' decision to grant or withhold the all-important visa is based on 'satisfactory' visual and written proof that a 'genuine' marriage has taken place. Thus, this is a vital aspect of the immigration process.[1]

As part of the process of deciding on the validity of a marriage, the immigration officer who looks into the wedding albums and other documentation of the marriage seeks evidence for whether: a) specific customs had been followed according to the Tamil culture, b) certain rituals had been performed and c) the photographs taken reveal the presence of a large number of family members. It appears that immigration officers do not accept a civil marriage as valid, unless evidence of Tamil customary marriage ceremonies is furnished. An important question that arises then is: Why do immigration officers seek evidence of customary marriage ceremonies over and above the evidence of a civil marriage? Other scholars have pointed out how the immigration rules and procedures are set to restrict marriage migration to the host countries (Gell 1994; Hall 2002). The host countries' immigration procedures, in order to validate a marriage as genuine, set out to operationalise the perceived 'traditional' and 'cultural' norms of the migrants' own community (Palriwala and Uberoi 2008).[2]

Interestingly, the discussion on Tamil customary marriage ceremonies and the debates surrounding the validity of 'legal' Tamil marriages according to the Tamil tradition had taken place in courtrooms during the colonial era in Sri Lanka in the early twentieth century (Goonasekera 1984).[3] Thus, questioning the validity of a legal Tamil marriage in the eyes of the immigration laws is not a new phenomenon. It is clearly a new phase of an old, unsettled issue from the colonial past of Sri Lanka. While the relationship between the colonial laws of Sri Lanka and the immigration laws of Western countries is a fascinating study in its own right, it is not the focus of this essay.

This essay is a detailed exploration of the growing phenomenon of the transnational marriage between Tamils who live in host and home countries. I explore how wedding photographs have become a form of authentic evidence that proves the genuineness of the marriage. How have these documents emerged to determine the genuineness of the marriage? How does the production of such visual documents and the people involved in their production (e.g. photographers and witnesses of such documents, such as state officials) come together to create a specific notion of what a 'Tamil marriage' is and what the specific 'Tamil marriage traditions' are? What kind of visual images of Tamil 'traditional' marriages and romance and intimacy between two people are necessary to satisfy the immigration officer? I also seek to understand the logic by which wedding photographs are able to function as 'witnesses' of a 'genuine' Tamil wedding'.

Movement and Marriage

The Tamil diaspora is not a mono-directional phenomenon; rather, it is circulatory in nature (Cheran 2004). For Cheran, the circulation does not mean that people live both in host and home countries at different time periods; it means that even though a member of a community lives in the host country, he/she continuously has strong material and immaterial relationships with his/her home country. Cheran points out that even while being away from Sri Lanka, members of the diaspora continue to invest (in property, business and marriage) in Sri Lanka and have close family ties in Sri Lanka. He argues that the Tamil diaspora cannot be studied only in the host country, but needs to be understood in terms of the circulation of people, money and goods between the 'host' and 'home' countries.

I hold, however, that the ideas of dispersion and that of the circulation of people, goods and obligations are not completely new. Banks (1960), who studied marriage and kinship among Jaffna Tamils, points out that their marriages do not take place only within the village, but across villages. Marriage, for instance, ensures the movement of people across villages rather than only within a village. Moreover, land transfers as part of dowry transactions mean that even as women move away from their villages, their rights in the natal village are retained (Tambiah 1973). Furthermore, cross-sibling relationships are important because of the claim a sibling has over cross-siblings' children as potential marriage partners for their own children (Yalman 1967). It is clear, then, that marriages which can lead to people leaving a domestic setup can also ensure their possible return to their place of origin in the future, because of ties to property and sibling obligations. It highlights the fact that a form of movement had been associated with marriage among the Jaffna Tamils even before war and displacement. The location in which a marriage takes place has shifted from the village to other spaces. Most of the marriages of the Tamil diaspora take place either in Colombo or in India. Often, since the bridegroom does not have citizenship in his adoptive country, he can only travel to countries other than Sri Lanka.

Story 1: Cross-border Marriages and Documents

Kayal was living in Jaffna with her parents. Kayal's marriage was arranged by her parents. Her future husband is a refugee in country X and did not have the required documentation to travel to Sri Lanka. As a result, Kayal's marriage took place in Chennai where the bridegroom travelled to from country X for the marriage. They invited as many people as possible to the wedding in order to produce photographs for the immigration officials at the country X's embassy, so that they could prove that the marriage was 'genuine'. After the marriage, Kayal returned to Sri Lanka and made arrangements to join her husband. She produced several documents for the embassy, such as photographs of the wedding ceremony, detailed telephone bills and personal letters along with the marriage certificate as a proof of her marriage. She was called for an interview at the embassy. During the interview, the immigration officer had asked her whether she had given a dowry and she said that she had not. The immigration officer then told her that in a traditional Tamil marriage it is important for the bride to provide dowry to the bridegroom and since she has not given a dowry, it makes him think that the marriage was not 'genuine'. Further, he said that the personal letters sent by her husband to her sound too 'official' and lacked romance. Based on this, he put her case on hold for a few months.

Like Kayal, the visa applications of many Tamils to rejoin their husband or wife in the host countries were rejected, because they could not satisfy the immigration officer's notions of Tamil customary wedding ceremonies and performances. In another instance, a letter of refusal given to a Sri Lankan Tamil by country X's embassy refers to a 'definition' of a Sri Lankan Tamil arranged marriage:

> In my opinion, the circumstances of the marriage between you and your sponsor are not consistent with Sri Lankan arranged marriages. In a culture where an arranged marriage is considered to be bringing together of two families, and greater emphasis is placed on compatibility and knowledge of the other party as essential.
> (Extracted from the letter provided to Y by country X's immigration authority, dated 22 May 2006)

Kayal's case points out how notions of a 'traditional' Tamil wedding are constructed by the immigration officers and various embassies of the foreign states. In addition, the embassy dictates what love should be like within Tamil culture. The visa officer expects that the personal letters have to explicitly express in romantic language that the couple is deeply in love. In the course of my fieldwork, I have compiled examples of ten such cases where visas were rejected on the basis of insufficient documentary evidence being provided of the marriage's authenticity. Interestingly, photographs often seemed to carry the greatest weight in providing documentary proof of a valid wedding or a legitimate marriage. The immigration officers look at the wedding photos for how many people participated in the wedding and the details of customary ceremonies conducted during the wedding to validate the marriage. In other words, if you cannot prove that your marriage is socially accepted and that customary rituals were performed at your wedding, you fall outside the institution of Tamil marriage (Maunaguru 2009).

In the case of Kayal, whole documents—including the wedding photographs—have become authentic evidence of a genuine or false marriage. The next story will focus on how and why wedding photographs have become the authentic evidence of a genuine marriage over any written document, and how it has been called on by state officers to validate a marriage as being genuine.

Story 2: Wedding Photographs and the Notion of Witnessing

Ramani, a Sri Lankan Tamil woman, went to country X in 2002—along with her mother, two sisters and brother—as a refugee from Sri Lanka and obtained refugee status. In 2006, her marriage was fixed with Nithi, her cross-cousin (her father's sister's son). Nithi's parents had died in the war and, as a result, he left for India in 1990 with his grandparents, as a refugee. His brother and sister, both married, continued to be in Jaffna. Nithi's grandmother and Ramani's mother had arranged his marriage with Ramani. Ramani and Nithi had not been in contact since 1990 when, due to the civil war in Sri Lanka, both families separated.

Nithi's brother and sister could not attend the wedding because of the war in Sri Lanka. Ramani's mother and remaining siblings could not attend the wedding either. Her mother was in the process of obtaining her citizenship in country X during that period and Ramani's siblings could not obtain Indian visas in time. Therefore, Ramani arrived in India accompanied only by her sister and cousin. Ramani and Nithi wed in 2007. Ramani and Nithi's wedding was performed according to 'Hindu custom' at a marriage hall in Chennai followed by a civil marriage on the same day. They had to invite at least 75 people to the wedding to prove to the embassy of country X that their marriage was 'real' by providing photographs of their marriage ceremonies as evidence of a 'genuine' Tamil marriage. Ramani returned to her host country, where she made arrangements for her husband to join her. In the meantime, Nithi applied for a visa to join his wife in her host country. Nithi had to produce clearance reports from the police, photographs of the marriage ceremonies and personal letters/cards and gifts, along with a marriage certificate at the embassy. However, even after producing all the above documents, he was refused a visa.

The visa officer explained in a letter the grounds on which the visa was refused. The letter states: 'The circumstances surrounding your marriage cause me to doubt that it is a genuine marriage.' The officer goes on to point out that the marriage was arranged too hastily, that the couple did not meet prior to the wedding, and especially stressed that the wedding was not attended by important family members.

> Parents play an important role in the marriage ceremonies according to the customs prevalent in your community .... All relatives, friends and acquaintances are gathered on this occasion to witness the event and bless the couple. On the contrary, there was a low gathering at your wedding, and you could not provide any reasonable explanation. Your wedding appeared staged. Photographs submitted in support of your marriage do not show you and your sponsor appearing natural and comfortable. The photographs suggest lack of solemnity, spirit of celebration and festivity customarily seen in marriages in your community. Though stated that your wedding was attended by 70–75 persons, the wedding photographs show a much smaller gathering. In these photos you and your sponsor appear disjointed. The natural level of closeness and comfort as seen in newly married couples is not visible.
> (Extracted from the letter provided to Nithi by the immigration officer, dated 14 December 2007)

Therefore, he concluded, that this marriage was entered into by the applicant primarily for the purpose of obtaining permanent residence in country X.

Many of the official visa refusal letters describe how the particular marriage is not 'genuine' or was performed under questionable circumstances. One such letter states: 'As seen in the photographs, your registration was at home with no older married person assisting with the tying of the *thali* as is the custom in the Tamil community.' In other words, it is clear that not only is the visa officer looking for evidence of particular ceremonies being observed according to the customs of the Sri Lankan Tamils, but also for evidence of who performed these ceremonies during the event in the photographs. This raises the question of why wedding photographs, a visual medium, have become a form of authentic evidence over a civil marriage document in the visa officer's determining if a marriage is genuine.

Unlike other representational forms, Ronald Barthes (1981) insists photography holds a unique relation to the real, defined not through the discourse of artistic representation, but that of magic, alchemy and indexicality:

> I call "Photographic referent" not the *optionally* [emphasis in original] real thing to which an image or sign refers but the *necessarily* [emphasis in original] real thing which has been placed before the lens, without which there would be no photograph ... in Photography I cannot deny that the *thing has been there* [what I see in the photograph has been there]. (ibid.: 76–77)

Therefore, it is the conclusion of a truth in the past that cannot be questioned. Moreover, he says:

> The important thing is that the photograph possesses an evidential force, and that its testimony bears not on the object but on time. From a phenomenological viewpoint, in the Photograph, the power of authentication exceeds the power of representation ... [Therefore] ... Photograph cannot be penetrated—because of its evidential power. In the image, the object yields itself wholly, and our vision of it is *certain* [emphasis in original]—contrary to the text ... (1981: 88–89, 106)

In the context of the visa office, wedding photographs function for the immigration officers as a witness to a wedding—somewhat like a live being—as well as authentic evidence that captures and shows within its frame that the families, relatives and friends of the bride and groom took part in the wedding ceremonies and witnessed the event. The dual role that photographs play here are: 1) as a medium of witnessing the event itself (freezing the moment and capturing the event), and 2) capturing the presence and involvement of witnesses at the wedding (relatives and parents of the couple).

Nithi's story highlights that the immigration officers were looking for specific clues in the wedding album. It appears that immigration officers do not accept a civil marriage as valid unless evidence of Tamil customary marriage ceremonies are performed, and presented to the visa officer through the eyes of the camera. Further, the visa officer looking for a 'romantic' expression and close intimacy between the couple in the photos, seeking a performance of romance and affection in the newly-married couple (who have never seen each other before the marriage), shows a projection of the cultural norms of the host societies onto the newly-married couple from a different culture (Palriwala and Uberoi 2008).

The Notion of Witnessing among Tamils

In the case of Nithi, even after he had submitted the civil marriage form, his visa was rejected, not because the civil marriage document was forged or wrong, but because the wedding photographs showed 'insufficient' intimacy between the couple and highlighted the absence of relatives, especially that of Ramani's mother, who were unable to attend the wedding and consequently, to participate in the ceremonies. Therefore, the visa officer concluded that the key family members had not witnessed the event. The notion of witnessing a marriage can be traced back to two sources in Jaffna Tamil cultures. One is in the early Tamil literature (which is always referred to, whenever I ask people to describe Tamil marriages and ceremonies); the other is in the court cases of the colonial period in Sri Lanka, especially cases regarding property disputes, where the court had to validate marriages in order to determine the property rights of the parties concerned.

In mapping out Tamil marriage rituals stated in early Tamil literature (between 13 BC and AD 200) one sees the diversity of marriage rituals and forms of marriage that existed. A helpful illustration can be seen from Sangam literature. Sangam poems were written prior to the second century AD. Many themes run through these poems. According to these poems, there are two kinds of marriages: one is the so-called 'arranged marriage' (where a man actually marries the woman he falls in love with, with the acceptance and in the presence of villagers, relatives and parents); the other is the 'love marriage'. A particular point I wish to highlight from these poems is that in all of these marriage forms, the idea of staging the marriage for the community or for the gods and goddesses was obviously demonstrated. Even in the *kalavu manam*, love marriage, a friend of the bride witnesses the marriage of the couple. Moreover, the Sangam poems describe that *kantharuva* (love marriage) was witnessed by the *aimpoothankal* (five elements of nature) i.e. air, water, earth, sky and fire. By their presence, these witnesses transform what could just be a sexual relationship into a marriage and give it the status of a public event. The notion of 'public' includes the presence of (and witness by) gods and goddesses, relatives of the bride and groom or even a single friend of the bride or groom.

Further illustrations are seen in the *Tholkappiyam*, another work of early Tamil literature. Here, two forms of marriage are described: kalavu manam and *karppu manam*. The literary translation of kalavu manam is 'love marriage', where the male and the female are in a relationship without the knowledge of the people except a female friend of the woman. Karppu manam refers to a situation where, after a man and woman fall in love with each other, they make a public announcement to the village and marry each other in public. Tholkappiyar, author of the *Tholkappiyam*, notes that the friend of the girl pressures the couple to disclose their love to the public and to start their life with a public marriage. This, then, converts the kalavu manam into karppu manam. While there are no descriptions of marriage rituals in this text, it states: '*poyium valuvum thonriya pinarr iyar yathanar karaman enpa*', which may be translated as, 'The elders have made the rule that the marriage has to take place in front of people in public for, if not, a person involved will not take responsibility for the love marriage in cases where cheating, or abandonment has taken place'.

Therefore, these works show that the witnessing of a marriage is important, not only because the formation of a new kinship relationship is as much a public event as it is a private one, but also because witnesses to the union can be called upon at times when injustice occurs to one of the parties in the marriage contract (e.g. in cases of infidelity or denial of marriage). This same notion regarding the witnessing of a marriage was expressed by those who spoke to me about Tamil marriages and they often made references to Tamil literature in support of their view. In other words, it seems like the work of the witness is to change a private affair into a socially accepted institution that can be recognised and validated.

This idea of witnessing is not only seen in literature but also in many decided colonial court cases related to Jaffna customary marriages in Sri Lanka. For example, the decided court case of *Selvaratnam vs. Anandavel* (*Selvaratnam vs. Anandavel* 1941 42. N. L. R. 486) clearly demonstrates how the colonial courts considered the marriage as legal, based on the criterion of social acceptance. The judge took into consideration that there was no evidence that a thali had been tied at the marriage ceremony. Moreover, a priest had not been present at the alleged ceremony and neither a *dhobi* (washerman) nor a barber had taken part in the rituals. There was no evidence of camphor being burnt, coconut being broken or the presence of a brass pot with mango leaves, all of which were thought to be necessary in a Hindu marriage ceremony. Therefore, the judge, J. De Krester, held that, 'the account of the marriage reads like a farce than a reality'. He goes on to say,

> Under the Hindu system, the marriage was arranged by the parents; the contract was made by them, and implemented by the children. One of the inevitable concomitants of the ceremonial being the presence of the relatives and friends of the two contracting parties.

The ruling was based on the facts that: a) there were no relatives and family members present at the wedding ceremony and b) no proper Hindu ceremonies took place. According to the Vellalar (a high Tamil caste) wedding traditions, a dhobi and an *ambatan* (barber) had to be present, because the dhobi and ambatan castes are service castes to the Vellalars, are responsible for decorating the house and the marriage place and doing the bride's and groom's makeup, respectively. On this basis, the judge held that the marriage was not valid because most of the rites and ceremonies performed at Hindu marriages had not been observed.

The absence of relatives, family members and service castes as witnesses of the marriage and participants in the customary ceremonies, as in the case cited above, serves to highlight the importance of a marriage being accepted by the 'public' (i.e. family). Thus, a marriage is considered valid only if two conditions have been fulfilled: the observance of certain customs, and the acceptance by parents and relatives. Viewed through a different lens, it could be said that marriage ceremonies serve to provide a public face to the marriage. When the colonial laws could not rely on civil marriage, they relied on specific customary ceremonies to validate the marriage. Thus, the validation of a marriage was based on public, societal and parental acceptance. The social acceptance of a marriage is shown through the observance of proper customary ceremonies in which all the relatives and friends take part and witness them.

Even the move by the colonial regimes in Sri Lanka of having a marriage registered by the state was an attempt at bringing a marriage into the public domain. Yet, even for the same state, the practice of registering the marriage became unreliable for, as the judges pointed out, in certain cases,[4] it could be forged. Consequently, the state called upon the authority of the community or the family to validate the marriage. Thus, marriage was still brought into the public domain by the colonial state through the notion of societal acceptance, in order to validate a marriage. This is a significant clue as to why visa officers still call for proof of the observance of customary marriage forms, even where a civil marriage has been contracted, in order to validate a marriage. However, 'public' in this case is not constituted through the presence of random individuals or strangers who witness the event, but through the presence of parents, specific relatives and close kinsmen. Thus, the criterion used by immigration officers and colonial judges in assessing the validity of a marriage, i.e. the presence of witnesses, brings back into the arena notions of blood ties and affinal relationships, and their role in marriage rituals in deciding the validity of a marriage. The presence of these close relatives as witnesses is what is required to form the 'public' entity in the validation of a marriage. In the case of Nithi and Ramani, the visa officer was skeptical about the marriage, because Ramani's mother was not present at the wedding.

It seems that, here, wedding photographs are replacing the notion of 'witnessing' from the human eye with the eye of the camera. The notion of witnessing, in this context, is not only about capturing a particular past and witnessing the event but also, for ensuring a certain future for the bride and the groom by helping to reunite them in the groom's or bride's adoptive country.

The stories of Ramani and Kayal above illustrate how the visual documents are called upon, read and interpreted at the place of immigration. How are these wedding albums created by the photographers? The next story describes how the technique of capturing wedding photos and the figure of the photographer come together to produce wedding albums, allowing us to explore how the act of witnessing an event is transferred from the human eye to the eye of the camera.

Story 3: Photographers and Wedding Albums

I met with several wedding photographers who are Sri Lankan Tamils and discovered that an essential aspect of their services is that of creating beautiful wedding albums. These photographers are highly professional. They either run their own family businesses or have learned their trade by assisting established photographers. They either have studios or they run their businesses out of their homes. Such a photographer's main customers are grooms or brides from overseas, who have their marriage performed either in India or Sri Lanka. One such photographer is Rajan, a Sri Lankan residing in India.

When I met Rajan, he and his three assistants were actively involved in photographing and video-taping a wedding. Rajan, like the director of a movie, was calling the shots and giving advice to his assistants. He told them where to focus, from which angle to take the shots, when to take a close shot and if the shots should be long or short for a given event. For example, before the groom was asked to tie the thali, Rajan told the groom how he should look into the camera while tying the thali. Also, Rajan and the priest, who performed the ceremony, were in constant communication with each other. The priest was ensuring that the important events in the ceremony were captured by Rajan. Also, after each important event, the priest asked the groom and bride to face the camera. At times, Rajan asked the wedding couple to repeat certain aspects of the ceremony if he was not satisfied with the outcome of the photographs. He took more than four or five shots of every single event of the ceremony; he told me this was so that he could select the best one, the one that looked the most 'natural'. At times, he even challenged the authority of the priest, telling him that he was not performing the rituals according to the 'real' tradition or, complaining that the priest was hurrying certain ceremonies.

After the ceremony, Rajan asked the bride and the groom to hold each other. He asked the groom to put his arms around the bride's shoulder or around her hips, and asked the bride to hug the groom and hold him tight. When the couple was shy or uncomfortable, he would constantly tell them, 'Relax, you are married now. Come closer and smile, do not be nervous, you are a hero today.' He attempted to put them at ease, to make them feel comfortable, for these intimate photographs. At times, when Rajan wanted to capture more intimacy in the photos, he would take the couple to a corner of the wedding hall and would ask others in that area to leave. He informed me that if the others were present, the bride and groom may feel shy to hold each other. He said, 'You know, they should look natural in the photos.'

Rajan claims that he knows the ceremonies very well. When he was showing his wedding albums, he said that he tried to make the wedding albums into story books. He generally takes around 400–500 shots of the event, and selects the best photos out of them. Each album looks like a moving picture. The way the photos are arranged tells a chronological story: from morning to evening, from the groom's family to the bride's family, how two families come together, from the minute details of the ceremonies to how two individuals at the end of the wedding become intimate and close to each other. He also captures important symbols or events, such as the tying of the thali or wearing of the *meddi* (the toe-ring that the groom places on the bride's toe). He enlarges these photos and places them next to the photos of particular rituals or ceremonies. He says he enlarges these photos because a non-Tamil person who looks at the album might not exactly know or see these symbols and recognise their importance.

Rajan is also aware that these photos are to function as crucial evidence to obtain a visa. Further, Rajan said that it is much more difficult to take wedding pictures now than it was in the past. He said that nowadays, he has to take an almost 180 degree angle shot in order to show the gathering of a larger crowd who are attending the wedding on the one side of the photo, and the bride and groom who are performing the ceremony on the other side of the photo. He has to do this, he explained, so as not to create any doubt in the mind of the visa officer about the marriage. This, then, is what I call the 'double move' of the photograph: it functions both as a medium that witnesses the event, while at the same time capturing the act of the guests at the marriage witnessing it.

Rajan asks the bride and groom to relax, look 'normal' and 'real' for the camera. He creates a certain kind of intimacy between the bride and groom through the medium of photographs, anticipating that the visa officers will look for such moments that 'capture' romance. By asking the couple to look directly into the camera when they perform important rituals during their wedding, Rajan provides facial evidence to the visa officer(s), indicating that the people who are applying for the visa are the same people 'truly' marrying each other. By looking directly into the camera, the groom and bride seem to be looking directly at the visa officer through the medium of the photograph. Through such photos, the photographer, the camera and the people in the photos come together to create a face-to-face relationship with the visa officer in the visa officer's office. It creates an illusion of presence of the bride and/or groom in the visa officer's office or the visa officer's presence in the wedding, when the visa officer asks questions about the wedding photos to the bride or the groom. The photographs come alive, creating a certain level of intimacy between the bride and the groom. Marianne Hirsch, in her book *Family Frames*, points out:

> Photographs immobilize the flow of the family life into a series of snapshots; it perpetuates the familial myth while seeming merely to record actual moments in family history ... the still picture is captured by a single camera eye, whose point of view, that of the photographer, determines the viewer's position ... but the structure of looking is reciprocal: photographer and viewer and the recorded object, the viewer encounters, and/or projects, a screen made up of dominant mythologies and preconceptions that shape the representation (1997: 7)

Even though photographers have the power to immobilise events into snapshots—freezing the past and capturing the event—the wedding photos I encountered carry a certain sense of the future. The photograph should not end with the captured event; rather, it should have the power to come alive and recreate the effect (that of tradition and intimacy in this case) in the presence of the visa officer, so that he is convinced that this particular wedding is 'true', has followed all the 'Tamil traditions' and that there is an 'intimacy' between bride and groom, and, therefore, is not staged.

In the case of wedding photography, unlike what Barthes says on photography, it seems that the visa officer scrutinises the photos, searching for evidence of specific wedding traditions and customs. At the same time, I also learned from Rajan that no matter how carefully he takes the photos, with the same priest performing the same ceremony, there have been instances where visas were refused on the basis of the marriage being perceived as staged. Therefore, until the wedding photos are actualised in the present in the visa officer's office, a high degree of uncertainty surrounds the wedding photos. It seems that similar photos from the same photographer become illegible at the office of the visa officer.

Adrian (2003) argues that the uniqueness of photography is not its ability to capture reality, but its propensity to mediate and manipulate reality while passing the photograph off as truth. Adrian points out,

> Countless observers have documented the myriad ways that photographs can lie, cheat and steal. The camera de-contextualizes; it fragments space, freezes time, manipulates light and settings in which they were photographed and in the way photographs are displaced, captioned, sequenced and viewed. (ibid.: 205)

A photograph's tendency to serve as an invisible medium makes it doubly powerful. Here, the medium of wedding photographs carries the double burden: both as an 'evidence force' and as an 'invisible medium'. It can be read and unread at the same time. The photographs in the visa officer's office come alive and break away from the frozen time (past); it becomes penetrable evidence. The temporality surrounding these photos opens the possibility that it can be false and true simultaneously. It is possible that the question for us is not that 'this thing has been there' (Barthes 1981), but why and how these things would have been there to make it readable in the future.

Conclusion

Recent anthropological work on the state has attempted to plot the presence of the state within everyday life (Ferguson and Gupta 2002). Das and Poole (2004) argue that the modern state constitutes itself through writing practices. However, not only do modern states constitute themselves through the 'legibility' of their written forms and genres but also through the 'illegibility' of their documents and deeds. I am inclined to see that the illegibility of the state's written legal documents requires the state(s) to call for visual documents, which are then incorporated into a legal documentation regime. According to Barthes (1981), photographs are evidential proof, which cannot be penetrated and so, bring out the real past and truth. This is probably the reason that visual documents have become authentic proof of a genuine marriage. The ability of the eye of the camera to witness an event, even as a human eye, and the ability of a photo to reproduce minute details of an event in a realistic image form brings about a contraction of the distance between the viewer and the people in the photographs and the past event. Yet, we have seen in this essay, how these photos are produced, the different ways in which tradition and romance are portrayed and captured, not only during the wedding ceremony but also at the site of the embassy. Further, we have seen that photos can be read in multiple ways. Thus, the production of the wedding photos and the interplay between the camera, the photographer and the visa officers show me that the wedding photos that are submitted to the embassies by the bride and/or groom, simultaneously contain both the legibility and illegibility of the state's practices.

By the visa officer calling for their witnessing capability, the photographs are, on the one hand, being required to do more than they are able to. On the other, the use of photographic evidence as a witness of the wedding, and the visa officer's questioning of the validity of a marriage on the basis of the absence of relatives and close family members at the wedding or the absence of particular kinsmen, who are supposed to perform certain customary rituals, reinforces the importance of blood ties and affinal relationships in the marriage ceremony. Visual documents are asked for, to help create the notion of a 'Tamil marriage', to capture the essence of a Tamil marriage and to show the key participants at the event and the active roles they play according to the customs of Tamils in Sri Lanka. In other words, the notion of witnessing the wedding (both by the eye of the camera and the human eye) not only brings back the importance of the blood and affinal relatives in the marriage rituals, but also brings back the idea of social acceptance of the marriage by the community or family as a way of validating the marriage. Does this mean, then, that when state practices and documents become unreadable for the state itself, the state calls up on the authority of the family and community to revise its mode of law-making?

Anthropological literature has long focused on the 'middleman' to understand how the state becomes a presence in the everyday life of people (Gupta 1995; Das and Poole 2004). While the traditional focus has been largely to show how official agents of the state, such as that of the police or revenue collector, insert themselves into everyday life (Gupta 1995), more recently there has been new interest in the appearance of the figure of local strongmen (Poole 2004), as well as the economic broker (Roitman 2004). Furthermore, these studies suggest how the figure of the state may not be so much situated in the centre, but as something that becomes visible in the margins, embodied within new and extant localised figures of authority. The figure of the photographer has changed during the thirty years of conflict in Sri Lanka. He is now marked by professionalism, commercialisation of the trade and brings with him/her the knowledge and experience of making a number of wedding albums for transnational Tamils weddings. Unlike old photographers, the wide expertise (in computers, computer programmes and access to new technologies) of new photographers makes them important figures. Further, the fact that the photographer comes from the same community and social space and that the families involved in marriage negotiations know him/her through personal networks provides a certain accountability and authority to the figure of the photographer. The photographer operates as a public authority providing both evidence and state-sanctioned authenticity to wedding ceremonies and enabling partners to unite across space and time. In my study, the figure of the photographer becomes representative of a different state power, not through his incivility or a mode of violence, but through the knowledge and information 'power' he has at his disposal. He is the 'holder' of information regarding requirements made by the various states for legitimising marriages. Since this validation is a crucial step in the process of brides and grooms leaving or re-inhabiting dislocated social landscapes, he becomes an important figure in bringing individuals together. However, despite such official recognition and professionalisation of the trade, the fact that photographers accrue benefits from the misfortunes of others (i.e. arising from the contemporary situation of political instability) has given the profession a somewhat dubious reputation. The dual characteristic of the Sri Lankan Tamil photographer opens up questions on how traditions are produced, circulated and contested through visual spaces.

Notes

[1] In addition to the above-mentioned documented proof, the host countries require that a marriage should not only be valid under the laws of jurisdiction where it took place, but also under the laws of the migrating country, in order to accept that the marriage is legal.

[2] The virginity test administrated on south Asian brides by the British administrative officers between 1979 and 1981 is a celebrated example. For further discussion on this, see Palriwala and Uberoi (2008) and Hall (2002).

[3] It is interesting to note that in Sri Lanka, the colonial state implemented civil marriage as a compulsory requirement for a marriage to be recognised as legal in 1847. However, the failure to register a marriage, and the concerns voiced by various colonial authorities regarding the rigidity of the new civil marriage, eventually brought about an amendment of the marriage laws in 1870. Thus, the ordinance of registration of a marriage as a compulsory requirement for legal marriage was done away with. In other words, a marriage did not need to be registered to be legally valid and, in such a case, the validity of a marriage was based on other evidence. Even though the colonial authorities did away with the mandatory registration of a marriage, they brought back a different form of validating a marriage: proof that either the marriage had taken place according to traditional custom, or there had been long-term cohabitation (Goonasekera 1984).

[4] See in the case of *Chettiar vs. Nagamotto in 1843: No 3690* (quoted in Mutukisna et al. 1862: 215).

References

Adrian, Bonnie. 2003. *Framing the Bride: Globalizing Beauty and Romance in Taiwan's Bridal Industry*. Berkeley: University of California Press.

Banks, M. 1960. 'Caste in Jaffna'. In *Aspects of Caste in South India, Ceylon, and North Pakistan*, ed. E. R. Leach. Cambridge: Cambridge University Press.

Barthes, Roland. 1981. *Camera Lucida*. New York: Hill and Wang.

Cheran, R. 2004. 'Multiple Homes and Parallel Civil Societies'. Paper presented at the Solomon ASCH center at University of Pennsylvania, Pennsylvania.

Daniel, Valentine. 1996. *Charred Lullabies: Chapters in an Anthropography of Violence*. Princeton: Princeton University Press.

Das, Veena, and Deborah Poole. 2004. 'State and its Margins: Comparative Ethnographies'. In *Anthropology in the Margins of State*, ed. Veena Das and Deborah Poole. Oxford: School of American Press.

Ferguson, James, and Akhil Gupta. 2002. 'Spatializing the State: Toward an Ethnography of Neoliberal Governmentality'. *American Ethnologist,* 29 (4): 981–1002.

Fuglerud, Oivind. 1999. *Life on the Outside: The Tamil Diaspora and Long-distance Nationalism.* London: Pluto Press.

Gell, Singh Man Simeran. 1994. 'Legality and Ethnicity: Marriage among the South Asians of Bedford'. *Critique of Anthropology* 14 (4): 335–92.

Goonesekere, Savitri. 1984. 'Some Reflections on Solemnization of Marriage in the General Law of Sri Lanka'. *Mooter: Journal of the Moot Society* 1:24–38.

Gupta, Akhil. 1995. 'Blurred Boundaries: The Discourse of Corruption, the Culture of Politics, and the Imagined State'. *American Ethnologist* 22 (2): 375–402.

Hall, Rachel A. 2002. 'When is a Wife Not a Wife? Some Observations on the Immigration Experiences of South Asian Woman in West Yorkshire'. *Contemporary Politics* 9 (1): 55–68.

Hirsch, Marianne. 1997. *Family Frames: Photography, Narratives, and Post Memory.* Cambridge, Massachusetts and London: Harvard University Press.

Jaganathan, Pradeep. 2004. 'Checkpoint: Anthropology, Identity and the State. In *Anthropology in the Margin of State*, ed. Veena Das and Deborah Poole. Oxford: School of American Press.

Lawrence, Patricia. 2000. 'Violence, Suffering, Amman: The Work of Oracles in Sri Lanka's Eastern War Zone'. In *Violence and Subjectivity*, eds. Veena Das, Arthur Kleinman, Mamphela Ramphele and Pamela Reynolds. New Delhi: Oxford University Press.

Maunaguru, Sidharthan. 2009. 'Brides as Bridges? Tamilness Through Movements, Documents and Anticipations'. In *Pathways of Dissent: Tamil Nationalism in Sri Lanka*, ed. Dr. R. Cheran. Delhi, London: SAGE publication.

Mody, Perveez., 2008. *Intimate State: Love-Marriage and Law in Delhi.* London: Routledge.

Mutukisna, Francis Henry, Robert Atherton, and Class I Saakzoon. 1862. *A New Edition of the Thesawaleme or The Laws and Customs of Jaffna.* Ceylon: Ceylon Time Office.

Palriwala, Rajni, and Patricia Uberoi. 2008. 'Exploring the Links: Gender Issues in Marriage and Migration'. In *Marriage, Migration and Gender*, eds. Rajni Palriwala and Patricia Uberoi. London, New Delhi, and Singapore: SAGE Publication.

Perera, S. 1999. *Stories of Survivors: Socio-political Contexts of Female-headed Households in Post-terror Southern Sri Lanka.* New Delhi: Vikas Publication.

Poole, Deborah. 2004. 'Between Threat and Guarantee: Justice and Community in the Margin of the Peruvian State'. In *Anthropology in the Margin of State*, eds. Veena Das and Deborah Poole. Oxford: School of American Press.

Roitman, Janet. 2004. 'Productivity in the Margins: The Reconstitution of State Power in The Chad Basin'. In *Anthropology in the Margin of State*, ed. Veena Das and Deborah Poole, Oxford: School of American Press.

Tambiah, S. J. 1973. 'Dowry and Bridewealth, and the Property Rights of Women in South Asia'. In *Bridewealth and Dowry, Cambridge Papers in Social Anthropology*, ed. Jack Goody and Stanley. J .Tambiah, Cambridge: Cambridge University Press.

Tambiah, S. J. 1965. 'Kinship Fact and Fiction in Relation to the Kandyan Sinhalese'. *Journal of the Royal Anthological Institute of Great Britain and Ireland* 95 (2): 131–73.

Yalman, Nur. 1967. *Under the Bo Tree: Studies in Caste Kinship and Marriage in the Interior of Ceylon*. Berkeley: University of California Press.

Surfing for Spouses

Marriage Websites and the 'New' Indian Marriage?

Ravinder Kaur with Priti Dhanda

Introduction

In India, as in much of South Asia, marriage remains an important rite of passage in an individual's life. To the vast majority, it grants social adulthood and sets the stage for the *grihastha* (householder) stage of life, across regions and religions. The marriage ceremony calls up every possible social obligation, kinship bond, sentiment and economic resource. Almost 90 per cent of marriages in India remain arranged (Mullatti 1995) and family, particularly parental, involvement in arranging marriage is a continuing norm.[1] Writing recently, Sharangpani notes, 'The arranged marriage system is a patriarchal artefact invested in maintaining caste purity, class privileges and gender hierarchy' (2010: 270–71). While this description correctly implies that arranged marriages are endogamous, within class, and retain the superiority of wife-takers over wife-givers and of husbands over wives, it fails to capture two other important aspects of marriage in India. First, arranging marriages of their adult progeny is a peculiarly south Asian 'inter-generational contract' entered into by parents, leading to a sense of mutual obligation between the generations.[2] Indeed, children may resent parents who 'fail in their duty' to find them spouses, and society holds such parents responsible for having reneged on this important duty. Equally, the obligation of parents to arrange matches confers on them the opportunity to exercise power and control over children and provides them with avenues to further personal welfare and family mobility goals (Bourdieu 1977).[3] Hence, parental involvement in arranging matches remains a tightly protected privilege in India.[4] Second, Sharangpani's description (2010) does not pay sufficient attention to the deviations from the norm that are beginning to challenge traditional boundaries of caste, community and family arranged marriages as well as equations within marriages.

It is in these contexts that an analysis of the contemporary modes and processes of arranging marriages assumes great importance. Matchmaking in India has evolved over the decades from being a face-to-face process in which family and community were intimately involved, to one in which more anonymous media such as newspaper advertisements (which emerged during the colonial period), and most recently, technically sophisticated, internet-enabled matrimonial websites are involved. In addition to the above, marriage bureaus and marriage fairs of various castes and communities[5] provide other modes of arranging matches. India's culturally and developmentally varied landscape ensures that multiple modes of matchmaking continue to survive side by side.

This essay is about matchmaking through internet websites, a new mode that is finding rapid and widespread adoption among families and marriageable youth. From a single matchmaking website, shaadi.com, set up in 1996, the industry has proliferated rapidly to include about 1500 such websites (Pal 2010). The most popular are shaadi.com (the pioneering website), bharatmatrimony.com,[6] jeevansaathi.com, simplymarry.com, lifepartner.com, etc. According to the market research 'A Web Partner for Life', the online matrimonial industry was expected to reach 20.8 million registrations with revenues of $ 63 million by 2010–2011 (EmPower Research LLC 2008). The IT recession of 2000 which devastated many industries under its ambit, left the matrimonial website business untouched. Such websites are also increasingly the most popular mode of matchmaking among diasporic Indians.

Do Modern Technologies Yield Modern Marriages?

Matchmaking through internet websites raises several important questions about the nature of contemporary marriage in India. If matrimonial websites represent a globalising face of marriage, are marriages arranged through the use of this sophisticated modern technology—which allows easy maintenance of large databases of eligible grooms and brides, and boasts of the 'state of art' proprietary algorithms driving the matching process—'modern'? If individualism, choice and equality are considered central features of western modernity, in what ways is Indian marriage moving towards the above ideals? Do website-based marriages unite like-minded persons across barriers of class, caste, community, region and religion? Has agency in matchmaking shifted substantially from parents to the marrying individuals? Are more such marriages based on self-choice? Are the resulting marriages more gender equal? (Giddens 1994) How different is such matchmaking from that mediated by newspaper advertisements, marriage brokers, extended family, friends or traditional 'go-betweens'? Do changing ideas and ideals of courtship, intimacy and conjugality make the internet a preferred mode? Is the technology itself facilitating incipient new ideas of intimacy and marriage? How does the interactive nature of the medium influence the matchmaking process?

In order to answer some of these questions, the essay does three important things: first, it explains how marriage websites work as matchmakers. Second, using data obtained from one national matrimonial website, it explores the social profile and trends among users of this technology. Third, based on analysis of profiles posted on a popular website and interviews with couples who looked for spouses on the internet or whose marriages were arranged through the internet, the essay explores answers to some of the questions raised.

Our study finds that a prominent reason for seeking matches through the internet is to access a greater selection of marriage partners and to find spouses who fulfill an ever growing and diverse wish list of spouse characteristics. We also find that the technology of internet matchmaking seems to result in two distinct kinds of marriages—those that re-inscribe traditional community norms and criteria of caste, region, religion, language, class and those that transgress many of these. In the former, despite the fact that the new technology places greater power and agency in the hands of youth, the family continues to play a large role, while in the latter, the role of the family is drastically reduced and often nullified. We also find that the latter set of marriages involve somewhat older individuals in their 30s, who are generally urban professionals and for whom individual compatibility matters more than social conformity. For such individuals, the meaning of marriage has definitely transformed and ideas of self-choice and companionate marriages seem to have taken hold. Both types of marriages employ modernity in different ways—the first, through their use of modern technology to arrange marriages in which marriage fundamentally remains a family strategy to pursue individual and collective mobility goals and to reproduce the social group (Bourdieu 1977) and the second, in allowing individuals to challenge traditional marriage and pursue a vision of more egalitarian marriage. The process of matchmaking through the internet remains, however, a gendered one, privileging men more than women.

Emergence and Growth of the Web-based Matchmaking Industry

Narrating how he came up with the idea of shaadi.com, the founder, Anupam Mittal, explains that it was a chance encounter with a marriage broker that led him to the idea of starting a marriage website. He researched the 'business model' of the traditional matchmaker to discover that the latter went door to door within his community and to people he knew, and carried resumes with him. Essentially, the choice of a life partner was determined by how far the matchmaker could travel and how much weight he could carry. He wondered what would happen if one did away spatial and geographical limitations by putting up profiles on the internet instead (Roy Choudhury 2007).

The idea was so successful that by 2008, shaadi.com had over 10 million members and claimed 8,01,764 success stories. The online marriage websites service appeared to respond to the needs of an ever growing tech-savvy population located anywhere in the world. Shaadi.com was quickly followed by bharatmatrimony.com. Once their success became evident, a veritable proliferation of websites took place exploiting every angle of a segmented and checkered marriage market. Specialised matrimonial websites catering to groups and categories of people based on caste, ethnicity, region and religion have sprung up with great rapidity. Some examples are jatland.com, brahminsmatrimony.com, chennaimatrimony.com, tamilmatrimony.com, sindhimatrimony.com, etc. New 'boutique' websites such as indianmillionairemarriages.com cater to very rich, busy people or to those holding or seeking spouses with H1B (US work visas) status. Some websites focus on those on the margins of 'normal' marriage, such as secondmarriage.com, nodowry.com, etc. The popularity of secondmarriage.com may suggest a lifting of taboos against remarriage of divorcees, widowers and widows.

Web use surveys suggest that between 12 and 15 per cent of internet users in India now search for spouses online (Mathur 2007). Most of them are well-to-do, upwardly-mobile professional youth between the ages of 21 and 35 (Adams and Ghosh 2003; Chatterjee 2007; Shukla and Kapadia 2007). Seventy per cent of users of marriage websites are from the 'urban consuming class', according to the *2008 Online Matrimony Report* (JuxtConsult 2008). According to this report a little more than half of all internet users are under 25 years of age. Most net users are salaried workers, automobile owners and have personal computers or laptops at home, implying a fairly high level of income irrespective of location. According to the same report, only 11 per cent of matrimonial website users visit generic portals for seeking spouses. The bulk 89 per cent opt for 'specialised' matrimonial websites. In 2008, 49 per cent of people going online visited a matrimonial website; this being one of 10 most popular online activities.

Expanding Geographic Reach of Marriage Websites

With the growth of internet in the country, users of matrimonial websites have spread from metropolitan cities to non-metros, with the percentage of non-metro users increasing to about 60 per cent of the total registrants on websites in the past few years. Interestingly, the bulk of regular internet online users come from non-metro towns (JuxtConsult 2008). As a result, internet matrimonial websites are beginning to compete successfully with other matchmaking channels. In our sample from one national website, while 40 per cent of the registrants were from metros, 60 per cent came from non-metros. Websites are able to spread their network into small towns and rural areas by providing offline assistance to people though kiosks. Thus, kiosks, such as 'ShaadiPoints' by shaadi.com, fulfill the needs of those who lack net access or computer skills. Advertising on television channels by many marriage portals has further extended their reach.

Compressing Space: The Transnational Middle Class

The compression of space and time resulting from the internet revolution has reconfigured human life in many ways. And marriage is no exception. Marriage websites have transformed the marriage market from a local, regional and national to a global one. NRIs, as an ethnic transnational middle class,[7] comprise a large section of the users of matrimonial websites (Sharma 2006; Adams and Ghosh 2003; Chatterjee 2007). Sites specifically dedicated to NRI brides and grooms are extremely popular in the southern states of India, where bharatmatrimony.com is a favourite website. Such marriages lend credence to the claim of portability of the Indian family system and Indian values outside India (Uberoi 1998).[8] Matrimonial websites allow NRIs a means of reproducing such values and traditional marriage. Sharma (2006) argues that they also provide diasporic south Asians loci for practising identity and producing community, in the face of assimilation or acculturation by host cultures. At the same time, it allows them to practise 'nation' with the homeland no longer being a distant memory, but to be actively engaged with. In India, websites allow Indian parents and youth easier access to green card holders or foreign spouses; it allows them to fulfill dreams of mobility through spatially hypergamous marriages. Yet, the dangers inhering in international marriages, where verifiability remains inadequate, do not vanish and individuals face the same vulnerabilities as in broker-arranged NRI marriages.

'Doing' Matchmaking through the Internet: Finding the 'Right' Person

Can machines replace the indigenous knowledge bank of the *ghatak* or the *vichola* (Majumdar 2004), the community matchmakers who carried around portfolios of grooms and brides, and who knew family histories going back several generations? The role of the internet in matchmaking begins with potential brides and grooms posting profiles on a selected website. Most marriage websites are keen to distinguish their identity from dating websites. They actively discourage 'non-serious' users who may not have marriage in mind. They also take great care to ensure that misuse of profiles does not take place and seek to establish the trust of the spouse-seekers. Thus, websites make available stringent security settings to their clients, allowing access only to those who pay to register, and communication is allowed only after mutual consent. Given the sensitivity of reputations in the marriage market, and until recently, the stigma associated with looking for a match through the internet, establishing trust and confidence becomes essential for such websites.

Websites use sophisticated mathematical formulae to match characteristics and make information available to clients.[9] A proprietary algorithm is used through which websites generate similar matches in the hope that this will give them an edge over competitors. A simple search can be performed based on caste or religion; a more complex one allows matching of education, occupation, income and other such criteria. To fine tune the match even more closely to desired characteristics, people can also perform searches based on 'lifestyle' attributes such as diet, smoking or drinking habits or search for only *manglik*[10] profiles or those based on marital status. All these search criteria can be mixed and matched to filter out the profiles fitting a user's choice. This search optimisation is so efficiently developed that users get to see the results in a fraction of seconds, eliminating 'undesirable' profiles and giving users access to the profiles suiting their criteria. This increases the efficiency and reduces the 'residence' time, i.e. the time gap between registering and finding a match through the website.

While allowing users to search for matches by themselves, the websites also recommend 'potential matches' among other users/members based on the member's description of his/her desired partner through a psychometric study of the members—the kind of profiles they visit, searches they make and members they accept for further communication. The websites provide members with recommendations/match alerts. Most often these match alerts are very helpful in bringing more profiles to the user from the huge database that these portals possess. While websites definitely provide greater choice, and of the desired sort, spouse-seekers and their families still need to protect themselves against fraudulent profiles and be discriminating enough to make the right choice.

User Patterns and What They Tell Us About Spouse-Surfers

Who are the people who seek brides and grooms through the net? Based on a sample of 1300 individuals who posted their profiles on a major national website on a single day, this section looks at age, gender, caste, religion and income profile of this user group.

Age and Marital Status

Most of the registrants belonged to the age groups 18–27 (54 per cent) and 28–37 (42 per cent). Thus, roughly half were in the expected age range for marriage for the urban middle class and half were older. Ninety-five per cent of the total number of the members registered had never been married and divorcees/widow(er)s formed the rest. All were above 18, the legal age for marriage in India where 35 is often considered as the outer edge of being eligible for marriage. A small percentage of people (4 per cent) were over 38 years of age. The internet thus seems to be opening up possibilities for older individuals, who can rely on their own agency to seek a companion or a spouse. Websites like secondmarriage.com also provide opportunities to individuals who may have lost their spouse or got divorced late in life and wish to marry again.[11]

Gender

Our data show that searching for a spouse through an internet portal is heavily skewed in favour of males, with males representing 73 per cent of those posting profiles, while females represented a meagre 27 per cent of the total members.[12] This is easily understood in the context of prevailing family, kinship and gender norms, especially as they shape the social construction of women's marriage. The marriageable girl is seen to be much more vulnerable and there is need to protect her reputation, which has an important bearing on her marital prospects. Women worry about the misuse of their internet profiles and providing access to those whose attention is unwelcome. Many women initially post themselves under a pseudonym. Yet, the fact that 27 per cent of profiles posted were those of women implies that a sufficiently large number of parents/women perceive gains from seeking a spouse through the net as outweighing the risks of tarnishing their reputations. What may further signal a trend towards change is that a significant 43 per cent of the women had posted their profiles themselves.[13] Interestingly, NRI women replicate the national trend with fewer posting on matrimonial websites than males. Of the

13 per cent, who had posted on this website between 2005 and 2007 and were NRIs, only 20 per cent were women.

Some respondents interviewed informally confirmed that marriage websites were the last resort while looking for a spouse and this was even more so with women. Chatterjee (2007: 23) also mentions that 'social stigma' may be attached to the use of websites for marriage. Many people shy away from revealing that they have posted profiles on marriage websites. Yet, our case studies reveal that women persuaded parents to post their profiles on websites to look for more suitable grooms.

Education, Occupation and Gender

Women posted on the website had higher educational qualifications than men. Over 45 per cent of the women held a Masters degree and 38 per cent had a Bachelors degree, whereas in the case of men these numbers were 33 per cent and 44 per cent respectively. Even though women's education remains oriented to marriage among a large section of Indians (evident also in the fact that 25 per cent of the women in the sample showed no income of their own), it is more likely that better-qualified women have greater difficulty in finding appropriate matches and hence are turning to the net for greater choice. Thirty per cent of these women were employed in areas of education, medical and health services and in the IT software industry. Most of the male applicants also held jobs in the services sector of the economy. In our sample, over 12 per cent of the women posted on the net were students. Interestingly, 95 per cent of the male members either did not state a preference for a working/non-working wife or did not care about the working status of the prospective bride, which appears contradictory, given the educational profile of those posting and the desire for upward mobility in the middle class.

Income and Class

As the JuxtConsult (2008) report states, most internet users are members of the 'urban consuming class'. It is obvious that those who are using the internet to seek a spouse are individuals with fairly high education, income and class status. The majority of users in our sample fell within a wide range of monthly income between INR 50,000 and INR 3,00,000. Of the total women members 25 per cent reported no income, while only a miniscule percentage of men did so.

Most of the registered members described themselves as belonging to the upper middle (38 per cent) and the middle class (32 per cent), though 25 per cent of the users decided not to disclose their family class status. In summary, most registrants on websites were 21–35 years old, generally male, upwardly mobile professionals, and familiar with the internet. A large number of these were NRIs, for whom this provides a way of connecting with the community back home and in other parts of the world (Chatterjee 2007; Adams and Ghosh 2003). Given the large number of people in the Indian middle class now, this profile is not surprising.[14]

Caste

Caste remains a crucial variable in finding a match; the websites have space to specify caste and sub-caste and as many as 248 caste names were available in a drop-down menu for registrants to choose from, including castes among Hindus, Muslims, Christians and Sikhs. Websites derive this data by researching castes listed by people on various other websites. The greatest specificity in the data pertains to the Brahmin castes, where around 30 sub-caste names appear. Although it is difficult to analyse social status from caste names, it is clear that castes across the spectrum—high and low, and spread all over India—are represented. Registrants from Dalit castes also appear on the website. While members from among all castes thus appear to have access to the net and are keen to use internet technology, the great variety of Brahmins reiterates the pattern whereby the educated and elite Brahmins have always been the first to access new channels of education and communication for upward mobility, while at the same time emphasising and maintaining caste and class exclusivity. Given the great number of subdivisions and related status distinctions among Brahmins, they appear to be keen to retain these. Websites make it easy to practise caste and sub-caste endogamy, as they allow access to a greater number of individuals of the same caste or sub-caste. Some profiles make it a point to list the *gotras* (clan or lineage) to be avoided by a prospective partner. Contrary to the conclusion one arrives at from a study of the profiles, in Mathur's study of marriages through websites (2007: 26) only 23 per cent of the participants married within their caste and just 29 per cent within the community of the same mother tongue. However, Mathur's upper- and middle-class sample from Mumbai may account for the greater deviation from norms. Contrastingly, a study by Banerjee et al. (2009) of marriages through newspaper advertisements among middle-class Bengalis in Kolkata found that there was a strong preference to marry within caste. Parents tended to accept a groom or bride with fewer years of education if the caste was the same. The essay concludes that the 'cost' of marrying within caste is low for families when other social group attributes are homogenous, explaining the persistence of caste in the marriage market. A study of newspaper matrimonial advertisements by McCann Erickson's Consumer Insights (Sethi 2000) showed that caste remains resilient in matchmaking.

Distribution by Religion

The distribution by religion among the members was highly skewed towards Hindus. Almost 80 per cent of the registrants were Hindus, followed by 7 per cent Muslims. The proportion of Muslim users is, however, a little over half of their presence in the Indian population. It is also possible that Muslims may be posting exclusively on websites such as MuslimMatrimony.com. Interestingly, the data reveals that there are as many Muslim women posting their profiles as there are Muslim men, pointing to the fact that they face the same difficulties as educated Hindu women in finding compatible spouses. Posting on websites also points to a weakening of consanguineous marriages among educated Muslims, as they look outside the extended family for suitable partners (see Vatuk, this volume). This is not surprising considering the income-education profile of registrants. Yet, community remains important; Muslims also seek spouses from specific denominations such as Shia, Sunni, Dawood, Bohra, etc.

FIGURE 12.1: Distribution by Religion

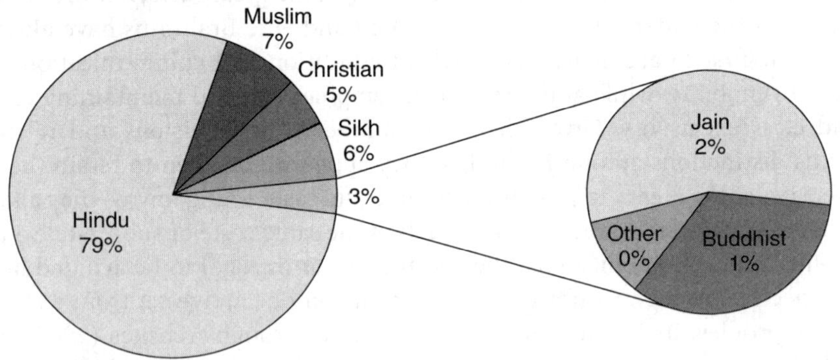

Source: Drawn by author based on data from a national matrimonial website

The percentage of Christians, Jains and Sikhs was higher than their presence in the Indian population, reflecting higher incomes, education and hence greater access to internet technology. Religious groups such as Hindus, Christians, Sikhs, etc. also further differentiate themselves along sectarian lines, as reflected in specific labels such as Digambar and Shwetambar Jains, 'Born again', Catholic, Evangelical, Syrian, Nadar Christians, etc. Despite being modern enough to post on the net, specification of denomination implies that people are looking for spouses within narrowly-defined communities.

Practising the Self: Are Marriage Websites a Site for the Emergence of Individuality?

Several clues to whether the new technology is initiating marriage change can be derived from interrogating the data from various vantage points. For example, who posts the profile? Interestingly, a high proportion of the total profiles (65 per cent) were posted by members themselves followed by 21 per cent posted by parents. Eleven per cent of profiles were posted by siblings and friends. Over 73 per cent of the men posted their own profiles; the corresponding percentage for women being 43 per cent. Thirty-nine per cent of female profiles were posted by parents and 11 per cent by siblings; in contrast, for males, 14 per cent were posted by parents and only 3 per cent by siblings.

Figure 12.2: Profiles Posted by Guardian

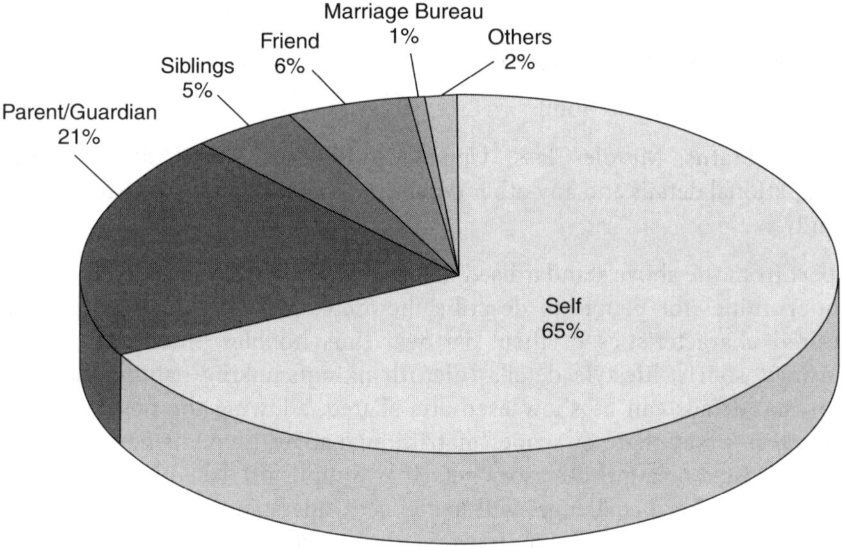

Source: Drawn by author based on data from a national matrimonial website.

Who posts the profile may be an important indicator of shifts in generational participation in the match-making process. Middle- and upper-middle-class youth, more proficient with internet technology, are likely to post their own profiles. The high number doing so indicates significantly greater agency on their part. Equally, the participation of a greater number of younger people such as siblings and friends may signal a greater trust in one's peer group while deciding on a spouse. Yet, the fact that 21 per cent of the profiles are being posted by parents, and 11 per cent by friends and siblings of users underlines the continuing importance of family in the matchmaking process.

While marriage websites provide standardised formats for uploading information, the scope for the amount and kinds of information that can be provided is much greater than in newspaper advertisements. Website profiles make a significant break from the latter by allowing for more information to be conveyed. Conventionally, the following information is requested to create a profile of the user:

General: Age, Date of Birth, City, Profession, Marital Status, Income.

Religion and Ethnicity: Religion, Mother Tongue, City of Birth, Caste, Sub-caste, Gotra, Time of Birth, Manglik Status.

Lifestyle and Attributes: Diet, Smoking/non-smoking, Drinking/non-drinking, Complexion, Body Type, Challenged (Physically or Mentally).

Education and Occupation: Education Level, Qualifications, Occupation.

Family Values: Liberal, Conservative, Orthodox, Moderate.

Family Type: Nuclear, Joint

Family Status: Middle-Class, Upper-Middle-Class, Rich/Affluent, family occupational details and any other details the user wishes to furnish about the family.

Apart from the above standardised details, the website format provides ample opportunities for people to describe themselves as individuals and list the desired characteristics of their partner. Thus hobbies, interests, favourite cuisines, sports, lifestyle details (diet, drinking/smoking habits) and other personal details can be showcased and shared, allowing the presentation of the self in a way that newspaper matrimonial advertisements never could. A profile posted by a girl describes herself as 'simple girl, faced hard situations, ready to face hard challenges with patience. Understanding; Respect towards elders.' She states that she plans to work after marriage and is open to marrying a person from any one of several Hindu or Sikh castes. Many websites advertise themselves as a space where people can find a 'soul mate', underlining a new emphasis on individual compatibility with a new emphasis on conjugal intimacy.

Is the Modern Anxiety Not About Making the Right Marriage but about Finding the Right Person?

Many individuals now seek individual compatibility rather than purely family compatibility based on standard matching criteria. Somewhat older spouse-seekers for whom conventional matchmaking has not worked, especially seek a private space or platform to express their views on the kind of person they want as a marriage partner. For such individuals, the family plays a lesser role than in the case of younger spouse-seekers.

Women posting their own profiles are quite explicit in their expectations of minimum professional qualifications or the income they expect their prospective partner to have. This is a change from the trend observed in the past,[15] when women had little encouragement to express their desires. Women also clearly state their own career goals (planning on doing a Ph.D., for instance) and income status in their profiles. Urban, educated women's agency in deploying the strategy of arranged marriage to fulfill their own goals and desires is also a result of their increased bargaining power in the marriage market (Sharangpani 2010: 253). In our case studies of such women we found that they pushed their parents to register them on internet sites in order to enlarge their choice of suitable spouses and took active interest in selecting or rejecting potential candidates.

Despite such agency, the entire process of the use of web space and display of the self remains an unequal one for the genders—clearly seen in the elaboration of the profiles and also the role taken by women once mutual interest is initiated. Men feel freer to state their desires and describe themselves, while women are far more restrained in what they or their parents/siblings post about them. Further, in consonance with newspaper advertisements from the 1990s, even as professional characteristics and income and education of girls have attained importance, physical attributes, like skin colour (fairness being an explicit demand) and body type (slim being sought after) continue to be desirable attributes.[16] Website advertisements generally show pictures of very fair, pretty women as objects of desire. Interestingly, virginity, which was explicitly mentioned in newspaper advertisements of the 1960s, is not mentioned any longer (Sethi 2000). The demand that women be prepared to take on domestic duties and adopt the home-maker role, even while contributing financially to the household, is made clear in both newspaper advertisements and web profiles.

The gendered nature and weaker agency of women in web-based matchmaking, however, goes deeper than this, as revealed in a case related here. Anjali's brother placed her profile on the net. Ram, the groom, whose family had failed to find a satisfactory match for him (he said, 'no good proposals were coming through family and friends' and that, 'the internet provided a larger platform to meet people and to choose from'), and who was already located abroad, decided to put up his own profile on several websites. The girl's family gave minimal information, while the boy posted a fleshed out resume. While the girl relied on her brother (even though both her parents are alive) to initiate and handle the process, the boy surfed the potential choices himself, being open to the development of a love relationship that could blossom into marriage.

While the boy corresponded with several girls (keeping his parents informed), the girl did not correspond with any one and it was her brother who approached Ram for a potential match. While Anjali's brother executed the search, keeping caste, profession and their native city in mind, Ram's only expressed concern was that the girl be a Hindu. For him, 'looks' were important, while for the girl's family, the groom's social and economic status was more important. Ram claimed that he wanted to project 'who he was as a person, and convey a true sense of himself'. Such an opportunity was not available to the girl, since a conventional, minimal, conservative profile of her was posted by her brother. However, despite Ram's desire to display a modern self and marry on the basis of 'knowing himself and the other individual', the match was fixed without the couple talking on the net.

The meeting in person took place after complete verification of backgrounds through a common acquaintance. The families ascertained that they were closely matched in caste (both being Maithili Brahmins from Bihar), class, native place, desired levels of education, etc. The couple then developed a 'liking' for each other against this secure background, the sealing of the match being dependent only on 'the gaze' or *dekhna* (seeing or viewing) which the couple directed at each other in their first and only personal meeting. While this may sound no different from a traditional matchmaking exercise, what made it different was the boy's stated desire to project his 'self' and the girl's claim later that 'basically he was looking for someone like me'. This could be seen as a post-facto rationalisation but reflects new desires of the matrimonial project. The couple claimed that they would recommend the same route to others seeking a match; the girl however emphasised that it was important to ascertain that the profiles on the net were genuine as the virtual nature of the net made deceit quite possible. The role of the parents and family loomed large in the matchmaking. The girl moved to USA after marriage; ironically, the marriage did not last long despite the detailed matching of family backgrounds and of desired spousal characteristics, the couple ultimately found that they were personally incompatible.

Reproducing Class Through Marriage and Family

Despite the increased space given to the individual, does the Indian marriage remain a family strategy at heart? Websites provide more space for display of the 'self', but at the same time they provide more space for the display of the family as well. Matching caste, community, religion and region is almost automatic through the new technology. Matching family is being made equally easy and allows for the reproduction of class.

Internet profile formats allow extensive highlighting of family background which helps maintain class endogamy. Besides an individual's own qualifications, those of the parents and siblings can also be included; for instance, whether a parent or sibling is an IAS officer or an IIT graduate, or employed with a highly-rated MNC.[17] In one profile, the individual mentions that his mother hails from a royal family, another lists the achievements of his uncles. Through such details, the individual not only enhances his own profile, but also successfully makes status claims. While details of certain characteristics provided by the individual pertaining to himself/herself—such as physical characteristics, hobbies, desired characteristics of spouse, etc.—may support a greater emphasis on the suitability of the individual person, the provision of information about other family members strengthens a conservative reproduction of class. Matching of a great number of variables through the internet technology also ensures that parents' choices and proclivities will be met without them having to take the lead or initiative.

Two interesting attributes in the profiles pertain to 'family values' held by the individual and the type of family s/he belongs to. The choices provided to describe family values are: orthodox, liberal or moderate and, for the type of family, nuclear or joint. This additional information being provided by both parties enables people to sort profiles based on whether families are considered 'modern' or 'Western' or 'traditional' in their outlook. In many cases, couples tend to refrain from moving further in the process if family type or values do not match, even if characteristics of the individuals are compatible. While caste and community remain fundamental to the matching process, family values essentially refer to the internal class-based differentiation occurring among families within such groups. Upbringing, socialisation and cultural capital denote different degrees of personal freedom and individualisation, signalled through family values.

The type of family, joint or nuclear, is another important consideration. Even in the past, parents queried the size and type of family (nuclear or joint, many or few siblings, married or unmarried siblings) of a prospective partner to gauge the future quality of married life for the girl, while parents of boys calculated how much parents of daughters would be able to give in marriage. In contemporary marriages, women have strong views about living in joint or nuclear families with educated, working women rarely wishing to move in with a joint family; joint living becomes acceptable only when children are born. Co-residence with the spouse's brothers' families is almost never desired, while co-residence with in-laws is tolerated when needed. Spouse-seekers are explicit about wanting to know the type of family even before considering a prospective partner.

Among the class of people using the net for matchmaking, it is no longer politically correct to mention dowry expectations in the posting. It does not, however, mean that dowry is not negotiated in such marriages. It is most likely relegated to the second phase of matchmaking. The public nature of the internet and the desire to present a modern front pushes such discussions behind the scenes. Dowry remains an important consideration in most Indian marriages and many negotiations break down precisely on the question of dowry demands.

Despite the modernity of the internet technology and its users, horoscope matching remains a very important element in the matchmaking process. Websites enable users to create their horoscopes easily by feeding in the date of birth, time, city and country of birth. The importance of matching horoscopes indicates the need to control the uncertainty around the fate of a marriage as marriage essentially remains a lottery with unknown individuals and families. As one mother who arranged her daughter's marriage through a website said, 'Horoscopes were matched; it narrows down the choice somewhat but we felt it was important.' The girl's parents were both professionals, and the couple had MBA degrees and were working in the corporate sector.

That marriage remains an important strategy for individual and family mobility is illustrated by several cases of web-based marriages. In two of three such cases documented for this essay, mother and daughter decided to post the latter's profile on the net; in the first, because they found proposals through other routes 'scanty' and not 'up to the mark' and in the second, because the daughter announced that she had not met anyone she wanted to marry and was ready for an arranged marriage. In the third case, having tried other routes, the brother of the girl took the initiative to search for a spouse for her on the internet. All three couples are well educated, for whom profession and educational qualifications followed by family background were important criteria. In a fourth case, the marriage was cross-regional (west and north) even though the caste was the same; the net thus opening up possibilities of finding a suitable match across cultural regions, though from the same community.

As an example, we look at the case of Lata, whose mother took the initiative to post her profile on the net despite opposition from the father. Her father remained sceptical and didn't wish to waste money by becoming a paid subscriber. Lata said, 'When we started seeing better offers from more educated people with better profiles, we were encouraged.' Finally, the mother and daughter (who was on her way to qualifying as a doctor and hence keen on finding the right match) prevailed upon him and a paid account was opened. To make the initial contact, the mother and brother corresponded with the people whose profiles interested them. They had specified that the groom had to be a doctor, from an educated family and located in the National Capital Region (NCR) of Delhi. After the initial phase, the girl would communicate with the boy; the discussion would be around education and dowry did not figure at all. In her profile, her education, fair complexion, her parents' education and her brother's qualification as an IIT graduate were emphasised. For the girl, the groom's education, caste and height (after making sure that he too would be a doctor) were important characteristics. She was very clear that she was not looking for a 'soul mate' and left our question on romance in marriage unanswered. Lata's agency in the groom search is apparent in her selecting the profiles that interested her, after short-listing by her mother and brother, and rejecting those who she thought did not meet her expectations or would not be compatible.

Negotiating Diverse Intimacies

The language of matchmaking in websites is an important indicator of shifting sensibilities around marriage. While newspaper advertisements talk about 'seeking a match', internet websites talk of 'seeking a life partner' or a 'soul mate'. Such rhetoric may be mere gimmicky advertising, but in many cases the internet is providing individuals with a way to express new desires.

An example is of a North-Indian Bengali Catholic woman who married a Protestant Christian man she met through a marriage website. Although community was not an issue with her because of her secular upbringing, somewhere along the way she felt that she would be more comfortable with a person from a similar religious background. The woman is in her mid-30s and the man in his 40s. There was family pressure to get married but, more importantly, she too was keen to get married as the biological clock was ticking. Her extended family had tried looking for a groom for her, but she did not find any of the candidates suitable. She had not wanted to seek a match through a newspaper matrimonial ad. Being busy professionally, she found little time to meet people. Finally, she decided to sign up on a 'free' marriage site which she found user-friendly. She posted her own profile and adamantly declared 'I was not going to let anyone else do it'. She corresponded with about five people by email. It was the persistence of her future spouse that impressed her and she responded to him. Her spouse, in turn, found her profile witty and intelligent. After conducting a courtship on the net and over the phone, they decided to meet and then marry. According to her, neither set of parents would have had the right to veto the marriage once the couple had decided as they were old enough to make the decision themselves. The role of parents in this particular marriage was thus, totally absent. According to the woman, other friends of hers had also found the same route to matrimony; she felt that if one was level-headed, one could find a spouse through a website, or else 'you could simply waste your time'. The success of such young, professional women in finding suitable spouses is emboldening many others to take the same route. As she said, 'they don't need to feel guilty about it'.

In another such case, the woman posted herself on the net, initially 'for fun', and was by her own admission not preoccupied with the thought of marriage as such. She corresponded with many men, some of whom became good friends even though nothing romantic developed. Although information on caste, religion, etc. was available, she did not think of it as being of great consequence because she was more interested in a potential spouse's personality, his outlook on life and his achievements. After conducting a courtship on the net and over the phone (he turned out to be an NRI), they decided to meet and then to marry. He first met her parents and then they announced the decision to his parents.

These last two cases represent a process of matchmaking different from the ones outlined earlier, in that the process is not family-controlled. Rather, the family plays a secondary role, entering only to celebrate the marriage. In the former kinds of cases the internet expanded traditional choices, whereas in the second type, the internet enabled an expansion of the parameters for selection and type of choice to include modern ideas of suitability, compatibility, intimacy and a couple's life together. In the first set of cases, women denied ever having been romantically involved with anyone. While men admitted to posting on several websites simultaneously and pursuing their own searches, women were generally posted on a single website and rarely conducted the search independently.

Some other stories we learnt about did not have such happy endings—individuals seeking each other out, but the match being rejected by the family—revealing the resistance to both the new mode of finding a spouse and the new independence demanded by marriageable individuals. In one case, the girl, an orphaned child brought up by two sisters, put up her own profile and after corresponding with several men, fell in love with one of them. The boy's mother, however, summarily rejected the girl.

In another case, a couple entered their second marriages after conducting a search on the net. Marriages in which couples find each other independently of family involvement are often across caste and community, as in another case where the man is a Bengali and the woman a Maharashtrian, both NRIs. In such cases, the couple is typically older, may have been spouse-searching for some time, and considers compatibility in terms of education, profession and personality more important than traditional community-defined criteria. Among couples interviewed for this essay, most got married within four to six months of posting their profiles. However, conversations with several unsuccessful registrants revealed that many were never able to find a satisfactory match despite being posted simultaneously on several websites.

While men seek both intimacy and marriage when posting their profiles on the net, most women in parent-driven matchmaking may create a post-facto romanticisation of the relationship. In cases where individuals seek partners themselves, the internet technology allows desire to become one of the ingredients of matchmaking; the displayed self is a sexualised self in posting profiles describing an attractive personality. Thus, the professional Catholic woman, who was adamant on posting her own profile, and whose courtship moved from 'furious email chatting to telephone and finally meeting in person', actualised a possibility not available through newspaper advertisements or marriage bureaus. The technology also represents the possibility of bypassing the traditional requirement of confining sexuality to marriage. Of course, this particular engagement with the technology does not come about in a vacuum. Many couples in urban areas today are experimenting with live-in relationships and pre-marital sex before tying the knot. A cultural appropriation of the new technology has taken place, which functions to keep older requirements of matching intact while allowing certain new elements to be added.

Global Choices, Local Marriages?

The process of globalisation has been characterised by scholars such as Giddens as compressing time and space (1999). The fact that the internet endlessly expands the horizon over which brides and grooms can be 'surfed for' is what appeals most to families and individuals taking this route. This modernity is thus one of expanding choice and possibilities, and overcoming barriers of geography and physical location and expanding the marriage distance. Yet, this modernity does not necessarily encompass seeking marriage partners across traditional criteria of caste, class, religion and region. What drives the need to have a wider choice than that provided by marriage brokers, newspaper ads, and family and community contacts? Is it a crisis of matchmaking? As arranged marriage remains resilient and community ties weaken, matrimonial websites have opened a new frontier for aspiring couples belonging to the middle classes. In contemporary marriages, choice itself is being redefined in the context of the marriage market and changing notions of conjugality and intimacy. It may either be self-choice resulting from a romantic relationship or, as is the case most of the time, it is more a market style 'informed choice' that the internet provides. Such choice opens up greater possibilities, yet prevents individuals from making wrong choices—such as falling in love with the 'wrong' type of person, of the wrong caste, class or religion—while picking the most suitable boy or girl. As important shifts surely take place in marriage, in the matchmaking process and in the marriage market, any structural break remains caught between the conservative and radicalising possibilities of this new technology.

Notes

[1] See Khandelwal (2009) for a discussion on how arranged marriage is positioned as a symbol of Eastern or Indian/south Asian marriage, implying parental control and a lack of agency on the part of the marrying individuals. She argues that the contrast between arranging marriages in the East and love marriages in the West is overdrawn, with agency being overestimated in the latter.

[2] See Kabeer (2000) on inter-generational contracts. The parental contract with sons is the assumption that they will provide old-age support to them. The gendered nature of roles in society extends this duty to daughters-in-law, who are seen as being responsible for domestic tasks, including provision of care to in-laws.

[3] A paper by Mathur (2007) highlights that parents tend to choose daughters-in-law who will look after them rather than have compatibility with the sons.

[4] Honour killings in North India are a reaction to the loss of control which families and communities experience when young adults marry out of caste or repudiate other community norms (Chowdhry 2007; Kaur 2010).

[5] Please see Sharangapani (2010) for marriage bureaus and Pache (1998) for marriage fairs.

[6] Recently, bharatmatrimony.com has overtaken shaadi.com in market share. bharatmatrimony.com is especially popular among NRIs and in South India.

[7] Biao (2005) formulates the concept of 'ethnic transnational middle class'; members of this middle class are active users of marriage websites.

[8] Uberoi (1998) points to the role of media and the Indian cinema in perpetuating Indian family values among Indians abroad.

[9] 'Operation Match' was the first dating computer program set up by Harvard students, which was followed by Project TACT-Technical Automated Compatibility Testing—New York city's first computer-dating service (Paumgarten 2011).

[10] Among Hindus, there is a belief that a person who is a *manglik* is born under an inauspicious astrological configuration with negative consequences for marriage. This configuration is supposedly one for widowers. Hence, it is believed that the spouse of a manglik partner will be in danger of prematurely losing her/his life. If two mangliks marry each other the effect is cancelled out.

[11] A recent news report from Gujarat described a marriage mela organised by an NGO for older individuals, who were looking for partners; such melas may eventually afford greater legitimacy to live-in partnerships.

[12] In 2012, Shaadi.com had 20 million plus users of which 65 per cent were men and 35 per cent were women (Poonam 2012).

[13] In 2012, SimplyMarry.com reported that earlier 80 per cent of girl profiles were posted by parents, but now it had gone down to 50 per cent (Poonam 2012).

[14] A report by the National Council for Applied Economic Research's (NCAER) Centre for Macro Consumer Research states that by 2015–16, India will be a country of 53.3 million middle-class households, translating into 267 million people falling in the category. As per the study, which uses 'household income' as the criterion, a family with an annual income between INR 3.4 lakh to INR 17 lakh (at 2009–10 price levels) falls in the middle class category (*PTI* 2011).

[15] See Liddle and Joshi (1989) on women's greater assertiveness in choosing the family they wish to marry into.

[16] In a survey of 203 advertisements in contemporary English dailies, 59 per cent of the advertisements by men or their parents mentioned their salary, while only 11 per cent of the women did so. Skin colour was mentioned for 42 per cent of the women and for 18 per cent of the men. Thirty-eight per cent of the women mentioned body type as being slim while only 3 per cent of the men gave this information (Fargette and Marchal 2008).

[17] IAS (Indian Administrative Service), IIT (Indian Institute of Technology), MNC (Multinational Corporation).

References

Adams, Paul C., and Rina Ghosh. 2003. 'India.com: The Construction of A Space Between'. *Progress in Human Geography* 27 (4): 414–37.

Banerjee, Abhijit, Esther Duflo, Maitreesh Ghatak, and Jeanne Lafortune. 2009. 'Marry for What? Caste and Mate Selection in Modern India'. *NBER Working Paper* No. 14958. Available at: http://www.nber.org/papers/w14958. Accessed on: 30 June 2013.

Biao, Xiang. 2005. 'Gender, Dowry and the Migration System of Indian Information Technology Professionals'. *Indian Journal of Gender Studies* 12:357–80.

Bourdieu, Pierre. 1977. *Outline of a Theory of Practice*. Cambridge: Cambridge University Press.

Chatterjee, J. S. 2007. 'The Internet as Matchmaker: A Study of Why Young Indians are Seeking Marriage Alliances Online'. Paper presented at the annual meeting of the International Communication Association, TBA, San Francisco, CA. Available at: http://citation.allacademic.com/meta/p_mla_apa_research_citation/1/7/2/1/3/pages172135/p172135-1.php. Accessed on: 27 February 2013.

Chowdhry, Prem. 2007. *Contentious Marriages, Eloping Couples*. New Delhi: Oxford University Press.

EmPower Research LLC. 2008. *A Web Partner for Life: Indian, Matrimony Web Sites are Modernizing Matchmaking for the Offline World and Positioning to be Lifelong Portals for the Online One*. 20 October. Available at: http://www.marketresearch.com/EmPower-Research-LLC-v3570/Web-Partner-Life-Indian-Matrimony-1920947/. Accessed on: 20 February 2013.

Fargette, Camille, and Julien Marchal. 2008. 'Matrimonial Advertisements: Content and Analysis'. Unpublished student paper, Indian Institute of Technology, Delhi. September.

Giddens, Anthony. 1999. *Runaway World: How Globalisation is Reshaping Our Lives*. London: Profile.

______. 1994. *The Transformation of Intimacy: Love, Sexuality and Eroticism in Modern Societies*. Cambridge: Polity Press.

JuxtConsult. 2008. *India Online 2008 Online Matrimony Report*. 1 June. Available at: http://www.marketresearch.com/JuxtConsult-v3690/India-Online-Matrimony-2196564/. Accessed in: February 2013.

Kabeer, Naila. 2000. 'Inter-Generational Contracts, Demographic Transitions and the "Quantity-Quality" Trade-off: Parents, Children and Investing in the Future'. *Journal of International Development*, 12 (4): 463–82.

Kaur, Ravinder. 2010. 'Khap Panchayats, Sex Ratio and Female Agency'. *Economic and Political Weekly* 45 (23): 14–16.

Khandelwal, Meena. 2009. 'Arranging Love: Interrogating the Vantage Point in Cross-Border Feminism'. *Signs: Journal of Women in Culture and Society* 34 (3): 583–609.

Liddle, J., and R. Joshi. 1989. *Daughters of India: Gender, Caste, and Class in India*. New Brunswick, New Jersey: Rutgers University Press.

Majumdar, Rochona. 2004. 'Looking for Brides and Grooms: Ghataks, Matrimonials and the Marriage Market in Colonial Calcutta, circa 1875–1940'. *Journal of South Asian Studies* 63 (4): 911–35.

Mathur, Divya. 2007. 'What's Love Got to Do With It? Parental Involvement in Spouse Choice in Urban India'. Department of Economics, University of Chicago. Available at: http://ssrn.com/abstract=1655998. Accessed on: 27 February 2007.

Mullatti, L. 1995. 'Families in India: Beliefs and Realities'. *Journal of Comparative Family Studies* 26 (1): 11–25.

Pache, Veornique. 1998. 'Marriage Fairs among Maheshwaris: A New Matrimonial Strategy'. *Economic and Political Weekly* 33 (17): 1970–75.

Pal, Jiban K. 2010. 'Social Networks Enabling Matrimonial Information Services in India'. *International Journal of Library and Information Science* 2 (4): 54–64.

Paumgarten, Nick. 2011. 'Looking for Someone: Sex, Love, and Loneliness on the Internet'. *The New Yorker*. 4 July. Available at: http://www.newyorker.com/reporting/2011/07/04/110704fa_fact_paumgarten. Accessed on: 27 February 2013.

Poonam, Snigdha. 2012. 'Casting the Net'. *The Caravan* 4 (3): 48–59.

PTI (Press Trust of India). 2011. 'India's Middle Class Population to Touch 267 Million in 5 yrs'. *The Economic Times*. 6 February.

Roy Choudhury, Pritha. 2007. 'Interview: *Shaadi.com* is the leading online matrimonial service'. *Merinews*. 16 June. Available at: http://www.merinews.com/article/interview-shaadicom-is-the-leading-online-matrimonial-service/125367.shtml. Accessed in: February 2013.

Sethi, Kapil. 2000. *Branding Brides and Grooms in Asia: An Analysis of Matrimonial Advertising in India 1967–1997*. McCann Erickson's consumer insights. Available at: http://www.brandingasia.com/columns/mccannerickson5.htm. Accessed on: 27 February 2013.

Sharangpani, Mukta. 2010. 'Browsing for Bridegrooms: Matchmaking and Modernity in Mumbai'. *Indian Journal of Gender Studies* 17 (2): 249–76.

Sharma, Archana. 2006. 'Girl Seeks Suitable Boy: Indian Marriage Dot Com'. Ph.D. Dissertation. University of Toronto.

Shukla, Sonal, and Shagufa Kapadia. 2007. 'Transition in Marriage-Partner Selection Process: Are Matrimonial Advertisements an Indication?' *Psychology & Developing Societies* 19 (1): 37–54.

Uberoi, Patricia. 1998. 'The Diaspora Comes Home: Disciplining Desire in DDLJ'. *Contributions to Indian Sociology* n.s., 32 (2): 305–36.

'WHY DID YOU SEND ME LIKE THIS?'*

Marriage, Matriliny and the 'Providing Husband' in North Kerala, India

JANAKI ABRAHAM

INTRODUCTION

'Enthina nee ingane ayachatu' 'Why did you send me like this?' Shobha would repeat, asking her mother why she had got her married to the person she had. During fieldwork in North Kerala among a formerly matrilineal[1] caste called the Thiyyas,[2] I was struck by how a woman's shift in residence at marriage was highlighted. This shift in residence at marriage and the norm of virilocality, residence in the husband's house, is firmly embedded in language. *Kalyanam kazhichayakkanam* (get her married and send her) is what people would say when referring to the marriage of a woman. This is often shortened to just *ayakkanam* (must send) or the past tense *ayachu* (sent) so that marriage

* The research on which this essay is based was part of my doctoral work. A version of this essay was presented at the conference *Marriage in Globalising Contexts: Exploring Change and Continuity in South Asia* held in September 2008 at IIT, Delhi, and also at a colloquium in the Anthropology Department, LSE, London. I thank the audiences in both these places for many useful questions. I am grateful to Prof. A. M. Shah, Ravinder Kaur, Rajni Palriwala and Shalini Grover for comments on this essay. I would also like to acknowledge Aaradhana Dalmia for assistance. A longer version of this essay appeared in the *Asian Journal of Women's Studies* (*AJWS*), 2011.

itself is referred to in terms of the rule of residence, i.e. a woman is 'sent' in marriage. In turn, the words used for separation or divorce of a woman refer to returning, *madangi vannu* (returned) or *thiruchu vannu* (came back) or *poyitu konduvannu* (went and brought back). In contrast, the terms used for the marriage of a man do not indicate a change in residence. And the term for divorce refers to a woman being 'sent away'.[3]

For a woman being 'sent' in marriage is not only about a shift in residence. It also critically expresses the idea that the husband is to 'provide' for her while they are married. In this essay, I consider the idea of the 'providing' husband as both characterising the image of a normative conjugality among the Thiyyas and also as an idea that has characterised changes in matriliny and marriage since the late nineteenth century. In doing this, I look at ideas of a normative conjugality, especially as expressed in marriage customs and rituals and in ideas of post-marriage virilocality. Simultaneously, I point to what makes the context of matriliny and virilocal residence different from a patrilineal patrilocal context—most importantly, women's inheritance of property—and seek to understand how the norm of post-marriage virilocal residence is lived and negotiated in a context in which women inherit property and have a right to return to their natal house. Looking at negotiation in everyday life is crucial because so much of the focus in kinship studies has for long been on rules rather than the messiness of practice.[4]

One of the problems with much of the literature on matriliny in Kerala has been an almost exclusive focus on upper-caste and landed Nayars and particularly the exotic conjugal arrangements of central Kerala, described as 'visiting' husbands and polyandry (Thurston 1906; Gough 1961b; Jeffery 2004). In these descriptions, the focus was on contexts in which matriliny was coupled with post-marriage matrilocality or duo-locality in which women lived in their matrilineal *tharavad*s (joint family houses) and husbands visited.[5] Marriage was seen as a slim tie and fathers and husbands were seen as having a minimal presence and role. In fact, *Here comes Papa*, a Ravi Varma painting done in the late nineteenth century is seen as representing the emergence of new conjugal and familial relationships for those following matrilineal kinship (e.g. Arunima 2003; Kodoth 2003).

In anthropological literature, matriliny was assumed to be generally accompanied by a weak marital tie (Radcliffe-Brown 1950; Schneider 1961). This was seen as a way of ensuring that there was no contradiction between the authority of the mother's brother and that of the husband. The central-Kerala case was seen as an extreme or thorough case that exemplified this relationship of matriliny and marriage.[6] The idea of a weak marital tie and the descriptions of visiting husbands and polyandry, led to considerable curiosity and myth-making about the implications of this system for women and for gender relations. In fact, feminist scholars explored matrilineal contexts to see if they provided an alternative to what was being described as the universal subordination of women (Reiter 1975).

At a popular level, one of the conceptual confusions made was between matriliny and matriarchy and scholars have had to clarify that even though inheritance and descent was through women, authority rested with men. The implications of the overwhelming focus[7] on the formerly matrilineal and matrilocal, or duo-local, Nayars in central Kerala has been an inadvertent furthering of this myth. What it has also done is overshadow an understanding of kinship among matrilineal castes, including the Nayars in Kerala, who follow a different post-marriage norm of residence.[8] In fact in discussions on matriliny in Kerala insufficient attention has been paid to residence. As Palriwala points out, 'structuralist analyses tended to take locality as subordinate to marriage and descent in making kinship structures' (1999: 237).

A large heterogeneous caste, the Thiyyas were seen as ranking below the Nayars in the caste hierarchy and have suffered disabilities due to practices of 'untouchability'. Although associated with the 'traditional occupation'[9] of toddy-tapping (toddy is the sap from the coconut palm), members of the caste have been engaged in occupations ranging from agricultural labour and Ayurvedic medicine to modern bureaucratic jobs from roughly the middle of the nineteenth century. A range of social processes, including educational and occupational opportunities made accessible through the Basel German Mission and the British in Madras Presidency, led to the formation of a sizeable elite among the caste during colonial rule. Thiyyas are now scattered all over the country and the world.

This essay is based on intensive fieldwork done primarily over two years (1996–98) in Thalassery (also known as Tellicherry), North Kerala, and also in other cities in Kerala, and in Chennai, Bangalore and Delhi. However, fieldwork has continued since then, through regular visits and phone calls. In Thalassery, I concentrated on two neighbourhoods: a ward in the Thalassery municipality, which I call Pattamkunnu, and a panchayat or village area adjacent to the town of Devaloor. These two neighbourhoods are distinct with respect to the class and occupational status of households. This study focuses primarily on the broad category of the middle class.

Legislative Changes and the Imperative of the 'Providing' Husband

The twentieth century witnessed the dramatic erosion of matriliny in legislation and in everyday life. Starting in 1896, the Malabar Marriage Act was the first law passed for Hindus following matriliny or *marumakkathayam* in Malabar. A series of laws followed through the twentieth century, until the final legal axe came in 1976 when the Kerala Joint Family (Abolition) Act was passed. From then on matrilineal joint family tharavad properties could not accrue new members, while existing tharavad properties were deemed to be divided among all existing members.

The impetus for the first marriage legislation at the end of the nineteenth century came from elite Nayar men who sought to legitimise their conjugal arrangement called *sambandham* (literally, connection). They thus turned to the colonial state and demanded a marriage law that would recognise sambandham as marriage. This demand came in the face of a popular conception, expressed in writing by travellers, colonial ethnographers and anthropologists, that Nayar sambandham was a form of concubinage. While the motivation for the legislation came from some Nayars and while the debate was centered on Nayar sambandham, the Bill and subsequently the Act passed in 1896, brought under its purview all Hindus following marumakkathayam[10] (or matrilineal) law of inheritance domiciled in Madras Presidency. It thus applied to matrilineal groups with diverse kinship practices—most prominently the difference in kinship practices between north and south Malabar and differences in practices of various castes. What all the groups shared at the time under the matrilineal system was that descent and inheritance was through women. The property of men devolved to their sisters and their sister's children. Marriage did not lead to rights in property, for a woman to her husband's property or a child to his/her father's.

What was central to the Malabar Marriage Act, and to subsequent legislation, was the idea that marriage should result in the husband 'providing' for his wife and children, not only during his lifetime but critically 'after' his death as well. It was this idea of a 'providing' husband that was seen as central to a legitimate marriage. The Act was a permissive law that stipulated that if a man and a woman registered their marriage under it, on the former's death, the woman and their children would be entitled to half his self-acquired property.[11] The Act and the ideology informing it were clearly influenced by ideas of the modern patri-centred family (Arunima 2003; Kodoth 2003). This idea of providing was strengthened through the twentieth century, so that by 1933 the legal provision was that all of a man's self-acquired property would go to his wife and children. However, the relationship of the 1896 Act to kinship practices in the area was extremely varied. This is clear from opinion collected by the Malabar Marriage Commission and compiled in a report published in 1891. All Thiyya respondents were categorical regarding the ways in which their marriage was both in nomenclature and practice different from that of the Nayars. They argued that they had a 'substantial marriage', which was referred to as *mangalam* and not sambandham or *pudamuri*, as it was for the Nayars. 'It is not a binding marriage in the legal sense. [But] among Tiyans

[Thiyyas] the union lasts for life.'[12] All respondents said that after marriage the bride moved to the husband's house. These testimonies thus suggested that the practice of virilocality and a 'lasting union' indicated a 'substantial marriage'.

The idea of a 'providing' father was expressed not only through the practice of growing up in the father's house, but also through the devolution of a tharavad name from the father, and fathers who gifted property to their children. A few respondents said that they had taken their fathers' name because their father had 'educated and protected' them. In some cases a father had educated his children and also given them a fraction of his property. However, the picture of who provided and when, was quite mixed. From the respondents it was clear that some men provided for their wives and children both during their lifetimes and later by gifting self-acquired property to them, while others were taken care of by their maternal uncles. All respondents were categorical that self-acquisition should not go to the *karnavar* (the eldest male and head of the matrilineal tharavad). In fact, the testimonies express a strong sense of antagonism towards the karnavar. What is significant then from these testimonies is that shifts in ideas about who constituted the family, who lived with whom, and who should be provided for by whom, were already underway even before the legislation.

In fact, while the legislation was scarcely used,[13] it was not necessarily because a man did not want his wife and children to inherit half of his self-acquired property. Rather, it was because the Malabar Wills Act passed in 1898, could be used to will self-acquired property or could be given through a gift deed. However, in evaluating the legislation, there has been a tendency to focus primarily on the south Malabar Nayar case and, in doing this, overstate the divergence of the legislation from practice. In the next section, I look at the context of virilocality and seek to understand expectations of a husband to provide and the normative structure of conjugality that has accompanied it.

'Providing' and the Normative Structure of Conjugality

The obligation of the husband to provide for his wife during his life time has been central to the meaning of marriage among those who followed marumakkathayam in Kerala. In fact, irrespective of the norm of residence, symbolically providing was central to the marriage ceremony and was seen as an indication of the continuation of a marriage and of the acceptance of paternity. Thus, among the Nayars, sambandham was contracted through a ceremony called the *pudumuri*—in which the groom gifted a sari or length of cloth to the bride. Further, as Kathleen Gough argues, the legitimacy of a child was established through gifts from the father (1961b: 359–60). However, for matrilocal Nayars, it appears from the descriptions that these gifts were symbolic; they established marriage and the legitimacy of the child. The responsibility for everyday care of a woman and her children remained with her tharavad where she lived. This was quite different in the virilocal case.

Before I discuss issues of providing in everyday life, I would like to look at expressions of a husband providing in marriage rituals and customs. Among the Thiyyas in Thalassery, the expectations from the groom start even before a woman is married. After the *nischeyam* (the ceremony when it is agreed that the couple will get married) and before the marriage, if there is a festival that is commonly observed by both or specifically in the bride's region or locality, the groom is expected to give new clothes to the bride, her parents and her unmarried siblings. When a woman gets married, all the clothes and accessories she wears for the wedding ceremony, other than the gold jewellery and the flowers on her hair, come from her husband's house. An attaché case is brought to the bride's house with every stitch and pin that the bride will need: clothes, shoes, hair clips, safety pins and even the thread needed to tie the gold jewellery at different lengths. Thus, when a bride goes to her husband's house after the wedding the only things she takes with her from her house is the gold jewellery she is wearing on her body and the jasmine flowers she wears on her hair. At her husband's house, a cupboard is prepared and generally placed in the room allocated to the newly-wed couple. This has all the things that she will need such as clothes, a comb and hair accessories, sanitary towels and until mobiles became popular, it often even had stationery for her to write home! Both the attaché case and the cupboard are shown to people who visit, especially women. These seem to reflect the money spent by the husband's family, the care taken in choosing items, and may be seen as reflecting how well she will be provided for. Most of all, these things reflect the status of the groom's family.[14] This is the reverse of the trousseau and dowry display that takes place at the bride's house and again at her husband's house after the marriage in North India and among some communities in South India.

In addition to the clothes and other things for the bride, there are two gifts that the groom gives at the marriage ceremony which are important. The first is the gold chain and pendant called the *tali* which he puts on the bride;[15] the second is the gift of saris (*ammai*'s *pudava*), which he gives to the bride's mother's brother's wife and the bride's father's sister. The mother's brother's wife (the bride's karnavar's wife) represents a woman whom the bride's tharavad provides for. The father's sister, a member of the bride's father's tharavad is someone whom her father has to provide for as a tharavad member, while at the same time providing for the bride's mother (while he is alive) as well as for the bride and her siblings. Thus, the groom has to symbolically provide for two women who do not belong to the tharavad of the bride and are provided for by the men who have been providing for her. This can be seen as marking a shift from the everyday provisioning that the father and the karnavar are responsible for. However, it does not mean that her rights in her natal house or in her mother's tharavad cease. Nor do the obligations of these homes towards her cease.

Under the old system centered on land, a nephew or brother who worked on the land was maintained by his tharavad. He often did not have an independent income. In such a situation, a man's wife was maintained by the tharavad and I was told stories about how a man would instruct his wife to wear her most tattered sari when appearing in front of the karnavar so as to impress on him that she needed a new sari! Thus, a man here was unable to provide for his wife and children directly and was dependent on his tharavad and in particular the karnavar to do so. This old system, wherein men worked on the land and were maintained by their tharavads, broke down in and around Thalassery town, well before it did in the hinterland. In Thalassery town and adjoining areas, new forms of paid employment and the partition of property brought considerable changes in residence and in 'providing' observances. Furthermore, with the break-up of tharavads over the twentieth century the right to residence and the nature of obligations of kin and households has changed significantly.

In the 1990s it was clear that the responsibility of providing was focused much more on the husband. Women generally returned to their mothers' homes for the delivery of their children and at the time of childbirth, the husband was expected to give a lump sum towards meeting the hospital and other expenses of his wife and child. Similarly, he was expected to support his wife and children even if they were staying in her natal house. Thus, for a woman and her children who lived in her natal home while her husband was away—say, in the Gulf—he was expected to pay for all the expenses of his wife and children. In the household survey I conducted, women who lived duo-locally—i.e. the woman lived in her tharavad and her husband lived in his—felt they must explain that their husbands paid for all their expenses. This was often said to indicate that the marriage was still on.

Obligations of a mother's brother to provide have not gone away despite the break-up of tharavads. These and the obligations of other kin—tharavad members and the father's family—are evident in gift-giving at certain occasions such as marriage or house-warming functions. The nature of gifts depends not only on the genealogical relationship, but critically on sentiment and the nature of residence in the past or present.

While a husband is expected to provide money for the running of the house and for meeting expenses, it is the responsibility of women to do all of the domestic work. Although a man may help with cleaning or with taking care of the children, these are considered as 'helping' his wife or the other women in the house. Despite the large number of women who work outside the home in Kerala, there is no public discussion on housework.[16] This sexual division of labour is part of a normative structure of conjugality in which men are considered bearers of authority and responsible for earning. The idea of the 'providing husband' and post-marriage virilocal residence are therefore coupled not only with the strong sense of a dependent wife, but also by the husband's unequivocal authority.

In Thalassery, a man's authority over the woman he is going to marry is asserted (at least symbolically) from the time the marriage is fixed. From then on, the woman needs to get his or his family's permission to go anywhere that is not part of her everyday routine. *Chodikonum*, to ask or seek permission, is a principle that recurs throughout a woman's married life and I would often hear women saying that they will 'ask'. Although, this authority is negotiated by women in a variety of ways and changes with time, the birth of children, age and earning capacity, what is considered the norm and the public face is the image of the husband who has authority over his wife. This public face was evident when I was doing the household survey. In the course of a conversation with a couple, Vimla and Mukundan both in their 70s, I said that only one (currently married) woman in the neighbourhood had said that she was the head of the household. I reported that she had said, 'The men bring in the money but I manage it.' Vimala was quick to respond, although half swallowing her words so her husband could not hear, 'Oh that is because we don't want the man to feel bad.' In presenting the image of the 'norm,' women save face for their husbands and in turn for themselves. While women negotiate this authority, the normative structure of conjugality wherein the husband has authority substantially reduces the bargaining space of women. Kerala's high level of domestic violence presents one face of the constraints of this norm.[17]

The idea of the 'providing husband' also needs to be seen within a larger context in which men are seen as primary players in public spaces. Although girls and women may have greater physical mobility in Kerala than women in many other parts of the country, and Hindu women do not observe veiling or seclusion, public spaces in Kerala are predominantly male and women have to appear to be purposefully traversing these spaces.[18] A strong public morality regulates dress and interactions in public.[19] This heightens the idea of respectability attached to conjugality, especially for young women. Further, critical to the dependence is the gendered structuring of spouse selection such that a man is expected to be better qualified, earn more than the woman (if she is working), and be taller and older.[20]

However, what marks out North Malabar Thiyyas from patrilineal groups in Kerala and elsewhere, is that women not only have a right to inherit property, they do inherit property and have a right to live in their tharavad or natal house. Below, I turn to looking at how, despite the strong rule of virilocality, women's inheritance enables flexibility in residence and has important implications for marriage.

The Rule of Virilocality, Women's Inheritance and The Negotiation of Residence

Virilocality is critical to the understanding of marriage among the Thiyyas. This is expressed not only in language, as described earlier, but also in marriage rituals. The marriage ceremony is not considered complete without the couple leaving after the ceremony for his house,[21] wherever they may leave from—the bride's house, a temple, an auditorium or a hotel. This was brought home to me at a marriage I attended in Delhi between a Thiyya woman and a Maharashtrian Christian man in which the couple were going to live independently in a flat. A church wedding was followed the next day by a Hindu and predominantly Thiyya ritual at the bride's house. After the wedding and lunch, suddenly there was talk about how the couple must leave before *rahu kalam* (an inauspicious period of the day) or else they could only do so after rahu kalam and that would be too late. As the couple was walked out toward the gate I could hear the bride saying loudly 'why are you pushing me out ... I haven't even taken my pair of shorts to change into! ... I am coming right back.' Her mother repeatedly said, 'They are waiting for you.' In the evening the couple was back, and in the course of conversation, the bride said something about how she had been 'pushed out of the house.' The marriage ceremony was not considered complete without the bride leaving her house.

Where a bride goes to live depends on where her husband lives at the time: with his parents in his father's tharavad, in his tharavad (his mother's tharavad), in neo-local residence set up by his parents, or in a separate residence if he has a job away from his parents' house. While hierarchies based on age and gender in tharavads are discussed in the literature (Arunima 2003; Fuller 1976), the focus on duo-locality, or the neglect of norms of residence implies that there has been little discussion on the experience of a woman in her husband's tharavad, especially as a young bride. Many women I spoke to in Thalassery in the 1990s spoke about how everyday life for a woman in her husband's house was not always comfortable. They would be the last to eat in these large tharavads and this was particularly so for young in-marrying women. A recurring comment in conversations about tharavad living was that often there would be no curry left for the women who ate last and they would have to make do with rice and pickle. Further, a great deal of housework had to be done by them, including cooking, grinding, cleaning, washing clothes and so on. A woman would go to her mother's house for a period of a month[22] once a year to have a break and be 'fattened up'. The normative idea of the husband who provided appeared completely at odds with these images. Of course, women's experience of the virilocal tharavad house was dependent on the composition of the household, the number of women in it and the nature of the relationships between its members.

Under the old system, a woman living in her husband's joint-family house, on being widowed, was expected to return to her matrilineal joint-family tharavad house with her children (who were considered members of her tharavad). Otherwise, she returned to her parents' house. If the couple had set up their own house then on the death of her husband, a woman would not have to move in with her children. If they had not set up neo-local residence and her mother's tharavad had been partitioned or for some other reason she could not return there, then a woman had to negotiate residence in a context in which her options were very limited.[23] This was one reason why women were often keen to acquire their own homes. In fact, through the twentieth century, men and women often set up new households. Often a couple built a house on the woman's share of the tharavad property and this came to be seen as a *thavazhi* or matriline.

The idea of the 'providing' husband, coupled with his unequivocal authority, is reflected in the notions attached to the norm and ideology of virilocality. For a man to live in his wife's undivided house is considered *koravu* (a matter of shame). Men who do so, or did so at some point, are often somewhat hesitant to talk about it or feel compelled to explain or justify this. Thus, for instance, when I was filling out a questionnaire in a house in Devaloor, I noticed that when I got to the question of who lived in the house, the brother of the woman I was interviewing seemed to be trying to persuade her about something. She told me a few minutes later that he wanted his name included in her household rather than in that of his wife, where he actually lived. He was clearly uncomfortable with the idea of my documenting him as a resident in his wife's household. Despite the strong norm of virilocality, women's inheritance of property and her right to residence in her natal house, expand the possibilities for residence. Even those residence patterns that are considered stigmatised are negotiated. This has important implications for the lived experience of marriage.

A look at residence practices[24] indicates the ways in which these are negotiated in everyday life. Data from the household survey I conducted in two neighbourhoods, which I call Pattamkunnu and Devaloor in Thalassery, shows that in fact a large number of women do live virilocally with one or more of her husband's relatives. Further, one finds that in a majority of cases the houses in which couples live, with or without their children, have been built on land owned by the husband. While these cases do indicate the strength of the norm, the small number of instances (even though a minority) of women living with one or more family member or on land she inherited, indicates the multiplicity of available possibilities for residence and property ownership when the woman inherits property.

What is significant about the cases in which a couple lived with one or more of her relatives was that a large number of these were where the woman was the sole owner of the property or will be the sole inheritor, either because she was an only child or because her siblings were single or had no children. Such cases are frequent and are considered respectable. In fact, among the instances of couples who lived in her undivided property, a distinction was often made between a man living in his wife's house, with one or more of her relatives, where he was the only man in the house, and in other cases where there were other men in the house, such as his wife's brothers. To live in your wife's undivided house, or a house that will not belong to her exclusively, is a comment on the amount of power the man will have in the house and especially over his wife. Thus, for example, Madhavan, who retired from the army, told me that while he had been away on duty, his wife and children had lived in her tharavad house. When he retired and came back, 'there were no men there, so I lived there', he said. The absence of men in the household was seen as the rationale for why he stayed in his wife's undivided tharavad. This is one way in which residence in one's wife's house is justified, in order to counter the idea that a man living in his wife's house is powerless. The one case in which the couple lived with a relative of both the husband and the wife is worth noting. This was a case of cousin marriage, a marriage type that has reduced dramatically over the last few decades.

It is important to note here that not only does the composition of households change over time, but often people may move between two homes in the course of a week. In Devaloor, for example, in one particular household a woman, Prema, lived at her parents place, which her father described as 'her house.' When I asked who lived in the house he named himself, his wife and daughter and said his son-in-law lived there for three days of the week, spending the rest of the time in his tharavad. I would in fact often see Prema's husband returning in the evening and then leaving in the morning, his clothes in a polythene cover. Prema, too, would sometimes go to his house for a couple of days, carrying a similar polythene cover. The polythene cover is in fact symbolic of the flexibility of residence and expresses part of what enables this flexibility, i.e. women's inheritance and her right to residence.

In contrast then to practices in North India—for example, where the *bidai* (the bride's departure from her parents' house) marks a permanent shift in a woman's membership from her natal house to that of her husband's—among Thiyyas a woman's right to a share of the property ensures that a woman can return[25] to her natal home. This she can do in the event of a separation or divorce or even while she is married.[26] In fact, when Shobha said, 'Why did you send me like this?' she was not commenting on where she lives. She, her husband and their children had been staying with Shobha's mother for several years. Women's inheritance of property thus enables flexibility in residence despite the strong norm of virilocal residence.

However, there are several processes that threaten this flexibility. In the case of migration to another town, a woman's share of property may be sold and a house bought elsewhere, which may not necessarily be in her name. Similarly, when women inherit property, but do not have an income that would enable them to obtain a loan from a bank, the property may be registered jointly in the names of the couple so that the husband can avail of a loan. Such a situation diminishes the security that a house of her own would provide a woman. In fact, such instances point to the importance of not only women's right to property, but also to their earning capacity.

While many women support their husbands with their incomes or with revenue from their property or their natal families, this is not an expectation either at the level of traditional norms or in law. It is interesting to note that while all the legislation through the twentieth century has focused on increasing the amount that the husband should 'provide' for his wife, not only in his lifetime but after his death as well, this expectation of providing, via property or wealth is not considered symmetrical. Women may be expected to provide domestic services, but her wealth is still seen to devolve to her children and not her husband. In fact, as Jeffrey (2004) points out, in the 1956 Hindu Succession Act there was a clause of exception for those observing matrilineal kinship, which stated that if a woman died intestate, her property would devolve to her sons, daughters and mother, rather than her husband.

Conclusion

While the idea of the 'providing husband' was critical to the modernist argument for a marriage legislation that would link marriage with rights in property, I argue in this essay that among those who have a history of matrilineal kinship in Kerala, there is and has been considerable heterogeneity in kinship practices. This heterogeneity is based on, for example, region, caste and crucially the nature of post-marriage residence norms. While matrilineal inheritance and descent had important consequences for women, there has been undue romanticisation of what matriliny has meant to women. The comparative neglect of virilocality as a post-marriage residence norm has only exacerbated this. Furthermore, I hope this essay will help complicate those observations that name matriliny as one of the factors that has contributed to the so-called Kerala Model, referring to the state's positive social indices of development,[27] which is accompanied by the image of its 'high status women' (Jeffrey 1993, 2004).[28]

In this essay I have tried to understand the norms that have structured conjugality in the context of the matrilineal North Malabar Thiyyas. I argue that among them, virilocality is accompanied by obligations of the husband (and his family) to 'provide' for his wife. This idea of the 'providing husband' and the corresponding 'dependant wife' has characterised changes through the twentieth century. In addition to economic and social changes, I would like to argue that a congruence with pan-Indian marriage norms of residence, for example, and the structure of conjugality in which the husband carries authority, has enabled a process of mimesis from rituals and practices of patrilineal and patrilocal conjugality. Thus, while the only symbol of marriage a woman wore was her tali, now most women also wear *sindhur* (a red mark in the parting of the hair). The influences that have led to this are many and include migration and television. In addition, the practice of women using their husband's first name as a surname and dropping the tharavad name as an initial preceding the personal name is another indication of the way in which pan-Indian[29] and international conventions have influenced local practices. This style of naming is seen to be modern.

While the husband is seen as the provider and although the Thiyyas pride themselves on not giving dowry, the amount of jewellery a woman will be given and the amount of property she will inherit, are important considerations in a marriage. A significant change has taken place in terms of the amount of gold[30] women are given when they get married. In fact, one change that has crept in is that some people refer to the jewellery and even land sometimes as dowry, indicating again the way dominant discourses that associate marriage and dowry elsewhere in India creep into the meaning of both gifts of gold given to a daughter and to her inheritance. Further, Kodoth (2008) suggests that in the areas of North Malabar, dowry is being asked for even among castes and communities that were matrilineal. She argues that dowry is demanded or promised in instances where a woman is seen to be lacking in some way and suggests that the 'respectability' that women are seen to gain through marriage sustains the institution of dowry. It is then the idea of compulsory marriage for women that fuels this and may in fact underlie the redefinition of gifts of gold to the bride and her inheritance as dowry.

The idea of compulsory marriage and the stress on marriage itself now appears in contrast to what genealogical charts and stories about who lived in the tharavads indicate. From these it appears that there was often an unmarried woman in a tharavad. Some women chose not to get married because they wanted to pursue careers. In other cases, I was told of women who were unwell or for whom a proposal 'just did not work out'. What is clear is that the breakdown of the tharavad and the security it provided for the care of women[31], single or widowed, no matter how troubled that care may have been, has only led to strengthening the idea of compulsory marriage.

Continuity in the practice of women's inheritance of property and the right, again however troubled, to residence in her natal home is what enables greater flexibility in residence and negotiation within marriage. Instances of couples and their children living on women's properties and therefore near her kin, indicate this. Thus, despite ideas of a 'dependent wife' and norms of conjugality, wherein at least in its public face authority lies with men, women's access to property provides a space for negotiation in marriage.[32] This is important in the given context of India, where women may have a formal right to inheritance, but in practice few actually receive it. The cases of matrilineal communities or formerly matrilineal communities are instructive for understanding the implications of women's property ownership in the lived experience of marriage.

Notes

[1] Both property and descent was traced through women. The matrilineal joint family and house were both referred to as a *tharavad*. A woman's children belonged to her tharavad, a man's to his wife's tharavad. I say formerly matrilineal because in 1976 Kerala abolished all joint-family property and thus the matrilineal joint-family tharavad stopped accruing new members.

[2] In contrast to North Malabar, Thiyyas of South Malabar follow patrilineal inheritance.

[3] *Kalyanam kazhichayachu* (got married) and *ozhivakki* meaning sent her away, out-casted.

[4] In this regard it is unfortunate that Kathleen Gough never published her doctoral work as a book. The thesis is full of rich ethnographic description indicating precisely the messiness of practice. However, the force of the structural functionalist method in the 1950s led to her writing a series of articles in the book she co-edited called *Matrilineal Kinship*. These tended to concentrate far more heavily on the normative.

[5] The visiting husband could have been Nayar or a Namboodiri Brahmin. Namboodiris had a system of property devolution such that only the eldest was allowed to marry a Namboodiri woman, while the younger brothers were expected to have *sambandham* with Nayar women.

[6] In fact, there was a long debate among anthropologists on whether there was marriage among the Nayars at all. See for example Gough (1959).

[7] Exceptions are Dube (1969, 1996) on the Lakshwadeep islanders, den Uyl (1995), and Gough's brief discussions on matriliny among the Thiyyas (1961a) and Mopallas (1961c).

[8] The Nayars of North Malabar, for example, follow post-marriage virilocal residence, as do the Thiyyas. Mappilla Muslims of North Malabar who follow matrilocality are an exception in North Malabar (Gough 1961c).

[9] The Thiyyas share the same 'traditional occupation' with the Ezhavas, who have been better studied. While both castes have come under the Sree Narayana Guru movement, they are quite distinct as a result of different political, economic and social histories, and the different geographical regions they have been concentrated in.

[10] The Act also covered those following an equivalent law—Aliyasanthana in south Kanara, which was a part of Malabar. The Bunts of South Kanara are an example of a community that followed Aliyasanthana law.

[11] The Act introduced the idea of the state legitimising marriage. A legitimate marriage was defined as monogamous and the termination of a marriage that had been registered was to be sought through legal divorce. The husband was bound to 'maintain' his wife and children.

[12] Testimonial of P. V. Kunyambu to the Malabar Marriage Commission (1891). These statements of 'difference' simultaneously seem to be assertions of the status of Thiyyas in relation to the Nayars, who were seen to rank above them in the caste hierarchy.

[13] Edgar Thurston's tabulation of applications registering sambandhams between 1897 and 1904 shows that while 36 people filed applications in 1897 a decreasing number did so thereafter (1906: 128).

[14] A woman therefore is expected to wear the new clothes provided by her husband after she gets married. Married women would talk about how they gave away all their clothes to younger sisters or cousins living in their house. In a marriage I attended, the bride had decided not to give away much. She said she could wear them when she came to her mother's house and a few she would gradually take to her husband's house. She commented on how she was unsure of what kind of 'dresses' they would buy for her. We laughed when she said they might be *jaga boga* or garish! A husband buying all the clothing for his wife was then sometimes anticipated with some trepidation. In so far as clothing is an expression of an individual or group's identity, the groom and his family buying clothes that the new bride would wear after they were married, can be seen as a way of giving her a new identity.

[15] The tying of the *tali* at the marriage ceremony dates to the beginning of the twentieth century. Prior to that, the tali was tied at a pre-puberty ceremony called the *talikettukalyanam*.

[16] This is not unlike elsewhere in the country where the debate on women's unpaid housework is no longer a focus of the women's movement, nor of feminist scholarship.

[17] However, a study done by Panda (2004) shows that women's property ownership enables women to negotiate situations of domestic violence better.

[18] The idea that women cannot loiter in public is of course not unique to Kerala. See for example, Phadke et al. (2011) on Mumbai. However, in Thalassery, as elsewhere in the state, Kerala's high unemployment rate is tangible and visible in the large numbers of men hanging out at tea shops or street corners. It is the presence of these men, often staring and making comments, not to mention more violent forms of sexual harassment, that seems to shrink public spaces for women.

[19] These ideas about women's behaviour in public spaces are not new and are clearly informed by ideas of caste and class respectability. Writing on the basis of her fieldwork in Kerala soon after India's independence, Kathleen Gough says '[Women] do not stop to talk to people in the streets, and despise those who do as being low caste and unmannerly' (1950: 219). More recently, photographs of women in public spaces (Mukhopadhyay 2007) are illustrative of the gender segregation and the constant attempt to project respectability.

[20] This is of course neither unique to the Thiyyas nor to Kerala.

[21] The groom's family and friends generally leave with them, accompanied by an odd number of people from the bride's house. This is referred to as *penine koottipokanam,* i.e. to take the bride to the house of her husband (the last four words are implied). A little later, another group of people from the bride's house follow and they return on the same day. If the groom does not live in the same town or city as the place of the wedding then generally the house of a relative serves as the 'groom's house' and is the place where the couple go to after the marriage.

[22] During the month of *karkadam*, which falls during the monsoon. This is believed to be an inauspicious time, and particularly one when women should not conceive. Woman would therefore often go back to their homes at this time.

[23] Women who had young children were dependent on a brother or a brother of her mother to support them. In a study of liaisons that some Thiyyas had with British men during colonial rule, I argue that one of the reasons people gave for why women entered into such liaisons was that there were no men in their tharavads and therefore no breadwinnners (Abraham 2006).

[24] The study of practices in everyday life is an attempt to critique and move away from the understanding of people as automatons, governed by a set of rules. Instead, the focus is on understanding the ways in which a rule is lived, broken and negotiated.

[25] In Thalassery, while a woman may have tears in her eyes as she leaves her mother's house after the marriage, the scene of her leaving is dramatically different from that of the north Indian *bidai* in which not only the bride but many of the women and men cry.

[26] This is often the case when the husband lives and works in the Gulf; Kerala having a very high level of employment migration to countries in the Gulf and the Middle East.

[27] For example, according to the 2001 census, Kerala had a high sex ratio (1058 females to 1000 males), a low level of infant mortality (11 per 1000 live births), high life expectancy for women and men (73.1 and 67.1, respectively), below replacement level of fertility (1.7 children per woman), high levels of literacy among women and men (88 per cent and 94 per cent, respectively), and high levels of health and nutrition among women and children.

[28] It is another story that the euphoria over the Kerala Model, in recent years, has been followed by observations of a 'gender paradox' and an understanding that these indices of development do not adequately reflect the everyday lives of women in Kerala (Kodoth and Eapen 2005; Panda 2004; Saradamoni 1999).

[29] By pan-Indian I do not mean to suggest a uniformity of practices in India but refer to dominant practices that also tend to find representation in mass media.

Patrilineal naming practices, wherein a woman is seen as completely incorporated into a husband's lineage and therefore must take on his name, are examples of such change.

[30] Apart from other factors, a shift away from cousin marriage has heightened this.

[31] It is worth stressing that the idea of the 'providing husband' was mitigated by the responsibility a tharavad had towards its members.

[32] See Agarwal (1994) for an exploration of the implications of women's access to property in India.

References

Abraham, Janaki. 2006. 'The Stain of White: Liaisons, Memories, and White Men as Relatives'. *Men and Masculinities* 9 (2): 131–51.

Agarwal, Bina. 1994. *A Field of One's Own: Gender and Land Rights in South Asia*. New Delhi: Cambridge University Press.

Arunima, G. 2003. *There Comes Papa: Colonialism and the Transformation of Matriliny in Malabar, Kerala. c.1850–1940*. New Delhi: Orient Longman.

den Uyl, Marion. 1995. *Invisible Barriers: Gender, Caste, and Kinship in a Southern Indian Village*. Utrecht: International Books.

Dube, Leela. 1996. 'Who Gains from Matriliny? Men, Women and Change on an Indian Island'. In *Shifting Circles of Support: Contextualising Gender and Kinship in South Asia and Sub-Saharan Africa*, eds. Rajni Palriwala and Carla Risseeuw. New Delhi: Sage.

———. 1969. *Matriliny and Islam: Religion and Society in the Laccadives*. Delhi: National Publishing House.

Fuller, C. J. 1976. *The Nayars Today*. Cambridge: Cambridge University Press.

Gough, Kathleen E. 1961a. 'Thiyyar: North Kerala'. In *Matrilineal Kinship*, eds. David M. Schneider and Kathleen Gough. Berkley and Los Angeles: University of California Press.

———. 1961b. 'Nayar: Central Kerala; Nayar: North Kerala; The Modern Disintegration of Matrilineal Descent Groups'. In *Matrilineal Kinship*, eds. David M. Schneider and Kathleen Gough. Berkeley and Los Angeles: University of California Press.

———. 1961c. 'Mappilla: North Kerala'. In *Matrilineal Kinship*, eds. David M. Schneider and Kathleen Gough. Berkeley and Los Angeles: University of California Press.

———. 1959. 'Nayars and the Definition of Marriage'. *Journal of the Royal Anthropological Institute* 89:23–34.

———. 1950. 'Changes in Matrilineal Kinship on the Malabar Coast'. Ph.D. dissertation submitted to Girton College, Cambridge University, UK (in 1950 she went by the name Kathleen E. Miller).

Jeffrey, Robin. 2004. 'Legacies of Matriliny: The Place of Women and the "Kerala Model".' *Pacific Affairs* 77 (4): 647–64.

———. 1993. *Politics, Women and Well Being: How Kerala became 'A Model'*. New Delhi: Oxford University Press.

Kodoth, Praveena. 2008. 'Gender, Caste and Matchmaking in Kerala: A Rationale for Dowry'. *Development and Change* 39 (2): 263–83.

Kodoth, Praveena. 2003. "Here Comes Papa': Matriliny, Men and Marriage in Early Twentieth Century Malabar'. Paper presented at *Exploring Masculinities: Travelling Seminar*. Shillong: North East Hill University.

Kodoth, Praveena, and Mridul Eapen. 2005. 'Looking beyond Gender Parity: Gender Inequities of some Dimensions of Well-being in Kerala'. *Economic and Political Weekly* 40 (30): 3278–86.

Mukhopadhyay, Swapna, ed. 2007. *The Enigma of the Kerala Woman: A Failed Promise of Literacy*. New Delhi: Social Science Press.

Palriwala, Rajni. 1999. 'Transitory Residence, Invisible Workers: Rethinking Locality and Incorporation in a Rajasthan Village'. In *From Myths to Markets: Essays on Gender*, eds. Kumkum Sangari and Uma Chakravarti. New Delhi: Manohar Publishers.

Panda, Pradeep Kumar. 2004. 'Domestic Violence against Women in Kerala'. *Discussion Paper No. 86*. Thiruvananthapuram: Centre for Development Studies.

Phadke, Shilpa, Sameera Khan, and Shilpa Ranade. 2011. *Why Loiter? Women and Risk on Mumbai Streets*. New Delhi: Penguin.

Radcliffe-Brown, A. R. 1950. 'Introduction'. In *African Systems of Kinship and Marriage*, eds. A. R. Radcliffe-Brown and D. Forde. London: Oxford University Press.

Reiter, Rayna R., ed. 1975. *Toward an Anthropology of Women*. New York: Monthly Review Press.

Malabar Marriage Commission, The. 1891. *Report of the Malabar Marriage Commission, 1891*. Madras: Lawrence Asylum Press.

Saradamoni, K. 1999. *Matriliny Transformed: Family, Law and Ideology in Twentieth Century Travancore*. New Delhi: Sage Publications.

Schneider, David M. 1961. 'Introduction'. In *Matrilineal Kinship*, eds. David M. Schneider and Kathleen Gough. Berkley and Los Angeles: University of California Press.

Thurston, Edgar. 1906. *Ethnographic Notes in Southern India*. Madras: Government Press.

'Purani aur Nai Shaadi'*

Separation, Divorce and Remarriage in the Lives of the Urban Poor in New Delhi

Shalini Grover

Conjugal Stability, Social Change and the Rise of Legal Divorce in India

In the 1980s, barring the Shah Bano controversy over Muslim women's maintenance claims, divorce in India had provoked little public interest. On the other hand, the enormous debate that modern dowry generated, marital dissolution, and divorce clearly has not. This is partly because the prevailing view has been that, unlike in western countries such as the United States and Britain,[1] official divorce rates in India have remained low. According to conventional wisdom, the institution of family-arranged marriage is responsible for preventing high divorce rates and for ensuring socio-cultural compatibility between spouses. Similarly, caste status has been attributed as a factor in impeding divorce. In her book *Hindu Divorce*, Livia Holden discusses the persistent high-caste disclaimer of divorce:

* I would like to thank the *Asian Journal of Women's Studies* (*AJWS*), 2011, for permitting me to reproduce a modified version of this essay. I am grateful to Caroline Osella, Rajni Palriwala, Ravinder Kaur and Orlanda Ruthven for their valuable comments.

> Divorce is very often declared to be unknown within Hindu tradition. Such a purported absence is framed within the notion of Hindu marriage as conceptualised in the classical Hindu texts: the union sanctioned by the performance of the sacred rites that bring a permanent change to the spouses and yield a sacred and indissoluble union. Accordingly, once the rituals are properly accomplished, the conjugal bond is established for eternity because of the indelible and internal changes produced within the spouses by the very performance of the rites. (2008: 1)

Given that the indissolubility of marriage axiom has dominated the public discourse over the span of pre- and post-independence India (Holden 2008), in the current era of globalisation in the early twenty-first century, the character of the debates is somewhat changing. Legal divorce is gaining prominence in the media, and amongst writers, family counsellors, lawyers, feminists and the state. The media is reporting how in Indian cities divorce has become a modern conundrum. English-language magazines catering to the middle classes report that parental separation has devastating effects on children. The rising divorce rates are attributed to various factors, including women's increasing economic and sexual emancipation, the collapse of the traditional joint family, socio-legal advancements and pre-marital relationships. Two aspects need to be addressed here. First, much of the media reportage and the public perception of mounting divorce rates are based on simplistic assumptions that remain unsubstantiated by strong empirical evidence. Nonetheless, what this denotes is that from the earlier strident discourse claiming that divorce is not an Indian or high-caste Hindu phenomenon, the tide has now turned; rather than a rise in the rate of divorce, we see a rise in the recognition of, and a discourse around, divorce.[2] Second, the topical interest in divorce, rapid social change and modernity is focused on the metropolitan middle classes and on their shifting marital practices. The Indian middle class imagines itself as larger than it is, as representative of national trends (Deshpande 2003, 2006). A very small segment of society represents itself here as the 'average', and proclaims that its ideals and practices are 'normal and good for society as a whole'. It is pertinent that divorce is being subjected to scrutiny at a time when marital dissolution is being allied to the middle classes. India's poor and migratory population seems to be residual in this modernising narrative. My case material attempts to rectify this elision by chronicling the significant permutations that subaltern groups in Delhi are experiencing and the institutions that are shaping their marital lives.

The Anthropology of Divorce and Remarriage

Barring a few studies,[3] jural and ethnographic records of various modalities of divorce still remain fairly under-developed in India. For this reason, anthropology and sociology have been slow to comment on suppositions about contemporary divorce trends. Recognising the neglect of data pertaining to marital breakdown and divorce, Parry (2001: 785) has postulated that 'the recent literature has largely lost sight of the issue'. He observes that it is possible to be legally married to somebody one has not seen for years and, therefore, a demarcation needs to be made between jural and conjugal stability:

> And if we are interested in the latter, in whether the couple actually remain together, it is obvious that in contemporary India the legal divorce rate is an extremely poor guide. Though in much of the 'traditional' high-caste Hindu world the jural relations of marriage have indeed been very stable, it is unlikely that conjugal relations were ever equally so. (ibid.: 785)

Identifying another lacuna, Simpson notes:

> The early interest in divorce thus focused on what it revealed about marriage in broadly functionalist terms rather than on divorce as a process in itself which involved actual relationships and arrangements concerning people and property, negotiated in particular contexts of power and gender relationships. (1994: 833)

In this regard, Holden (2008) offers one of the first detailed feminist accounts of divorce in India. She argues that the scale of divorce amongst Hindus has been underestimated. Not only have modes of divorce existed amongst the high castes, but customary divorce also receives recognition in the existing law. Holden portrays the expediency of customary divorce and its availability for rural low-caste women in Madhya Pradesh. More revealing and counter-intuitive is her contention that Hindu women of varied social backgrounds are often the ones who navigate and pursue divorce. This essay also sheds new light on female initiative and constraints in divorce and remarriage. In several of Delhi's low-income neighbourhoods, remarriages are a striking part of everyday marital practice. This urban phenomenon is itself worthy of inquiry. My contribution thus lies in exemplifying various unexplored aspects of informal remarriages and their gendered implications in a north Indian milieu.

A multiplicity of case studies, personal narratives, official applications and ethnography relating to sojourns at police stations and women's organisations form the principal sources for contextualising low-caste intimate lives. I begin by describing the poor urban community whose marital practices form the subject of my discussion. I then unravel women's remarriage narratives and the rationale behind the regularity of successive unions. Subsequently, I discuss the role of state and non-state actors, illustrating how the latter are powerful mediators and advisors.

Delhi's Lower Castes and their Marital Practices, Working-class Lives and Subaltern Modernity

It is estimated that New Delhi, the national capital, has the country's second largest slum population, totalling about 68.1 million people (Page 2007). Both permanent and makeshift slums are noticeable even at the edges of affluent colonies, as poor migrants desperately try to stake a claim over open spaces in the city. I conducted fieldwork in a large working-class neighbourhood in South Delhi, which I call Mohini Nagar.[4] As per the 2001 census, the population of Mohini Nagar is roughly 1,00,475. Mohini Nagar comprises many *bastis* (semi-permanent shanty settlements or slums). Basti homes, known as *jhuggis*, are usually single- or double-room structures where several family members cohabit. Inhabitants live in highly congested conditions, with access to minimum amenities. The illegal status of their settlements prompts frequent eviction and relocation orders from the Delhi authorities. Adjacent to the bastis are 'resettlement colonies' where housing consists of solid structures or *pucca ghar* (permanent homes). Residents of the resettlement colonies have more secure housing, as they are in legal possession of their properties and this makes them slightly better off vis-à-vis basti-dwellers. Nevertheless, both bastis and resettlement colonies are characterised by overall low standards of living and residents share similar caste backgrounds.

The local population of Mohini Nagar comprises Scheduled Castes (SCs), Other Backward Castes (OBCs) and regional groups. This heterogeneous mix is unified through cultural practices such as the north Indian rule of patrivirilocal residence. Similar patterns of marital breakdown, divorce and remarriage seem widespread and conspicuous across Mohini Nagar and in nearby neighbourhoods. They are visible even amongst the upwardly mobile, some of whom have jobs in the private sector. As for other resettlement colonies and unauthorised neighbourhoods in Delhi, with which I familiarised myself (e.g. Sangam Vihar and Khanpur), I also noticed the pervasiveness of marital instability, particularly through my documentation of women's periods of refuge in the natal home (Grover 2009). Mohini Nagar residents are the urban-born children and grandchildren of migrants who came to Delhi in 1975. Some basti-dwellers in the vicinity have a different migration trajectory, having arrived in Delhi in 1982–84. Consequently, certain bastis in Mohini Nagar were consolidated only during the 1980s. For the purposes of marriage, a handful of women from rural North India continue to migrate to Delhi, as some families in the vicinity are eager for village brides and alliances.

Mohini Nagar's adult population works in the informal sector, in insecure, unskilled and low-paid jobs. Men work as auto-rickshaw drivers, sweepers, scavengers, bus conductors, construction workers, daily labourers, mechanics, contractors and market vendors. It is noteworthy that despite insecure male employment, the dominant ideology is that men should be the sole bread-winners in marriage while women should perform household chores. The exemplary husband is a 'successful and stable provider'. The urban poor cling to such ideals, which are often unattainable. Married women in Mohini Nagar may commonly enter the labour force in times of acute financial crisis or when their husbands can no longer provide. Women seek employment as sweepers, housemaids and massage ladies (masseuses), and with non-governmental organisations (NGOs), beauty parlours and export companies.

Although Mohini Nagar is a deprived neighbourhood, it is situated in a modern matrix and is well connected to the main roads of South Delhi. A number of women's organisations have set up offices in the area. The neighbourhood is in close proximity to large hospitals, markets, middle-class colonies and malls, which have sprung up in the last five years. The middle-class colonies, being a hub of employment opportunities (e.g. recruitment of domestic workers), facilitate interaction across social classes and offer exposure to affluent consumerism and cosmopolitan lifestyles. Local residents, however, exhibit low-intensity consumption patterns, such as the use of inexpensive televisions, mobile phones and automobiles. Consequently, while Mohini Nagar residents are poor, as part of a modernising economy they witness rapid urbanisation, such as the construction of the metro system in south Delhi, the rebuilding of roads for the Commonwealth Games 2010, and the induction of many new services across the city.

Women's Trajectories of Remarriage

In a poor setting, successive and frequent remarriages seem to have a functional and purposeful role in the lives of low-caste women. In the following narrative, Reena explains why she left her husband from her arranged marriage and promptly remarried. Her narrative introduces a discussion about women's choices, subjectivities and motivations for entering into new marriages.

Reena's Second Marriage and Surender's Third Marriage

Reena, a migrant from Bihar, is in her early 20s. She says that her husband, Raju, is having an affair with a woman from a nearby *gali* (by-lane): 'My husband is roaming around with a Dhobi-caste woman. We belong to the much higher Kumhar caste.' Realising that her husband may abandon her, and with no natal kin in Delhi, Reena had taken up employment to support herself. Two months later, I hear that Reena had remarried. She says, 'Look, this *doosri shaadi* [remarriage] happened because I was *majbur* [compelled]. In previous months, Surender, who lives three galis away, saw how I was struggling and the topic of marriage arose.'

Surender, who by caste is a Jatav, declares that Reena is his *teesri biwi* (third wife). His *pahli biwi* (first wife), with whom he had three children, died some years ago. He recalled his *doosri biwi* (second wife):

> I met her when I was employed as a cook. Somebody informed me that there was a woman who had left her husband and is unhappy. So I asked her to live with me. I could not say how many days or months she would remain with me. As she was beautiful, I thought some day she would meet someone else. Her husband lived in a nearby neighbourhood, and word got to him that she was with me. He convinced her to return to her conjugal home.

When I asked how he had met Reena, he responds, 'I knew she was majbur, and so I began to help her. My children needed looking after, so it suited us both.'

In the vicinity of Mohini Nagar, neighbours often enter into remarriages. In densely populated shanty settlements, relationships of intimacy and friendships based on mutual dependency burgeon easily on account of the rich affective ties between neighbours and the close sharing of communal resources and spaces. Despite neighbourhood codes of basti exogamy, Reena's remarriage within the same basti where her first husband continued to live did not provoke a strong moral reaction. Reena emphatically portrays herself as having been left with no choice but to remarry. She asserts that her remarriage to Surender is a substitute to facing continuing marital instability. From Reena's narrative, and from those of other basti women, it is apparent that remarriages are motivated by, and anchored in, practical everyday needs as they are tied to extreme hardship. As a survival mechanism women actively exercise their agency to initiate new marriages. The stigma attached to being *akeli aurat* (a single or divorced woman) becomes a prime catalyst for remarrying. The detrimental consequences of remaining unmarried, single, divorced or widowed have been widely acknowledged in different south Asian settings. Interesting research on nuns, yoginis, saints, and singers (Khandelwal, Hausner and Gold 2007) describes how south Asian women from disadvantaged groups choose the act of renunciation to subvert unsupportive relationships and conventional feminine roles and expectations. Hausner (2007) argues that while female *sadhus* (Hindu ascetics) intend to pursue religious lives, being in an unhappy marriage influences their choices. Knight (2007) discusses how Vaishnava and Muslim Baul women adopt the path of renunciation to avoid the stigma attached to their unmarried status. Renunciation, as Hausner and Khandelwal (2007: 7) write, is 'about mitigating social, economic and religious circumstances that make life as a solitary woman, or single mother, or poor widow, very difficult.' Remarriage, which is a distinctly different practice from renunciation, nonetheless also affords an opportunity for escaping and altering difficult or intolerable circumstances.

Mohini Nagar women justify their remarriages with reference to *majburi*, a vernacular term signifying vulnerability, powerlessness and helplessness. The declaration of majburi can be read as a statement that a woman is experiencing a tumultuous phase, that she lacks alternatives, and that she is no longer in control of her life. She is compelled to choose a set of actions to resolve this crisis. Women use the discourse of majburi to emphasise their current constraints, and while majburi conjures powerlessness, it paradoxically also signals their agency, as they are strategising on pursuing other possibilities in their lives. Women's narratives of majburi evoke considerable sympathy from the local community, and majburi discourses endorse justification for acts that might otherwise seem contentious. Men empathetically and opportunistically respond to confessions of majburi when women approach them during times of crisis. They are ready to assist women, as majburi elicits an emotional response framed within an appropriate moral discourse. To defend mutually beneficial relationships, they, too, resort to the idiom of majburi. A situational ethics and a pragmatic set of norms are then applied here by both men and women. Subsequently, majburi generates new relationships and becomes a legitimate choice.

Although women explicate their remarriages through majburi discourses, their narratives conceal manifestations of desire, consensual love and the impetus for greater freedom in mate selection. Let us note that Reena does not attempt to return to her natal family in Bihar. She discusses how the Bihar environs constrain women and states that she is happier in Delhi. She has found a spouse on her own, stressing that he is of a lower caste than hers. Her migration from Bihar via an arranged alliance has been an empowering experience, one that has opened up a new world. On further probing, Reena defends her decision to remarry on the ground that her arranged marriage was unsatisfactory. She is extremely forthright about her emotional needs and romantic longings. Several Mohini Nagar couples who have remarried voiced dissatisfaction with their arranged marriages, arguing that they had no choice but to abide with parental mate selection, which prioritises endogamous alliances and economic considerations. As a consequence, many women and men readily terminate parental matches to find more companionate and supportive relationships. Some married women who have separated from their spouses decide not to remarry. Having lost faith in marriage, they make a concerted attempt at being financially self-reliant and prefer remaining single. Accordingly, despite the constraints faced by these women, it is apparent that low-caste women make diverse choices. Although the trajectories of single women are a critical area of inquiry, they do not constitute the topic of this essay.

At this stage, it is imperative to bring to the fore other functional options that married women can exercise besides rejecting or endorsing remarriage. What support structures are available to local women born and raised in the city? Usually, local women in unhappy marriages mobilise their natal kin and brothers for support and succour. In Mohini Nagar, generous parental support and refuge in the natal home is recognised as a 'right', a moral and social entitlement (Grover 2009). Natal families offer refuge and shelter, for they recognise the social hazards their daughters might encounter if they were to form independent households. Unlike recent migrants like Reena whose natal communities are afar, local women are fortunate to have strong mechanisms of support from their natal families. Many secondary unions are concretised when a woman's parents are not alive and she is left to manage on her own. They are also concretised when married daughters have exhausted the refuge option. Evidently, secondary unions serve as critical exit options.

The Continuities and Realities of Remarriage

Women's narratives of remarriage also reveal complex continuities; former husbands do not simply fade away from their lives. Surender's account attunes us to the immediacy and malleability of 'primary' and 'secondary' marriages.[5] In relation to his second wife, he recalls how 'he could not even conjecture as to how many weeks or months she would remain with him'. Ultimately, his second wife returned to her first husband. Similarly, Ramu, a Municipal Corporation sweeper, alleged that his wife had left him for other men ('she has had three marriages'), but once her secondary unions were effectively terminated, she would return to him. Mamta, a masseuse or 'massage lady' from whose life story I was able to identify a parallel pattern of serial monogamy, ultimately also returned to her first husband with whom she had strained relations. Mamta stressed her love for her children and stated that her secondary unions were unstable, being devoid of male commitment. While Simpson (1994) introduces the notion of the 'unclear family', Mamta's account establishes how the family unit in low-income settings is fluid, adaptable and unfixed, manifesting unclear and uneven demographic patterns. Moreover, rather than there being a clear-cut divide or a severance between primary and secondary marriages, as is normally assumed in anthropological literature, we observe instances of spouses returning to each other when their remarriages fail. Parry (2001) describes the fluid nature of secondary unions in Chhattisgarh. He cites the example of a woman who, after a series of secondary unions, ran off with none other than her first husband (ibid.: 794)! My findings also indicate that after long interludes of separation and periodic infidelity, there is scope for husbands and wives to pursue a successful and practical renewal of their relationship. The shuttling between primary and secondary partners suggests that remarriage may be a temporary option and that relationships are being reversed, sustained and renegotiated. Separation and divorce may produce continuities (Simpson 1994) such as intermittent joint cooperation over child care and flexible residential arrangements. As a consequence of the intermittent shuttling, many children thus grow up in their mothers' natal homes. Not surprisingly, terms such as *talaak* or divorce are not invoked by couples to describe marital break-up or where there are signs that the marriage has collapsed. The more standard epithets are '*meri purani shaadi*' ('my old marriage'), '*meri nai shaadi*' ('my new marriage'), '*meri doosri shaadi*' ('my second marriage'), or '*alag hona*' ('we left each other' or 'we have separated').

While the urban poor enter into a series of remarriages over their life courses, what are the underlying socio-economic consequences of this phenomenon for women? It suffices that poor women who are not normally entitled to inheritance (i.e. their parents' resettlement plots) and have few possessions besides their jewellery and dowry, entering into a secondary union may not substantially deprive them of material comforts. Socially, remarriages also carry no negative connotations. Yet, there are occurrences where a woman's remarriage has precipitated angry rejoinders from her natal kin. More conspicuous are the disappointments faced by many women once they remarry. While a new marriage may initially afford the space for escaping unfavourable circumstances, relationships with new partners are not necessarily safer or more egalitarian. Primarily, secondary unions reproduce the violence and gender asymmetries of arranged or primary marriages (Grover 2011). Nor do they entirely mitigate domestic or sexual vulnerability, for they tend to be temporary and short lived. For women, the search for better relationships and consensual love could eventually further hardship. The dark side of remarriage could, in some instances, mean forfeiting natal kin and children; indelible discontinuities in family ties are therefore also markers of female remarriage.[6] While women appear as active agents in remarriage portraits, the reality is that for low-caste women, remarriage can have debilitating and unpredictable implications. This gendered prognosis of low-caste divorce is at variance with Holden's (2008) Madhya Pradesh ethnography, which suggests that customary divorce and remarriage enable favourable outcomes for low-caste women.

Divorce and Remarriage as Public Matters

So far the ethnographic picture of remarriage has been one where the state has been absent. I now examine the role of the state, legal institutions and women's organisations in matters pertaining to remarriage. I also bring into focus the specificities of low-caste customary divorce. The ensuing elopement story pertaining to two generations of families that reside in the same basti sets the stage for the exploration of these themes.

Elopement with Close Neighbours

Two Generations: Vijay, Seema and Rakesh, and Rakesh's Parents

On a rainy August morning, in Mohini Nagar's largest basti, there is gossip and talk about an elopement. Vijay informs me that Seema, with whom he had an arranged marriage eight years ago, has run away with Rakesh, their unmarried neighbour. He has filed a Missing Persons Application at the local police station. Vijay says that he has been a good husband. 'We were not lacking in anything. Look, Seema used to tie a *rakhi*[7] on Rakesh, as they shared a brother-sister relationship. Our children would call him *mama* [mother's brother], so why would I have suspected an affair between them?' Vijay's brother adds that if Seema was unhappy in her marriage, she would have taken refuge in her natal home, but instead she eloped with her jewellery and the household savings.

Rakesh's father has interesting things to say about his son's elopement. He insinuates that his wife has played a central role in this elopement. He makes other allegations against his wife. A couple of years ago, while employed as a housemaid, she left him for a Muslim man, who was working as a security guard at a hospital. He immediately submitted a Missing Persons Application to the police, but no action was taken. His wife eventually returned to him as pressure was put on her Muslim lover by his family to remarry. Rakesh's father claims that she is now having another affair.

On being introduced to Rakesh's mother, I ask whether she is in any way responsible for her son's elopement. She says, 'Why should I encourage an alliance between my unmarried son and a married woman? Would I not want my eldest son to have a respectable arranged marriage?' Nonetheless, Rakesh's mother defends Seema by arguing that she had a good reason for eloping. 'Her husband would beat her and pour kerosene oil over her. She had no choice but to elope.'

I accompany Vijay to the police station to inquire about his Missing Persons Application. A senior police officer tells us that Vijay's case is invalid. Seema is a consenting adult and has eloped on her own accord. The police do not take responsibility for such cases. Vijay complains that he needs another wife, as he cannot cope with the housework. The police officer confidently advises him to remarry according to local customary rules. The Missing Persons Application will provide proof that his wife left him.

The above events illuminate yet another example of a female-initiated divorce where the couple has eloped. Seema terminates her arranged marriage for a young unmarried man. Seema and Rakesh's elopement has become a public matter, as the incident has been reported to the police and a Missing Persons Application has been filed. Meanwhile, Seema's elopement has caused consternation amongst the elderly basti residents, as she has overtly formed a sexual bond with her 'rakhi-brother'. Elderly folk inform me that rakhi-tying is taken seriously by their generation, as it creates a 'blood' relationship. In their view, the younger generation is not committed to the true spirit of rakhi. Young people, however, have long known that rakhi-tying enables hetero-social interaction (Abraham 2001). Conversely, as a counter current, the older generation hopes and presumes that rakhi-tying will vitiate sexual overtures. Nevertheless, while the elderly were scathing in their criticism of Seema and Rakesh's elopement, in reality, remarriages and extramarital affairs prevail across all age groups. A brief examination of the marital history of Rakesh's parents suggests that marital instability and infidelity are features of both the young and the old in Delhi.

Overall, men and women who form temporary or permanent remarriages rarely proceed to dissolve their first marriages through legal means.[8] Parry notes that in Chhattisgarh, while people routinely resort to the courts and the police, legalised divorce remains a rarity (2001: 808). In Delhi, people like Vijay and Rakesh's father will try to involve the police and solicit advice from local lawyers. Yet, legal divorce remains uncommon, even when particular elopements and break-ups become public episodes. In this regard, we do not see fundamental legal transformations touching the lives of the urban poor.

What explains the absence of formal divorce practices amongst the urban poor? As mentioned before, given the continuities and temporality of marriages and relationships, legal divorce is not initiated frequently for practical purposes and mutual reasons. Next, the majority of basti and resettlement colony inhabitants simply cannot afford the high financial costs of litigation.[9] They also associate the courts with complicated, protracted and corrupt procedures. Holden (2008) has shown how divorces are easily manipulated by male notaries and lawyers, who dominate public offices. In addition, the contemporary law on divorce is itself fairly convoluted.[10] We have seen how the police, recognising the impediments that low-income residents might face in dealing with the legal system, impart advice on remarriage according to customary modes. These include a private exchange of garlands between the couple in a temple whereby the husband puts *sindoor* in the parting of his wife's hair (symbolising her status as a married woman) and presents her with a *mangalsutra* (a sacred necklace indicating a woman's marital status). It could also mean hosting a reception (get-together) for family, friends and neighbours to make the relationship official. Other ways in which couples convey that they are together is by signalling to the world that they are committed to each other. Gestures of commitment such as the employment of spousal epithets are powerful ways of displaying loyalty and togetherness that constitute a symbolic form of informal remarriage (Grover 2011).[11] The high incidence of remarriage and the diverse forms of cohabitation and conjugal arrangements are permissible in deprived neighbourhoods through the deployment of such low-key customary practices.

Furthermore, it is common practice for married men to file Missing Persons Applications at police stations and to plead with state officials to locate their wives. While I will elaborate on the minutiae of a Missing Persons Application and how it serves an important purpose for the subaltern male, it is important to recognise that such public applications drafted by husbands do not prompt any state action. Conversely, if a married man were to 'go missing', to elope or to desert his wife, police officials will react somewhat differently. At the Mohini Nagar police station, I run into Asha. She says. 'For two years my husband and I have not had sexual relations. He has been seeing a widow. Last week, they ran away. He has left me with four hungry children.' Thereafter, Asha rallied the police, who traced her husband and gave him a warning by citing the legal implications of bigamy. In the presence of the police, Asha's husband categorically stated that he will not return to his wife. They can pursue legal action, but he will continue living with the widow. Asha's case discloses how poor deserted wives have some form of state protection, the logic being that destitute women and children need economic protection and succour. In addition, it demonstrates that when women are unable to negotiate favourable outcomes with their spouses through custom and informal negotiations, deploying the state and other agencies becomes a necessity (Parashar and Dhanda 2008). In many instances of bigamy and male-initiated divorce and desertion, women are keen to use formal institutions to pursue legal action. Only those women who have the financial means actually manage to appeal for justice.

The Significance of Written Proofs, Missing Persons Applications and Letters

Mahesh, a basti-dweller, takes out a Missing Persons Application from a rusted, decrepit steel trunk. His application states that his wife left him seven years ago. He has kept this application safely for the last seven years. Time and again, men like Mahesh submit Missing Persons Applications at police stations. For an abandoned husband, a Missing Persons Application has a significant intent. While applications describing how a wife has gone missing convey part of the story, in addition they represent documentary evidence of marital break-up and divorce. While I have described how many remarriages are negotiated and approved through custom, written proofs of the break-up of the primary or first marriage should ideally complement the customary process. The original Missing Persons Application submitted by Vijay when his wife, Seema, eloped reflects the multiple purposes of such applications.

Vijay's Application

Applications are handed in at police stations and are registered with the details of the case in a 'Missing Persons' file. Those who submit applications receive a photocopy with a signature and a date, officially stamped 'Received'. In most applications, the person introduces himself, giving his father's name, his address, and stating how long he has lived in the neighbourhood.

> Dear Sir,
>
> Subject: Complaint against my wife for the offences of theft and criminal misappropriation.
>
> I have two children. I have been married for approximately 8 years. Some time back, I noticed that my aforesaid wife is having illicit relations with one (son of so and so), who resides in my neighbourhood. I objected to the same and informed to her mother who also made her understand but of no use. My other neighbours also made my wife understand but she was not prepared to listen to anybody and have not given any heed to any one of them. And today she ran away around 2 PM. I am absolutely sure that my wife has run away with that man. She has also run away with all her jewellery and our savings off Rs 5000. It is my sincere hope that you will do everything you can to find my wife.

Vijay's application is an urgent and emotional plea. He notifies the state that he is powerless and explains the efforts he has made to salvage his marriage. He absolves himself of any responsibility for the situation, insinuating that he has the support of the neighbourhood community ('Everyone, the neighbours, as well as Seema's mother, tried to appeal to Seema'). Other applications that I gathered read as lengthy narratives wherein men highlighted the salient incidents in their married lives, such as the birth of their children and certain conflicts of a repetitive nature during which the husbands tried to reason with their wives. Besides reporting that a wife is missing, a Missing Persons Application and other letters are submitted in anticipation of future eventualities. When Vijay alerted me about Seema's elopement, he said that a Missing Persons Application protected him. In the event that Seema should commit suicide or be harmed, he would not be held responsible. The importance of this protection was strongly emphasised by the men who submitted such applications. Consequently, Missing Persons Applications function as a written form of self-protection, and the police receive them on a regular basis. It suffices that police stations are chiefly used to negotiate socio-cultural eventualities. The police warn that applications are not always genuine, and may be exaggerated to prompt police action.[12]

Vitally, within the local community, the Missing Persons Application is viewed as proof of separation and divorce, as few residents have official documentation of their marital break-ups. The Missing Persons Application represents a form of state attestation (accompanied by the stamp and signature of the police) that a wife left the conjugal home on a certain date. A woman who is contemplating remarriage is likely to want assurance that her partner's former wife will not resurface to create trouble or raise objections. Some form of written proof is likely to strengthen and influence negotiations leading up to the remarriage. It is at such junctures that men will furnish a Missing Persons Application to signal their 'availability' and commitment to the relationship. Missing Persons Applications are preserved by men for long periods and they (or their copies) are distributed or shown to neighbours and relatives. This reveals the significance that written proof, documents and paperwork have come to acquire in the marital lives of the residents of Mohini Nagar. In relation to their intimate lives, the urban poor's most regular contact with the state is in the form of preparing and submitting paperwork and applications to the police, which is a current and frequent practice in low-income neighbourhoods (cf. on the state's insistence and proclivity of legal marriage documents, in the context of Jaffna Tamil marriages, see Maunaguru, this volume. The practice of filing paperwork is also being heavily promoted by women's organisations whose ideological affiliation lies with the Indian women's movement.

Mahila Panchayats as Advisors and Mediators

The landscape of Mohini Nagar is dominated by women's organisations. Action India and the Janwadi Mahila Samiti (JMS) have on-going projects in the area, having established a prominent base there. Since the year 2000, my interaction has been with Action India, a dynamic grass-roots community-based organisation that has developed the *mahila panchayat* (Women's Council) concept. There are four mahila panchayat branches in Delhi's resettlement colonies. Specifically, mahila panchayats represent a type of *nari adalat* or 'women-led arbitration court' (Bhatla and Rajan 2003; Merry 2006), which offer a different system of resolving marital disputes vis-à-vis mainstream law.[13] These panchayats specialise in informal dispute settlement, and counselling aimed at reconciling poor couples whose marriages have disintegrated. Through negotiations with estranged spouses, they tackle cases of domestic violence, male alcoholism, *kharcha-pani* complaints (conflicts over family budgets and provisioning) and so on. The Mohini Nagar mahila panchayat is run by four low-income counsellors, employed as permanent staff. While Action India is supervised by a middle-class woman, the functioning of the mahila panchayat is delegated specifically to activist women from the resettlement colonies who have received legal and gender training. As activist counsellors, these women have intimate knowledge about marital disputes in the area and are familiar with the caste and religious structures of their clients. The eldest counsellor is in her 40s, the youngest in her early 30s, while the other two are in their early 40s. The panchayat also comprises 20–30 volunteer women in the age group 40–55 years, drawn from the local community. Although mahila panchayats are not legal courts, they have built an authoritative reputation for handling conflict resolution in cases of marital discord. In addition, these bodies are besieged by local women and men who want advice on their relationships. Client inquiries normally pertain to how lovers may be made to commit to new relationships and whether it is a feasible option to obtain a legal divorce before remarrying. To illuminate the nature of client inquiries and to trace how mahila panchayats have emerged as key advisors, I shall describe the strategies they propose. A dialogue between Rakesh's father and the mahila panchayat reveals the contribution and role of non-state actors.

Seeking advice, Rakesh's father visits the mahila panchayat in Mohini Nagar. He wants to remarry and his queries revolve around the legality of secondary unions.

> **Rakesh's Father:** My wife has left me twice. I am a lonely man. I want a wife who will live with me permanently. Can I remarry when my first marriage has not been legally dissolved? I have written proof that my wife has left me (shows his Missing Persons Application).
>
> **Mahila Panchayat Counsellors:** If your wife has left you permanently, you can remarry. But maintain your duties towards your daughters. You need not do much for your sons, but you must marry off your daughters.

After being reassured by the counsellors, Rakesh's father announces in his basti that he is seeking a wife. Later in the month, he has news. He has found a widow, a woman called Geeta. However, Geeta stipulates the following conditions, 'I want it in writing that he [Rakesh's father] will not leave me. I am a widow with two young children.' Rakesh's father revisits the mahila panchayat.

> **Rakesh's Father:** Geeta wants written proof that we are married.
>
> **Mahila Panchayat Counsellors:** Go and buy stamp or bond paper (i.e. paper used for official transactions, available from documentation centers and special shops). Call your neighbors and relatives. In their presence, sign a paper saying that you have married Geeta and that you will not

> leave her. Take photos as well. Go to the police station and hand in an application [stating] that your previous wife has left you many times.

Two days later, I receive an urgent phone call from Rakesh's father. His first wife, Dharmanti, has stormed into his jhuggi with two policemen, accusing him of bigamy. She has told the police that they are not legally divorced. They are estranged because of his drinking problem. When Rakesh's father produces his Missing Persons Application (stamped with a date), with details about how Dharmanti has left him several times, the police back off. However, the situation does not end here. Dharmanti shows up several times and demands her stake in the conjugal home. They have children together and she wants her share in Rakesh's father's Life Insurance Policy (a pension scheme). In a novel twist of events, Rakesh's father says that he will keep both his wives. On hearing this, Geeta decides to leave him.

Rakesh's father's example substantiates how basti-dwellers dynamically and actively approach women's organisations that have a wide outreach in the area. Compared to the state, women's organisations with their limited resources offer personalised services, extending their time and expertise to helping the marginalised. These organisations offer advice confidently, making decisions on behalf of men and women, while couples request their presence at remarriage functions. Subaltern groups are cognisant of many legal concepts: bigamy, court marriage (state-sponsored civil marriage) and legal divorce. They absorb information on existing laws through local activists and counsellors, which they then use to their benefit (e.g. Dharmanti who colluded with the police in accusing her spouse of bigamy). The importance and widespread recourse to paperwork is emphasised by mahila panchayats; events related to remarriage, elopement and desertion result in individuals making several trips to police stations and counsellors to submit applications, photographs and photocopies. As the normal modus operandi is to submit applications at police stations, counsellors do not dismiss these procedures. However, as the mahila panchayat's main interest is helping women, counsellors have also been aiding their clients, especially widows, to 'secure' and register their remarriages through written proof, court marriage and other documentary evidence.[14] Female-initiated marriage contracts, encouraged by mahila panchayats, are aimed at fortifying conjugal stability through entitlements that can safeguard women financially. So, while counsellors acknowledge that women often initiate divorce and marital break-up, they see their action as a strategy for majburi and as a consequence of the everyday violence they face. Concurrently, counsellors also identify women as being highly vulnerable in new relationships. They have witnessed instances where women have been jilted by their partners, prompting a return to their former abusive arranged marriages (i.e. former husbands and affines). Holden (2008) highlights how women in Madhya Pradesh successfully deploy affidavits and contracts on their own terms and conditions to negotiate better remarriages. Compared to the first marriage, contracts and customary divorce in connection with remarriage entail better scope for financial bargaining, facilitating rights to inheritance, and promising stronger protection for these women. Negotiating remarriages through proof is one of the mahila panchayat's advisory strategies. Written proof, resembling a contract, have some of the following features:

> 1. I have married so and so [person's name] in the presence of my neighbours and the mahila panchayat.
> 2. My husband will provide for me fully. [It will be stated that the husband will provide for their offspring, should they have any in the future. He is also obliged to provide for stepchildren.]
> 3. As a wife, I am entitled to a share in my husband's resettlement plot and his life insurance policy. This is to ensure that I have financial security and that in the event of my husband's demise, his affines will not harass me.

Many women feel that such proof of marriage confers stronger validity compared with informal ceremonies that involve merely an exchange of garlands between the couple. Younger generations of women in Delhi are increasingly wary of customary norms of marriage. Equally, they are conscious of the need to portray their remarriages as respectable; trust, commitment and intimacy need an official persona in the form of contracts and photographic evidence. However, in the long run, the outcome of female-initiated contracts in remarriage negotiations is unclear. Endorsing this view, the mahila panchayat argues that while documentation and marriage contracts may not guarantee economic safeguards or the permanence of a union, they can nonetheless aid abandoned children and women. Mahila panchayats and women's groups in Delhi are thus re-adapting customary divorce and emphasising marriage proof so that poor women can have greater protection in their conjugal unions. In terms of a broader critique, mahila panchayats often deal with the problematics of divorce and remarriage in rather confused ways. They hastily advised Rakesh's father to remarry without unearthing all the facts about his first marriage. As it emerged, Rakesh's father has a serious drinking problem, which has impelled his wife not to leave him permanently but to live apart. Crucially, mahila panchayats are neither addressing the structural roots of serial remarriage nor finding fundamental ways of easing women's socio-economic constraints. Primarily, they work to smoothen out women's lives, which may often involve encouraging local women to accept certain unequal, and even unjust, situations for the greater good of maintaining peace and ensuring the children's welfare. Interestingly, Basu (this volume) delineates how Kolkata counsellors in the family courts purport patriarchal ideologies of marital stability to middle and lower-middle couples. Analogous to what

Basu finds, the mahila panchayat's strategies rest upon the need to fortify remarriage through male financial security. Encouraging female economic independence and obliterating the stigma attached to being a single woman are not on their activist agendas. These are the serious limitations exhibited by mahila panchayats, which at times give rise to tensions between counsellors and the local women who see the mahila panchayat as a place for raising critical concerns.

Remarriage as a Site for Intervention

In this closing section, I want to focus more on the gendered ramifications of remarriage. While increased importance is being given to the rising rate of divorce at the national level, I have illustrated how separation, divorce and remarriage have long prevailed amongst the urban poor. The life histories of those above the age of 60 confirm this. For the urban poor who live on the margins of modernity, remarriage is mainly an in-formalised process, devoid of legal divorce practices and court settlements. Yet, police stations, women's groups, and most importantly the Missing Persons Application play a pivotal role in shaping everyday marital practices. Accordingly, we also observe great flexibility in cohabitation arrangements and in the domestic realm. At times, there is ambiguity as to where and with whom a woman is residing. For low-caste women in a patrilineal setting, remarriage has a distinct rationale; it is interwoven with hardship, survival and the pursuit of consensual relationships. This aspect needs to be urgently recognised by policy makers. As is apparent, female-initiated remarriages are also temporary exit options, for there is shuttling and continuity aplenty between primary and secondary partners. A key finding is that while the freedom to remarry appears liberating and synonymous with unequivocal post-marital choice, it nevertheless has grave risks for women, as it puts them in a position of vulnerability. Holden has examined the potential of Hindu customary divorce to promote gender equality or to perpetuate the oppression of women (2008: 159). She argues that customs offer wider scope for women's agency and constitute an attractive option for both lower- and upper-class women. In the Madhya Pradesh regions of Piparsod, Gwalior and Shivpur, remarriage through customs provides a strong basis for renegotiating better lives for women. The Mohini Nagar data illuminates interesting gendered contrasts for the northern region and a different scenario; informal remarriages through customary modes are marked by bold female initiative, instability, flexibility and inequality. Remarriage with close neighbours and with men of similar or even lower caste backgrounds does not necessarily result in egalitarian relationships or stronger entitlements. A lot would, of course, depend on the stage at which a woman is in her life cycle and on her fallback position, such as the support she has from her natal kin, women's organisations and her immediate environs. We need to reaffirm that many remarriages in low-income settings are prompted by unsatisfactory primary marriages. Herein lies the problem. In terms of gender asymmetry, there are stark continuities between primary and secondary marriages. Successive remarriages and open-ended informal relationships are therefore critical sites for feminist intervention and further debate, and much still remains to be understood about women's choices, desires and subjectivities.

Notes

[1] In a vivid account of divorce in Britain, Simpson (1994: 831) charts the emergence of large-scale divorce in western societies: 'Divorce rates which were marginal at the turn of the century have become central demographic features of most European countries.' Simpson describes how multiple partners and children, and extended kin are the product of modern-day divorce. These developments make the definition of the 'British family' highly ambiguous. Simpson shifts the analytical focus from the normative 'nuclear family' to the 'unclear family'.

[2] For instance, in their study on 'companionate marriage', Fuller and Narasimhan (2008: 747) discuss how for the urban middle-class Tamil Vattimas, divorce is still a rare phenomenon. However, divorce is being discussed as a potential risk in their community.

[3] See, for example, Dumont (1964), Gell (1992), Jeffery and Jeffery (1996), Kapur and Cossman (1996), Parashar and Dhanda (2008), Parry (2001), Shah (2006), Uberoi (1993, 1996) and Vatuk (2008).

[4] The data-collection process took place in Mohini Nagar between 2000 and 2002. For a more detailed account of the physical description of Mohini Nagar, see Grover (2011).

[5] The urban poor habitually refer to their primary (first) and secondary (subsequent) marriages. The latter distinction has been made by Dumont (1964). As per Dumont's interpretation, the primary marriage is a woman's proper and first marriage. The secondary union or remarriage, which could take place on account of divorce or the death of a spouse, is legitimate, but is often less strictly regulated in terms of ritual and caste. For the Mohini Nagar neighbourhood, Dumont's distinction holds validity. A number of secondary unions are inter-caste remarriages that involve minimal rituals. These are rarely seen as violating codes of familial honour.

[6] Women who leave their first husbands often forfeit their children for fear that a new partner will not accept their offspring. If children are born into an inter-caste secondary union, they take on the caste identity of their father. If a widow forms a secondary union, her children from her primary marriage will marry within their mother's rather than their stepfather's caste. There are no local customs pertaining to which parent should have custody of their children. In a situation of 'temporary separation', women stress that it is essential to leave children with their fathers so that the latter will not abdicate their responsibilities completely.

[7] In northern India, *rakhi*-tying is an important festival observed to celebrate the brother-sister bond.

[8] The practice of financially compensating a divorced spouse through a *panchayat* (council) is also something I did not encounter. I was told that some *biradari* panchayats (caste associations) in South Delhi issue financial compensation to the aggrieved party. Yet, as per my understanding, these male-dominated biradari panchayats have lost their credibility and women rarely approach them. Moreover, biradari panchayats in the capital do not function as a 'parallel judiciary', as is the case with the *khap* (caste council) and other panchayats in Haryana and Uttar Pradesh. The demise and ineffectiveness of biradari panchayats in Delhi may be attributed to the heterogeneous character of urban neighbourhood (i.e. the regional and caste mix) where one particular caste is unable to dominate the social landscape.

[9] See Chowdhry (2007: 135) for a description of how the 'financially draining' courts remain out of reach for a large proportion of people in rural North India. Disputes and grievances pertaining to marriage continue to be handled by the caste group. See also, Holden's (2008: 123) ethnographic contributions describing how official law is often a means of last resort.

[10] Under the Hindu Marriage Act of 1955, while divorce can be granted through mutual consent, some of the following reasons are generally accepted as sufficient grounds for divorce: adultery, desertion, cruelty, chronic disease, mental disorder, the physical inability of the couple or of either spouse to consummate the marriage and religious conversion. These grounds make it difficult for a poor person to obtain a legal divorce as this involves cumbersome procedures, requiring the individual to muster proofs of various kinds.

[11] Couples who remarry without the involvement of their parents do not usually enact elaborate marriage ceremonies. The latter may feature in a 'secondary arranged marriage,' where the union has been arranged by parents the second time round.

[12] Note that Vijay's application has the subject 'Theft and criminal misappropriation'. Most other applications have the subject 'My wife has left me/gone away with someone'. The police describe how men hastily write these applications; a small altercation with a wife, following which she leaves her conjugal home for a short period, can prompt a comically long and tearful Missing Persons Application.

[13] For an in-depth analysis of the genesis of Delhi mahila panchayats, the types of cases they arbitrate, and their political orientation, praxis and ideology, see Grover (2011). This section contributes to an understanding of the mahila panchayat's advisory capacity, a subject I have not previously discussed at length.

[14] Other women's organisations in Delhi also encourage written proofs. As a cursory passerby at the Janwadi Mahila Samiti women's grievance cell, I observed how an anxious Rani was imploring counsellors for advice. Five years ago, she had married her partner in a simple ceremony at which he had presented her with a *mangalsutra*. She had taken photos of this ceremony. She now feels that it is imperative to have written proof. 'One day, he may throw me out of the house. If I were to get ill, he may find someone else. I want my share in having looked after him.' According to Rani, her partner's friends have persuaded him against the idea of arranging proof. He is showing signs of betraying her. 'My partner does not smoke, drink or gamble and so

I want to retain this marriage. There are many women on the outlook for such men. That's why I want it in writing that we are a couple.' Later when I spoke to a counsellor, I was told that they were going to persuade Rani's partner to have a 'court marriage' and that they had recommended this course of action some years ago.

References

Abraham, Leena. 2001. 'Redrawing the Lakshman Rekha: Gender Differences and Cultural Constructions in Youth Sexuality in Urban India'. *South Asia: Journal of South Asian Studies* 24 (1): 133–56.

Bhatla, Nandita, and Anuradha Rajan. 2003. 'Private Concerns in Public Discourse: Women-initiated Community Responses to Domestic Violence'. *Economic and Political Weekly* 38 (17): 1658–64.

Chowdhry, Prem. 2007. *Contentious Marriages, Eloping Couples: Gender, Caste, and Patriarchy in Northern India.* New Delhi: Oxford University Press.

Deshpande, Satish. 2006. 'Mapping the 'Middle': Issues in the Analysis of the 'Non-Poor' in India'. In *Contested Transformations: Changing Economies and Identities in Contemporary India*, eds. Mary E. John, Pravin K. Jha, and Surinder S. Jodhka, 215–36. New Delhi: Tulika Books.

———. 2003. *Contemporary India: A Sociological View.* New Delhi: Penguin.

Dumont, Louis. 1964. 'Marriage in India: I. The Present State of the Question, Postscript to Part I; II. Marriage and Status, Nayar and Newar'. *Contributions to Indian Sociology* 7:77–98.

Fuller, Chris J., and Haripriya Narasimhan. 2008. 'Companionate Marriage in India: The Changing Marriage System in a Middle-Class Brahman Subcaste'. *Journal of the Royal Anthropological Institute* 14 (4): 736–54.

Gell, Simeran Man Singh. 1992. *The Ghotul in Muria Society.* Chur, Switzerland and Reading: Harwood Academic Publishers.

Grover, Shalini. 2011. *Marriage, Love, Caste and Kinship Support: Lived Experiences of the Urban Poor in India.* New Delhi: Social Science Press.

———. 2009. 'Lived Experiences: Marriage, Notions of Love, and Kinship Support Amongst Poor Women in Delhi'. *Contributions to Indian Sociology* 43 (1): 1–33.

Hausner, Sondra L. 2007. 'Staying in Place: The Social Actions of Radha Giri'. In *Nuns, Yoginis, Saints, and Singers: Women's Renunciation in South Asia*, eds. Meena Khandelwal, Sondra L. Hausner and Ann Grodzins Gold, 162–79. New Delhi: Zubaan.

Hausner, Sondra L., and Meena Khandelwal. 2007. 'Women on Their Own'. In *Nuns, Yoginis, Saints, and Singers: Women's Renunciation in South Asia*, eds. Meena Khandelwal, Sondra L. Hausner and Ann Grodzins Gold, 1–47. New Delhi: Zubaan.

Holden, Livia. 2008. *Hindu Divorce: A Legal Anthropology.* Aldershot, England and Burlington, Vermont: Ashgate.

Jeffery, Patricia, and Roger Jeffery. 2006. *"Don't Marry Me to a Plowman!" Women's Everyday Lives in Rural North India.* New Delhi: Vistaar.

Kapur, Ratna, and Brenda Cossman. 1996. *Subversive Sites: Feminist Engagements with Law in India.* New Delhi: Sage Publications.

Khandelwal, Meena, Sondra L. Hausner, and Ann Grodzins Gold, eds. 2007. *Nuns, Yoginis, Saints, and Singers: Women's Renunciation in South Asia*. New Delhi: Zubaan.

Knight, Lisa I. 2007. 'Renouncing Expectations: Single Baul Women Renouncers and the Value of Being a Wife'. In *Nuns, Yoginis, Saints, and Singers: Women's Renunciation in South Asia*, eds. Meena Khandelwal, Sondra L. Hausner, and Ann Grodzins Gold, 245–87. New Delhi: Zubaan.

Merry, Sally Engle. 2006. 'Transnational Human Rights and Local Activism: Mapping the Middle'. *American Anthropologist* 108 (1): 38–51.

Parashar, Archana, and Amita Dhanda, ed. 2008. *Redefining Family law in India*. New Delhi: Routledge.

Parry, Jonathan P. 2001. 'Ankalu's Errant Wife: Sex, Marriage and Industry in Contemporary Chhattisgarh'. *Modern Asian Studies* 35 (4): 783–820.

Shah, Alpa. 2006. 'The Labour of Love: Seasonal Migration from Jharkhand to the Brick Kilns of Other States in India'. *Contributions to Indian Sociology* 40 (1): 91–119.

Simpson, Bob. 1994. 'Bringing the "Unclear" Family into Focus: Divorce and Remarriage in Contemporary Britain'. *Man* n.s. 29 (4): 831–51.

Page, Jeremy. 2007. 'Indian Slum Population Doubles in Two Decades'. *The Times*. Delhi edition, 1. 18 May. Available at: http://www.defence.pk/forums/world-affairs/5365-indian-slum-population-doubles-two-decades.html. Accessed in: 2013.

Uberoi, Patricia, ed. 1993. *Family, Kinship, and Marriage in India*. Delhi: Oxford University Press.

———, ed. 1996. *Social Reform, Sexuality and the State*. New Delhi: Sage Publications.

Vatuk, Sylvia. 2008. 'Divorce at the Wife's Initiative in Muslim Personal Law: What are the Options and What are their Implications for Women's Welfare?' In *Redefining Family Law in India*, eds. Archana Parashar and Amita Dhanda, 200–35. New Delhi: Routledge.

Multiple Ironies

Notes on Same-Sex Marriage for South Asians at Home and Abroad

Ashley Tellis

I

In the summer of 2006, I was volunteering for a non-profit group in New York City called Queers for Economic Justice (henceforth, QEJ). I was assisting a Fellow with QEJ, who had an independent fellowship, which he was routing through them. He worked on queer immigrant rights and I knew him from the loose *desi*[1]/Leftie/queer network in and around New York, of which both of us were a part. I volunteered as his assistant and helped with many of the activities of QEJ that summer. It happened to be the summer when QEJ launched a campaign against, or modifying considerably, the demand for gay marriage, which—within the epistemically limited sphere of US gay politics dominated as it was (and is) by the demand for gay marriage—was quite momentous and courageous.[2]

QEJ put out a campaign document entitled 'Beyond Same-Sex Marriage' and the first few lines of it succinctly explained what it was about:

> We, the undersigned—lesbian, gay, bisexual, and transgender (LGBT) and allied activists, scholars, educators, writers, artists, lawyers, journalists, and community organizers—seek to offer friends and colleagues everywhere a new vision for securing governmental and private institutional recognition

> of diverse kinds of partnerships, households, kinship relationships and families. In so doing, we hope to move beyond the narrow confines of marriage politics as they exist in the United States today.
>
> *We seek access to a flexible set of economic benefits and options regardless of sexual orientation, race, gender/gender identity, class, or citizenship status.*
>
> We reflect and honour the diverse ways in which people find and practice love, form relationships, create communities and networks of caring and support, establish households, bring families into being, and build innovative structures to support and sustain community.
> In offering this vision, we declare ourselves to be part of an interdependent, global community. We stand with people of every racial, gender and sexual identity, in the United States and throughout the world, who are working day-to-day—often in harsh political and economic circumstances—to resist the structural violence of poverty, racism, misogyny, war, and repression, and to build an unshakeable foundation of social and economic justice for all, from which authentic peace and recognition of global human rights can at long last emerge. (emphasis in original)

The document, as expected, raised a lot of hackles, especially among the religious Right in what is essentially a Christian fundamentalist country, but I was, and am, more interested in the battle from within by a group of white gay men, that beleaguered category within the US. These men, all in their late middle-age and older, comprise the cutting edge of LGBT scholarship in the US, are mainly academics and do what is called in the US 'high theory.' All of them refused to sign the document. There are many reasons for this.

These are men from the lost generation, the survivors of the AIDS pandemic that swept North America and western Europe in the 1980s and 1990s. Most of their friends, their lovers and their networks were wiped out by the first few waves of AIDS in North America. Most of these men had terrible histories with their families as men open about their sexuality. They lost their families, were alienated from them and were disowned by them. Understandably, then, they were not going to sign any document that celebrated kinship of any sort. Kinship to them was, and is, anathema.[3]

One of them got into an unfortunate battle with a lesbian academic from the city who did sign the petition and who was his closest friend. She was also his health proxy (the person in charge of the medical decisions around a figure who has no next of kin/spouse). She broke up with him as a friend, painfully, and argued that as his health proxy, she was part of a kinship bond with him and for him not to sign was for him to deny that and, therefore, in some sense, deny the bond they shared. As a feminist, she was also making the argument that this was a classically male thing to do, to depend on a community or a relationship, but to pretend one was autonomous and self-sufficient. To her, it is what hetero men did; she did not expect it from her gay best friend.

I signed the document but I saw the point these men were making. I know the wages of marriage and family through my own history and the histories of those around me, across the world. I would never choose to be part of marriage and family. I found these men courageous and, in this essay, I want to explore, in the context of the global call that QEJ makes, the meaning of same-sex marriage and family for Indians and Indian immigrants, based on fieldwork in New York, Kerala and Bangalore.

II

Every other evening, after work at QEJ, I would go to see my friend B in Queen's, New York's most diverse and most ghettoised borough. B is a Bangladeshi Christian who I had, once again, met on the desi queer scene as lawyers, who were part of it, were helping him get immigration into the US. Indeed, when I first met him, he had just got his green card and soon he was to get citizenship and a US passport, which he did in the months to come. I was helping him with English, with a nursing exam he wanted to do to get out of his job at Dunkin' Donuts (henceforth, DD), where he had to stand up all night; and his knees, which were destroyed, would not let him do it anymore. He wanted out and he wanted to move up, but it was proving difficult. Over the days that I met him, B and I became close friends and he shared his life story with me. I would go home to my hovel in Brooklyn, from his hovel in Queens, crying every night at the sadness of his stories. B sent his meagre DD savings home to his large Christian family of parents, brothers, sisters, the children of brothers and sisters and so on, but not just home. He also sent some to a man he considered his husband, who worked in the Gulf. He was not out to his family. He was not a real part of his husband's life.

Nevertheless, he considered this man his husband. They had loved each other and had a relationship for years, from 1976 to 1994, when the husband entered a heterosexual marriage. The man was now married with a child of his own and worked in the Gulf as a labourer, a common destination for many lower-middle class and poor South Asians. B and he still spoke over the phone regularly. B had attended his own husband's marriage and gave it his blessings back in Bangladesh. B carried his husband's photo around in his wallet. B said that he, himself, was this man's wife and would love him till he died. B said he did not need anyone else. But B was alone and sad, and did not like the Bangladeshis who shared his basement because they did not care. He kept them at a distance, using his seniority and his properness, but they smelled a gay rat and they treated him badly, he said.

B also asked me to take him to gay bars because he did not speak good English and did not know whether he could ever go himself. B also told me he liked black men and wanted a black boyfriend. He said he wanted only a straight boyfriend. He said gay men were terrible and he wanted only a real man. I told him that while he was likely to find straight men in a black gay bar, they would be on the down-low, messed up and bad news. He said he was up for it. I took him to the only black gay bar I knew on Christopher Street. It was a weekday evening (the only day B was off) and there were not many people in the bar. He was disappointed and quickly his mood turned foul; he told me how much he hated gay men, gay bars, gay sex and that I should take him home.

B took me one evening to a white man's house. He said he was scared the white man might make a sexual pass at him and so he wanted me along. I suggested it might be a good idea for the white man to make a sexual pass at him. He said that he hated white men and that this white man was not really a man, but one of 'us' (by which he meant homosexual and for him the object of desire was always and only the straight man).

The white man turned out to be a priest, or a lapsed priest, but one who still worked with a church and tried to build community spaces for gay men of colour. The white man had a boyfriend of some indeterminate, non-white colour and region at home. It seemed unlikely B was going to be sexually approached as long as I was there, though the white man clearly wanted B. He invited B and me to church and to meetings. B and I went home. On the way back, I asked B what he thought of religion. He said he was a believer. I asked him about his husband. His husband was also Christian and Bangladeshi. B was part of some Christian group in New York. B made me *daal-chaaval* (cooked lentils and rice) in his basement and we talked about his nursing exam, as I pondered the various co-ordinates that made up his life, the differences between his understanding of his gayness and the dominant understanding of the country he adopted to avoid persecution and loneliness. The facts were that he was terribly alone and would have found no place in the gay world of New York.

III

One of my friends in the desi queer network is HIV positive. I will call him Q. Q had been a pioneering LGBT organiser and activist in Calcutta, but had moved to the US over a decade earlier. At the point when I began hanging out with him, he lived in AIDS-assisted housing in a really rough part of Brooklyn. On certain days, I went home with him to that frightening place, where he was once mugged, and almost every day was homophobically abused by rowdy

Latino boys. He had an addiction problem or some addiction problems. People said it was crystal meth. He had no work culture then. He had no control over his life and no one could help. I tried and failed. He had moved into this assisted housing because he was thrown out of his last place of residence by his activist room-mates—accused of stealing, using, abusing them. I did not put any of it past him. He was out of control. He spent most of his money in the first week of the month on clothes and shoes, neither of which he could afford, neither of which were more important than material he should have bought for a clean toilet and to make himself some soup.

He looked for sex on the net all the time. He said he had a lot of it and I often wondered whether he told people about his status, especially because he was into anal sex and fisting or so he claimed. It was painful to read the contradictions of his life and even more painful to be unable to help at all. Q had a remarkable reputation as a queer immigrant organiser in the US. He came from high Brahmin, cosmopolitan stock in Calcutta, went to Calcutta's most prestigious college. I don't know how he saw that past from his urine-smelling, fetid Brooklyn dive. He never washed his clothes. He pissed in a bottle by his bed. Q was out of control and none of his 'friends' seemed to care. They just pretended not to see it. That he was difficult, compulsive, disorganised and not seeking any help, but pretending that all was well made it easier for them and exceedingly difficult to help him.

One evening, sitting in a bar in Chelsea, the uptown gay neighbourhood neither of us could afford to be in, downing drinks in a bar whose drinks neither of us could afford, he told me, half-jokingly (but it staggered me), that he was looking for a white boyfriend to marry. He wanted a rich boyfriend, someone who would pay all his debts, his bills, fund his education and whom he would love. I said that figure was likely to be a sugar daddy and half-cheekily added that for that he would have to move to San Francisco; but he told me he wanted a lover, not a sugar daddy. He wanted his lover to be a twink, a white boy, out of an Abercombie ad. I sipped my orange juice in silence. It was a neoliberal fantasy, articulated in a moment of despair. I did not have the heart to break his bubble. He is not stupid. He knew it was a bubble. But I also knew he really wanted it. The ironies of his life and his dream were rising around me and I thought that he would dissolve in them, that I would dissolve in them. I took the train home as he waited for more friends and more drinks. On the train, I wondered how different Q's fantasy was from many upper-middle-, middle- and lower-middle-class gay and straight South Asians in the US and in India. Q had studied sociology in Calcutta; he knew his Marx. He had spent years in the US; he knew his race politics. Yet, he persisted in this fantasy and his innermost psychic space was colonised by the most obviously unreal fantasy of marriage and settling down. Differently located from B, his access to that fantasy seemed equally removed, yet his attachment to it equally unquestionable.

IV

I moved back to India in 2007. I resumed my activist work here. I sought to finish the book I had begun when I first went on a postdoctoral fellowship to the US in 2004. I wanted to understand the phenomenon of what were being fancifully called 'lesbian marriages' and 'lesbian suicides' in Kerala. I took the trip to India's version of God's Own Country finally in 2009. I was only hoping it was not like the original I had just fled from.

It is a universally acknowledged truth that Kerala is a strange sociological space. Sharmila Sreekumar (2009) has made this strangeness clear. She shows, through close textual readings, how the Kerala model of development is constructed on the figure of the woman. Examining material across a variety of sites—letters between young girls, public advertisements about sexual violence against women and AIDS, and finally the private diaries of middle-class women—Sreekumar shows how women are the pivot on which narratives of this model move.

From these explorations, Sreekumar discerns the twin hegemonic and seemingly contradictory formations of Kerala as utopia and Kerala as dystopia, and shows how despite appearing contradictory, they cohere and, centrally, how women are the lynchpins of this coherence (ibid.). The utopia model is then delineated and deconstructed through the letters; the dystopia through the advertisements, and their coherence through the diaries of the middle-class women and the central trope of domesticity. But Sreekumar's book was not yet out while I was doing fieldwork.

My starting point was the group Sahayatrika, which against all odds was helping women who ran away with each other, preventing them from committing suicide. Sahayatrika had just shifted base to Thrissur from Kottayam. They had just received some funding via the Bangalore-based NGO Sangama and the Bill Gates foundation, and could now therefore afford an office.

The high court judgment reading down Section 377 was just out and queer activists were thrilled; I remained unmoved. Women in Thrissur (where I was located) did not even know what Section 377 was. When Sreekumar told them about the judgement, they were not impressed.

V

I met Y and Z in a rented room in the house of a feminist advocate in Thrissur, who was to be my translator and facilitator as well.[4] Y and Z were dressed in a sari and salwar-kameez, respectively. They looked like any other two women in Kerala and have been together for the past ten years. When Z came to Thrissur Y was already there, and when they met Y asked Z to stay over and they became close. Y's parents died young, she lost her property and came to the orphanage at a young age. From a very young age, she felt she was a man, not a woman, and did not want to dress like a girl.

I asked them a series of fairly straightforward questions. They answered with great equanimity and did not seem offended at all. Here are excerpts of the conversation:

> **Q**: What do you think about marriage?
>
> **Z**: I am not interested in marriage. If a marriage happens, it gets into the media, one becomes famous. I am not interested in any of that. I am not interested in a secret marriage. Living together is enough for me.
>
> **Y**: I would like to be married. I do not like the publicity around it, but I would like to tie the *tali* on Z. Even if we do not marry, we will always be together.
>
> **Q**: (to Y, in response to the answer above) Why do you feel the need to marry?
>
> **Y**: A registered marriage provides a certificate; a proof. Marriage also prevents couples from separating. The tali keeps women together.
>
> **Z**: I guess it gives strength, certitude. Anyway, whether or not we are married, I want to live with her, die with her.
>
> **Q**: So, then, you are no different from a man and woman marrying?
>
> **Z**: We are like a man and a woman. She works, I am at home.
>
> **Y**: Z is my wife. She also wants it.
>
> **Q**: Isn't that buying into the heterosexual and patriarchal idea that lesbians are just failed heterosexuals?
>
> **Y**: Z has options, but she did not choose to marry a man. She has a relationship with me and she is happy with that.
>
> **Z**: I have no interest in men. I had it in school, but not now.
>
> **Y**: I have been lesbian since childhood, Z has not. She is my wife, she does household chores.
>
> **Z**: I am happy. Earlier, we had so many quarrels. She insists on my being at home, not going out, not meeting other people.

The feminist lawyer, sensing that they did not quite get my question intervened here and rephrased it

FL: But the man-woman relationship is a power relationship. Why do you want to replicate it?

Z: Y is in control and this is okay with me. There is a power struggle, but we adjust. I am ready to forgive her because I love her so much.

Q: In an ideal world, would you live your life together differently?

Z: If such a world existed, our relationship would change. Y is a typical man. She is possessive and even if I talk to the *paanwalla* [local cigarette or betel leaf store], she gets suspicious and jealous. I do not like this. I hope that she will change, if the world changes. There is hierarchy now, but hopefully that will not be there in the ideal world. I am faithful and loyal, but Y is still insecure.

Y: In an ideal world, I would cut my hair. I would not wear a sari, but man's clothes. I would have freedom of movement like men do; independence. I am deeply insecure about Z, because everyone wants to part us. That is why I am possessive of her.

The differences between Y and Z, that I had made them articulate on the ideologies that bound them, gave me some breathing space from the otherwise claustrophobic narrative of their 'married' life.

VI

I was told that it was imperative that I meet U. U is Dalit, feminist, lesbian and saw the intersections between these identities clearly and politically. She was in Kottayam and I was to go there. But when contacted, U said she would prefer a telephonic interview and also made it clear that this could happen only when she was outside the house as she could not speak about any of these issues from home. Over the phone in Kottayam, this is what U said:[5]

Q: What do you think of the institution of marriage? What does it mean to you?

U: Marriage should cease to be a social compulsion; instead it should be based on individual choice and on mutual love and consent. I have been married to my partner and no one had a say in it or knows about it except for us; it was similar to the *Gandharva Vivah* [love marriage, without rituals].

Q: Why do you think women from Kerala and elsewhere who want to be with each other seek to marry first?

U: Mainly marriage is considered in our society as a means of gaining social and legal sanction. We are so engrained in the norms of the heterosexual society that we invariably seek the same in our own relationships. People who are in homosexual relationships are not recognised by the family or the law. It is also to gain the right to family property and legal protection that they are demanding for the constitutional approval of homosexual marriages.

Q: Why do you think these women play the roles of man/woman, and not try and live on their own terms, without these roles?

U: Having been born and brought up in a hetero-patriarchal system, we tend to follow the same model in homosexual relationships too. My partner identifies himself as a male, although he is not completely male. He has gone through counselling and is preparing for surgery to become completely male. We are in a heterosexual relationship and play the roles of man and woman.

Q: In defining themselves as man and woman are they not playing right into the hands of heterosexuality, which sees lesbianism as failed heterosexuality?

U: It is not a bad thing to be in a heterosexual relationship as long as it is based on love and trust. Ours is not a power relationship, but is based on friendship. I have known my partner for 20 years and have had a monogamous relationship.

Q: How do you and you partner identify?

U: We identify as a heterosexual couple, playing the parts of husband and wife.

Q: In an ideal world, would you define your relationship differently?

U: Yes. I would want my partner to be completely male as we have faced a number of problems owing to his confused gender identity.

VII

I took the bus to Bangalore. On various earlier trips to Bangalore, at demonstrations against right wing forces or around Koshy's (an old-world coffee house in downtown Bangalore where a section of Bangalore's 'queer' set regularly hang out), I would notice what looked like a group of young boys, dressed to kill, bristling and confident, belts and boots, hanging out together on the fringes of these events and spaces. My friend and gay activist, Nithin Manayath, pointed them out to me once and informed me that they were all Malayali lesbians. They came to Bangalore, many stayed at the on-off lesbian shelter offered on the outskirts of the city by Sangama. (When I was in Bangalore, there was talk of it shutting down, because Sangama did not have the resources to run it, ensure security for the women there and so on.)

Manayath also told me interesting stories of how many of these boy-girls came to Bangalore as couples, but the introduction to Sangama, to the city's queer subculture and to each other, led to these relationships breaking, re-forming, led to forms of sexual and social experimentation that was transforming the dominant ideas of rural women from Kerala who, if they did not commit suicide, came to Bangalore. Many found living there impossibly expensive and adjustment difficult and returned to Kerala. Others stayed on.

Through Manayath, I got in touch with Sunil, who works with Sangama, and expressed my desire to meet at least one 'couple' among this interesting set, preferably who were still a couple and 'ideally married' or interested in the project of marriage. Sunil said marriage was not on the minds of most of these folk and it was difficult even to find couples, but he had one couple in mind of which I could meet one partner. I met and spoke with S, who has spent the last 14 years with J, a traumatic 14 years. Both S and J are Dalit and J is also Christian. This is the pattern for most of these women in Kerala and Bangalore. They are most often from Dalit or adivasi and poor backgrounds, and this in itself is in need of investigation, but it does put paid to the populist idea that 'lesbianism' is a strange western import. Here are women making these choices with little, sometimes no knowledge of the word 'lesbian' or its western associations.

S says the model for 'him' (and he was dressed as a man, had short hair and saw himself as a man, though he looked more of a boy) was the same as heterosexuals. He dreamt of living together with J, married and happy, but he got no acceptance. Both of them come from Trivandrum, lived in the same area and met in school. Their parents got wind of the relationship, shifted J to another place and they did not meet for seven years.

They met again and resumed their relationship, and family resistance led to the filing of a court case against them. The Kerala high court ruled that they were adults and could live together. When they threatened to die together, the parents appeared to relent, after which they lived together in S's house for a year. His parents deemed it a 'friendship' and tried to adjust to it. However, things proved difficult yet again, and they left and decided to live on their own. They slept on the roads as they found it difficult to get employment and were not offered support from anyone. They developed health problems: S had a stone in the kidney and serious eye problems; J developed mental health problems and, most recently, has developed piles.

They, or S at any rate, kept getting thrown out of jobs in Kerala. For the last five years, they have been in Bangalore where they have taken up jobs. S lives in fear of people finding out about his relationship with J. When I met him, he was a driver for Sangama (he said people would usually not hire him as a driver once they discovered he was a woman) and Sangama supported both of them.

'Love and care has kept us together. I am the man of the relationship and there is no need for an alternative model', said S quietly. He was laconic through the interview.

VIII

Destabilising questions are what plagued me before, through this fieldwork, and continue to do so. While the pain and difficulties in the lives of B, Q, the women in Kerala, the boy-girls in Bangalore, S and J, all upset me, their unquestioning assent to the hegemonic model of organising intimate relations upset me equally. All the ironies of their lives, which appeared painfully visible to me, seemed somehow invisible to them.

While the naturalised and well-ensconced nature of the institutions of family and marriage allow for such an invisibilising of one's life's ironies, what struck me was the failure of the women's movement to create spaces for women outside marriage and family, outside the heterosexual imperative. Unlike in the West, there was never a radical feminist moment here, run by self-identified lesbian women, imagining utopias without men or lives without marriage. Not just that, there was no serious engagement with a large body of socialist-feminist work which critiqued the institutions of marriage and family from a feminist perspective. It seemed to me that the dead bodies of several women in Kerala weighed upon the Indian feminist movement, but nobody seemed to care.[6]

The NGOised, urban, male-dominated Indian 'queer' movement lapped up the idea of gay marriage, though for them a figure like B does not exist or, at any rate, does not matter and is ignored. They were embarrassed by the periodic stories of mofussil and rural women marrying. They ignored the women committing suicide (no funding is forthcoming for that) and celebrated the idea of marriage, without even pausing to examine what the institution and its corollary, the family, had done to them. It was another cascade of ironies here.

As an activist, not only was I unwilling to allow myself the standard anthropological piety of merely listening to these voices, recording them, being sympathetic and understanding, I was also unable to understand how to read this investment in marriage and family—institutions that practised the worst forms of exclusion and violence on these subjects. Even as these marriages and desires and longings for marriage might be read at one level as an opting out of the political economy of compulsory heteronormativity and reproduction, at another might not they also be read as upholding precisely the institution that is fundamentally anti-democratic, which naturalises heteronormativity?

IX

Marriage is the most burdensome model on same-sex loving people in India. It is as though there is no other imaginable mould in which to place human relationships. If the women's movement never went far enough to fundamentally question the institution and blow it out of the water, then the burden must fall on a same-sex politics that must know that the only way the pile of women's dead bodies will stop rising and the only way we can imagine intimate and meaningful relations between same-sex subjects is when we can imagine structures and spaces outside the institution of marriage. But must that necessarily be outside marriage?

Clearly not for Vanita (2005), who has upheld the idea of same-sex marriage in India in a book and several articles on the issue. For her, there is no better institution for same-sex subjects. For a feminist, it is remarkable how she does not engage with feminist critiques of the institution and reduces it to a matter of individual choice and practice. Vanita speaks of 'several feminists and queer theorists in the West' (ibid.: 17) but cites only Michael Warner's *The Trouble with Normal*. Further down, she speaks of 'a few theorists' (and cites no one), who are against monogamy. A body of feminist work over more than a century critiquing marriage and family is dismissed on the following grounds: a) that critiques of marriage 'do not probe deep enough', though it is not clear into what. This is followed by a critique of a reductionist account of radical feminism. Vanita writes: 'If the oppressiveness of marriage were based largely on male domination, would that domination disappear if marriage as an institution was abolished?' (ibid.: 18)

Socialist-feminism has offered a much more serious and structural critique of these institutions in a long tradition. One can think of Alexandra Kollontai's *Communism and the Family*, Rosa Luxemburg's 'Women's Suffrage and Class Struggle', Clara Zetkin's 'Lenin on the Women's Question' and within the Anglo-American tradition Emma Goldman's 'Marriage and Love', Charlotte Perkins Gilman's *Women and Economics*, and a later work by Angela Davis on the black family or the work of lesbian poet and activist Audre Lorde. In England, the rich body of feminist-socialist work, from Juliet Mitchell's *Women's Estate* and *Women: The Longest Revolution* and her *Psychoanalysis and Feminism* to Michele Barrett and Mary McIntosh's *The Anti-Social Family* with various texts in between like Sheila Rowbotham's *Woman's Consciousness, Man's World*, Denise Riley's *War In The Nursery* and, in continental Europe, the works of someone like Frigga Haug.[7]

None of this work dismisses marriage or family altogether, but they seek to offer a structural critique of these institutions, their relationship to capitalism, and its repercussions on men, women and children. To take just one example: Juliet Mitchell has, since *Psychoanalysis and Feminism*, looked at lateral relationships, particularly with siblings and peers, in her more recent books like *Mad Men and Medusas* and *Siblings: Sex and Violence*, and offered a powerful critique of the organisation of sexuality within the family. She argues that the focus on reproduction and the vertical organisation of power prevents the recognition and management of crucial lateral relationships based on a non-reproductive sexuality, and has sought to redefine family and gender relations through an exploration of these relationships.

Vanita does not engage with this work and arguably the Indian women's movement has not either. But to continue with Vanita's grounds for dismissing the critique of marriage: b) a boycott of marriage is unrealistic; c) marriage aspires towards and embodies friendship and love; d) people choose monogamy because it offers other freedoms and pleasures.[8]

For the moment, it is important to note that for Vanita, everything is a matter of choice and best practices. Further on she argues that if Foucault taught us anything, it is that eradicating power is impossible[9] and that not all 'hierarchy or inequality' is 'inherently negative' even as this follows, inexplicably, with the need for a keen awareness 'of the constantly shifting power balance in any relationship' and 'equitable sharing of resources in forms that are backed up by society and state', which will 'check abuses of power within relationships' (2005: 19). It would have been productive if the last rather utopian statement was embedded in a discussion of what would make such a world possible.

The disciplines of sociology and anthropology in India have also been culpable in leaving the foundations of institutions like marriage and family unquestioned. A recent book on marriage and intimacy does a survey of sociological work on the family from A. M. Shah to Patricia Uberoi and does not feel the need to remark that it is strange that the institutions were never questioned, but merely described and reviewed (Sen, Biswas and Dhawan 2011). Neither do the editors do it themselves in their introduction. Of the two essays on same-sex marriage in the volume one relies wholly on western feminism (lesbian standpoint theory) showing a complete lack of awareness of the contexts of same-sex women's lives in India[10] (Biswas 2011: 414–35), the second hints at the fact that there is another sociological universe to be uncovered in these tales and that western identity politics will not help us uncover it, but does not offer any dense or detailed critical analysis of what exactly this universe comprises (Mokkil 2011).

As my fieldwork in Kerala has shown, such an alternative universe might be one of our own fantasy. What we do find is a messy sociological terrain sought to be steamrollered into uniformity, not just by western-style identitarian politics, but also by the dominant heteronormative framework of marriage and family. In fact, I would argue that marriage and family are far more oppressive on these subjects than the 'queer movement's' hegemonies, not least because the latter has not really engaged with these subjects. Dead women don't make good subjects for NGO funding or cool copy about how we have liberated ourselves into twenty-first century modernity with a half-baked court judgment.

So, my answer to the question of whether our discussion of same-sex relationships must take place outside the frames of marriage, family and kinship is a resounding Yes. What we need is a serious engagement with the body of feminist work to which I referred earlier and the creation, at the ground level, of spaces outside marriage within which same-sex subjects can breathe and imagine their lives in the ways they want.[11] They might well still choose these institutions and they might still subscribe to deeply oppressive ideologies outside these institutions, as Vanita informs us, but at least the choices will be based on a real structural diversity of cosmological conceptions.

X

Judith Butler, in 'Is Kinship Always Already Heterosexual', has offered a powerful critique of what she calls 'the normalizing powers of the state'—if we seek legitimation from it—and the dangerous patriarchal and patrilineal nationalism behind the need to defend the state from same-sex forms of kinship (2002). Her comparativist argument shows how the potential radicalism of non-heteronormative cultures is stymied by our demand for, or celebration of, same-sex marriage. Butler is careful not to romanticise these cultures as some unutterable space of otherness, but speaks of them as political non-places from where to begin.

One of the fundamental questions Butler asks is why we presume kinship is at the base of social organisation or provides 'the rules of intelligibility for any society' (ibid.: 249). Questioning heterosexuality as 'the founding and pervasive symbolic law', she calls for 'a re-thinking of culture itself'(ibid.: 254).[12] To argue that we are normal, that we have families too, is to leave the framework of normality and marriage and family unquestioned. To structure the debate within the polarities of for or against gay marriage, or for or against gay family is to 'constitute a drastic curtailment of progressive sexual politics' (ibid.: 255) as we allow marriage, family and kinship 'to mark the exclusive parameters within which sexual life is thought'(ibid.).

While Butler ends with an implicit romanticisation of 'progressive sexual politics', what we may learn from her account is that both as subjects and theorists of same-sex marriage, we must begin from the productive non-place she speaks of, where the ground beneath our feet has broken and we are destabilised. We have a rich (mainly feminist) tradition showing us what is wrong with marriage, kinship and family. We have to have the ability to imagine our lives outside the normative frameworks of heterosexuality, modern marriage and family.

It is a difficult fight (undoing the rigidity of psychic formation is always difficult),[13] and Butler's non-place is more of a political-rhetorical flourish than an achieved position. Harder-working materialist feminists like Gayle Rubin and Juliet Mitchell have given us more concrete roadmaps toward this even as they have also shown us how difficult the road is.[14]

There is no non-place from which to begin that is absolutely free of kinship and the structuring of the social. The multiple ironies of my title constitute the non-place from which such imaginings might begin. Mitchell, in the work referred to earlier, has asked us to look at gender in psychoanalytic terms as having, in many instances, nothing to do with reproduction, but definitely always including sexuality, and necessarily being disruptive of the hegemonic framework of marriage and reproductive sexuality. She locates this in the self-preservation and survival drive, and in relation to siblings and peers and not, therefore, in vertical and reproduction-based relations, but rather in lateral and non-reproduction based relationships.[15]

The movement from coupledom to multiple lateral relationships among the Malayali women moving from Kerala to Bangalore, in a crucial sense, bears Mitchell out. It shows that marriage is not a framework engraved in stone for these subjects and not the only framework either. Unlocking gender from sexuality, Mitchell imbues gender with radical, non-reproductive possibilities. It is up to us to break out of marriage and bring back the polymorphously perverse adults in us.

Notes

[1] By *desi* is meant south Asian and, in the context of the US, this includes Indians, Pakistanis, Sri Lankans, Bangladeshis, Nepalis, south Asian Fijians and south Asian populations from Caribbean countries. In the LGBT context, many of these come under umbrella groups like SALGA—the South Asian Lesbian and Gay Association—based in New York.

[2] QEJ works mainly with the homeless in New York and were arguing, among other things, that kinship patterns among the homeless do not follow the nuclear family model which is the only model the US state recognises and on which it confers benefits.

[3] This set of scholars has been termed the 'anti-social school' and they are pitted against the affective school of queer theorists in the US. For a useful summary and complication of the binary relationship between these two schools, see Halley and Parker (2011)

[4] I thank Asha for agreeing to be facilitator and translator.

[5] I thank Renu Elizabeth Abraham in Kottayam for conducting this interview for me.

[6] The Indian women's movement has had certain moments when it did approach a serious critique of marriage as an institution. Two examples would be: (a) the first editorial of the feminist magazine *Manushi*: 'Right from childhood, marriage is posed as the be-all and end-all of a woman's life' and 'Let us re-examine the whole question, all the questions. Let us take nothing for granted' (Kishwar and Vanita 1984: 242, 245), and (b) People's Union for Democratic Rights, PUDR 1984 report *Inside The Family: A Report on Democratic Rights of Women* which states, 'inequality ... [is] inherent in such a structure' and 'The structure of the family, and the social norms and values that are built around it, are thus completely against the democratic principles our republic stands for'. I thank Uma Chakravarti for pointing out these references and Rajni Palriwala for pushing me on this question. I still stand by the reading that the women's movement in India did not follow through this critique and have left the family more or less uninterrogated as an institution to be opted out of.

[7] This is just a random sampling of a rich and vast body of work which offers powerful critiques of the institutions of marriage and family and many ways of negotiating the foundational violence of these institutions, both conceptually and empirically.

[8] There are many more problems with Vanita's book, which requires a more sustained engagement. Two salient ones I want to highlight in the context of this paper's argument are: a) the contradiction between Vanita's indictment of the West for the bringing of homophobia and her simultaneous claim that as India modernises, it becomes more and more accepting of same-sex love and marriage, and b) her claim that only Hinduism offers the space for same-sex marriage in India, which is in keeping with a position not so different from the same Hindutva parties she now and then condemns. At the end of the day, it is an argument of their Hinduism versus hers, but both positions implicitly and explicitly demonise other communities. One major shortcoming of Vanita's book is that all her evidence is based on newspaper reports. She conducts no ethnographic fieldwork, neither with these women whose unions and suicides she celebrates nor at the sites where they are located. Such fieldwork might have complicated her celebration of the 'Hindu' love between these women. There are two more recent and equally problematic writings on the subject by Vanita. In one (2007), she recycles most of the historically muddled arguments of *Love's Rite*. In the second, she argues for 'Hindu ideas about love' (2009: 49–60), which she sees as inclusive and accepting, and claims a doctrinal debate is developing within Hinduism on the question of same-sex marriage. This is on the basis of one decades-old interview conducted by Shakuntala Devi, one self-conducted interview with a swami and a journalistic interview with some swamis in the US, published in *Hinduism Today*—a US-based newspaper run by the Hindu diaspora.

[9] This is an untenable reading of Michel Foucault. Foucault moves from a somewhat problematic conception of power to an ethical reconsideration of the concept in his later work. In both phases, he is never less than absolutely careful to show how power works in all its complexity and his own activist work shows his urgent belief in the need to alter power relations.

[10] Further, Biswas reiterates the Us (heterosexuals) and them (queer) throughout the essay thereby defeating the whole point of a lesbian standpoint position. Even Western ethnographies on same-sex marriage and family, most famously Kath Weston's *Families We Choose: Lesbians, Gays, Kinship* does not question the very framework of marriage and family, but instead, (understandably perhaps given the time it was written and the context) works within the institutions of marriage and family, and merely stakes a claim to them. More recent anthropological work on same-sex marriage and family in non-western contexts remains deeply problematic in its negotiation of same-sex marriage, family and kinship, either valorising its sexism and deep conservatism under the sign of the postcolonial (see, for example, Boellstorff 1999) or anthologies like Murray and Roscoe (1998). These are just two examples of a large body of work, from full-length studies to individual essays, on same-sex marriage and family almost none of which question these structures at all or the conceptual frameworks of these institutions and practices.

[11] Even Flavia Agnes in her recent two-volume study *Family Law* does not engage with this body of feminist work or offer any conceptual critique of marriage and family as institutions (2011). This, of course, has to do with the fact that she works within the domain of the law which does not allow such questions, and is part of the normatising apparatus of the state, but why is that not questioned?

[12] For an overview of debates around kinship and same-sex marriage, see Levine (2008).

[13] It is interesting that Butler (2002) turns to psychoanalysis for help with such a project. Juliet Mitchell and Gayle Rubin can be seen to have been critical of Butler's earlier somewhat voluntarist re-writing of kinship through a perhaps too malleable conception of gender.

[14] See 'Sexual Traffic: Interview with Gayle Rubin' by Judith Butler in Rubin (2011), especially pages 299–300. See also Juliet Mitchell's new Introduction to the 2000 edition (25th year edition) of *Psychoanalysis and Feminism*.

[15] See 'The Difference between Gender and Sexual Difference' (in Mitchell 2003).

References

Agnes, Flavia. 2011. *Family Law Volume I: Family Laws and Constitutional Claims* and *Volume II: Marriage, Divorce, and Matrimonial Litigation*. New Delhi: Oxford University Press.

Biswas, Ranjita. 2011. 'Of Love, Marriage and Kinship: Queering the Family'. In *Intimate Others: Marriage and Sexualities in India*, ed. Ranjita Biswas, Nandita Dhawan, and Samita Sen. Kolkata: Stree.

Boellstorff, Tom. 1999. 'The Perfect Path: Gay Men, Marriage, Indonesia'. *GLQ* 5 (4): 475–510.

Butler, Judith. 2002. 'Is Kinship Always Already Heterosexual?' In *Left Legalism/Left Critique*, ed. Wendy Brown and Janet Halley. New York: Routledge.

Halley, Janet, and Andrew Parker. 2011. 'Introduction'. In *After Sex: On Writing Since Queer Theory*, ed. Halley, Janet, and Andrew Parker, 9–10. Durham: Duke University Press.

Kishwar, Madhu, and Ruth Vanita, ed. 1984. *In Search of Answers: Indian Women's Voices from Manushi*. London: Zed Books.

Levine, Nancy E. 2008. 'Alternative Kinship, Marriage, and Reproduction'. *Annual Review of Anthropology* 37:375–89.

Mitchell, Juliet. 2003. *Siblings, Sex and Violence*. Cambridge: Polity.

Mokkil, Navaneetha. 2011. 'Lives Worth Grieving For: Lesbian Narratives from Kerala'. In *Intimate Others: Marriage and Sexualities in India*, ed. Samita Sen, Ranjita Biswas and Nandita Dhawan, 391–413. Kolkata: Stree.

Murray, Stephen O., and Will Roscoe, eds. 1998. *Boy-Wives and Female Husbands: Studies in African Homosexualities*. New York: Palgrave.

PUDR (People's Union for Democratic Rights). 1984. *Inside The Family: A Report on Democratic Rights of Women*. Delhi: PUDR. Available at: http://www.pudr.org/content/inside-family-report-democratic-rights-women. Accessed on: 31 May 2012.

Rubin, Gayle. 2011. *Deviations: A Gayle Rubin Reader*. Durham: Duke University Press.

Samita Sen, Ranjita Biswas and Nandita Dhawan. 2011. 'Introduction'. In *Intimate Others: Marriage and Sexualities in India*, eds Samita Sen, Ranjita Biswas and Nandita Dhawan, 1–31. Kolkata: Stree.

Sreekumar, Sharmila. 2009. *Scripting Lives: Narratives of 'Dominant' Women in Kerala*. Hyderabad: Orient Blackswan.

Vanita, Ruth. 2009. 'Same-Sex Weddings, Hindu Traditions and Modern India'. *Feminist Review* 91: 47–60.

———. 2007. "Living the Way We Want': Same-Sex Marriages in India'. In *The Phobic and the Erotic: The Politics of Sexualities in Contemporary India*, eds Brinda Bose and Subhabrata Bhattacharya. Calcutta: Seagull.

———. 2005. *Love's Rite: Same-Sex Marriage in India and the West*. New Delhi: Penguin.

Weston, Kath. 1991. *Families We Choose: Lesbians, Gays, Kinship*. New York: Columbia University Press.

DREAMING A BETTER COURT FOR WOMEN

Adjudication and Subjectivity in the Family Courts of Kolkata, India

SRIMATI BASU

INTRODUCTION

The Bankshall courts complex in Kolkata, housed in an old building credited to belong to Siraj-ud-dallah in the eighteenth century, is part of an extended law complex in the heart of the city, minutes from the high court building and the modern city civil court. A vibrant legal culture thrives here on weekdays: the clatter of manual typewriters from petition writers in tables and chairs set on the pavement; the call of touts who follow around those who look like potential litigants, promising everything from stamps and petitions to lawyers; the low-slung blue plastic sheets hung over benches that serve lawyers' al fresco offices; clusters of black-and-white where lawyers confer interspersed with the more colourful garb of clients.

In one wing of three rooms on the second floor in the court complex, the family courts or *Parivarik Adalat*, a different form of legal process is allegedly at work. These are trial courts which deal with matters of divorce, custody and maintenance through a direct relationship between the judge and the litigants. They are imagined to be lawyer-free spaces; where lawyers are allowed in only in advisory capacities, with litigants managing their own cases. The wide corridor in front of the courts is largely occupied by couples going through marital dissolution, stealing furtive glances at each other while trying to put space between themselves, occasionally re-enacting domestic quarrels in public, quite loudly as mediation sessions revisit touchy ground.

Most women litigants continued to wear signs of marriage, like vermillion on the forehead and conch bangles (which of course may be read as the safety of appearing married as much as a sign of preserving the marriage). Many carried folders where bright red and gold wedding cards (that serve as standard evidence) stood out against a fat pile of court papers, the juxtaposition of the religio-social against the legal poignantly marking failing marriages. A large number were almost permanent visitors, sitting hopelessly on one of the benches day after day to recover maintenance money, or to begin criminal recovery procedures for habitual non-payers. Non-custodial parents, often fathers, stood clutching bundles of brightly wrapped presents for their children, following which there would be a short visit at the back of the courtroom, the parent striving for moments of connection and the child shy or awkward or petrified by this encounter that was being monitored by court counsellors, police, grandparents, even other litigants not too far away. Paralegal helpers called 'counsellors', black-and-white clad lawyers, and assorted family members and neighbours both fomented and held off further conflicts, frequently joining the fray with advice, admonition and occasional physical intervention.

Amid the tension and terror of public spectacle that palpably haunts the court corridors, it is sometimes hard to remember that this is visualised as a utopian site of new meanings of marriage and empowerment. The existence of the family courts, of a venue for litigants to directly bring their grievances before the law, is a triumph of the Indian women's movement's negotiating power. The courts were built to emphasise efficiency, economic redress for women's financial hardships caused by divorce or separation, conflict resolution and women's legal agency. However, the court profiled in this essay also exemplifies the problems with enacting such institutional legal reform: the intransigence of gendered norms, the ambivalence of being lawyer-free, and the problems with adjudicating violence alongside divorce and maintenance.

Legal reform, turning to the state to ask for changes in legal standards that affect women's material options and mark a symbolic transformation in meanings of gender, has been a critical strategy of feminist groups internationally (Rai 1996; Kapur and Cossman 1993; Smart and Brophy 1985). Rai argues that the postcolonial state is, particularly, 'of critical importance in women's lives both public and private', citing the example of India where there is 'a considerable emphasis placed on the power (or lack of power) of the state to formulate, legislate and enforce laws regarding equality between men, and women' (1996: 11). But legal reform constantly carries with it the shadow of vigilance, because reforms visualised as part of feminist social movements also unravel in unforeseen ways as they are interpreted through existent legal structures and discourses. They may create new forms of dependence and protection while redressing older forms, or invite prescriptive gendered behaviour that is scarcely different from previous scripts, even though the laws under which this behaviour is judged may be egalitarian.

In India, reforming women's lives by resorting to the law has been a critical project of both colonial regimes and the postcolonial state. Interventions 'in the name of women', from widow immolation to widow remarriage to temple dancing to regulation of sex work, were the hallmark of 'civilising' colonial action that justified intrusion into personal law (Tambe 2009; Nair 1996; Kumar 1993; Sarkar 1993). Historians contend that the uneven nature of the reforms indicate that women were the proximate site of colonial governance (and of resistance from colonised male elites) rather than sustained beneficiaries (Nair 1996; Mani 1989), but it set the pattern for invoking gender as the grounds of drastic social change. In the immediate postcolonial period, there were several dramatic reforms in Family Law, Hindu Family Law specifically, including monogamous marriage, adoption, inheritance of property in intestate succession. As feminist scholars have documented (Parashar 1992; Agnes 1999), at this time discourses of modernity for women were deployed to bring about change even as male/upper-caste landed privileges were systematically validated, in provisions such as women's exclusion from ancestral property, the primacy of fathers as 'natural' guardians of children, and married women's inability to adopt children on their own. The robust Indian women's movement since the 1970s, as accounts like Kumar's (1993) make clear, has similarly worked in circumstances where calls for feminist reform are negotiated through legislative settings which reformulate original goals, and cultural practices which resist legal transformations of gendered behaviour.

This essay profiles the institutionalisation of one such demand from the women's movement: the relatively new experiment of mediation-based family courts as a feminist legal-reform strategy. Using ethnographic data, I consider whether these courts can provide better access to the law for women, or indeed better justice, as the rationale for family courts claim. The cases illustrate that new forms of legal subjectivity and modalities of justice are created through this innovative venue, but that legal outcomes are not correspondingly transformative, grounded as they are in juridico-social conceptions of family and marriage. The challenges of enacting substantive versus innovative gender justice, serving strategic and not just practical gender interests, can thereby be considered.

Marriage law is a critical site for examining the workings of gendered equality and subordination. There seems to be wide consensus that recent changes to marriage and divorce laws indicate loosening state control on the marriage tie and an assumption of equality among spouses (McIntyre 1995;

Fineman 1991; Buchhofer and Ziegert 1981; Glendon 1980). While Glendon argues that there is also a corresponding loosening of familial units and a greater reliance on individual property (1980), Buchhofer and Ziegert view the state as being thoroughly involved in the 'social safeguarding of family' (1981: 407), especially 'children and the economic support of the family' (ibid.: 404). The problem that emerges is one of nominal versus substantive equality: while women are formally equal in divorce, the economic consequences of divorce are disproportionately impoverishing for them, and the evaluations of atypically gendered practices often negative. Indian marriage law aptly illustrates this trend, because postcolonial law posits equality across gender for most religious groups, but women confronting divorce face disastrous losses of home and economic support. As the cases examined below demonstrate, women constantly tread the contradictions between being allegedly empowered legal subjects availing of laws with face-value equity, and the social and economic constraints that govern marriage, employment and residence.

Family Courts: History and Background

Family courts refer to a variety of institutions, depending on the national context. The US or Australian or Hong Kong model represents one of the types: these courts are for the most part descriptive of the issues they address, viz., matters related to family and children. There are a growing number of family courts which include special pre-trial mediation programmes to resolve issues, typically done by mediators, but these programmes are not innate to the nature of the court. By contrast, in Japan and India, family courts are not only courts that deal with particular 'family' matters, but are also cast as informal, comfortable spaces where litigants frame their own issues before judges or 'counsellors' (paralegal mediators), and where conciliatory rather than adversarial practices are to be employed.

The primary rationale for the establishment of family courts has been: women and other marginalised social groups who have historically had less access to the law often recount that they find formal legal proceedings in courtrooms alienating and incomprehensible; their claims for justice have to be translated into specific legal provisions and mediated through lawyers, and they feel little connection to the issues that brought them to court. To mitigate this alienation, some legal theorists have suggested a more holistic and direct approach. As family law almost always involves women, there have been recommendations to create family courts where parties would express their grievances and rebuttals in their own words and without lawyers, making legal decisions more meaningful to the parties and the law a less intimidating entity. In advocating for family courts in the UK, Peter Smith narrates litigants' 'sense of unreality, the invasion of privacy, followed by distress and finally humiliation'

(1988: 153) and the recurrence of the words 'frightening' and 'terrifying' in describing court experiences (ibid.: 157), arguing that 'the introduction of family courts would be the most effective and sustainable means' of addressing litigants' problems and ensuring 'greater sensitivity' from 'court officials', 'less intimidating' courtrooms, and procedures that would 'facilitate participation and communication' (ibid.: 159).

In part, the popularity of family courts is tied to the rise of Alternate Dispute Resolution (ADR) methods in the 1970s, with their focus on decreasing the volume of cases being litigated and reducing delays by creating set-aside courts on particular issues, as well as achieving outcomes better tailored to both parties (Nader 1997). The development of comparative jurisprudence and emerging US discourses of arbitration in business and investment contributed to this atmosphere as well.[1] But the UN Decade for Women beginning in 1975 is also credited with giving the idea of family courts great visibility—while family courts have been in existence since the 1950s in Japan, the CEDAW (Convention on the Elimination of All Forms of Discrimination Against Women) recommendation that nations take steps to make access to legal provisions easier for women spurred several nations to institute family courts based on the model of unmediated access to the law. Leonie Star describes the establishment of Australian family courts that were to be attentive to women's and children's financial problems and to no-fault divorce as 'revolutionary' and 'perfectionist' (1996: 1, 183).

There are reports that these courts have indeed cut down on the length of proceedings, simplified logistical procedures, and granted greater agency to the parties to a complaint by engaging them more directly in the process and using everyday language (Mir-Hosseini 1993: 31). But family courts have also created new forms of control. Leonie Star's historical study of the family court of Australia concludes that the model of the 'helping court' is beset with legal and structural problems pertaining to legal authority, administration, finances and mediation procedures (1996). Ziba Mir-Hosseini's work (1993) on the Iranian family courts shows that women are constrained by religio-legal provisions, economic priorities and the personalities which they have to assume in court. The research on Canadian, Australian and English courts (Sangster 1996; Star 1996; Eaton 1986; Buddin 1978) indicates that ideological apparatuses through which gendered behaviour is evaluated don't change simply because the format and even the content of laws change. An important corollary is also the growing feminist skepticism with mediation-based divorce programmes which are seen to provide insufficient protection of women's legal rights, and a call for engagement either with the public legal system or with systems of alternate dispute resolution that can better attend to issues of power, resources and accountability (Edwards 1997; Presser and Gaarder 2000).

In India, the establishment of family courts is explicitly tied to demands arising out of the feminist movement of the 1970s and 1980s. *Towards Equality* (Committee on the Status of Women in India 1974), the comprehensive documentation and policy analysis on women's status produced in preparation for the 1980 UN conference, as well as numerous women's organisations and social work organisations in India, strongly urged that the model of family courts be adopted. Family courts were also championed by legal scholars who favour ADR methods to counter bureaucratic complication, delays and corruption in the courts, and were seen as parallels to other new legal ventures such as consumer courts, traffic courts and Lok Adalat or people's court (specifically focused on rapid resolution of cases). The results of such sustained campaigning were seen in the passing of the Family Courts Act in 1984 (Law Publishers 2001), which decreed that special courts were to be created for the disposal of divorce, maintenance, adoption and custody cases. These were to be courts where litigants would express their concerns to judges in 'plain language'; lawyers were generally forbidden, although they could appear as 'amicus curiae' (friend of court) by petition. Clients were to work first with 'counsellors' (paralegals or social workers and not lawyers): these counsellors were to help negotiate settlements, try to bring the parties back together and advise about legal issues. Setting up actual courts proved to be a slow process, one major obstacle being opposition from lawyers' groups (Jha 1996), but by 2002, at least 13 major metropolitan areas had family courts.

In reading the feminist policy documents and legislative debates on family courts in the 1980s, I was struck by the palpable energy and optimism incorporated in the idea of this experiment, particularly the sense that this would be a radical measure to destabilise the patriarchal nature of legal discourse. But almost immediately, newspaper reports began to show that it was not that easy to transform modes of power or create alternate legal structures; while reports described the ease of access in the courts, they also pointed out that women are often vulnerable to judges' mercies in these courts, and that these courts are not necessarily a supportive atmosphere free from expectations of gendered behaviour (Vatuk 2006; Das 1996; *The Hindu* 1996; Singh 1996; Anjali 1995).

In my fieldwork conducted in the Kolkata courts,[2] I was interested in mapping the workings of the family court ethnographically, tracing the contours of power and the embodiment of the feminist vision. The Kolkata court came into being on 12 September 1994, and a second judge was assigned to the job in 2000. Lawyers stormed the court and charged at the judge on the first day it was open, but it has continued to function since then.[3] By Agnes' reckoning (2004: 25), the jurisdiction of the family courts covers about 20 per cent of Kolkata's population, and the court handles four per cent of the matrimonial litigation of the state of West Bengal (the Kolkata metropolitan area has 37 per cent of cases of the state, the rest being heard in the Alipore district courts where matrimonial legislation is mixed up with all other district court cases). According to Agnes (2004), the court has a relatively small caseload compared to other courts in India, but calls to expand its scope and size as originally announced have so far met with no response from the government.

A quantitative portrait of the Kolkata court culled from Flavia Agnes' report (2004: 26–31) commissioned by the West Bengal Women's Commission points to some telling factors that illumine the conflicts described below. Twenty per cent of cases are dismissed at the preliminary stage for want of prosecution, but 75 per cent of cases that continue are cleared within the first year of filing, and another 13 per cent by the second year—only three per cent of cases take more than three years, unlike the district courts where matrimonial cases are part of the larger pool. Claims of 'speedy disposition' are thus generally merited. Nine per cent of cases are filed within a year of marriage, 19 per cent within 1–2 years of marriage, 22 per cent within 3–5 years of marriage, 19 per cent within 5–8 years of marriage, 17 per cent within 8–15 years of marriage and 14 per cent after over 15 years of marriage. That is, there is a fairly even distribution between length of marriage and ensuing matrimonial problems.

The attempts to minimise the adversarial nature of divorces also seems valid to some extent. Of all cases, 9.5 per cent are deemed to be 'reconciled, settled or withdrawn', 13.4 per cent are granted an ex-parte decree and in 33.6 per cent cases there is a matrimonial decree. Almost half of the cases where decrees are granted (48 per cent) are mutual consent divorces, and in another 17 per cent of cases contested matrimonial cases are converted to mutual consent divorces. Along with the 'settled' cases, these mutual consent divorces signal the new horizon of non-adversarial divorce; often, the agreement comes at the end of numerous highly contested legal showdowns, but usually the monetary agreement struck at the end brings a resolution to the process (though attempts to recover money and negotiate custody can be ongoing).

The breakdown of the rest of the decrees also reveals gendered patterns and strategies: 24 per cent pertain to granting of divorce, one per cent to judicial separation, eight per cent to annulment and two per cent to restitution of conjugal rights. While far more women than men file for divorce (71 to 39), annulment (75 to 25) and judicial separation (78 to 22), men overwhelmingly file for restitution of conjugal rights (91 per cent). Because women overwhelmingly file for maintenance, the latter category is a mirror-image suit, in which the legal clause seeks to ask women to return to the marital household in lieu of seeking maintenance while being away from it, or else to forfeit the marriage through divorce. Agnes contends that many of these cases do get converted either to divorce or mutual consent petitions, and thus the total number in this category is small.

The family courts, while emphasising a different kind of adjudication method, are fundamentally a lower-level court. This means litigants have no choice but to show up once cases are filed, and are subject to fines and imprisonment if they fail to fulfill orders against them, even when these are ex-parte orders. Maintenance cases, a full 43 per cent of the cases in the court, exemplify this compulsory punitive dynamic. Every day, a large number of women come to court, often repeatedly, to find husbands defaulting on payments. This begins a retaliatory, potentially criminal hearing against the husbands, who typically show up at the hearing, make a variety of excuses and pay what is minimally necessary, then often promptly begin the process of defaulting on payments all over again. Fifty-eight per cent of these maintenance cases are filed under Section 125 of the Criminal Procedure Code, i.e. they relate to penurious circumstances, and 30 per cent deal with 'recovery' or the failure to obtain funds according to the judgment. The economic difficulties of divorce for women are perfectly reflected here in the demographic of women's penury outside of marriage, and the rituals of men's recidivism and the humiliation and harassment faced by women. Agnes argues that given the dominance of these issues in the court, streamlining methods to directly attach income would vastly improve the efficiency and workload of the courts (2004: 27), but that elegant solution does not account for the ways in which the end-runs around maintenance orders serve as deliberate signs of disentitlement for women.

Cases are filed by either the husband or wife; maintenance cases typically by wives, restitution of conjugal rights cases typically by husbands, children's visitation requests typically by fathers. But it is vital to recognise that cases in the family court are only one aspect of a well-choreographed series of cases in various legal and non-legal venues, such as mediation centres in neighbourhoods and women's organisations (political or independent), local police stations which register first information reports (FIRs) of violence, special women's grievance cells which mediate domestic violence cases, and criminal courts where 'torture' or domestic violence is also adjudicated. As I have explored elsewhere (Basu 2007), families try to manipulate the timing of these various cases to their advantage, often to the great irritation of judges and counsellors. These processes are of a piece with recent ethnographies of gendered mediation of marriage in India (Holden 2008; Grover 2006; Moore 1998), which vividly document the role of court officials, prominent local personages and non-governmental organisations in inventing quasi-legal resolutions which both incorporate legal categories and work around them.

In various Indian venues, family courts are talked about as spaces where women have an advantage (although this view is strongly contested by judges and counsellors who see themselves being fair to both genders). In Mumbai, they are referred to as '*baikanche* courts' (women's courts). There may indeed be a few advantages, such as speedier disposal of cases and a direct venue for obtaining maintenance (despite delays and resistance). I consider in this essay whether these factors make the court a more empowering space of gender justice. New ways of speaking and judging may be enabled by this innovative format, but do socio-economic/cultural structures of gender and class change alongside?

The Transformation of Judicial Authority

The double-edged protection and patronage of the family courts is exemplified in the attitudes of the judges. The courtroom here is largely unmediated by lawyerly interjections, so judges directly speak with litigants, conduct most depositions and cross-examinations, and dictate (sometimes simultaneously translating) cases to create the legal record. Judges and counsellors frequently speak of themselves as being involved in a satisfying new experiment of better and more meaningful access, of moulding and facilitating law and culture in important ways. As the female judge of the Kolkata court said to me in 2001, 'I am very pleased with working in the family court, because I like to talk with people and here I am very patient, though not otherwise in life.' In addition to having an expanded set of legal roles, the quality of their authority has supposedly changed as well: they are able, indeed encouraged, to get into the work of family reconciliation. This same judge said to a male client, 'this is not like other courts, here I will talk to you in my chamber like a member of your family, this is what your elder sister should have been saying to you if she was thinking about what was best for you.' The statement invokes the signature informality and ease of access of the family courts cast in deliberate opposition to the impersonality of other courts; but, is impersonal justice necessarily worse? Is justice ever impersonal? The analogy of family advice also signals that the court becomes a space where customary expectations of gender norms may prevail.

A more extensive look at the judge's rhetoric of persuasion in this case reveals the contours of the authority exercised by the female judge over the male respondent alongside the power assigned to husbandly authority. Here the husband Babu had come to court to be able to meet his child as part of a formal visitation on her birthday.

In her chambers, the judge asked about the couple getting back together, commenting on how happy they seem in each other's presence. She advised them to make up, telling Babu he would have to change his ways a bit. 'Why not her ways,' he asked. 'I'll tell her too on my own,' she said, 'but you're the only child of your parents and you have to realise it can't always go your way in the husband and wife relationship.' She told him he was a good person because he didn't drink or do drugs ['you don't, do you?' she asked after a moment] or smoke. 'I don't even have an addiction to tea,' he said. The judge backtracked to ask: 'So then why do you say in your complaint that she refuses to make tea for guests, when she isn't used to it because her husband doesn't drink tea?' 'But she drinks tea,' he said. The crux of the problem is that Babu had certain demands and behaved badly when thwarted. One major issue is that he refuses to allow his wife, Indrani, to work outside the home, although she has a good job at the Titan watch showroom and he only makes about INR 3000. The judge told him resolutely, 'I can't ask her to quit a good job when things are so unsettled.'

The case echoed a dominant theme of the family courts, that 'marital reconciliation' is the optimal good not just for the child's well-being but for the couple as well. Here the judge appears to be chastising the husband fondly and speaking in the wife's interest; at first glance, she seems to be enacting the perception that legal recourse is liberatory for women, that judges are favourably biased towards women's needs. But she scolds him while deferring to his expectations of the wife's responsibility for domestic service and his right to control her occupation and mobility. When she seeks to modify his opposition to his wife's paid work, she does so by emphasising the instability in her life for which he is at least partially culpable (both because of the unsettlement of the separation and his meagre income), thus invoking his failed role as breadwinner and head of household to bargain for his wife's claim.

Even though women's options within marriage appear to be negotiable, the ideological consensus required to keep her in the workplace so that she may economically fend for herself relies upon a normative patriarchal contract around men's control of labour and movement. To invoke Molyneux's formulation (1985), the wife's 'strategic' gender interests had to be undermined in the interest of attaining any benefits related to 'practical' gender interests; the domain of strategic gender interests were beyond legal formulation here. This judge told me in a candid moment in an interview, 'It was a good thing to have the courts, but their purpose is not being implemented, because the gender bias is still there.'[4] A juxtaposition of this statement with the negotiation above might indicate that using the kinship model is a strategic move to make some improvements in the women's situation, similar to the conversion narratives by counsellors that follow; but as in those cases, gendered juridico-economic-sexual hierarchies of marriage are not destabilised.

The Triumph of (Re)Conciliation

Like the judges, counsellors also often speak of themselves as being involved in an important social experiment. This seems a particularly important point of validation for the Kolkata counsellors who basically perform honorary service, being paid a very low fee for their services, and reimbursement for expenses which often takes years. Unlike other family courts (where elite women dominate as counsellors, see Vatuk [2006]), most counsellors and judges are from lower-middle to middle-class backgrounds, and counselling serves to affirm their influence and identity contrary to their relative economic marginalisation. Most of the Kolkata family court counsellors were associated with 'women's wings' of Left political organisations (including the main party the CPI(M) but other Left auxiliaries as well), as active party workers. The counselling structure, which they describe as a powerful social intervention instituted by a progressive government, also validated their political identities.

Family courts therefore serve as an apt extension of the counsellors' skills of negotiation, a vivid demonstration of their cultural capital. As Mrinal, a counsellor, said to me,

> The thing about family courts is that people's idea of what a court is does not mesh with what we have here, because the self-interest of lawyers doesn't work here. The government-appointed women like us are counsellors here, who were sent by women's organisations as representatives. Because we've come from these organisations and we've had a long experience of doing this kind of work, we have a responsibility to our organisations and to society. To do these cases properly, we need to find out everything correctly, and for that we go as far as we can, going to people's houses and offices, helping out people as much as we can. Unlike lawyers, we don't support one side, we want the best interest of both sides to be served. This is very hard work, takes a lot of time, you also need the personality to get along with all the people. But when we can see the work has gone well, when we see the couples become one again, then that is such a huge mental peace, you can't compensate for that with a lakh of rupees. And that is the meaning of family courts. Counsellors and also judges work towards this.

Another counsellor Shukla said, 'our biggest difference with lawyers [is] that we are appointed by the court and don't represent any one side, I see both sides and also the court's interest, for example to curb delays, all of that. What do lawyers do? They look out of one eye only, not both eyes.' Mrinal described helping a friend's mother die in peace because she knew her daughter's case was in Mrinal's hand; Sadhana, another counsellor, was visited almost daily by a young man who she felt she had rescued from profound depression brought on by his wife's manipulations. While the opposing parties in these cases likely disagreed with these characterisations, the counsellors' accounts nonetheless underline their own sense of pivotal social work and complex sets of social skills. But they also point to the fundamental purpose of the job, that of marital reconciliation and negotiating with families, which may serve to underline gender and class hierarchies.

According to the 1984 Act, family courts are set up 'with a view to promote conciliation in, and secure speedy settlement of disputes related to marriage and family affairs' (Law Publishers 2001: 1). 'Conciliation' is a slippery concept here, while a few practitioners take it to be a mode of conflict resolution, an antonym of 'adversarial process'[5] it is commonly interpreted to mean that 'reconciliation' must be tried to the utmost extent before divorce. The language of the Act (Section 9), and the parliamentary introduction of the Bill, both ambiguously refer to 'conciliation in marriage' and the latter frames it in terms of 'preserv[ing] the institution of marriage and promot[ing] the welfare of children' (ibid.: 192). [6] Thus, not only might these two stated purposes—efficiency and preservation of marriage—be seen as contradictory interests for the state, but the goals of preserving marriage and serving women's best interests are also potentially contradictory. The driving rationale for reconciliations may be economic or social pragmatism, and stated intent of litigants, in the absence of a radical transformation of labour market conditions and the stigma of divorce. However, in effect the legal directive places women back in superficially changed domestic conditions, and the cost of preserving the institution of marriage is often literally borne on women's bodies.

The contradictions and potential harm of the conciliation standard is best exemplified by the enthusiasm for 'reconciliations' seen in the Kolkata courts: counsellors typically measured their success by promptly and proudly recounting the number and kinds of 'reunions' they had brought about. Shopna, a counsellor at the Kolkata courts triumphantly described a case in a home where the daughter-in-law was being physically tortured by her parents-in-law. Having received several frantic calls from the woman, she had rousted the municipal councillor and arrived at the home with him and some police officers, and taken the woman home in a grand rescue scene. But then, 'The next day we sat down with the parents and also her husband, we all talked, I did some counselling for two or three days, and then I sent her back home. Her husband is a good person, it's the parents-in-law who are violent, but he is economically totally dependent on the family business and they cannot move away. I will try to check up on her, see if she and her husband can have some separate space in the house.'

In another case, Shopna described bringing together a couple where the husband was extremely paranoid and jealous, routinely violent, and finally slashed her, causing her to lose 'three bucketfuls of blood'. The woman allegedly told the police that she fell on the blade, because otherwise her husband would have lost his good government job and then she wouldn't be able to get maintenance for herself and their two children. Shopna described to me that she persuaded the man to see a psychiatrist for his paranoia, and to allow his wife a little freedom (for example, 'let her go to your daughter's school at least, there'll be another five parents sitting there and she can converse with them'), and that the couple were reunited and continued to be ecstatically happy.

These two narratives are part of a prevalent genre among counsellors, who often describe complicated negotiations with influential and intransigent people, and similar conversion tales of axe-wielding violent husbands. But reconciliation is always the optimal outcome, and the greatest triumphs are instances where women get slightly greater mobility or independence within the patched-up marriage. The narrative focus of these parables, conveyed through detailed dramatic descriptions of arrangements and conversations I have not reproduced here, is not the frustration of gendered economic dependency, but rather, counsellors' sense of accomplishment at their new jobs and the skillful negotiating tactics required, including, importantly, a sense of ensuring a better deal for women clients and leaving them with a sense of having a vigilant ally.

As in Brazilian police stations for women, the concrete work of mediating marriage was initially taken on by those who do not identify with feminist analyses of marriage, such that 'it was not surprising to hear statements from policewomen that clearly undermined the original goals of the women's police stations', demonstrating 'how the interests and culture of state actors are, or might be, transformed by interactions between state and civil society actors' (Santos 2004: 43, 51). In the Kolkata courts, counsellors enacted broader social norms, inscribing the reconciled family as an optimal economic, emotional and residential solution, violence a bad habit to be eradicated by appropriate counsel. For litigants, violence was thus routinised as a form of conjugal authority to be kept in check by other forms of surveillance, including patriarchal surveillance within marriage.

Organisations that deal with violence against women, such as Swayam in Kolkata, have been vocal in their opposition to lawyerless family courts and have alleged that some counsellors have asked for bribes in kind if not cash. Maitreyi Chatterji of Nari Nirjaton Pratirodh Mancha (Forum against Torture of Women) spoke about the validation of patriarchal attitudes in the family courts, the problematic emphasis on reconciliation, the heightened vulnerability of their clients if they cannot have their lawyers emphasise their interests.[7] Krishna Roy of Swayam pointed out, 'Laws and procedures stay same, but women fight own cases: that's the theory. This doesn't strengthen women's position in itself—only if a judge really tries. A judge will ask women to file petitions, but women don't know what it means. They need a lawyer behind them, for example, Swayam lawyers have drafted cases. Lawyers have to be paid, but judges are also afraid of lawyers watching, can't do illegal things.'

The solution, she says, 'would be implementing maintenance efficiently in all courts. Women at all levels need empowerment, education, health, skills development. The idea of a speedy trial is ok but counselling doesn't seem very valuable. Counsellors should get training in how women can become independent, not in how to patch-up marriage.'[8]

While greatly in sympathy with Swayam's views, and concurring that some bribery complicates the situation, I want to emphasise that the counsellors represent a different sort of feminist agency. They see themselves as helping women concretely on a daily basis, and devote a great deal of time and mostly unpaid labour to the effort. The bind of empowerment within which counsellors find themselves is that they are in the line of work with the avowed intention of helping out women and bettering social relations, but they are limited by the alternative economic and cultural spaces that can be imagined for women. Moreover, they may themselves not entirely be in disagreement with ideologies of gender and class. Helping poor women pursue their claims and setting things right in families are often cited as the high points. It is important that we validate this energy and effort, and not simply cast their work in opposition to that of lawyers or women, while also recognising the struggles between scripts of feminism and femininity in the inscription and development of their attitudes (Nelson 1996; Santos 2004).

Owning the New Legal Subjectivity: Differential Access

Theoretically, women and men litigants are supposed to be persons with voice and presence in these courts, persons in charge of their lives; they are meant to conduct their own cases by putting together their own petitions, asking for relevant court documents, organising and maintaining their files, showing up at hearings, cross-examining witnesses, managing appeals. In practice, of course, few are able to negotiate these steps without the help of lawyers and relatives, regardless of their level of education. Still, involvement in this sort of litigation does transform women's engagement with the public sphere; many women accustomed only to the home now have to learn about public transportation and important locations within court buildings, cultivate good terms with court personnel so they can ask for occasional favours, and train themselves to speak up and make their point in front of the judge. Even interactions with other litigants, such as through daily prolonged conversations on the court benches, open them up to other narratives of violence, conflict and corruption.

On the one hand, judges were routinely careful to pay attention to issues of women's economic maintenance; they often referred to this task as the most important aspect of their jobs. I witnessed one case where the woman had left her husband and was living with another man, another where there were numerous reports (and evidence in court) of a woman's querulous and erratic nature. The judges were annoyed by these women who were clearly not models of ideal feminine behaviour (in the latter case she was even removed from the courtroom), but always insisted that the bottom line was providing her a liveable allowance as part of the solution.

Yet the knowledge that women may have filed parallel charges of 'physical and mental torture' in the criminal courts (under section 498A CrPC) often made the judges react very unsympathetically to women, the implication from judges (and counsellors) being that the woman's invocation of Section 498A was a willful destruction of her marriage and an unforgivable embarrassment to her husband and affinal family. In one case, a judge was visibly contemptuous of the woman's Section 498A case (which was dismissed because of insufficient evidence), 'What a blow! He was just about to lose his job, and such a good senior job in the Railways. If I sent a qualified young man to you now, could you find him that good a job?' Then with a pause and a very sarcastic smile, 'But you want maintenance from him all right, and he has the job so he can pay it.'

There is a sense in such cases that the judge's role as sole authority has been insulted because litigants have taken some matters into their own hands and initiated criminal prosecution to leverage the civil case, and also that women litigants have asserted themselves in ways that are at odds with their roles as economically vulnerable entities in need of the court's protection. The implication is that women's empowerment can best be achieved second-hand, through the judge's benevolent patronage.

Social privileges do strongly influence litigants' power and comfort within the courtroom. Litigants' new powers of engagement in the family courts is best availed of by those who have some educational and cultural power. Those with minimal literacy skills often suffered frequent rebukes or ridicule for the way they spoke as well as more tangible consequences, such as ignoring court summons that read like gibberish to them. I observed a woman who had been given an ex-parte divorce without getting the chance to oppose or to apply for maintenance. Another man faced a criminal sentence for non-payment of maintenance granted through an ex-parte order because he had simply ignored the registered court summons. I visited him with the counsellors in distant Machlandapur, a three-hour train ride from Kolkata, to find that he had simply tucked away the papers in a trunk full of discarded stuff, assuming it was a summons for recovery of dowry. He believed he was in no danger from not acting on it because he had received his cash dowry through a very indirect route that could not be traced back to him.

Among those who were educated, there were several women who took to the court process with gusto, reading up on the details of the law, gathering thorough evidence, filing a range of complaints in civil and criminal venues. These women seized on litigation as a process of public retaliation against their husbands facilitated by the courts, as a space to expose financial and moral hypocrisies and bear testimony to violence or neglect, with the triumph of evidence and the backing of legal sanction. Even this potential empowerment, however, was limited by the expectations of judicial control of the courtroom.

A case in point involved a youngish man who had a high-end job at a reputed bank, and a woman who had occasionally earned money by tutoring. On the day of the husband's testimony, the wife was intricately prepared with questions, and was actually using a style of questioning that mimicked lawyers. [9] She asked him about his hidden bank accounts, his recent attempts to obtain an expedited passport, his drunkenness and violence, his irregular maintenance payments (she called him a 'habitual offender' at this, using those English words). The words of her relentless questioning were, 'Did you have money in that bank or not, Mr Roychoudhury, you must answer' and 'Do you regularly pay maintenance, you must answer.' He was usually non-responsive, at which she would turn to the judge and tell him to direct the witness to answer. However, her questions could only be asked as interjections to the judge's questions; he had already decided to cross-examine on her behalf, and had been going through the plaint asking the husband to confirm or deny allegations, and thus was increasingly irritated by her active role. When she grimaced/smirked as she directed one of her questions to her husband, he scolded, 'don't laugh, this is a courtroom,' and he finally silenced her by saying, 'So do you want to do all the asking? Then I can just let you do this job and not say anything.'

A genuinely active role assumed by clients is thus perceived as disruptive and inappropriate, despite the leeway provided in the Act; clients' activity has to be scripted within the context of the judge's power, and the docility of putting oneself in the judge's hands is very important for currying favour. In the final analysis, legal structures of authority still determine all important outcomes; opportunities for clients to speak directly to judges merely provide conduits to channel judges' perspectives rather than enhanced legal agency for litigants.

Conclusion

Family courts are not merely a facade of change, because they are indeed the space of apparently new forms of cultural negotiation, new opportunities to directly avail of legal rights. However, this seeming newness is profoundly entangled with existent institutional and ideological structures. The form of legal contest is apparently changed, but in fact, these are lower-level district courts operating with identical structures of deposition, precedent, evidence and appeal, which mean that the seeming informality must finally be rendered into the customary just-so legal formality. Judges, lawyers and counsellors still work through the ways in which they themselves were disciplined to learn about rights or entitlements. Even where the alienation of speaking through a lawyer may have been removed, litigants are subjected to judge-directed techniques of disciplined legal response in the courtroom, and are expected to be best represented through the judge's mediation rather than their own. Those with few educational and financial resources were still clearly at a disadvantage in the legal realm, unable to fully avail of newly available resources. Ironically, this format has vastly increased judges' powers in exchange for lawyers', with fewer checks and balances, such that individual personality traits can play an even greater role.

Women, too, could carve out a space where they could directly confront husbands and affines about private grievances with the backing of the law, especially if they were wealthy or educated. But this space existed within a cultural and legal framework where being 'woman' included: women's economic dependence on marriage for both food and housing, male control of women's decisions and movements, domestic violence as personality-related aberrations, and wifehood and motherhood associated with high levels of tolerance and sacrifice. Women thus bore the primary cost for keeping the institution of marriage viable in its present form. Any 'successes' for women usually had to be constituted through these ideologies. While provisions surrounding marriage and divorce were conceptually cast as equitable, partners were in fact vastly differently situated with regard to their economic capacities and the cultural expectations. Altering the mode of speaking or litigating was thus not a sufficient condition either for overcoming the alienation of legal process or for transforming the differential privileges of marriage.

Notes

[1] Upendra Baxi, personal communication, June 2005.

[2] I have been working on an ethnography of family law and family violence in Kolkata—in two extended periods of fieldwork in 2001 and 2004–05—with ongoing annual investigations since 2001, involving participant observation of numerous legal and quasi-legal venues, including the family court, the women's grievance cell, and various organisations dealing with family mediation. My fieldwork consisted of participant observation of the courtrooms, field visits to litigants' homes with counsellors and observation of other family law legal aid venues, plus interviews with judges, counsellors and feminist activists.

[3] In fact, however, lawyers continue to be involved at every stage of the proceedings, both because they write the petitions and frame the cases, and because litigants can formally apply to be represented by lawyers.

[4] Agnes (2004: 26) quotes a similar comment from the principal judge at the time.

[5] Pratibha Gheewala, retired chief counsellor of Mumbai family courts, personal communication, December 2002.

[6] Legislator Susheela Gopalan's objection to the Bill on the grounds that 'conciliation' might expose some women to further violence further indicates that 'reconciliation' is very much signified by the word (Family Courts Bill 1984: 192).

[7] Interview, October 2001.

[8] Interview, October 2001.

[9] Most litigants, invited by the judge to cross-examine, were at a complete loss; typically, they would repeat the complaints they had against the opposing party and the judge would try to translate this back into questions for the witness.

References

Agnes, F. 2004. *A Study of Family Courts, West Bengal*. Kolkata: West Bengal Women's Commission.

———. 1999. *Law and Gender Inequality: The Politics of Women's Rights in India*. New Delhi: Oxford University Press.

Anjali. 1995. 'The Pathos of Family Courts'. *The Pioneer*. 9 April.

Basu, S. 2007. 'Playing Off Courts: The Negotiation of Divorce and Violence in Plural Legal Settings in Kolkata, India'. *Journal of Legal Pluralism and Unofficial Law* 52:41–75.

Buchhofer, B., and K. A. Ziegert. 1981. 'Family Dynamics and Legal Change: Empirical Sociology in Search of a General Theory on the Effects of Law on Family Life'. *Journal of Comparative Family Studies* 12 (4): 397–412.

Buddin, T. 1978. 'Counsellors, Lawyers and Custody Disputes in the Family Courts'. *Australian Journal of Social Issues* 13 (3): 217–31.

Committee on the Status of Women in India. 1974. *Towards Equality: Report of the Committee on the Status of Women in India*. New Delhi: Ministry of Education and Social Welfare, Government of India.

Das, P. 1996. 'For and Against Family Courts'. *The Hindu*. 30 September. Delhi edition.

Eaton, M. 1986. *Justice for Women? Family, Court and Social Control*. Milton Keynes, UK: Open University Press.

Edwards, Patricia E. 1997. 'Gender Issues in Family Law: A Feminist Perspective'. *Family and Conciliation Courts Review* 35 (4): 424–43.

Family Courts Bill. 1984. Lok Sabha Debates 15th Session. V LI #25: 181–241.

Fineman, Martha. 1991. 'Introduction'. In *At the Boundaries of Law: Feminism and Legal Theory*, ed. M. A. Fineman and N. S. Thomadsen, xi–xvi, New York: Routledge.

Glendon, Mary A. 1980. 'Modern Marriage Law and its Underlying Assumptions: The New Marriage and the New Property'. *Indian Socio-Legal Journal* 6: 113–29.

Grover, S. 2006. 'Poor Women's Experiences of Marriage and Love in the City of New Delhi: Everyday Stories of Sukh aur Dukh.' Unpublished Ph.D. dissertation, University of Sussex.

Holden, L. 2008. *Hindu Divorce: A Legal Anthropology*. Aldershot: Ashgate.

Hindu, The. 1996. 'Family Court Act Change Flayed'. 24 April. Delhi edition: 2.

Jha, S. 1996. 'Family Courts Still Remain a Distant Dream'. *Indian Express*. 29 April. Delhi edition.

Kapur, R., and Brenda Cossman. 1993. *Subversive Sites: Feminist Engagements with Law in India*. New Delhi: Sage.

Kumar, R. 1993. *The History of Doing: An Illustrated Account of Movements for Women's Rights and Feminism in India, 1800–1990*. London: Verso.

Law Publishers. 2001. *The Family Courts Act 1984: Bare Act 2001*. Allahabad: Law Publishers.

McIntyre, Lisa J. 1995. 'Law and the Family in Historical Perspective: Issues and Antecedents'. *Marriage and Family Review* 21(3–4): 5–30.

Mani, L. 1989. 'Contentious Traditions: The Debate on Sati in Colonial India'. In *Recasting Women: Essays in Colonial History*, eds. K. Sangari and S. Vaid. New Delhi: Kali for Women.

Mir-Hosseini, Z. 1993. *Marriage on Trial: A Study of Islamic Family Law*. London: I. B. Tauris.

Molyneux, M. 1985. 'Mobilization without Emancipation? Women's Interests, the State and Revolution in Nicaragua'. *Feminist Studies* 11 (2): 227–54.

Moore, Erin P. 1998. *Gender, Law and Resistance in India*. Phoenix: University of Arizona Press.

Nader, L. 1997. 'Controlling Processes: Tracing the Dynamic Components of Power'. *Current Anthropology* 38 (5): 711–37.

Nair, J. 1996. *Women and Law in Colonial India*. New Delhi: Kali for Women.

Nelson, S. 1996. 'Constructing and Negotiating Gender in Women's Police Stations in Brazil'. *Latin American Perspectives* 23 (1): 131–48.

Parashar, A. 1992. *Women and Family Law Reform In India: Uniform Civil Code and Gender Equality*. New Delhi: Sage.

Presser, L., and Emily Gaarder. 2000. 'Can Restorative Justice Reduce Battering? Some Preliminary Considerations'. *Social Justice* 27 (1): 175–95.

Rai, S. M. 1996. 'Women and the State in the Third World: Some Issues for Debate'. In *Women and the State: International Perspectives*, eds. Shirin M. Rai and Geraldine Lievesley. London: Taylor and Francis.

Sangster, J. 1996. 'Incarcerating Bad Girls: The Regulation of Sexuality Through the Female Refuges Act in Ontario, 1920–1945'. *Journal of the History of Sexuality* 7 (2): 239–75.

Santos, C. MacDowell. 2004. 'En-gendering the Police: Women's Police Stations and Feminism in Sao Paulo'. *Latin American Research Review* 39 (3): 29–55.

Sarkar, T. 1993. 'Rhetoric Against Age of Consent: Resisting Colonial Reason and Death of a Child-Wife'. *Economic and Political Weekly* 28 (36): 1869–78.

Singh, K. 1996. 'Family Courts'. *The Pioneer*. 17 April. Delhi edition.

Smart, C., and Julia Brophy. 1985. 'Locating Law: A Discussion of the Place of Law in Feminist Politics'. In *Women-In-Law: Explorations in Law, Family and Sexuality*, eds. Carol Smart and Julia Brophy. London: Routledge and Kegan Paul.

Smith, Peter M. 1988. 'Families in Court: Guilty or Guilty?' *Children and Society* 2:152–64.

Star, L. 1996. *Counsel of Perfection: The Family Court of Australia*. Melbourne: Oxford University Press.

Tambe, A. 2009. *Codes of Misconduct: Regulating Prostitution in Late Colonial Bombay*. Minneapolis: University of Minnesota Press.

Vatuk, S. 2006. 'Domestic Violence and Marital Breakdown in India: A View from the Family Courts'. In *Culture, Power and Agency: Gender in Indian Ethnography*, eds. Lina Fruzzetti and Sirpa Tenhunen. Kolkata: Stree.

When Marriage Breaks Down How do Contracts Matter?*

Marriage Contracts and Divorce in Contemporary North India

Katherine Lemons

In 2008, the Lucknow-based Indian Muslim woman's rights activist Shaista Amber and her organisation, the All India Muslim Women's Personal Law Board (AIMWPLB), unveiled a new *nikahnama* (marriage contract). I had been anticipating this moment for several years, as the new nikahnama was a frequent topic of conversation during the time that I was conducting fieldwork in Delhi and Lucknow and getting to know Amber between 2005 and 2007. In our first formal conversation, Amber had told me that one of the AIMWPLB's strategies for improving women's conditions was to write a marriage contract that would be ubiquitously available in mosques and courts and that would be required to execute a legal Muslim marriage in India.[1] One of her aims, which became the first clause in the marriage contract, was to require that all Muslim marriages be registered by submitting a copy of the nikahnama to the state marriage bureau. Requiring registration would standardise the terms of Muslim marriage by drawing the state in as a mechanism of enforcement. This

* Numerous people have provided critical feedback on this essay. I would like to thank especially Dace Dzenovska, Mengia Hong Tschalaer, Arzoo Osanloo, Rajni Palriwala, Ravinder Kaur and Shalini Grover. For financial and institutional support of the research and writing of this essay, thanks to the Woodrow Wilson Foundation (Charlotte Newcomb Fellowship), UC Berkeley Center for Middle Eastern Studies and Jacob Javits Foundation.

approach, Amber argued, relies on the established Indian legal structure in which the state upholds religious laws in personal law matters.[2] The nikahnama named specific rights granted to women by the Quran and Hadith and called on the state to guarantee these rights to its Muslim citizens.

The AIMWPLB is neither alone in pursuing a new marriage contract nor did they invent it as a strategy of intervention (Vatuk 2007). In the 1990s, a group of scholars and activists hoping to codify Muslim women's rights in marriage presented just such a model nikahnama to the All India Muslim Personal Law Board (AIMPLB) for their consideration (Vatuk 2007: 505). Although the model nikahnama was not implemented, it set in motion a series of attempts to rewrite the nikahnama to include a provision allowing women to dissolve their marriages through a *talaq-e-tafwiz* (a delegated right of divorce) (ibid.). Delegated divorce grants a woman the right to unilaterally divorce her husband under conditions enumerated in the nikahnama (Carroll 1982). This earlier model nikahnama also initiated attempts to give women greater negotiating power in polygynous marriages.

Shaista Amber's nikahnama is among a new wave of such attempts to improve Muslim women's status through apparently legal interventions (Hong Tschalaer 2011; Vatuk 2007). Seeking to rectify the problems that Amber identifies as confronting the poor women in Lucknow who seek her advice, her nikahnama exhorts spouses to live up to the ideals of Muslim marriage, details the conditions within which women and men can initiate divorce and delineates post-divorce issues.

Scholars and academics in India have identified legal, social, economic and familial reasons for the problems women face in marriage (Ahmed 1976, 2003). Many feminist organisations view legal change and legal literacy as tools for intervening in the other three domains. These organisations have struggled to make laws governing marriage more egalitarian and to improve women's legal literacy, enabling them to fight domestic violence and other forms of harmful treatment.[3] That is, they both seek to regender law (Lazarus-Black 2003, 2007) and to improve women's ability and willingness to use the law as an instrument of self-defence against what the members of these organisations often described to me as social and familial impediments to equality.[4] These organisations work with a dense concept of the law: law includes statutes and case law, legal practice and interpretation, legal access and consciousness. Numerous legal scholars also engage with the problem of marriage and law through this dense definition (Agarwal 1994; Agnes 1992, 1999, 2008; Basu 1999; Kapur and Crossman 1996; Mukhopadhyay 1998; Oldenburg 2002).

In this essay, I look at Amber's effort to alter gendered power relations within Muslim marriages through the new nikahnama. Juxtaposing her emphasis on the artefact of the contract with its absence in negotiations of marriage in several Islamic legal institutions, I first suggest that contracts, like law more generally, bind not by virtue of their letter, but as a consequence of their embeddedness in webs of social relations (Durkheim 1933). I argue that based on this understanding, it seems easy to dismiss the new marriage contract as a misfire that at once assumes too much and too little about what contracts do. Further, given the plural legal landscape in which Muslim men and women in India negotiate marital and divorce disputes, the nikahnama's focus on the state as the primary mechanism of enforcement appears to be misguided. In the second part of the chapter, I suggest that such a dismissal would, however, elide the importance of the interventions that such a contract can and does make, in lived realities. In spite of its inability to directly produce social change, the new marriage contract I consider here makes important hermeneutic and pedagogical interventions; it stakes out a crucial space of possibility for women by addressing clergy and lay women with alternative interpretations of Muslim women's rights granted in the Quran. It thereby lays the groundwork for a different kind of jurisprudential practice than is currently common in the part of North India I study. This new nikahnama should, therefore, be understood as a pedagogical, hermeneutic and legal intervention that builds on the feminist legal interventions I have just glossed and shows that law produces social change through rhetorical and social practices.

Contractual Marriage and Marital Breakdown

Shaista Amber's decision to intervene in marriage by writing a new nikahnama is predicated on her view of Muslim marriage as primarily a contractual relationship between spouses. Amber often reminded me that Muslim marriages were established as contractual relationships 'fourteen hundred years ago' in the Quran. This is significant for Amber's intervention, because it serves as the foundation for her argument that her work of enumerating the rights provided to women in marriage by the Quran is a faithful development of long-established Islamic principles. From this perspective, Amber's nikahnama teaches women the rights that the Quran bestowed on them, but that, she argues, are often unrealised. Further, her view of the marriage contract itself suggests that changing its terms ought to impact rights and power relations within marriage itself.

Through her explanations of the benefits of contractual marriage, Amber traced the contours of the concept of a contract more generally. A contract, she told me, is distinct from a sacrament because its terms can be negotiated. In making this argument, she focuses on one sense in which a Muslim marriage is contractual: at the outset it can be a private agreement whose terms are drawn up between two individuals (Mir-Hosseini 1993: 129). For example, a couple can write a nikahnama that stipulates the conditions within which the husband or wife can seek divorce. It can include a provision allowing women to dissolve their marriages through a talaq-e-tafwiz; it can restrict a husband's right to engage in polygyny.

Amber's nikahnama enacts yet a different aspect of contract. Her nikahnama does not explicitly encourage husband and wife to include additional stipulations, but instead begins with a clause mandating the registration of marriage following which it lays out the components of the rights and duties of Muslim men and women in marriage. The important feature of a contract in this sense is not that it originates in an agreement between two sovereign individuals, but that it sets out terms to which its signatories can subsequently be held accountable. It is this facet of the contract that makes marriage registration and rights education so important to Amber; once the contract has been signed and a copy filed with the office of marriage registration, any violation of its terms can be reprimanded if the couple concerned are aware of the stipulations of the contract.

My response to Amber's emphasis on and understanding of the marriage contract has been somewhat sceptical. The primary source of my scepticism was that her investment in this new contract seemed to me to elide both the peculiarities of the marriage contract and the lived realities of Muslim marital disputes that I was concomitantly studying. In my research in several Islamic legal institutions, I found that for Muslims (and others) dealing with marital disputes, the state was only one, and often not the most important, site of adjudication. It was thus unclear how registering marriages with the state using a common nikahnama would change these dispute resolution procedures. Further, the artefact of the nikahnama was never referred to and rarely included in case files in the non-state institutions I studied. Because the nikahnama was absent from these negotiations, I did not see how forbidding unilateral male divorce, the triple *talaq*, or laying out women's property rights in divorce in the nikahnama would affect these institutions. Amber herself has noted that in spite of an existing right to *mahr* (dower) upon divorce, few women receive it. Even as some of the nikahnama's provisions thus seemed ill-suited to the plural legal reality in which Delhi Muslims negotiate marriage and divorce, other provisions appeared redundant. Notably, the nikahnama's provisions about women's rights to initiate divorce in specific situations are already readily upheld in both state courts and in Islamic dispute resolution institutions. To illustrate this point, that the nikahnama appears to misfire, I will turn to one Islamic dispute resolution institution, the *dar ul qaza*, that frequently hears divorce cases.

Divorce in the Dar ul Qaza

Dar ul qaza literally means 'house of the judge'. Delhi's dar ul qazas are dispute resolution institutions run by *qazi*s (judges) trained in Islamic law and jurisprudence. These institutions are not part of the civil court system and their judgments are not considered binding by the state's legal apparatus. Delhi's three dar ul qazas were founded in 1973 by the AIMPLB, a non-state organisation of *ulama* (Islamic scholars), whose explicit statement of purpose at its founding was to 'defend Muslim personal law'. Initially, the AIMPLB laid out a number of objectives, among them establishing of committees of clerics charged with studying and interpreting Muslim law and with defending Muslim personal law against the threat by judicial or legislative changes. The AIMPLB established numerous dar ul qazas as alternatives to the civil courts for Muslim disputants.

Dar ul qazas are not regulated by the state, but their parameters are nonetheless framed by it. The dar ul qazas only hear cases that fall within the state's definition of personal law—including marriage, divorce, succession, adoption and inheritance. The vast majority of the cases in the dar ul qazas I studied limited themselves to divorce cases. I argue elsewhere that although dar ul qazas' judgments are not legally binding, they have a moral authority and a relationship to the state's civil courts that make them part of the larger legal landscape relevant to Delhi Muslims (Lemons 2010).

One exemplary case demonstrates the disjuncture between Shaista Amber's aspirations for her nikahnama and practices of marital dispute resolution in dar ul qazas. This case was among the numerous annulment petitions I observed or read that had been submitted by women to the dar ul qazas, which always involved or rested on allegations of abandonment. The woman who initiated this case had been married for six years at the time of the petition. Her husband was a researcher in Unani medicine[5] at a major Muslim university in North India. When she married, the woman moved to Delhi to live with her husband and his family. Two years later, her husband left and never returned. The court records indicate that the wife and her in-laws had no idea where he had gone. The wife continued to live with her in-laws, but complained that they did not treat her well. The wife's opening petition to the dar ul qaza states, 'If my husband returned, I would happily go back to him, but if he does not, I would like a *faskh nikah* [judicial divorce/annulment]. I would like to have a peaceful life.'

Faskh nikah is a woman-initiated divorce that can take place under specific circumstances, according to the Maliki school of Islamic law (Mahmood 2002: 89). Prior to 1939, Indian Muslims did not have access to this form of divorce and, as a consequence, women seeking to get out of troubled marriages often resorted to apostasy, which immediately ended their marriages (Agnes 1999: 70). With the passage of the Dissolution of Muslim Marriages Act of 1939, the Indian government made faskh nikah legal in specific circumstances, including abandonment (Agnes 1999; Mahmood 2002). The AIMPLB was supportive of the bill and the right to a faskh seems to have been adopted by many qazis (Vatuk 2008; Hussain 2007; Lemons 2010).

This case file resembles other petitions for faskh nikah on grounds of abandonment; it contains not only the petitions and letters typical of all dar ul qaza records but also statements from witnesses, who attest to the husband's disappearance, and notices from the local Urdu newspaper, *Nayi Duniya*, requesting the husband's presence at the dar ul qaza. The newspaper notice, which is written by the wife as a public summons, states, 'Since you left, I have not heard anything from you. Your brother told me you never arrived in Aligarh. We are all in a bad way, your parents, your brother and I; we do not know where you have gone.' The notice includes a telephone number where the family can be reached and a photograph of the missing husband. The notice is followed in the case file by another letter from the wife restating her situation. This time she adds, 'I have waited for him at the house, as have his parents. I have put an announcement in the paper. I have no idea where he is and I do not receive any *kharch* [allowance] from him or from his family.' A letter from her brother-in-law supporting the faskh nikah corroborates her allegations.

The summary and judgment in the case reiterate the wife's story and extensively cite corroborating statements by witnesses on both the wife's and the husband's sides of the family. The qazi also states that he has put an advertisement in the paper requesting the husband's appearance in the dar ul qaza, but that this effort was to no avail. Having summarised the case, clarifying that all proper steps were taken, the qazi issued a faskh nikah to the wife, releasing her from her marriage.

When I presented an earlier version of this essay at a conference, my discussant, Kirti Singh, a Supreme Court advocate, was disturbed by the account I gave of this case. She told me that under civil law, the disappearance of a husband constitutes abandonment and that the court would not demand that the wife provide proof of her husband's disappearance. To her, the search for the missing husband represented an unnecessary obstacle to finding a just solution and releasing the wife from her marriage. Given Singh's observation that the qazi collected an overabundance of documents in the case, it is perhaps surprising that the marriage contract is not among them.

I suggest that the absence of the nikahnama reflects an understanding of the 'conjugal contract' that has less to do with the specific conditions and entitlements laid out in the marriage contract than with the affective and financial expectations of marital relationships (Whitehead 1981). Reflecting an aspect of the conjugal contract about which her in-laws agree, the wife argues that her husband should support her financially (Grover 2011; Osella and Osella 2006). Both the wife and her in-laws support the divorce on the grounds that she is not receiving support from her husband. Also, the wife and her in-laws seem to agree that if her husband has abandoned her, her in-laws should take on the responsibility of providing for her unless she receives a divorce. This implies that the husband's family, with whom the married couple lives, also plays a role in the conjugal contract. The family's role in the conjugal relationship is also apparent when we consider how the wife makes her case. In the case file, she emphasises her patience, her perseverance in waiting for her husband and her willingness to remain married to him should he return; further, she notes her loyalty to her in-laws by repeating that she has continued to live with them since her husband left even though they have not provided for her. The argument that she has conformed to the expectations of a good wife—here, patience and loyalty to her husband and her in-laws—seems important to her success in attaining a faskh nikah.[6] Having convinced the qazi of her virtues as a wife, and of the reality of her abandonment, the wife is released from her marriage.

Yet, the contractual obligations that Amber is careful to lay out in her nikahnama, including a woman's entitlement to mahr and to reasonable post-divorce financial settlement do not even arise in the case. This silence on the matter of the financial implications of the divorce is notable, because according to Hanafi law, as interpreted by the qazi and according to Indian law governing Muslim marriage, Muslim wives are entitled to their mahr and to maintenance money for at least the first three months after a divorce, including a divorce by faskh, i.e. for the *iddat* period (Fyzee 2005b: 186). In this case, though, the wife is filing for divorce in part because she is not receiving the support due to her by her in-laws. She may view remarriage as the only avenue of financial stability, in which case an expedient divorce is more beneficial to her than a slow divorce in the courts through which she is granted small financial rewards. As Sabiha Hussain and others have shown, women rarely see the money they are granted in divorce settlements, which may disincline them from asking for it at all (2007). In this case, we may also read the silence on the issue of financial compensation as an indication that when she writes that her in-laws do not 'treat her well', she hints at abuse and not mild disagreement. Descriptions of domestic violence are rarely included in the dar ul qaza's records, but statistics on the frequency of domestic violence suggest that this only indicates that the dar ul qaza records remain silent on the matter.[7] In other words, there are reasons beyond securing rights that shape disputants' decisions; often, the way a disputant pursues her case suggests that she has made compromises.

If on the one hand it seems unlikely that the contract would have much effect on cases such as this one, on the other hand, some of the nikahnama's provisions granting women-initiated divorce appear already to be accepted without the new contract. The practice of giving faskh nikahs to women who had been abandoned was, for example, common. This court case, therefore, highlights not the importance of contracts as sets of stipulations available to enforcement, but an altogether different view of contracts in general and of marriage contracts in particular. It implies a more expansive view of the marriage contract as embedded not in the paper nikahnama, but in broader norms and ideals governing marriage. As was apparent in this and many other dar ul qaza cases I have studied, these norms and ideals are crucial to the way disputants negotiate their positions and to the outcomes of their cases. Judicial divorces were granted to women, who could demonstrate that they had lived up to the normative understanding of the good wife in spite of their husbands' and in-laws' failures.

The Peculiarity of the Marriage Contract

The absence of the nikahnama in divorce proceedings reflects an aspect of marriage that feminist theorists in several contexts have noticed: marriage appears not to be reducible to a matter of private contract. Numerous scholars of Islamic law have questioned the conventional wisdom that Muslim marriages are primarily contractual relationships (Ahmad 1976; Fyzee 2005a; Hidayatullah and Hidayatullah 2006). A. A. Fyzee and Hidayatullah and Hidayatullah, for example, emphasise that while the *nikah* (marriage) is a contract, it is not 'only' a contract, but also has theological and social (and I would add, emotional) elements that differentiate it from other kinds of contracts. Ziba Mir-Hosseini elaborates a similar critique to thinking of Muslim marriage as simply contractual. Although Muslim marriages are inaugurated through a private contract, Mir-Hosseini argues, 'In terms of the rights and duties that it entails, marriage is treated as a public institution: couples can appeal to the courts to enforce terms of the contract' (1993: 129). As a public institution, marriage is governed by laws and norms that exceed the explicit terms of the contract. Changing these broader legal norms is a challenge that cannot be met solely by altering the nikahnama.

The very legal position of marriage in Islamic law makes this clear. Legally speaking, marriage inhabits the border between the two major subdivisions of Islamic law: *'ibadat* or ritual acts and *mu'amalat*, or contracts (ibid.: 32). Mir-Hosseini has shown that marriage intervenes in both spheres of law, because 'in spirit, marriage belongs to the 'ibadat: it removes the sexual taboo between the sexes by making them licit (*halal*) to each other. In form, it comes under the category of *mu'amalat*: it is a civil contract and is patterned after the contract of sale, which has served as model for other contracts' (ibid.: 32). In practice, marriage is measured and marital disagreements adjudicated not solely or even primarily on the basis of the terms of contract, but instead on the ethical and religious norms that also govern it. Mere contract, this suggests, will be hard pressed to effect change in marital practice or in negotiations of divorce.

Mir-Hosseini is not alone in making this argument. Carole Pateman's critique (1988) of the marriage contract, and of the idea of marriage as contractual relationship, suggests one way of thinking about this broader marriage contract. Pateman argues that marriage relies on sexual difference and sexual subordination not only by means of the actual marriage contract, but also through the broader set of norms and ideals that constitute the institution of marriage. In her exploration of marriage, Pateman cites legal scholars, who have argued that the problem with marriage is the 'status' it appoints to women and men who have agreed to the marriage contract (ibid.: 166). This line of argumentation suggests that if all marital relationships were contracts entered into by consenting individuals, the patriarchal right inherent in marital 'status' would be eliminated. The approach of the AIMWPLB and other Indian feminists take up just such a position: if the nikahnama—which is a list of responsibilities and rights agreed upon by a couple as part of their marriage—included all relevant rights for men and women, then marriage would be a properly contractual relationship guaranteeing women their rights.

The problem with this approach is two-fold. First, as Pateman argues, marriage is not a contract like others. Drawing on the work of the nineteenth-century utilitarian, William Thomas, Pateman argues that the marriage contract, which is independent of the actual relationship between a particular husband and a particular wife, grants the husband a patriarchal right over the wife (ibid.: 158). The marriage contract is unique because it entails a set of norms and ideals that remain unstated in the document that the parties sign to initiate the contract. On the level of the contract, these rules stipulate that only two parties can sign. The legal relationship initiated by the contract also has, until recently, included the subordination of one party to the other (Agnes 2008). The contract still makes the parties into sexual property for one another, giving them the right to sue if deprived of that property, as Flavia Agnes has shown through her analysis of debates (ibid.) over the restitution of conjugal rights. Together, this means that the marriage contract is embedded in larger legal provisions about which the couple does not decide.

The second argument for thinking about the marriage contract beyond the nikahnama is that it rests on non-legal norms that are as real as they are uncodified. In Carole Pateman's work, this point emerges through her argument that the marriage contract ultimately rests on the sexual contract (1988: 171). Even as the contract appears, for social contract theorists, to provide the basis for perfectly equal social relationships, these same theorists paint 'pictures of the state of nature [that] contain the non-contractual conditions necessary for infants to thrive and grow; love, trust and family life are assumed to be found naturally' (ibid.: 182). Women are placed at the border between this natural, non-contractual scene, through which individuals capable of contract are reared, and the sphere of civil society, in which these individuals relate as equals through contracts. The marriage contract *qua contract* incorporates women into civil society while, in its particularity, it 'confirms patriarchal right' (ibid.: 181). The contract of marriage, therefore, rests on relations that are not strictly speaking contractual even as they serve as the basis for this contract.

Anne Whitehead's ethnographic account (1981) of the 'conjugal contract' provides a useful way to turn Pateman's criticism away from the question of whether marriage is truly contractual to the question of what kind of contract it is. Whitehead defines the conjugal contract as 'the terms on which products and income, produced by the labour of husband and wife, are divided to meet their personal and collective needs' (ibid.:113). Whitehead argues that a conjugal contract is at once necessary both for marriage and for the household 'as a collectivity concerned with the daily maintenance of its members' and that this contract entails certain conflicts of interest between husband and wife (ibid.: 93). The conjugal contract creates and maintains expectations about which member of the couple provides which labour and finances. One way to think about the dar ul qaza case I have summarised is as a negotiation about whether norms of provision have been met. While this makes clear how the dispute is about an agreement, or a conjugal contract, at the same time it throws into relief the socially embedded aspect of this contract and its distance from the actual terms enumerated in the nikahnama itself.

Rhetoric as Action

Although it may be tempting to conclude that the attempt to improve women's rights in and experiences of marriage through a written contract is simply misplaced, a closer look at the hermeneutic and pedagogical interventions of Amber's nikahnama shows that its rhetorical intervention is itself a crucial piece of creating social change. I analyse these interventions here by focusing on three specific provisions in the nikahnama: unilateral male divorce, women's rights in divorce and *halala*, a practice that requires a woman who wants to remarry her husband to first marry another man and be divorced by him. Each of these interventions represents a pedagogical and hermeneutic intervention aimed at convincing lay Muslims and clerics respectively to rethink the terms of marital disputes. In this way, I argue, each seeks to reorganise gendered power relations in marriage by changing how clerics and spouses think of its entailments. Knowing the terms and the rights entailed in the contract can change the way marriage itself is lived: recognising women's rights to financial security and to dignity at the termination of a marriage, for example, at the same time acknowledges her rights in marriage, which may in fact affect the way the conjugal contract is understood and marriage lived.

In one provision aimed at contesting common interpretations of Islamic law, the nikahnama forbids unilateral, extra-judicial divorce initiated by men, a practice often referred to as triple talaq. According to the Hanafi school of Islamic law—that most north Indian Muslims follow and that is the basis for Indian law governing Muslims—a man can divorce his wife by saying 'I divorce you' to her three times. This form of divorce is disapproved of in Islamic law and it has been the subject of much debate in the Indian judiciary, but it remains legal (Subramanian 2008). Amber's nikahnama states that to execute a unilateral divorce, a husband must declare, 'I divorce you' once a month for three months, which is less disapproved in Islamic and Indian law than giving the declaration thrice in one sitting. The nikahnama also clarifies that no divorce results if the husband utters 'I divorce you' when he is angry or drunk or when his ability to think clearly is otherwise compromised. It is also invalid if communicated by text message, videoconference or phone. In our conversations about this practice, Amber argued that allowing a husband to effect a divorce by uttering talaq in anger is both un-Islamic and *nainsani* (inhuman).

This interpretation contrasts sharply with the interpretations of triple talaq issued by the Islamic cleric whose *fatwa*s I studied even as it intersects with debates within the Indian state courts and between Muslim clerics. A fatwa is a non-binding but authoritative legal opinion given by a trained Muslim jurist in response to a specific question. Of the over one hundred fatwas I studied, well over half responded to questions about triple talaq. The cleric who wrote them consistently opined that the three-fold utterance 'talaq' results in divorce regardless of the man's state of mind, as long as the utterance is correctly executed (Lemons 2010). Amber and I discussed the differences between her interpretation of talaq and the cleric's and she argued that her interpretation was not only true to the Quran, but upheld by many Islamic jurists. On this issue, the nikahnama documents Amber's side of an ongoing debate in which she is engaged with several prominent clerics. Her expectation, then, is not that the nikahnama will immediately alter the practice of talaq. Instead, she hopes it will persuade fellow Islamic legal experts to consider different interpretations of the rights and duties marriage entails.

If the clauses about triple talaq appear to address her disagreements with leading clerics, the nikahnama's provisions on woman-initiated divorce address the difficulty securing nominal rights in divorce. The bulk of the nikahnama's section about divorce focuses on women's right to initiate divorce and their rights to property, maintenance and remarriage following it. The reasons for which a woman can initiate divorce include: if her husband is absent for four years, if he does not provide for her for one year, if he mistreats her, if he has an affair or if he contracts HIV or fails to disclose that he is HIV positive at the time of the marriage. In all of these situations, a woman can divorce her husband by *khul'*—a woman-initiated divorce in which a wife convinces her husband to unilaterally divorce her. Following a divorce, the nikahnama forbids a husband to throw his wife out of her marital home, a provision that echoes through recent domestic violence legislation in and beyond India (Basu 2008; Hodzic 2009; Lazarus-Black 2007).

Amber's concern with woman-initiated divorce centres on the problem of mahr. Striving to ensure women's financial wellbeing, the nikahnama declares that the mahr should be given to the bride by the time of the marriage. Amber explained her concern about mahr as follows: '... if you do a survey, ninety-nine per cent of women do not receive their mahr, either because their husbands are ill-behaved or because she does not know that it is her right.' While this statistic is a rhetorical device, it captures a situation that has been documented by social scientists. My own research in Delhi's dar ul qazas suggests that women rarely petition for or receive mahr; other recent studies corroborate the point that few women receive their mahr upon divorce (Agnes 1999; Basu 2008; Hussain 2007). The nikahnama goes so far as to specify a minimum dower to be given to the bride from her husband's family, as Amber and others have noticed that mahr amounts are often so low as to be meaningless to offset a divorced woman's financial needs (Agnes 1999; Basu 2008). Even as the nikahnama requires that the husband or his family provide dower, it prohibits *jahez* (dowry), which is also commonly given even in Muslim marriages, as un-Islamic. Amber's hope is that including these provisions in the nikahnama itself will make women aware of their rights in divorce, encouraging them to begin making such demands.

Finally, in a provision that is at once a critical intervention in clerical debates and a pedagogical statement, the nikahnama forbids the practice of halala, which 'requires a divorced woman who wishes to remarry her former husband to first marry and be divorced by another man' (Vatuk 2007: 507). The cleric whose fatwas I study prescribed this practice, leading me to ask Amber for her view of it. She argued that if a woman was more educated about Islamic law she would be better prepared to refuse a practice that she finds abhorrent. She told me that while educated women would refuse to follow the advice to perform halala, poorer, less-educated women would think that they had no choice. Whereas the cleric I spoke with in Delhi argued that halala was a punishment for a husband who had divorced his wife, Amber argued,

> Halala is a punishment for women but not for men. To do halala, the man has to give talaq to the woman whom he married, so what kind of marriage is that? How does the woman know with certainty that the second husband will grant her a divorce? The Quran is full of respect for women, so why would such an absurd practice be necessary? Whoever prescribes this is not acting in light of the Quran.

When I pressed her on this point, she said that although halala is discussed in the Quran, it is necessary to reinterpret the practice because,

> At that time things were different. But today's women ... I understand today's women. If they love their husbands and their children, they want to live together for their children ... and I am not ready to obey this, because if a woman and man love one another there is no reason that they should separate. Love does not come from halala.

In her discussion of halala, Amber's hermeneutic differences with the *mufti* becomes clear. Hers was a combination of pragmatic assessment—women who knew what was good for them did not go through with the practice of halala—and contextualising work—the Quran was not written to respond to the particular problems of twenty-first century Indian Muslims. She reads the practice of halala against the Quranic limits on divorce to argue that halala goes against the spirit of marriage, which is to make sexuality licit and to enable procreation and, she adds, to nurture the family.

Amber here introduces a conception of marriage and the family that has not thus far been apparent either in the nikahnama or in the dar ul qaza case or fatwas. The conjugal couple Amber describes here is a pair united by romantic love above all else. This bourgeois conception of marriage breaks not only with the emphasis on marriage as an institution of alliance with a financial facet, but also with her own premise that marriage is primarily a contractual matter. This explanation of the halala provision offers insight into the nikahnama's pedagogical project, which not only seeks to raise women's legal consciousness but also to educate men and women in the appropriate way to think about marriage.

The nikahnama's pedagogical project is evident throughout its contents and its material presentation, preceding its interventions into legal interpretation and legal consciousness. The document begins with an exposition of norms and ideals of marriage. It offers paragraphs of advice about how spouses should treat one another, speak to one another and cultivate an equitable relationship through a clear division of labour.[8] The materiality of the nikahnama also demonstrates Amber's attention to dissemination. Printed both in Urdu and in Hindi, the nikahnama is more broadly legible than most documents produced by the Muslim clergy, who primarily publish in Urdu. Amber told me that she finds that fewer and fewer women learn to read Urdu, making a Hindi version necessary if the nikahnama was to be accessible to the women and men she hopes will learn from it. From linguistic choices to instructional commentary, the nikahnama seeks to open up a space within which women can more effectively realise their entitlements in marriage and divorce.

In the essay thus far, I have argued that although it seems to misfire because it construes marriage as a strict contract that can and should be enforced by the state, if one sees the nikahnama as a hermeneutic and pedagogical intervention aimed at remaking how clerics and the lay—men and women—think about marriage, it is possible to identify the concrete interventions it makes. In the final pages of the essay, I will suggest that in Shaista Amber's hands, the nikahnama also serves as the basis for a different kind of local-level adjudication practice than those I have observed in dar ul qazas and in fatwas. In this way, the nikahnama is a multi-vocal intervention into a plural legal landscape.

Conclusion: A Nikahnama in Action

It was August of 2006 and I had come to meet Amber at her office in Lucknow. Tucked down a long road lined with government buildings, her office is in a cement block building surrounded by greenery. I followed Amber up two flights of stairs and she led me through one room, full of people waiting to meet with her. We walked down a hall to a room just big enough to hold a double bed, several chairs and a little dressing table. Amber had introduced the 'case' to me quickly on the way to the office, telling me that the disputants were poor and that the young woman, who had made the complaint, had been married some time ago. After the marriage, her husband *mar-peet kya* (beat her) and he began to see another woman. Finally, he divorced her in a way that Amber described as improper (she said: 'light of Koran *main nahein tha*'). Although it was not proper according to Amber, the divorce was completed when both sets of parents and a neighbour signed a *talaq nama* (divorce contract). The family had come to see Amber because, although the divorce had been executed in June, the divorcee had yet to receive her *zewar* (jewellery), her mahr or any of the support to which she was entitled during the iddat period. After speaking with the woman and her mother, Amber had convinced the ex-husband and his father to come to her office to settle the dispute.

Once everyone was assembled, the group began to discuss the situation. The main point of disagreement initially was whether the mahr was INR 3000 or INR 5000. Someone produced the nikahnama, however, which stated that the mahr was INR 5000. The real fight began when the wife's mother asked where the jewellery was. The husband said he did not have it and the wife also denied knowing where it was. Both mothers also claimed that they did not have the jewellery. A fight began in earnest and, as the noise level rose, Amber hopped up and told me to come with her to the office.

After some time, I returned to the room where the dispute over the jewellery had concluded when the husband's family confessed that they had it and would return it to the wife. As I re-entered the room, papers were being signed and the mahr was being given to the wife. To conclude the payment, both wife and husband wrote that they had exchanged the money. The meeting ended in a flurry of paperwork, with Amber suggesting that people sign a document of agreement, photocopy it and paste photos of the couple to it. The paperwork and negotiations finished, the meeting adjourned.

Although I did not realise it at the time, I had just witnessed the only post-divorce negotiation I was to see that included a nikahnama and that concluded with the ex-wife receiving financial compensation. There were numerous reasons that this was the outcome. The wife approached Amber who, in turn, approached the husband, convincing him that it was his duty to settle this dispute. Once the family was in the room, the debate over the mahr was settled by the nikahnama and that over the jewellery was settled through Amber's cajoling. Ultimately, the plaintiff received her mahr because Amber was able to convince her ex-husband that giving it to her was his obligation. The nikahnama had its place in that process, but it was not by itself sufficient to secure these ends.

I conclude with this anecdote because it demonstrates both the importance and the inadequacy of the new nikahnama in helping women achieve their aims in marriage and in divorce. To return to the feminist legal scholars with whom the essay began, what is required here is what Amber performs: intervention in the social, ethical and religious negotiations of marriage and divorce coupled with clear stipulations in such documents as the marriage agreement. Marriage is a contract that exceeds itself, a contract made in and through broader normative frames that themselves require attention and intervention.

Notes

[1] This initiative was also followed in the national English, Hindi and Urdu media. Some of the major English language articles include Mishra (2006), *The Hindu* (2008) and Ramakrishnan (2008).

[2] Personal Law is the semi-codified domain of law governing marriage, divorce, inheritance, adoption and succession, whose origins lie in the British colonial reorganisation of the Indian legal system (Kugle 2001; Williams 2006).

[3] Among such organisations are Flavia Agnes' legal advocacy and education group, Majlis (http://www.majlisbombay.org/index.htm; accessed in 2013); the

Multiple Action Resource Group (MARG), founded by the scholar and activist Vasudha Dhagamwar (http://www.ngo-marg.org; accessed in 2013); the network of *mahila panchayats* (women's arbitration centers) overseen by the NGO Action India (http://www.actionindiaworld.org; accessed in June 2011) about which I have written elsewhwere (Lemons 2010); the Legal Aid Centres of the All India Democratic Women's Association, the Muslim Women's Forum founded by Sayeeda Hameed; and the All India Muslim Women's Personal Law Board (AIMWPLB) discussed here.

[4] In my discussions with the staff at MARG and at Action India, I was struck that the law, and women's ability to engage with and use it in their own defence without the interference of uncooperative law enforcement officials, appeared to be the primary and most promising instrument by which marriage would be made more egalitarian.

[5] Unani medicine is a 'system of Greek medicine that has evolved within the Muslim world' (Fleuckiger 2006).

[6] The importance of such extra-legal, character, based arguments to women's success in adjudication proceedings has also been pointed out by Maitrayee Mukhopadhyay in her study (1998) of women's successes and failures in bringing marital disputes and suits for property before the civil courts.

[7] The statistics about domestic violence against Indian women vary widely, but the low estimate is that 37 per cent of married women suffer some form of physical and/or sexual abuse by their husbands (IIPS and Macro International 2007). A 2004 United Nations Population Fund report cited a multi-sited study that found that '52% of women reported at least one form of physical abuse or psychological abuse by their husbands' (UNPF and ICRW 2004: 7–8).

[8] As Mengia Hong Tschalaer has argued (2011), this nikahnama focuses on equity rather than on equality, insisting that there is a naturally gendered division of labour that must be upheld in the interest of domestic harmony.

References

Agarwal, Bina. 1994. *A Field of One's Own*. Cambridge: Cambridge University Press.

Agnes, Flavia. 2008. 'Hindu Conjugality: Transition from Sacrament to Contract'. In *Redefining Family Law in India*, eds. Archana Parashar and Amita Dhanda. Delhi: Routledge.

———. 1999. *Law and Gender Inequality*. New Delhi: Oxford University Press.

———. 1992. 'Protecting Women against Violence? Review of a Decade of Legislation, 1980–89'. *Economic and Political Weekly* 27 (17): WS19–WS21, WS24–WS33.

Ahmed, Imtiaz. 2003. *Divorce and Remarriage Among Muslims in India*. Delhi: Manohar.

———, ed. 1976. *Family, Kinship, and Marriage Among Muslims in India*. Delhi: Manohar.

Basu, Srimati. 2008. 'Separate and Unequal'. *International Feminist Journal of Politics* 10 (4): 495–517.

———. 1999. *She Comes to Take Her Rights*. Albany, NY: SUNY Press.

Carroll, Lucy. 1982. '"Talaq-i-Tafwid" and Stipulations in a Muslim Marriage Contract: Important Means of Protecting the Position of the South Asian Muslim Wife'. *Modern Asian Studies* 16 (2): 277–309.

Durkheim, Emile. 1933. *The Division of Labor in Society*. Glencoe, IL: The Free Press.

Fyzee, A. A. 2005a. *Cases in the Muhammadan Law of India, Pakistan, and Bangladesh*. New Delhi: Oxford University Press.

———. 2005b. *Outlines of Muhammadan Law*. Fourth edition. New Delhi: Oxford University Press.

Grover, Shalini. 2011. *Marriage, Love, Caste, and Kinship Support: Lived Experiences of the Urban Poor in India*. New Delhi: Social Science Press.

Hidayatullah, M., and Arshad Hidayatullah. 2006. *Mulla's Principles of Mahomedan Law*. Delhi: LexisNexis Butterworths.

Hindu, The. 2008. 'Muslim Women's Personal Law Board Unveils New "Nikhanama"'. 17 March. Available at: http://www.thehindu.com/todays-paper/muslim-women-personal-law-board-unveils-new-nikahnama/article1221572.ece. Accessed in 2013.

Hodzic, Saida. 2009. 'Unsettling Power: Domestic Violence, Gender Politics, and Struggles Over Sovereignty in Ghana'. *Ethnos* 74 (3): 331–60.

Hong Tschalaer, Mengia. 2011. "Nikahnama' Politics in Lucknow: The Interlegality of Islamic Family Laws in Postcolonial India'. Unpublished conference paper presented at the Law & Society Association Annual Meeting. San Francisco.

Hussain, Sabiha. 2007. 'Shariat Courts and Women's Rights in India'. Occasional Papers Series. Delhi: Center for Women's Development Studies.

IIPS (International Institute for Population Sciences) and Macro International. 2007. *'National Family Health Survey (NFHS-3) 2005–2006', India: Volume 1*. IIPS: Mumbai.

Kapur, Ratna, and Brenda Crossman. 1996. *Subversive Sites: Feminist Engagements with Law in India*. Thousand Oaks, CA: Sage Publications.

Kugle, Scott Alan. 2001. 'Framed, Blamed and Renamed: The Recasting of Islamic Jurisprudence in Colonial South Asia'. *Modern Asian Studies* 35 (2): 257–313.

Lazarus-Black, Mindie. 2007. *Everyday Harm: Domestic Violence, Court Rites, and Cultures of Reconciliationi*. Urbana: University of Illinois Press.

———. 2003. 'The (Heterosexual) Regendering of a Modern State: Criminalizing and Implementing Domestic Violence Law in Trinidad'. *Law and Social Inquiry* 28:979–1008.

Lemons, Katherine. 2010. *At the Margins of Law: Adjudicating Muslim Families in Contemporary Delhi*. Unpublished Ph.D. dissertation, UC Berkeley.

Mahmood, Tahir. 2002. *The Muslim Law of India*. Third Edition. Delhi: LexisNexis Butterworths.

Mir-Hosseini, Ziba. 1993. *Marriage on Trial: A Study of Islamic Family Law*. London: I.B. Tauris & Co. Ltd.

Mishra, Manjari. 2006. 'Muslim Women to pen "nikahnama"'. *The Times of India*. Available at: http://timesofindia.indiatimes.com/news/india/Muslim-women-to-pen-nikahnama/articleshow/1393482.cms; Accessed in June 2011.

Mukhopadhyay, Maitrayee. 1998. *Legally Dispossessed: Gender, Identity, and the Process of Law*. Calcutta: Stree.

Oldenburg, Veena Talwar. 2002. *Dowry Murder: The Imperial Origins of a Cultural Crime*. New York: Oxford University Press.

Osella, Caroline, and Filippo Osella. 2006. *Men and Masculinities in South India*. London: Anthem Press.
Pateman, Carole. 1988. *The Sexual Contract*. Stanford, CA: Stanford University Press.
Ramakrishnan, Venkitesh. 2008. 'Women's Charter'. *Frontline* 25 (7). Available at: http://www.flonnet.com/fl2507/stories/20080411250702800.htm; Accessed in 2013.
Subramanian, Narendra. 2008. 'Legal Changes and Gender Inequality: Changes in Muslim Family Law in India.' *Law & Social Inquiry* 33 (3): 631–372.
UNPF (United Nations Population Fund) and ICRW (International Centre for Research on Women). 2004. *Violence Against Women in India: A Review of Trends, Patterns, and Responses*. April. New Delhi: ICRW. Available at: http://india.unfpa.org/?publications=367. Accessed in 2013.
Vatuk, Sylvia. 2008. 'Divorce at the Wife's Initiative in Muslim Personal Law: What are the Options and What are their Implications for Women's Welfare?' In *Redefining Family Law in India*, eds. Archana Parashar and Amita Dhanda, 200–35, London: Routledge.
______. 2007. 'Islamic Feminism in India: Indian Muslim Women Activists and the Reform of Muslim Personal Law'. *Modern Asian Studies* 42 (2–3): 489–518.
Whitehead, Anne. 1981. 'I'm Hungry Mum: The Politics of Domestic Budgeting'. In *Of Marriage and the Market*, eds. K. Young, C. Wolkowitz and R. McCullagh. London: Routledge and Kegan Paul.
Williams, Rina Verma. 2006. *Postcolonial Politics and Personal Laws*. Delhi: Oxford University Press.

Websites

Majlis Bombay Legal Center: A forum for women's rights discourse and legal initiatives at http://www.majlislaw.com/ (accessed in 2013).
Multiple Action Research Group: Justice Through Legal Empowerment at http://www.ngo-marg.org/ (accessed in 2013).
Action India's Mahila Panchayat Network at http://www.action-india.org/mahila_panchayat.html (accessed in 2013).

Widowhood, Socio-cultural Practices and Collective Action*

A Study of Survival Strategies of Single Women in Nepal

Makiko Habazaki

Introduction

Marriage is an important life event for both men and women in many societies. In Nepal, as in other south Asian societis, getting married is particularly important for women. When women reach a marriageable age, relatives as well as parents take a keen interest in their eventual wedding. Most Hindu women, especially of the high castes, marry at the urging of their parents who decide when their daughter will get married and with whom. Therefore, marriage may be an inevitable fate for women, beyond their own desire. However, even though parents may compel their daughter towards a marriage, it cannot be solemnised without her consent. In addition to traditional arranged marriages within the same caste or the same ethnic group, love marriages

* Materials for this essay were collected in 2006–07 in Surkhet and Kaski districts through participant observation and interviews with members of the single-women groups in Women for Human Rights (WHR). Open-ended interviews were conducted with women individually. I wish to thank many colleagues who narrated to me their own life histories. Lily, who is the president of WHR, and the staff, gave me a great deal of information about the NGO. Pabitra helped me to understand the interview process precisely. I am also very thankful to the Japan Foundation that helped me financially as a research fellow.

have been increasing recently (Pettigrew 2000; McHugh 2001; Levine 2007). In contemporary society, women may express their views, decide their spouse and continue in paid employment after marriage, which was rare earlier.

While marriage is arranged and planned, a husband's death may come suddenly. The fact of the event cannot be changed in itself. Each society not only distinguishes those who have lost their spouse from those whose spouse is alive, but also assigns distinct norms and roles to be followed by widowed persons. In Nepalese society, especially among the Parbatias,[1] distinctions are made between a widow and a married woman, with restrictions on their behaviour and appearance through the ornaments, make-up and clothes worn. Widows are discriminated against and called *bidhuwa* or *radi*.[2] Widowhood takes precedence as a social identity, over motherhood or womanhood. Women are forced to be conscious of their widowhood always, as they cannot wear accessories, brightly coloured clothes, or attend auspicious rituals. Furthermore, they are accused by the deceased husband's parents and relatives of being the cause of his death.

The situation for widowers is quite different. Although there are words to indicate men who have lost their wife such as *bidhur* or *rado*, they do not face behavioural restrictions and are not differentiated from other men by their appearance; nor is being a widower their primary identity. Remarriage is not difficult for them and most widowers remarry soon.

This essay focuses on the work of a local NGO named Women for Human Rights (WHR), which helps widows and single women[3] deal with their circumstances. It attempts to show Nepalese widows' strategies and practices for survival, highlighting the processes of negotiation. In the process, four questions are addressed. How do widowed women experience their lives? What is their lifestyle after their husband's death? How can the strict norms for widows be negotiated? How can social views on women be modified? I attempt to show that widows' daily practices have the potential to bring about change. Additionally, the widows' movement, as a group, is 'the place of negotiation'. In enabling widows to assert their own identity and actively unite against discrimination,[4] it carries the seeds of possible change in society.

Studies on Widows

Widows in the Social System

Cultural anthropologists as well as sociologists have focused on widows in the context of kinship relations. They analysed marriage as a socio-cultural and functional union that connected kinship communities. In other words, marriage was a social system to maintain relationships or communication within communities, or an alliance that exchanged women and properties.[5]

Rights over a woman's sexuality were an important area of discussion. The literature concerning divorce and bereavement is scanty in comparison to that on marriage, perhaps because widowhood was considered a marginal issue.

In most societies, the wedding is an elaborate ceremony. The accompanying chanting, singing, dancing and the use of symbolic forms (or use of symbols) aroused the interest of scholars. The observance of the event of divorce is comparatively simple and may not involve any rituals. The rituals that transform a married woman into a widow are generally performed within the private domestic space, as just one part of the mourning process for the deceased. They do not seem to have had the same fascination or appeal as weddings had for scholars coming from other cultures. Within the culture they are seen as events to be quickly glided over. As a consequence, divorce and bereavement have not been studied in depth and the daily practices and the voices of widows have found little place in monographs.[6]

However, many societies have normative, socially approved ways of reincorporating widows into society. For example, the dead husband's brother or some other close kinsman marries the widow in the custom of the levirate.[7] The levirate system ensures not only that the contract between the husband's lineage and the wife's lineage continues, but that rights over her sexuality and future children remain in his lineage. Levirate is found in many parts globally, including among middle and lower castes in South Asia.[8]

Widows as a Social Issue

As the women's movement grew in the 1960s, so did studies of widows; Lopata's study (1987), for instance, which covered widows in various parts of the world. In India, a major debate with regard to widows was over the custom of *sati*. In this tradition, a widow immolates herself on the funeral pyre of her dead husband. Sati was seen as the only way for widows to get respected status. People believed that the woman who burned herself became Sati, a goddess. This was disputed by those who saw it as a violation of human rights and demanded that it be banned.[9] It has become a global issue of human rights and a symbol that speaks of the low status of widows in south Asian societies, the discrimination they suffer, and the widespread violence against women. However, there has been much variation between regions, castes and ethnic groups in the occurrence of the custom. In Nepal, sati has been known in the upper class, but it never became a custom.[10] Minority ethnic groups and lower castes did not practice it.

Most widows face various problems after their husband's death. In spite of a substantial proportion of widows living in society, relatively little is known about their actual living conditions.[11] A woman who loses her husband has to negotiate with her in-laws as well as the society at large. Who she lives with, how she earns her livelihood, and whether she has access to her husband's property are some of the major issues that she must immediately resolve. If she has adult sons or supportive male family members, the negotiation process becomes easier. Most widows receive very little support from their in-laws (Chen 1998: 13). According to Chen, 'While there is general public anxiety about elderly widows and while we hear the occasional public outcry when the treatment of widows takes a sensational form, such as that of sati (widow immolation), there is a striking lack of public concern for the quiet deprivations experienced by millions of widows on a daily basis' (ibid.: 19). She not only sees a silence in the literature on poverty and in public debates on social policy, she states that the women's movement, also, has rarely addressed widows' mundane concerns.

However, feminists in Western countries as well as South Asia have depicted the widow's situation as a terrible social problem and women's groups have struggled with this social issue and discrimination against widows. Many NGOs have become active in this field.

The Cultural Framing of Widows

While a married woman whose husband is alive is identified as a fortunate woman in Hindu societies, a widow is looked down upon as an inauspicious woman. A married woman can wear a brilliant red sari, beadwork necklace and *tika* (vermillion powder) in the parting of the hair as a symbol of a living husband. A widow is prohibited these adornments as not only do they signify auspiciousness, which she is the opposite of, it is believed to enhance a widow's sexuality. Widowhood is a 'dreaded time of life' (Lamb 2000), a life of asceticism and a 'social death' (Chakravarti 1998: 64–66).

In a Hindu worldview, a husband can control a woman's sexual energy, but this energy can also cause his death. Widows are seen to have special sexual and destructive powers which pose a threat to other individuals, to their husband's and their own families, and to communities (Yagi 2007). 'These powers are heightened expressions of women's innate power (*shakti*) which is considered sacred if controlled, but highly dangerous if not controlled. As a result of these perceived threats, special (often drastic) practices have been instituted to restrict the dress, diet, and behaviour of widows' (Chen 1998: 49). In Nepalese society too, a widow's sexuality is considered to be extremely dangerous and a social anomaly due to the lack of a husband's control. She represents a potential problem to both her affinal and consanguineal kin. For the affinal group, her fertility has become useless, and yet they have an obligation to support her (Bennett 1983: 243–44).

Much of the focus on the rigid behavioural requirements for widows, especially among the high castes, seem to imply that widows are merely subordinate subjects compelled to follow imposed norms. Widows are however, active, strategising agents. They live their lives supporting themselves, raising their children, and hewing out their own future. In recent years, articles written about widows' daily practices have increased. Galvin (2003) wrote of widows choosing their residence and religion. She described a widow who had resisted particular strictures placed on her (ibid.: 82–83). Yagi (2007) portrayed some widows who moved to urban areas in India and lived with their lovers. Also, worth noting is that the rigid requirements for widows are not true in every caste. 'Unlike high-caste women, low-caste women do not follow the food proscriptions or wear white clothing for longer than a month. Widowed untouchables find it relatively easy to remarry with few social proscriptions. A widow of any caste is considered inauspicious, but the lower-caste widow can shed this state relatively quickly by remarrying' (Cameron 1998: 149–50).

Sato (2007) argues against the victimised portrait of women in south Asian societies, in which they are presented as passive and submissive in the patriarchal system backed by ideology and tradition. 'Countering the dismal and static perception of female subjugation, women's "agency" was brought to the fore and became the central subject matter of a number of works' (ibid.: 207–08). This is the approach taken in this essay, which argues that attention must be paid to each individual widow's unique situation and life. Their lifestyle and their negotiation with society, their in-laws, and their own family may be examined to understand the changing perceptions of what it means to be a widow.

From Widow to Single Woman (*Ekal Mahila*)

The Single Women's Movement and the Single Women's Group (*Ekal Mahila Samuha*)

Since democratisation in the 1990s in Nepal, the women's movement became a vigorous social movement to ensure women's social, economic and political rights. Currently, there are thousands of registered NGOs belonging to the Social Welfare Council in Nepal. They focus on individual issues that women face; some on trafficking, others on domestic violence or legal discrimination, and yet others on customs discriminatory of women.

Ekal Mahila Samuha, meaning single women's group, is one of the most energetic NGOs organised by single women.[12] It battles against socio-cultural discrimination related to widowhood, and lobbies and mobilises to establish their human rights. They identify themselves as *ekal mahila*—single women—and hope to wipe away the negative meaning of the word widow or bidhuwa.

They recognise ekal mahila as a positive term and feel better than when known as a widow. Identifying themselves as single women leads them to join in the group and become active in joint enterprises with other widows. The term implies an active state, subject and agency partaking in the society, while bidhuwa is a passive term identified with an inauspicious woman who has lost her husband.

The objective of the single women's movement is to acquire human rights for the women. Of the NGOs for single women's rights in Nepal,[13] the most active is WHR led by Lily Thapa, who is herself a widow. It was established in 1994 and has a network of single women's groups all over Nepal. In 2007, the number of widow members was 14,000, spread over 36 of the 75 districts. It is currently the largest organisation for widows in Nepal. Each member belongs to one Ekal Mahila Samuha, all of which are linked to the centre or *Kendra*—the head office of WHR.

> WHR recognises some central issues concerning widowhood: (1) Widowhood is not viewed as a natural period in the life of a woman. It is marked by social and economic exclusion from society and family. (2) Widowhood has its own moral dimensions such as a behaviour code, dietary restrictions, dress colour-code and other traditional practices. (3) Lack of support from men implies the multiple burdens of child-rearing, caring and earning. (4) Most ekal mahilas have a hard time meeting the basic necessities of life. (5) Young ekal mahilas are often ridiculed and made objects of sexual harassment. (6) An ekal mahila is generally ignorant of her rights of inheritance and ownership. (WHR n.d.)

The main purpose of the NGO is to strengthen the lives of single women, raise their social and economic status, mainstream the rights of single women, and develop their confidence levels and self-esteem. They educate widows on their rights to empower individual widows, encouraging them to wear red sari and *tika*[14], save a little money through micro-credit, enable training for jobs such as making handcrafts, beauticians or driving. They lobby with the government[15] as well as with local authorities. They also have received donations from international NGOs and bilateral agencies.

Participating in the Single Women's Group

Any single women can join the movement regardless of age, ethnicity or caste. The single women's group is organised by widows who belong to many ethnic groups and castes, different generations, educational backgrounds, religious backgrounds and economic conditions. This women's group is centred on kin and residential networks. Motivations to join a group vary. Some hope to do something productive for single women, others come to get economic help. Some hope to work as a volunteer in the group, others have no such plans.

Although the process through which a group is established varies, we can classify them as being organised voluntarily or through WHR. The former is registered with WHR as a single women's group in the district by women concerned willingly. The latter is formed through the workshops WHR conducts or by its district offices. The WHR aims to establish at least one group in each district while conducting workshops and giving training. The most popular way to participate in the group-making process is to attend a workshop. Women are informed by neighbours or city-hall employees that workshops and trainings will be held. Not only are they strongly encouraged to attend the meetings, but the women themselves also think of it as a good opportunity to learn a new skill or obtain information.

Juna, a 29-year-old Chetri woman, who graduated from the 12th grade[16] and is a secretary in an office in Kaski district, said that, 'A teacher working at the neighbouring school informed me about the single women's group. He submitted my name to the village office when he was asked if widows lived in our region. He informed the WHR about me and suggested that I go to their meeting.'

Some women get information about the single women's group from natal relatives. After Devi[17] was informed of the curriculum at WHR, she was given a bright coloured sari to wear for going out by her elder brother and his wife. She decided to come to the single women's group and see what they had to offer.

Pramila,[18] a 39-year-old Newar[19] woman, decided to become active after listening to a talk about WHR on the radio. 'One day I listened to Lily talking about WHR and the single women's group on the radio. I was very interested in the group. I wrote down the telephone number of WHR, and I called the office to make my own group in the Kaski district. When we established a group in 2005, many widows only cried. We noted the skills and abilities of each woman to determine what they could and could not do. And when we talked about our troubles and suffering with each other, I understood that other women without husbands faced problems much more difficult than mine, and I decided to work for single women.'

The Single Women's Group: Individual and Collective Practices

Single women have drastically changed their daily lives after participating in a single women's group. Their legal knowledge, job training, and micro-credit savings lead to a change in their daily life and enable them to plan for the future. This section is a description of their new practices as related through the narratives of single women.

Acquiring Legal Knowledge

When a single woman participates in the single women's group, she starts with the study of human rights and civil law. She is taught that she can wear auspicious colours and that she has a right to inherit both her husband's property and her own parents' property. That the social discrimination the widows experience locally is not necessary, is discussed. By attending the single women's group, women acquire this knowledge and begin to exercise their rights practically.

Bisnu,[20] a 39-year-old Dalit woman, said that 'I have changed my thinking after learning many things that are in the curriculum. I had never known that a widow had equal rights to her husband's property, or that I could inherit it in my own name. I had suffered psychological trauma, been extremely stressed, and was supported until I could become independent. Nobody had taught me the widow's rights in property until that time.'

Studying to Become a Professional

WHR also offers many job-training opportunities through its district offices. The courses offered include that of beautician, automobile driving, making handicrafts, sewing, cooking, farming and so on. They send women to training courses arranged by municipalities and other organisations. Since admission to most popular courses is competitive, the single women's group negotiates with the host organisation to ensure that single women are accommodated in good numbers. WHR organises some courses itself, using financial support from international donations.

One woman got her driver's license and started working as a driver, another became a trekking guide after graduating from a guide-school; and still another woman became a beautician. They could not imagine working independently when their husbands were alive.

Some women transform the adversity of their husband's death into a whole new lifestyle. One method adopted is to go back to school and college. A young Chetri woman told me about her hope to go abroad. She was studying to get her bachelor's degree. 'I was denied my right to study further by my husband, but now I am free to go to university. I have been studying computers for six months in a private school. And I hope to go to Korea or Israel. I will ask my mother to take care of my son in my absence.'

Bimala is a 48-year-old Newar woman, educated and wealthy.[21] She is active in the local society for the fellowship it offers. She stated, 'In modern society no woman should be discriminated against after her husband's death. It depends on us. If we are afraid of society, people will discriminate against us. But if we get a job and become successfully independent, people in the society cannot look down upon us.'

Meeting to Share Suffering

Many single women come to the 'office'[22] even when they have no business there. Devi said,'In this space I can share my thoughts and make new friends. If I was not here, I would be passing my time watching TV, eating and sleeping all day inside the house. I enjoy my daily life now coming to the group. Other members' sons and daughters recommend to them that they go to the Ekal Mahila Samuha.'

The place that they call their office is the only space where they can feel some relief from strict social constraints. Women who have suffered from the vilification of society gather here. They chat about their daily lives, their children's future, job training, and even gossip together. They spend a few hours talking about their worries while sipping tea, and return home content.

Radhika, a Bahun 40-year-old woman who lives with two sons earns a little money by sewing clothes. She shared, 'I have known each of the single women's faces, who are experiencing troublesome circumstances, and I can get power from my sisters.' They comfort one another in their social suffering and sympathise with each other's situations. They believe single women have similar social pain and can share it. They regard the group as the space where it is not necessary to remember the differences between them and married women. By participating in the group, they are able to live their lives without being constantly reminded of the pain.

However, they do not all have similar experiences and do not always talk about their suffering. Their commonality is that they are all widows, but their socio-cultural background, their motivations and intentions vary. Some members know others' individual life histories, but others know little of each other. The space is also a place where they can imagine and hope beyond the shared suffering and common experiences of discrimination.

Wearing Favourite Colours

After participating in the single women's group, most come to an understanding that they may choose to wear their favourite colours even though they are widows. They had earlier believed that the colour red was an auspicious symbol of a woman whose husband was alive, and they gave up wearing that colour or ornaments. Hence, they had given their brightly coloured clothes to kinswomen.

A Bahun woman named Sumitra, who is in her 40s and lives with a son, was wearing a red sari at a wedding ceremony in her village. I had not seen her wear red after she became a widow. She told me, 'This sari was presented to me by my oldest daughter a few years ago. But I couldn't wear it. Do you want to know why? Everyone in the village knows I am a widow, and I was afraid that fingers would be pointed at me or bad things would be said behind my back if I put on a red sari. One day my daughter became angry with me for not wearing her gift and she told me that a widow can also wear red now. So, although fearful, I have put it on today. No one has rebuked me.'

Kokila, a 23-year-old Bahun woman with red tika on her forehead and wearing a brightly coloured *kurta-salwar*,[23] looks like an unmarried girl. She told me a Hindu priest had put the red tika on her. He emphasised that she was young so she could put on the red tika even though she was a widow. Her parents-in-law could not object to the priest's act.[24]

Widows may be chastised for inappropriate behaviour and forced to obey socio-cultural rules prescribed for them. However, the cases described above depict a trend in which widows choose their appearance themselves, setting aside or reinterpreting norms.

Independence from the In-laws

After a husband's death, most women experience problems with their in-laws which are difficult to resolve. One woman expressed the view that the experience was such as 'to make me clever'. Earlier, on widowhood, a woman neither wished to nor expected to live an independent life. However, increasingly they choose to live independently from their in-laws; widows can create their own future, negotiate with others, and live their own lives positively.

Juna had to negotiate with her community as her deceased husband's younger brother insisted that she was not actually his brother's wife. He was plotting to prevent her from getting his dead brother's pension from the Indian army. If she were not his wife, the right to the pension would devolve on his parents. She petitioned a government office to issue a paper confirming her marriage and succeeded in getting proof by collecting the neighbours' verbal evidence. Since then she has been able to live independently from her husband's family on the pension.

A Newar woman in her 30s transferred land in her deceased husband's name to her own name. His family opposed the registration of the property in her name, because, according to social custom, her son would inherit his parents' property. She, however, held firm to her decision. The reason she had registered the property in her own name was that her son was too young to manage the property. She was afraid that he would be deceived by her husband's relatives. Finally, she solved the problem by negotiating with her in-laws and now lives independently in her own house.

Many women move to urban areas from rural homes after their husband's death. They need to do this cleverly so as to avoid friction with others in society. One of the ways is to use the education of their children as a reason for the shift of residence. Before coming to Pokhara[225] Devi had lived with her parents-in-law for seven years. Her mother-in-law constantly complained to her father-in-law over money matters, resulting in discord. However, this was not good enough a reason for her to leave the marital home; it was not a reason her in-laws would have accepted. Therefore, she chose to stay until her son was old enough to go to school, and with this excuse she succeeded in obtaining their permission to leave. She had to wait for seven years for her desire to be fulfilled.

Single Women's Negotiations with the State

Single women need to negotiate not only with the local society, but also with the government over policies for widows. Through the use of collective power to promote their demands, they have succeeded in getting a special public budget, scholarships, and priority in posts in public service.

Gaining Public Budget as well as Assistance for Single Women

The single women's group negotiates with the political authorities and influential organisations in the society. Sometimes the single women's group acts as a lobby to make their demands heard in the government and the regional administrative offices. They have succeeded in gaining public space free-of-charge to build their offices, to get resources in the regional budget and priority in seats in job-training courses. They are able to ensure the help of regional leaders and authorities, such as the police and hospitals, and assistance from some public agencies, such as NGOs, associations and political parties.

Resolving Individual Problems

The following is a description of a case of a single woman who pursued and resolved her predicament through her own and the group's efforts. Shanti is in her 30s and is a teacher in Surkhet.[26] Her husband used to work at a village office, but disappeared during the civil war. Shanti heard from an influential person in the local community that her husband was killed by the police as he was suspected of being a Maoist. This was also reported in the newspaper, but was not confirmed because his corpse was never found.

Shanti visited the local police to try and learn the truth. She needed living and educational expenses for her children. She requested the local police to issue a certificate that her husband was dead so that she could get governmental compensation. At that time, the Nepalese government was disbursing payments to bereaved families, even of civilians. Though she went up to the police headquarters in Kathmandu, she could not get the death certificate. She asked for help from the single women's group and appealed to WHR. At last she got support from an international human rights organisation that agreed to look for him as a missing person.

Shanti worked painstakingly, appealing to the authorities and using as many resources as she could towards a settlement. The social tendency was not to attach so much importance to women negotiating in public spaces, especially if they were widows who were poor, illiterate, old, of low caste and provincial. They seldom stood up to the authorities, because they knew that they would be ignored. However, such women have begun to voice their problems after their husband's death in public spaces such as courts, village halls and the like.

How do Single Women Strengthen Unity?

Single women organise a group by using the identity of a woman without a husband. This is evoked to confirm their membership when they gather at meetings. They have no common identity other than being single, because they are from a variety of ethnic, economic, caste, age and educational backgrounds. Therefore, rituals to build solidarity are important for the single women's group. The main ritual is at Tij,[27] a popular festival and ritual for Hindu women. It is observed on the third day after the new moon in the fifth month, Bhadau (mid-August to mid-September).

Women perform rituals for the long lives of their husbands or future husbands, and redemption from the sin of menstruation on the days of Tij and Rsi Pancami, which is two days later. They celebrate it by fasting through the day to become ritually pure, wearing auspicious bright red saris, putting on tika and luxurious beadwork necklaces. After worshipping at the Siva temple, they sing and dance. Occasionally, some women improvise, adding irony or complaints about the parents-in-law, or issues of the community into the song. Tij is not an enjoyable day for women without a husband. They are reminded that they are widows. They are seldom observed singing and dancing on the day. After a husband's death, most women quietly stay in their own house on Tij.

However, ekal mahilas make it a point to celebrate Tij. They come to their office wearing red saris and beadwork necklaces; they put a red tika on each others' foreheads. Women who hesitate to put on the tika are encouraged to do so by their fellow sisters, who say that it can be a part of ekal mahilas' celebrations too. These single women then look the same as married women and they chant, dance and clap their hands to the sound of drums.

Ekal mahilas use the structure of the traditional Hindu ceremony—they celebrate Tij and put on the red tika. Through this they show that single women are no different from women whose husbands are alive. They thereby strengthen the unity of ekal mahila calling on known rituals.

The Changing Perspectives of Widows

The struggles of single women to survive and negotiate with society after their husband's death have been presented above. In the final section, their changing views on their widowhood as well as modification in social perspectives are discussed.

Empowerment of Single Women

The participants in Ekal Mahila Samuha not only gained in knowledge, but also learnt from other women how to take initiatives. Through others' narratives they felt empowered to make a change in society. The following story is narrated by Juna.

> I was a changed person after attending the single women's group. Before joining the group, I was fearful of society. Sometimes I heard a neighbour complaining about the look of my sari and red tika. She criticised me, saying, 'Juna is walking around wearing a bright coloured sari and red tika. What does she intend to do? Less than two years have lapsed since her husband's death.' But, I continued to wear them. I could go against her, because I know every ekal mahila wears clothes of any colour like other women. I have my supporters in the group of single women who wear a red tika. I know it is not her [the neighbour's] own view, it's society that makes her censure me. After a while, she stopped criticising me. Now, I don't worry about accusations at all. I think we can change the perception about widows in society if we, ourselves, have changed.

A lot of women lose their fear of society after joining the group. Gita[28], a 32-year-old Chetri woman, spoke of her dread that 'has been blown away. ... Now, I can talk in front of many people and not dread going out in society, because I became empowered'.

In Bimala's words, 'Their faces looks different from the faces they had when they just came to our group. Their minds changed so that they are able to do many things by themselves now. They know of many women's successes. I think their appearance influences positive practice and gives a lot of hope. Now, they must be empowered.'

'Single women' changed their behaviour. They imitated the social action of their sisters and came to understand that they do not need to fear society.

Modification in Society

Single women's practice and negotiation with a group have modified the social perspective on women without husbands. They used to be admonished for behaviour deemed inappropriate, such as wearing bright saris, talking with men, walking around and so on. Many single women have the experience of people speaking ill of them behind their backs. However, such social censure seems to have diminished. They believe that this is a direct result of the power generated through the single women's group.

Juna, mentioned earlier, said, 'No kinsman can any longer point a finger at me. When they saw me go out of the home alone, they used to call me radi—a prostitute. But, now I can tell them not to call me by that name. I sustain myself and have my own property. I am proud of my life. Therefore, nobody calls me radi any more.'

Not only Juna but many other women have also felt that there has been a modification in the views regarding widows. Ganga, a 48-year-old Dalit woman, described her experience.

> After organising the single women's group, I felt that society has changed its way of seeing me. I earn my living selling small prayer items to be offered to deities in front of a temple. One day a man who was jealous protested against my business. He sent me away from the front of the temple. Therefore, I talked to my associates in the single women's group. The leader of our group soon called him to come and discuss this issue. She is a creditable and educated woman. After all that, he did not come to meet us and sent his wife to the meeting instead. She promised to accept my business as a member of the local community. I continue my business at the same place now.

Ganga's case is one of many successful cases in changing social attitudes and actions with regard to a widow. Single women are not being disturbed as they conduct their trade, and are identified now as independent businesswomen. Formerly, their requests for small business loans were refused, but now they are encouraged to apply for them. As women have shown their ability to run a business, live independently and negotiate in the public space, it is seen that they are not without support and power. Social attitudes toward widows and that of single women themselves have altered.

Contradiction and Discord

With these shifts, however, single women face various contradictions. They use the red colour and ornaments as symbols for their movement. They show widows are not inauspicious by using the colour red. It may be unavoidable that they use these symbols, because they live in a traditional Hindu society. They cannot abandon the socio-cultural value, auspiciousness—which red represents—even though they have suffered due to the custom; for the red as a symbol separates them from women whose husbands are alive and indicates discrimination towards widows. Hence, they claim that the symbolic auspicious colour of red signifies 'all women'. They reject the dark colours that are tied to inauspiciousness and widowhood. Thus, in using the same customs that have been significant in the discrimination they experience in their attempts to give a new meaning to their status, they may reiterate aspects of them.

Furthermore, even as they reject the term 'widow', they do not identify themselves as 'women' but as 'single women', ekal mahila. Most women in the group found that the latter term suited them. However, as some women pointed out the term 'single woman' also segregates women into those who are married and those who are unmarried, perhaps privileging the former as women whose husbands are alive and living with them.

Single women try to alter the traditional system by working with the hegemonic Hindu customs, rather than constructing a new moral system. Therefore the more they use Hindu symbols, the more they feel discord and contradiction in their actions within society.

Single Women/Ekal Mahila as a Strategy for Change

Single women actively practice, strategise and negotiate in society so as to be able to live independently. In the process, they acquire the power to lessen the discrimination and social suffering they experience. They, thus, escape from their portrayal as social burdens. Changes in their outward appearance are just a start to the process of bettering their lives and creating their own future.

The single women's group is a group composed of women from many different backgrounds, with a thin common identity—that of widows or single women. Perhaps, they would not have come into such close contact if they had not lost their husbands. However, they have brought about small shifts in social attitudes and actions towards widows, using resources from the single women's group such as knowledge, power, money and networking. There have been changes in their own situation, in their daily life and the social value given to widows. They have transformed made the idea of the ekal mahila into a positive state and agentic subject, unlike the passive and negative state of the bidhuwa. This small strategy of a widow becoming a single woman has enabled new survival strategies for them and wrought changes in society.

Notes

[1] Parbatias are the Nepali-speaking Hindu majority in Nepal and are composed of Bahun, Chetri and Dalit castes. Bahun and Chetri are local terms in Nepal for *Brahman* (priestly caste) and *Kshatria* (warrior caste) respectively.

[2] *Radi* is a derogatory term for a widow, and sometimes implies prostitute.

[3] WHR had been established in the stream of the women's movement of the 1990s. In the beginning of the twentieth century, the Nepalese women's movement was started by politicians' wives to support the struggle against the autocratic Rana regime. The first women's organisation, *Mahila Samiti* (Women's Committee), was founded in 1917 by the mother of B. P. Koirala, who became the Leader of the Nepalese Congress

as well as a prime minister. The government set up the Nepal Women's Organisation under the panchayat system, which was a partyless electoral system established in 1960. When the latter ended in 1990, following a people's movement for democracy, the women's movement grew in numbers, activities and intensity. The number of non-governmental organisations (NGOs) for women's rights soared rapidly in the1990s, those registered with the Social Welfare Council increasing from 16 in 1992 to 5978 in 1997. Some have described this as a 'boom' in the NGO sector. There are some business elements behind this boom. Establishing and managing NGO seemed to be a useful means to get donation from foreigners for the cause of social justice.

[4] With reference to 'the place of negotiation', I refer to Escobar (1995) and Kitamura (2004).

[5] Radcliffe-Brown, Fortes, Levi-Strauss and Evans-Prichard are important scholars in this discussion.

[6] See Borneman (1996) for a different and important argument regarding this lacuna in anthropology.

[7] This was first described by Evans-Pritchard (1951) for the Nuer in Africa.

[8] See Chowdhry (1994), Wadley (1995), Kolenda (2003).

[9] There are many discussions of Sati. See Tanaka (2002), Sen (2001) and Hawley (1994).

[10] Majupuria (1991) points out that there is no official record of sati being practised in Nepal.

[11] Chen states that in India, among women over 50 years of age, the proportion of widows is as high as 50 per cent (1998: 19).

[12] In this essay the term 'single woman' is shown as an active word in the context of their social movement. Otherwise, 'widow' is the common word used for a woman after her husband's death.

[13] STEP Nepal, a group of NGOs, has also laboured to organise single women's groups and to manage some programmes for widows.

[14] *Tika* is a mark put on the forehead. Hindus often put it on daily or for special religious occasions.

[15] WHR passed a national declaration to use the word *ekal mahila* instead of using *bidhuwa*.

[16] She is one of the educated women in her affiliated group of which most have only elementary school education. She makes a living by renting some rooms in the house she inherited from her husband where she lives with her son and a co-wife.

[17] She is a 37-year-old Chetri woman, who passed her 10th grade qualification and lives with her two sons. She makes a living by sewing clothes and receives a survivor's pension because her husband had worked in the Indian army.

[18] She is a very active woman, who graduated 12th grade and lives with a daughter and a son in her own house inherited from her husband. She works in a university and runs an agency for money transfer and publication. She managed her own beauty salon before her husband's death. At that time she would do make-up for brides on the day of their wedding ceremonies. As a widow she became an inauspicious beautician and customers declined, forcing her to give up this enterprise.

[19] The Newars are the indigenous people of the Kathmandu Valley in Nepal. Although they are an ethnic people, they have power and a wealthy background compared with other ethnic societies.

[20] She doesn't have the experience of attending school. She lives with two sons and a nephew in her house built by her husband who worked in the Indian army. She doesn't have any income besides the pension.

[21] She lives with two sons and a daughter who make their own living as business people. They reside in the house she built after her husband's death. She had helped in contributing to her husband's business for many years and now she works as a leader of a group in the Kaski district.

[22] Single women call the room for the WHR district group by the English word 'office'.

[23] It is a popular outfit of long pants and loose shirt falling either just above or somewhere below the knees, the dress of women in the Punjab in particular. It is increasingly worn by unmarried women in South Asia.

[24] Sometimes priests as well as senior kinsmen influence to encourage behaviour not in keeping with social norms.

[25] Pokhara, a central city in the Kaski district, is the second biggest city in Nepal.

[26] Surkhet district is in western Nepal.

[27] Skinner et al. (1994) describes the Tij festival in detail.

[28] Gita has been living in a small rented room in Pokhara with her son since she left her father-in-law's house after her husband's death. She started a sewing job a few months ago.

References

Bennett, L. 1983. *Dangerous Wives and Sacred Sisters: Social and Symbolic Roles of High-Caste Women in Nepal.* New York: Columbia University Press.

Borneman, J. 1996. 'Until Death Do Us Part: Marriage/Death in Anthropological Discourse'. *American Ethnologists* 23 (2): 215–35.

Cameron, M. M. 1998. *On the Edge of the Auspicious: Gender and Caste in Nepal.* Urbana: University of Illinois Press.

Chakravarti, U. 1998. 'Gender, Caste, and Labour: The Ideological and Material Structure of Widowhood'. In *Widows in India: Social Neglect and Public Action*, ed. M. A. Chen, 63–92. New Delhi and California: Sage Publications.

Chen, M.A. 1998. 'Introduction'. In *Widows in India: Social Neglect and Public Action*, ed. M. A. Chen, 19–59. New Delhi and California: Sage Publications.

Chowdhry, P. 1994. *The Veiled Women: Shifting Gender Equations in Rural Haryana.* New Delhi: Oxford University Press.

Escobar, A. 1995. *Encountering Development: the Making and Unmaking of the Third World.* Princeton: Princeton University Press.

Evans-Pritchard, E. E. 1951. *Kinship and Marriage among the Nuer.* Oxford: Clarendon Press.

Galvin, K. L. 2003. *Life After Death: An Ethnographic Analysis of Widowhood in Urban Nepal.* UMI Dissertation Services.

Hawley, John Stratton, ed. 1994. *Sati, the Blessing and the Curse: The Burning of Wives in India*. New York: Oxford University Press.

Kitamura, U. 2004. *Indo no Hatten to Jenda: (Development and Gender in India)*. Tokyo: Shinyosha.

Kolenda, P. 2003. *Caste, Marriage and Inequality: Essays on North and South India*. Jaipur: Rawat Publications.

Lamb, S. 2000. *White Saris and Sweet Mangoes: Aging, Gender, and Body in North India*. Berkeley: University of California Press.

Levine, S. 2007. 'Parental Wisdom vs. Youthful Romance: Getting Married in Two Nepali Communities'. In *Nepalis Inside and Outside Nepal: Political and Social Transformations*, eds. H. Ishii, D. N. Gellner, K. Nawa, 223–53. New Delhi: Manohar.

Levi-Strauss, C. 1969. *The Elementary Structures of Kinship*. Boston: Beacon Press.

Lopata, H. Z. 1987. *Widows*. Durham: Duke University Press.

Majupuria, Indira. 1991. *Nepalese Women*. Bangkok: Craftsman Press.

McHugh, E. 2001. 'Sliding, Shifting and Re-drawing Boundaries'. *European Bulletin of Himalayan Research* 20 (1): 113–17.

Pettigrew, J. 2000. 'Gurkhas in the Town: Migration, Language, and Healing'. *European Bulletin of Himalayan Research* 19:7–40.

Sato, S. 2007. 'I Don't Mind Being Born a Woman: The Status and Agency of Women in Yolrmo Nepal'. In *Nepalis Inside and Outside Nepal: Political and Social Transformations*, eds. H. Ishii, D. N. Gellner, K. Nawa, 191–222. New Delhi: Manohar.

Sen, M. 2001. *Death by Fire: Sati, Dowry Death and Female Infanticide in Modern India*. New Brunswick: Rutgers University Press.

Skinner, Debra, Dorothy Holland, and G. B. Adhikari. 1994. 'The Songs of Tij: A Genre of Critical Commentary for Women in Nepal'. *Asian Folklore Studies* 53:259–305.

Tanaka, M. 2002. *Kugi Sekai no Henbou: Minami Ajia no Rekishi Jinruigaku (Transformation of the Sacrifice World: An Historical Anthropology of South Asia)*. Kyoto: Houzoukan.

Yagi, Y. 2007. '*Shiroi Sari to Akai Shinduru; Kita Indo Nouson no Kafu no Monogatari*, (White Sari and Red Sidur; Stories of Widows in a North Indian Rural Village)'. In *Yamome Gurashi: Kafu no Bunka Jinruigaku (Widow's Life; Cultural Anthropology of Widows)*, ed. W. Shino, 174–192. Tokyo: Akashi Shoten.

Wadley, S. S. 1995. 'No Longer a Wife: Widows in Rural North India'. In *From the Margins of Hindu Marriage*, eds. L. Harlan and P. B. Courtright, 92–118. New York: Oxford University Press.

Women for Human Rights (WHR). n.d. *Brochure of Women for Human Rights*. Naxal, Kathmandu, Nepal: WHR.

Contributors

Janaki Abraham is a Reader, Department of Sociology, Delhi School of Economics, Delhi University.

Sajeda Amin works with the Population Council in New York.

Lester Andrist is an editor on a website called 'The Sociological Cinema' (thesociologicalcinema.com) that he co-founded. The website promotes video and popular culture in teaching and learning sociology.

Manjistha Banerji is a researcher with Annual Status of Education Report (ASER) Centre, New Delhi.

Srimati Basu is Associate Professor of Gender and Women's Studies and Anthropology at University of Kentucky, USA.

Maitreyi Bordia Das is Lead Social Development Specialist in the Social Development Department of the World Bank in Washington DC, USA.

Sonam Chuki currently works as curricula developer at the Royal Education Council in Paro, Bhutan.

Sonalde Desai is Professor of Sociology, University of Maryland College Park and Senior Fellow, National Council of Applied Economic Research (NCAER).

Priti Dhanda is an MBA graduate from University of Virginia's Darden School of Business.

Quy-Toan Do is Senior Economist, Poverty Team of the Development Research Group, World Bank.

Shalini Grover currently holds a Senior Research Fellowship at the Institute of Economic Growth, Delhi.

Makiko Habazaki is Associate Professor in the Office of Diversity, Tsukuba University, Japan.

Shareen Joshi is Assistant Professor of International Development, Edmund Walsh School of Foreign Service, Georgetown University, Washington, DC, USA.

Sriya Iyer is an Official Fellow, Bibby Teaching Fellow, and College Lecturer in Economics at St Catharine's College, Cambridge; and an Isaac Newton Trust Affiliated Lecturer at the Faculty of Economics, University of Cambridge.

Ravinder Kaur is Professor of Sociology and Social Anthropology in the Department of Humanities and Social Sciences at the Indian Institute of Technology Delhi, New Delhi.

Pushpesh Kumar teaches sociology at the University of Hyderabad, Hyderabad.

Katherine Lemons is Assistant Professor of Anthropology at McGill University, Canada.

Johanna Lessinger is a social anthropologist and currently teaches in the Department of Anthropology at John Jay College, which is part of the City University of New York.

Sidharthan Maunaguru is Assistant Professor, South Asian Studies Programme, Faculty of Arts and Social Sciences, National University of Singapore.

Rajni Palriwala is Professor of Sociology, Department of Sociology, Delhi School of Economics, University of Delhi.

Amali Philips teaches socio-cultural anthropology at Wilfrid Laurier University in Waterloo, Canada.

Priti Ramamurthy is professor and chair of the Department of Gender, Women, and Sexuality Studies at the University of Washington, Seattle, USA.

Anwar Shaheen is an assistant professor at the Pakistan Study Centre, University of Karachi, Pakistan.

Ashley Tellis is Associate Professor in English at Jindal Global Law School, O. P. Jindal Global University, Delhi.

Sylvia Vatuk is Professor Emerita of Anthropology at the University of Illinois, Chicago, USA.

Index